Introduction to Accounting for Business Studies

F. P. Langley, MPhil, FCCA

and

G. S. Hardern, BA(Econ), LLB, ACMA

FIFTH EDITION

Butterworths
London, Boston, Dublin, Edinburgh, Hato Rey, Kuala Lumpur, Singapore,
Sydney, Toronto, Wellington
1990

United Kingdom	Butterworth & Co (Publishers) Ltd, 88 Kingsway, LONDON WC2B 6AB and 4 Hill Street, EDINBURGH EH2 3JZ
Australia	Butterworths Pty Ltd, SYDNEY, MELBOURNE, BRISBANE, ADELAIDE, PERTH, CANBERRA and HOBART
Canada	Butterworth Canada Ltd, TORONTO and VANCOUVER
Ireland	Butterworth (Ireland) Ltd, DUBLIN
Malaysia	Malayan Law Journal Sdn Bhd, KUALA LUMPUR
New Zealand	Butterworths of New Zealand Ltd, WELLINGTON and AUCKLAND
Puerto Rico	Equity de Puerto Rico, Inc, HATO REY
Singapore	Malayan Law Journal Pte Ltd, SINGAPORE
USA	Butterworth Legal Publishers, AUSTIN, Texas; BOSTON, Massachusetts; CLEARWATER, Florida (D & S Publishers); ORFORD, New Hampshire (Equity Publishing); ST PAUL, Minnesota; and SEATTLE, Washington

A CIP Catalogue record for this book is available from the British Library.

ISBN 0 406 51370 8

Typeset by Phoenix Photosetting, Chatham, Kent
Printed and bound in Great Britain by Mackays of Chatham PLC, Chatham, Kent

Preface

Originally published in 1970 the book has now been revised for the fourth time. It has been updated throughout, new material introduced and some omitted where it was becoming less relevant. However the aims remain the same and these may be inferred from the title —

An Introduction —

The text should provide a sound introductory study of accounting by explaining the basic principles and procedures and also developing an understanding of the reasoning behind them and the significance of the information produced. For students who do not plan to go beyond this stage it should give sufficient insight into accounting functions to appreciate their contribution to business affairs and their interaction with other areas of management responsibility. For others it should provide a firm foundation from which to proceed with more advanced studies.

— to Accounting

The text is an introduction to both financial and management accounting. Whilst data collection and recording procedures are included, the main emphasis is on the preparation of accounting reports for external and internal use and an understanding of their usefulness and limitations.

— for Business Studies

The text has proved to be well suited for courses such as Business Studies degrees, BTEC awards (National and Higher National), Accounting Foundation courses and a number of others of similar scope. Whilst the subject is developed mainly within the context of private-sector commercial organizations, the broader view of 'business' is recognized and opportunities are taken to refer to, and use examples from, some public-sector organizations. In particular there is a chapter to illustrate how the form and content of published accounts respond to the organization's form of ownership and its objectives.

In completing the revision we have been helped by constructive comments from several users of the previous edition. We are grateful for these contributions and would welcome others. Tutors will be pleased to know that a key to the additional questions at the end of each chapter is available free of charge from the publishers.

We acknowledge with thanks permission to use extracts from the financial statements of:

British Airways
Royal Insurance (UK) Ltd
British Gas
British Railways Board
Central Independent Television plc
Nottingham Health Authority
British Heart Foundation
Oxfam

F. P. Langley
G. S. Hardern

Contents

Chapter 1

The Scope of Accounting Work

No organization can operate on a sound basis for very long unless proper financial records are kept and financial reports made available to the management. What does the organization own and what does it owe? What should it cost to make the products or provide the services and what is it actually costing? Is the organization profitable and is it keeping to its financial objectives? Questions such as these are fundamental in business life and it is the function of accounting to provide the answers.

As an introductory illustration of the range of accounting activities we start with a simple business venture.

John Grieg had money and ideas but also a job which left him little spare time. His nephew, Will Shaw, on the other hand, was having difficulty finding permanent employment. John had constructed a bird table for his own garden with features which made it unique and attractive. After discussions with his nephew he agreed to finance a business to assemble and sell (by mail order) tables of a similar design. Will was to be the manager and sole employee — even so, the venture would probably provide only part-time work for the present.

The tables in basic form would be supplied by a local joiner. Steel shafts (coated to resemble wood) and accessories such as bird baths and peanut towers were to be obtained from other suppliers. John rented a small unit in a commercial enterprise centre. The tables were to be advertised in national newspapers, inviting bird lovers to send their payments in advance — £20 per table plus £3 for packing and postage.

John agreed to invest £2,000 in the business and to pay Will a monthly wage of £100 with a commission of 15% on the amounts received for tables. He also promised to give the venture a reasonable trial by keeping it going on these terms for at least a year.

You will see that some accounting work must already have taken place before operations began. Whilst the selling price of £20 per table was presumably decided after some research — at least by checking competing products — only by seeing the interrelationship of all the estimated sums involved would it be possible to assess the potential risks and rewards. As a first step John would compare the cost likely to be directly incurred in making and selling the tables with the proposed selling price.

	£	£
Selling price (each)		20
Direct cost (each)		
materials from suppliers	12	
commission to Will	3	
postage and packing (£3, but		
this will be paid by customer)	—	
	—	15
		£5

However, there will also be general expenses not directly related to the production or sale of individual tables to take into account. Each table sold will contribute £5 towards these expenses and to any profit. Assuming estimated sales for the first year of 900 tables, the budgeted result might be as follows:

	£	£
900 tables at £5 each		4,500
Rent of unit for year	1,800	
Advertising	1,000	
Miscellaneous expenses	300	
Wages (£100 × 12)	1,200	
		4,300
Budgeted profit for year		£ 200

In terms of monetary rewards this might just about justify the venture, though much depends on whether the estimates prove realistic, particularly the volume of business. You may like to consider what the expected results would be for sales of 1,200 — or for 600 tables.

Further estimating would have been necessary in deciding how much capital to introduce. Capital provides the resources to keep the business going. For instance, some stocks will have to be bought and held in advance of sales, and furniture or equipment may also be required. These amounts had to be anticipated, and apparently £2,000 was thought to be enough.

Let us now assume that operations have started — on 1 April. John has opened a bank account in the name of the business, Grieg Enterprises, and deposited £2,000. Some basic shelving and fittings have been acquired and stocks of tables and accessories purchased. Advertisements begin to have effect and orders are received, the tables assembled, packed and despatched. So what sort of accounting work should Will do? We assume that he is acting as accountant as well as everything else. Clearly, he must keep records of all transactions such as money received and paid, materials ordered and delivered and tables sold. We can identify three general reasons for needing these and other records.

(1) Figures must be available to calculate and report periodically what profit (or loss) has been made and to set out the latest financial position of the business. We return to this reason soon.

(2) The movements of money, of other assets and of liabilities will need to be controlled on a day-to-day basis. For example, a constant knowledge of the bank balance is essential, especially before writing further cheques, and Will should have his own up-to-date records of sums owing to suppliers (creditors) and of items held in stock. If the trading method ever changes and goods are sold on credit terms it will be important to know how much is outstanding from each debtor, so that action can be taken if any debts become overdue.

(3) Efficient management of a business also involves constantly reviewing activities and deciding what (if any) changes to make to improve results. Information about costs and earnings, both actual (past) and budgeted (future) will be required. A budget was prepared before trading commenced, and one method of review would be to see how actual results compare with the budget periodically, analysing the differences and deciding whether any remedial action seems necessary. There will be an opportunity to do this for Grieg Enterprises later in the book. John may consider such matters as sources of supply, the specification of components, the selling price, or possibly whether to expand or diversify the business. Records of past transactions in conjunction with estimates of the effect of alternative or supplementary actions will provide a basis for such decisions and plans.

In summary, then, accounting work can be thought of as having three main types of function:

(1) Preparing periodic (usually annual) reports of performance and position;
(2) Control of assets and liabilities (money, debts and tangible items);
(3) Contributing to management decision making by the provision and use of relevant financial information.

The first two are generally referred to as Financial Accounting and the third as Management Accounting, though the distinctions are often blurred.

A good starting point for studying accounting is the annual summary of financial position and calculation of profit, and the next two chapters explain how this is done, continuing with the affairs of Grieg Enterprises for illustration. From Chapter 4 the day-to-day record keeping and control aspects are linked with a further development of the theory and practice of profit and position reporting, management accounting principles and techniques being considered in Chapters 11 to 15.

Both financial and management accounting are essential activities in most organizations, whether they be small 'sole-trader' businesses such as Grieg Enterprises, partnerships, small or large limited companies, local or national authorities, charitable bodies or any other types you can think of. The constitution and objectives vary widely, and consequently the particular nature of the accounting contribution will also differ. In some organizations (for instance, social services and charities) profit or loss considerations do not apply: they are mainly concerned to keep planned expenditure and available income more or less in balance. How accounting functions and reports respond to the objectives of different types of organization is discussed in Chapters 9 and 18.

Before completing the introduction let us consider why Grieg Enterprises needs to prepare periodic statements of profitability and financial position. Will Shaw is managing a business owned by John Grieg and must be expected to report to him so that John can judge whether the affairs are being satisfactorily managed. For most organizations there is a legal obligation to prepare annual reports and to have them audited so that all of those with an interest can be assured that they are adequately informed. Whilst there is no such law governing the accounts of sole traders there is another type of legal requirement that cannot be avoided — to complete tax returns, so accounts must be drawn up as a basis for annual assessment. John will also need to decide whether to withdraw any of the profits, and he can only do this when he knows what they amount to. Again, if the bank was to be approached for a loan to provide additional capital the latest annual accounts would be an essential part of the evidence to support the application. With larger and more complex organizations a variety of people or groups make decisions on the basis of accounting information, and it must therefore be available to them in an appropriate form.

Chapter 2
Balance Sheets

2.1 Two types of financial statement

In the introductory chapter we referred to two financial statements produced for periodic reporting purposes, one showing the calculation of profit or loss and the other the financial position at the end of the period. The figures for both of these statements are drawn primarily from records of transactions taking place during the period. The PROFIT OR LOSS calculation sets the amount earned from the business activities *throughout the whole period* against the costs incurred in carrying out those activities, whilst the position statement, or BALANCE SHEET, summarizes the financial situation *at the end of the period* — a 'snapshot' taken at one point of time.

As a simple example of this relationship let us assume that I start a business with £800 in the bank representing my opening capital. In the first trading period the only transactions are that I buy some army surplus stores for £600 and later sell half of them for £500. The profit calculation for the period would show earnings of £500 less the cost of stock sold £300, leaving a profit of £200. At the end of the period the position is that the business has two assets, money in the bank of £700 (£800 − 600 + 500) and stock, which we assume is still saleable, of £300. The total of £1,000 assets is represented by my interest in the business, my capital, which has been increased from the original £800 by the profit of £200. It is the function of the balance sheet to summarize that closing position.

We can now return to Grieg Enterprises for a fuller illustration. First, we summarize all the transactions for the year's trading, then set out the profit calculation. The details of this are discussed in the next chapter, and we ask you to accept it as given for the time being so that we can concentrate here on the balance sheet.

GRIEG ENTERPRISES
Summary of the Transactions for the First Year

	£
Tables, shafts and accessories were bought at a total cost of	10,520
Most of this (£10,150) had been paid, but there were unpaid invoices outstanding at the year end of	370
All the items purchased had not been used — some were still in stock at the year end. At cost price these totalled	1,200

	£
820 tables were sold at £20 each and the cash received was	16,400

As well as the cheques sent to suppliers other payments
during the year were:

	£
Wages (12 × £100)	1,200
Commission (15% of £16,400)	2,460
Rent of premises	1,800
Advertising (in addition to the £670 paid, a further £170 was owed at the year end)	670
Other expenses	450
Shelving and equipment	420

(assume that payments for postage and packing were equalled by the
£3 per table received from customers)

GRIEG ENTERPRISES
Calculation of Profit for the First Year

		£
Sales		16,400
Cost price of goods sold (purchases £10,520 less items left in stock £1,200)		9,320
		7,080
Operating expenses for the year:		
Wages	1,200	
Commission	2,460	
Rent	1,800	
Advertising (£670 + £170)	840	
Other expenses	450	
		6,750
Profit for the year		£ 330

Had a statement of financial position been drawn up on the day the venture started it
would have shown:

GRIEG ENTERPRISES
Balance Sheet 1 April 19X1

	£
ASSETS	
Cash in bank	2,000
CAPITAL (contributed by John Grieg)	2,000

The business had one asset, money in the Grieg Enterprises bank account, and this
equalled the amount contributed as capital by John Grieg. One year later the position
has changed as a result of the various transactions and the statement now shows:

GRIEG ENTERPRISES
Balance Sheet 31 March 19X2

	£	£
ASSETS		
Shelving and equipment		420
Stock of materials		1,200
Cash in bank		1,250
		2,870
Less		
LIABILITIES		
Creditors for tables, etc.	370	
Owing for advertising	170	
		540
Capital (original £2,000 + profit £330)		2,330

Q.2a Check the amount of cash in the bank by adding to the opening balance the amount received and deducting the payments made during the year.

2.2 Defining the balance sheet

The balance sheet is a statement of the financial position of a business (or any other type of organization) at a particular point of time. Each element of the definition is important and must be looked at in detail.

The balance sheet is a statement . . .

This means that its purpose is to communicate information in summarized form so that the position will be intelligible to the intended reader. The statement is compiled by extracting information from records kept by the business. Provided that it communicates information of the right quality and detail the precise layout is not of paramount importance, though most balance sheets appear either in the vertical form as used above or in two-sided form, thus:

GRIEG ENTERPRISES
Balance Sheet 31 March 19X2

CAPITAL	£	ASSETS	£
(net worth	2,330	Equipment	420
of proprietor)		Stock	1,200
LIABILITIES		Cash at bank	1,250
Creditors (owing			
to other people)	540		
	£2,870		£2,870

Just as we drive on the left-hand side of the road in the UK, whilst the right-hand side is used in most other countries, so we have traditionally shown assets on the right of a two-sided balance sheet whereas most countries do it the other way round. This is of no consequence. In any case the vertical form is probably to be preferred as it highlights the important figure, £2,330, and in most of the examples in the book we shall use the vertical form.

... of the financial position ...

The basis on which the items in the balance sheet are valued will be dealt with later, but it should be noted here that since we are using money as the unit of measurement, only those aspects of the business which can be given a monetary value are included. There are other aspects which could well influence the status and prospects of the business but these are not shown in the balance sheet merely because they cannot readily be measured in monetary terms. For instance, the skill and loyalty of employees may be a very valuable asset in one sense, but could not very well appear in the balance sheet.

... of a business ...

The balance sheet shows the position of Grieg Enterprises rather than of John Grieg himself. As a person he may have other assets besides his investment in the business. In the two-sided balance sheet you will notice that the proprietor's interest in the business (his capital) appears on the same side as the liabilities. The capital is not itself a liability in the sense that it is an amount owing that must soon be paid, but like the other liabilities it represents a claim on the assets. Of the total of £2,870 assets, the creditors can claim £540, and the balance is attributable to John Grieg. If it was decided to discontinue the business the actual amount repayable to John would depend on what the assets could be sold for — he would get what remained after paying the creditors.

... at a particular point in time

In any balance sheet the date must be included as part of the heading, because the position applies at that point in time only. Immediately afterwards there will be new transactions affecting some of the assets or liabilities. The elements are constantly changing and the balance sheet only provides a summary of how they stood at a given date. If in May you look at a balance sheet dated 31 March you are examining the position retrospectively even though it may not have changed very much in the intervening weeks.

Q.2b Assuming that the only transactions affecting Grieg Enterprises during April are:

the amount owing for the advertisement is paid;
£300 worth of stock is bought on credit terms;

draw up a new balance sheet to show the position at the end of April. Use the balance sheet at 31 March as a starting point.

2.3 The accounting period

Whilst it is possible to extract a balance sheet at any date or moment in the life of a business, in practice it is only done in a formal way at the end of an 'accounting period'. This does not imply that information about the position of a business is available only

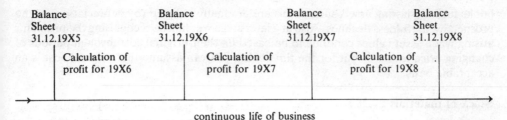

| Balance Sheet 31.12.19X5 | Calculation of profit for 19X6 | Balance Sheet 31.12.19X6 | Calculation of profit for 19X7 | Balance Sheet 31.12.19X7 | Calculation of profit for 19X8 | Balance Sheet 31.12.19X8 |

continuous life of business

Fig. 1

on such occasions. Records are kept on a continuous basis and can be inspected by the management as required, but the profit calculation is only summarized formally for an accounting period and the position stated again as a balance sheet at the end of it (see *Fig. 1*).

The accounting period is normally one year, which is both a convenient and a reasonable interval of time for reporting purposes. Most businesses do, of course, summarize their performance and position at more frequent intervals, but the formal reporting is still done annually.

The accounting year can end on any chosen date. For some businesses there is a natural business year, when the accounting period is chosen to cover the annual cycle of activity, and end at the slack time. For instance, a company selling fuel for heating purposes would probably have a 30 June or 31 July year end, and 31 January (after the 'sales') might be chosen by a department store.

2.4 Assets

Cash in hand or at the bank is an obvious asset, and there can be no argument about its valuation. We have only to count it, or get the bank to notify us how much is in our account, though this information should be available from the records we keep in any case. But what other items qualify for inclusion as assets, and how are they to be valued? An asset is some property or right acquired by the business as a result of a transaction, and which can either be turned into cash or otherwise used for the future benefit of the business. Buildings, machinery, tools, vehicles, stocks of goods and materials are all assets, if they have been taken over for use by the business and the purchase price has already been paid or there is an outstanding obligation to pay it. Buildings rented by the business or items of equipment hired do not come within the definition. The firm pays periodically for their use, but there is no contract to acquire the ownership of them and they still belong to someone else.

The method of valuation of assets is an important topic, referred to frequently, but as a starting point, let us look at how the assets of Grieg Enterprises have been valued at 31 March.

Equipment

This is an asset which Grieg hopes will last for a considerable time. The basis for entry in the balance sheet is its cost. To use the cost is a convenient way of putting a value on the future usefulness of the asset, though we shall see later that the values recorded in the books for long-lasting assets such as this are gradually reduced (by depreciation) as the prospective usefulness declines. Also at a later stage we shall be recognising the problems arising when asset values continue to be based on their original cost through periods of changing price levels — but for the time being you can assume that original cost is an acceptable basis.

Stock of materials £1,200

These are materials already purchased but still in stock at 31 March. The money paid for them has not been wasted because it is expected that they can be converted into saleable items. Again the basis of valuation is cost.

Bank £1,250

This is the amount which should be in the bank. John Grieg will be able to verify the balance from his bank statement.

To introduce another type of asset let us assume that four of the bird tables had been sold in March on credit terms — that is, despatched to customers who will pay for them at a later date — and the debts were still outstanding at the year end. There would be £80 (4 × £20) less in the bank but Debtors £80 would appear as an asset in the Balance Sheet. The business is justified in including this as an asset so long as it is expected to be received. When it is eventually paid the business will be no better or worse off — the debts will no longer appear as an asset but there will be £80 more in the bank.

2.5   Classification of assets

Assets are classified into two main categories, fixed assets and current assets. By fixed assets we mean those which have been acquired for continuing use by the business and which are likely to be employed for several accounting periods. Examples of fixed assets are buildings, equipment and vehicles. Current assets are those expected to be turned into cash or consumed in the course of trading operations in the short term. They include the stock of materials or goods, amounts owing from debtors and the cash and bank balances. In the main, current assets are those which circulate as part of the natural cycle of activity (see *Fig. 2*).

Fixed assets, on the other hand, are bought to facilitate such activity by providing the premises and equipment. They are expected to last over several accounting periods. In the balance sheet, fixed assets are shown in descending order of permanence (land and buildings would usually appear first), the current assets in descending order of liquidity (cash would usually appear last).

The importance of the distinction will be more apparent when we consider some aspects of interpretation of balance sheets, and sources of capital. Limited companies are legally obliged to distinguish between fixed and current assets in their balance sheets.

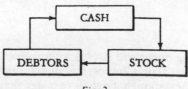

Fig. 2

See how this works with the aid of a simple example. Though balance sheets are usually prepared formally at the end of accounting periods we can use them to illustrate the changing position as new transactions occur. This time it is Roger Green starting in business.

(i) Green opened a business bank account and paid in £1,000 as his capital:

	£		£
Capital	1,000	Cash in bank	1,000

(ii) Equipment was purchased for £350 and paid for by cheque:

	£		£
Capital	1,000	Fixed asset	
		Equipment	350
		Current asset	
		Cash in bank	650
	1,000		1,000

(iii) Stock was purchased on credit terms for £400:

	£		£
Capital	1,000	Fixed asset	
Current liability		Equipment	350
Creditors	400	Current assets	
		Stock	400
		Cash in bank	650
	1,400		1,400

(iv) Green paid £250 of the amount owing to the creditor:

	£		£
Capital	1,000	Fixed asset	
Current liability		Equipment	350
Creditors	150	Current assets	
		Stock	400
		Cash in bank	400
	1,150		1,150

At this stage remember that in the Grieg Enterprises example the effect of making a profit of £330 was to increase the net assets (assets – liabilities) and therefore also increase the proprietor's interest (capital) by the same amount. So how would the position of Roger Green's business be affected if half of the stock was now sold on credit terms for £280? First, the stock reduces by £200, and there is now a new asset, Debtors, worth £280. The net assets are thus increased by £80, which will be reflected in the proprietor's interest.

	£		£
(v) Capital	1,080	Fixed asset	
Current liability		Equipment	350
Creditors	150	Current assets	
		Stock	200
		Debtors	280
		Cash in bank	400
	1,230		1,230

Q.2d Now restate the position after stages (vi) and (vii).
(vi) Stock originally costing £100 is sold for cash £145 and on the same day a further payment of £50 is sent to the creditor.
(vii) A debtor sends a cheque for £120 and on the same day we pay £30 wages to the part-time assistant.

If you completed the last stages correctly you should be showing capital of £1,095 (£1,000 + 80 + 45 − 30). Clearly, there would be no question of drawing up a daily balance sheet — it would be a tedious and unnecessary business — but this illustrates the effect on the assets, liabilities and capital. For the last payment of £30 there was no corresponding asset which could be recognized and it did not reduce an existing liability, so the amount was an expense to set against the profit. The profit for this short period could be summarized as

	£
Sale of goods	425
Cost of goods sold	300
	125
Wages	30
Profit (= increase in capital)	95

If the proprietor decided to withdraw some of the profit for his own personal use (let us say £60) his claim on the business assets is reduced by a corresponding amount. The balance sheet at this point would be as follows:

	£		£
Capital	1,035	Fixed asset	
(£1,000 + £95 − £60)		Equipment	350
Current liability		Current assets	
Creditors	100	Stock	100
		Debtors	160
		Cash in bank	525
	1,135		1,135

Before completing this chapter consider again what the figures in these balance sheets mean. The LIABILITIES are amounts owing to other people and represent claims on some of the assets. The ASSETS are physical items (such as equipment or stock), debts owing to the business or actual cash held. The physical items have at this stage been valued at their original cost but there will be more to say about this later. The CAPITAL is the residual claim on the assets by the proprietor. As a profit is made so the capital increases, but it is reduced if the proprietor takes money (or other assets) out of the business or if the business makes a loss.

Q.2e   On the basis of what we have done so far, would it be true to say that the amount of capital indicates what the business is worth?

2.8   Additional questions

[1]

    (a) What is the purpose of a balance sheet?

    (b) Suggest an alternative name for a balance sheet.

    (c) Why is it essential to include a date in the balance sheet heading?

[2]
Prepare a balance sheet in vertical form from the following information about W. T. Bray's business at 30 September.

	£
Cash in hand	50
Bank overdraft	190
Capital — W. T. Bray	29,000
Vehicle	6,340
Equipment	19,700
Creditors	830
Debtors	1,200
Stock in hand	2,730

[3]
Prepare a balance sheet in two-sided form from the following information about V. Carter's business at 30 April. The amount of the bank balance is missing so you will need to calculate and include it.

	£
Vehicles	12,700
Trade creditors	1,370
Stock of goods	3,120
Owing to T. H. Carter for a loan to the business	1,200
Debtors	480
Office equipment	5,400
V. Carter's capital	19,330

[4]

Prepare a balance sheet in vertical form from the following information about G. Wright's business at 31 May. The amount of Wright's capital is missing so you will need to calculate and include it.

	£
Vehicle	6,000
Trade creditors	3,400
Stock of goods and materials	4,620
Amount owing for telephone account	60
Debtors	900
Bank balance	740
Furniture and equipment	1,200

On the basis of the balance sheet figures, what do you think is the main problem facing the business?

[5]

Redraft the following balance sheet to correct any mistakes, and also to improve its form:

T. Paterson: Balance Sheet for the year ended 31 March

	£		£
Debtors	170	Cash (in cash box)	30
Bank overdraft	270	Furniture and fittings	770
Capital	3,000	Creditors	270
		Stock of goods and materials	1,620
		Tools and equipment	950
	3,440		3,440

[6]

Define in your own words what you understand by a business asset. Do you think that each of the following would be included as assets in the balance sheet of T. Thorpe's business at 31 March. Explain your answer in each case.

(a) New office equipment purchased and received during March but not paid for until May.
(b) New fur coat purchased by T. Thorpe for his wife out of the business bank account.
(c) A debt to the business from S. Short which has been outstanding for a long time, and is unlikely to be paid.

[7]

Define in your own words what you understand by a business liability. Do you think that each of the following would be included as liabilities in the balance sheet of T. Thorpe's business at 31 March? Explain your answer in each case.

(a) Amount owing for office equipment purchased and received in March.

(b) Amount payable under a contract signed by Thorpe for the erection of a new garage at the business premises. The work has not yet started.
(c) Amount owing for rates for Thorpe's house.

[8]
Indicate whether each of the following is a Fixed Asset, or a Current Asset, or a Current Liability, in the books of a garage proprietor.

New vehicle for sale
Breakdown truck
Amount owing to suppliers of petrol and oil
Stock of petrol in tanks
Electronic engine tuner
Amount owing by customer for repairs
Cash register
Spares in service bay stores
Bank overdraft

[9]
The following is the balance sheet of Pam Shaw, a retailer:

P. Shaw's Business Balance Sheet at 31 March

	£		£
CAPITAL	12,020	FIXED ASSETS	
LIABILITIES		Vehicle	8,420
Creditors	200	Shop fittings	3,210
		CURRENT ASSETS	
		Stock of goods	340
		Debtors	70
		Bank balance	180
	£12,220		£12,220

(a) Why is Pam Shaw's capital shown on the same side as the liabilities?
(b) What do you understand by the term 'Debtors'?
(c) What do you understand by the term 'Creditors'?
(d) Do you think that the shop premises are owned by the business?
(e) If at the beginning of this period Shaw's capital was £10,000 and she had withdrawn £7,000 during the period, what was the profit?

[10]
Calculate the missing figure for each of the following situations:
(a) Liabilities £560; Assets £4,060; Capital?
(b) Capital £3,540; Liabilities £960; Assets?
(c) Fixed assets £4,800; Current assets £2,600; Current liabilities £1,800; Capital?
(d) Capital £16,000; Current assets £9,000; Current liabilities £5,000; Fixed assets?
(e) Capital £10,000; Fixed assets £7,000; Working capital?

[11]

At 1 March the balance sheet of G. R. Marsh showed the following position:

	£		£
Capital	3,200	Equipment	840
		Stock	1,930
		Bank balance	430
	3,200		3,200

During March the following transactions took place:

Stock	£
More stock was bought	£300
Stock that originally cost £600 was sold for	920
Expenses were paid	80
More equipment was bought	100

(In each case the receipts or payments were made immediately by cheque.)

(a) Calculate the new bank balance at 31 March.
(b) Calculate the profit for the period.
(c) Set out the new balance sheet at 31 March.

[12]

In respect of each of the following statements, indicate which of the alternative wordings shown in brackets is the correct one.

(a) The difference between total assets and total liabilities is the (profit/capital).
(b) The people to whom the business owes money are its (debtors/creditors).
(c) Capital will be increased if the business makes a (profit/loss).
(d) A butcher's delivery van is one of his (fixed/current) assets.
(e) If a business hires machinery, the value of that machinery (will/will not) be shown in the balance sheet.
(f) If the business has any liabilities, the proprietor's capital must be (less/more) than the total assets.
(g) If £300 is spent on new equipment, the value of total assets (will/will not) change.
(h) By looking at a balance sheet of a business, we can tell its (financial position/profitability).

[13]

The following is the balance sheet of R. Taylor, a fruit and vegetable wholesale merchant:

R. TAYLOR'S BUSINESS
Balance Sheet at 31 March

FIXED ASSETS	£
Leasehold premises	62,800
Vehicles	11,340
Miscellaneous equipment	1,130
	75,270

CURRENT ASSETS

Stock in hand	3,740	
Debtors	3,030	
	6,770	

Less

CURRENT LIABILITIES

Creditors	2,840	
Bank overdraft	130	
	2,970	3,800
		£79,070

CAPITAL — R. TAYLOR

(a) Would it necessarily be true to say that Taylor as a person is worth £79,070 on 31 March? Explain.

(b) If, after drafting the balance sheet, Taylor discovered that the stock had been overvalued by £100, and that a debt owing from a customer for £120 had been omitted, what would the corrected figure for capital be?

(c) Taylor tells you that his main asset is the loyalty and skill of his manager and other employees. Why does this not appear in the balance sheet?

(d) Do you think that because there is a bank overdraft, the business is in a difficult position?

[14]

Balance sheets are usually formally prepared at the end of the accounting period of a business. However, it is possible to represent the position of a business at any point in time by a balance sheet. The following balance sheets show the position of G. Prior's business after each of the first few transactions have taken place.

After each balance sheet, describe the latest transaction. (The first one has been given as an example.)

		£		£
(a)	Capital	500	Cash	500

(Prior has started the business by bringing in £500 cash as capital.)

		£		£
(b)	Capital	500	Equipment	200
			Cash	300
		500		500

		£		£
(c)	Capital	500	Equipment	200
			Stock	100
			Cash	200
		500		500

		£		£
(d)	Capital	500	Equipment	200
	Creditors	80	Stock	180
			Cash	200
		580		580

		£		£
(e)	Capital	500	Equipment	200
	Creditors	20	Stock	180
			Cash	140
		520		520

		£		£
(f)	Capital	560	Equipment	200
	Creditors	20	Stock	80
			Debtors	160
			Cash	140
		580		580

[15]
You are thinking of buying a fruiterer's business and someone has told you that you must have sufficient working capital. Explain and illustrate what you understand by this expression. What could be the danger of having insufficient working capital?

Chapter 3

Measurement of Profit

3.1 A definition of profit

We now return to the calculation of profit for Grieg Enterprises. The first year's transactions were given in Chapter 2 and the profit calculated as follows:

	£	£
Sales		16,400
Cost price of goods sold		9,320
		7,080
Wages	1,200	
Commission	2,460	
Rent	1,800	
Advertising	840	
Other expenses	450	
		6,750
Profit		£ 330

The sales figure is the amount earned by the business during the year, sometimes referred to as the Revenue. In many businesses revenue is just the total value of goods sold, but in others it could include charges for work done or any other form of earnings. From this amount has been deducted the value of materials or services used up in the same period in order to achieve those earnings. For several transactions in this introductory example 'resources used up' happened to be the same amount as the cash paid during the year — this applied to wages, commission, rent and other expenses. However, for advertising, whilst £670 was paid in cash, an additional £170 of advertising services had been provided within the year and a liability for this sum incurred, so the total expense for advertising relevant to the year's trading was £840. Conversely, whilst £420 was spent on equipment, the items purchased would probably be expected to last for several years to come and were not therefore 'used up' in the course of the year's operations (for the time being, we are ignoring the fact that fixed assets depreciate over time). The cost of the equipment does not therefore appear in the profit calculation but remains as an asset at the year end.

What about the tables and accessories purchased? The amount for inclusion in the

21

calculation is the cost price of the items sold during the year. The total bought and received into stock was £10,520, but £1,200 of this was still an asset at 31 March and would form part of the profit calculation next year, assuming those items were sold. The fact that Grieg Enterprises still owes £370 to suppliers at 31 March does not affect the cost of goods sold — these items have been received as part of the total purchases and there is an obligation to pay for them, represented by the liability in the balance sheet.

All the figures deducted from the sales have been referred to as materials or services used up in the same period. It is convenient to introduce the term Expense to denote these amounts collectively. So we can express the calculation as:

REVENUE − EXPENSE = PROFIT
(total   (resources
earnings)   consumed)
(£16,400)   (£16,070)   (£330)

Q.3a   To check whether you can distinguish between these different terms try the following. During a given period a business sells some goods for cash, £800, and others on credit terms, £2,000. The goods sold had previously been included in the stock at a value of £1,900. During the same period wages and salaries of £400 were paid out of cash, and more stock was purchased for cash, £600. £1,000 cash was received from the debtors. Assuming nothing else happened, what is the total REVENUE, the total EXPENSE and the PROFIT for the period? Explain why two of the figures were not included in your calculation of revenue or expense. What were the total RECEIPTS and the total PAYMENTS?

The term Cost also needs a brief explanation. It is used to denote the amount of money paid or liabilities incurred in order to acquire some benefit for the business. So the amount of wages paid, or goods bought for cash or on credit terms, or equipment bought for cash or on credit terms are all examples of cost. Notice the relationship of Cost, Expense and Assets. The cost of goods purchased during the year was £10,520, £9,320 of which became an expense of the year and the remaining £1,200 was an asset at 31 March — an 'unexpired cost'. The cost of equipment £420 has not so far been expensed at all and remains as an asset, though we shall soon see that a proportion of the cost of fixed assets such as this usually represents a benefit to the period under review and has to be treated as an expense (depreciation), with the residual balance appearing in the balance sheet as an asset. The cost of wages, £1,200, was totally an expense of the year having no asset value at the end. Any cost incurred in acquiring goods or services will thus be treated as either an expense or an asset according to whether its value is used up during the period concerned or whether it remains at the end of the period.

The problem of identifying the revenues and expenses appropriate to particular accounting periods will be developed later but, whilst the Grieg Enterprises profit calculation is still fresh, let us next consider its form.

3.2   Form of profit calculation

You will have noticed that the calculation was made in two stages, first, deducting the cost of goods sold from the sales and then deducting all the other expenses. The difference between selling price and cost price (£7,080 in aggregate in this example) is referred to as GROSS PROFIT, whilst the final amount of £330 is the NET PROFIT. Those in business to buy and sell goods have to decide what 'mark-up' to add to cost prices when fixing selling prices, and the gross profit for a period represents the aggregate of these decisions for goods sold during that period. It is clearly a critical relationship for retailers or wholesalers, as selling prices have to be competitive enough to induce sales whilst leaving sufficient margin to cover all the other expenses and provide an acceptable profit. This also applies to manufacturers, but for them the costs of converting raw materials into finished products are part of the total cost of goods sold, so the gross profit results from both manufacturing and selling activities and the interrelationship of the elements is more complex than for a retailer.

Let us use another example to illustrate the distinction between gross and net profit. J. Green, a retailer, started an accounting period with goods in stock valued at £1,800 (their original cost) and during the period purchased more items for £36,400. The closing stock was £2,600. Sales for the period totalled £53,400 and the only two expenses were the wages of the shop assistant, £8,000, and the rent and rates of £5,000. The profit calculation would be as follows:

	£	£
Sales		53,400
Cost of goods sold		
Opening stock	1,800	
Purchases	36,400	
	38,200	
less Closing stock	2,600	
		35,600
Gross profit		17,800
Wages	8,000	
Rent and rates	5,000	
		13,000
Net profit		£4,800

In this case the gross profit margin is $33\frac{1}{3}\%$ of the sales value — or can be expressed as 50% mark-up on cost. Notice that the first part of the calculation compares figures which vary in more or less direct relationship to each other. If more goods are sold the cost of sales will rise proportionately (assuming that the selling price per unit and the cost price per unit each remain constant), whereas the two items of expense would presumably stay the same in this example, irrespective of the volume of the business.

Q.3b   If for J. Green's business the sales volume could be increased by 10% would you expect the net profit to increase by 10%, by more than 10% or less than 10%? First, think what you would expect to happen, then make the calculation.

How various types of expense respond to changes in the level of activity cannot usually be classified as easily as in this case (i.e. either varying directly with sales or remaining fixed) — in fact, even the Grieg Enterprises expense items had some different characteristics, and you might like to consider how each would respond to an increase or decrease in the number of tables sold. These relationships are a very important consideration in many management decisions, and we shall be dealing with them at some length later in the book.

Another aspect of the format is that you will usually see the calculation headed

'Profit and Loss Account for the year ended ...' In the next chapter we introduce ledger accounts — a system for showing cumulatively how each type of expense, revenue, asset and liability is affected by the business transactions. The fact that the summary of the profit calculation is styled 'account' merely indicates that the information in it is derived by transferring totals from other detailed accounts kept throughout the year. Sometimes you will find that for a retailer or wholesaler the first part, up to the gross profit stage, is called the Trading Account, the gross profit then being carried forward into the Profit and Loss Account. The principles remain the same, though different variations on the format may be used.

3.3   Profit and the proprietor's interest

Remember that the proprietor has invested money in the business and the Capital figure in the balance sheet represents the amount of the proprietor's claim on the assets at that date. We have already seen that he would be unlikely to receive back exactly this sum if the business closed down because the assets would be sold and the other liabilities paid off first, the proprietor then being entitled to what remained — so the claim is a residual one. However, the Capital balance does represent the amount of his interest on the basis of the present valuation of assets and liabilities. If a profit is made during a trading period the net worth of the business (assets — liabilities) increases and so does the proprietor's interest. If he withdraws part of the profits the claim is correspondingly reduced. Notice that such 'drawings' are not an expense to be included in the calculation of profit but rather an appropriation of that profit. In the case of a limited company the proprietors are the shareholders and the appropriation of profits is in the form of dividends — we shall be dealing with companies in Chapter 9.

If John Grieg had withdrawn £300 of the £330 profit, the closing balance sheet would show his capital as £2,030 and the bank balance as £950.

Any additional capital introduced by the proprietor during the year would, of course, also increase the Capital account. Even if no proper records were kept it would be possible to arrive at a profit figure by reference to the assets and liabilities at the beginning and end of the period. For example:

		£
	Net worth (assets — liabilities) of business X at 1 Jan.	25,000
	Net worth (assets — liabilities) of business X at 31 Dec.	32,000
	Drawings during the year	8,000
	Profit	15,000
Q.3c	Net worth (assets — liabilities) of business Y at 1 Jan.	70,000
	Net worth (assets — liabilities) of business Y at 31 Dec.	92,000
	Extra capital introduced during the year	20,000
	Drawings during the year	9,000
	Profit	?

Management and other interested parties do, of course, need information about the constituent elements of profit and not just its total amount. This relationship between profit and change in net worth does, however, demonstrate that measurement of profit on a transaction basis (i.e. deducting the expired portion of costs incurred from the revenue earned) is reflected in the valuation of the assets which include, apart from monetary items such as cash, the unexpired portion of costs incurred. For instance, if Grieg Enterprises had valued the closing stock at £1,400 instead of £1,200 the profit would have been £200 greater and so would the assets in the balance sheet. A higher proportion of the cost of materials purchased would have been regarded as unexpired.

3.4 Accounting for revenue earned

In many business situations it is not difficult to compute the amount of revenue earned within an accounting period. It is the total of goods delivered and charged to customers — or services performed and charged for — in that period. The usual critical events that allow revenue to be recognized (brought into account) are that either cash is received in exchange for goods or services or that a legal obligation to pay for them is established by means of an invoice. At this point an item sold ceases to be an asset and its cost becomes an expense to be set against the revenue earned. In some businesses there are problem areas for revenue recognition because of different trading arrangements — for instance, when goods are sold on hire-purchase terms or in connection with long-term contracts lasting over more than one accounting period. However, for the time being our illustrations will continue to deal with more straightforward situations.

Q.3d During its first accounting period a business sells goods to the value of £32,600 on credit terms. £30,400 of this is received during the period, £120 will have to be written off as a bad debt, and the rest is expected to be received in the next period. The business also received £300 cash during the period as deposits for goods which will not be delivered until the next period. Goods purchased during the period cost £19,800, of which £2,000 was still in stock at the end of the period. Wages and office expenses have been paid, totalling £9,600. What is the revenue for the period and how much profit was made? What balances will appear in the balance sheet at the end of the first period? (Ignore the cash balance.)

3.5 Expense chargeable against revenue

Whilst the amount of revenue earned in a period may be simply the total of all the sales invoices and cash sales, deciding what resources have been used up to achieve those earnings is often more difficult. Some costs will be wholly an expense of the period in which they were incurred but others may need allocating over two or more accounting periods, according to when the benefit is deemed to accrue. A few examples may help to explain this. For most of them we shall be developing the nature of the problem and the appropriate accounting treatment more fully later.

(a) Wages and salaries paid to administrative or sales staff during the year would be regarded wholly as an expense of that year — there is no problem here.
(b) Stock purchased by a retailer is held as an asset until sold, then becoming an expense. In principle this is simple enough, but it may be difficult to relate specific items sold to the corresponding purchases and there is also the problem of goods held in stock which are unlikely to be sold for as much as they originally cost.
(c) Materials purchased by a manufacturer are treated as an asset until the product in which they are incorporated is sold. Related production wages and some overheads also form part of the cost of the product, so the problem of identifying

expired and unexpired costs, reflected in the valuation of work in progress or finished goods, can be a considerable one.

(d) A fixed asset is usually expected to be of service for several years. The process of allocating its cost to the periods which benefit from its use is known as depreciation. Someone has to judge what proportion to charge as an expense in each year whilst the asset is still in service.

(e) A substantial advertising campaign might have beneficial effects beyond the year in which the costs are incurred, so in theory some part of the cost should be treated as an asset at the year end and matched against next year's revenue — but can the business be sure of future enhanced sales as a direct result, and what proportion of the cost should be carried forward?

(f) Some other costs are clearly related to time periods so, whilst an apportionment may be necessary, there is an objective basis for making it. For example, AB's accounting year ends on 31 December. A new insurance policy is taken out on 1 October 19X5, the annual premium of £600 being paid in advance. The cost in 19X5 is £600, but only £150 of this is chargeable as an expense in that year, the balance being shown in the balance sheet as an asset — a prepayment. In 19X6 this balance of £450 ceases to be an asset and becomes an expense because insurance cover is provided to 30 September 19X6. If the policy is renewed the same apportionment will again be necessary.

Q.3e   AB agrees to rent some equipment from 1 April 19X5 and £800 is to be paid annually in arrears. When is this chargeable as an expense? What entry will be included in the 31 December 19X5 balance sheet?

At this stage our purpose has been to illustrate the implications of determining profit by matching revenue with related expense, and you should be gaining the impression that it often depends upon judgement as to how costs are treated. We shall be developing this point later.

Sometimes where a cost should in theory be apportioned as an expense over two or more accounting periods, the effort of doing so might not be justified because of the small amount involved. The accountant would then charge it as an expense of the period in which the cost was incurred rather than carrying a proportion forward. This is one of the conventions accountants usually adopt — that matters of relative insignificance are dealt with in the most straightforward manner rather than having of necessity to conform to strict accounting rules. The convention may be referred to as *Materiality*. For instance, if XY Ltd bought £10 worth of stationery in February, and had not completely used it by the 31 March year end, the accountant would not attempt to value the amount left and treat it as an asset at 31 March, and then as an expense of the following year. Taking the two years together it would not make any difference whether part was carried forward or not, and the small amount involved does not warrant going through the necessary procedure. Whether apportionment is justified is a matter of judgement and depends on the degree to which the profits and position are affected. What might be very material in one business could be very insignificant for another.

3.6   Robin Black

A further example can now be used to illustrate some of the points made so far. To test your understanding, first mask the answer and attempt it yourself.

On 1 January 19X7 Robin Black starts business as a coal merchant, and opens a business bank account with £18,000. The following is a summary of his transactions for 19X7:

Bought lorry for £10,000 in January. (Ignore depreciation at this stage.)

Coal purchased and received during the year, £82,000. Black had paid invoices for £79,800, and still owed his suppliers £2,200 at 31 December 19X7.

Stock of coal in the yard at 31 December 19X7 he estimated to be worth £2,400.

Selling price of coal delivered and charged to customers during the year, £119,000. Of this, £112,000 had been received in cash. £400 was irrecoverable (a bad debt) and it was expected that the balance would be paid in full.

Fuel and oil, maintenance and taxation for the lorry cost £3,100 for the year, all of which had been paid.

Wages of assistant, earned and paid during the year, £7,800.

Rent of yard — £1,200 was paid in January, covering the period to 30 June, and a further £2,400 paid in July covered one year's rent.

Other expenses all relating to the year, and paid for during the year, £1,700 and a further £200 expense was incurred but not yet paid for.

During the year Black withdrew from the business bank account for his own personal use £20,000, in anticipation of profit.

From this information draw up a summary of changes in the bank balance, prepare a Profit and Loss account for the year, and a Balance Sheet at 31 December 19X7. Assume all money received was paid into the bank, and all payments made by cheque.

Solution

Changes in Bank Balance

	£	£
PAID INTO BANK		
Capital		18,000
Proceeds of sales		112,000
		130,000
CHEQUES DRAWN		
Lorry	10,000	
Coal	79,800	
Fuel, oil, etc.	3,100	
Wages	7,800	
Rent	3,600	
Other expenses	1,700	
Black's personal drawings	20,000	126,000
BALANCE AT 31 DECEMBER 19X7		£4,000

Profit and Loss Account for year to 31 December 19X7

	£	£
Sales of coal		119,000
Cost of coal sold		
Purchases	82,000	
Less stock at 31.12.X7	2,400	79,600
Gross profit		39,400
Wages	7,800	
Lorry expenses	3,100	
Rent	2,400	
Other expenses	1,900	
Bad debt	400	15,600
Net profit		£23,800

Balance Sheet at 31 December 19X7

	£	£
FIXED ASSETS		
Lorry		10,000
CURRENT ASSETS		
Stock of coal	2,400	
Debtors (£7,000 − 400)	6,600	
Prepayment of rent	1,200	
Bank	4,000	
	14,200	
Less		
CURRENT LIABILITIES		
Creditors (£2,200 + 200)	2,400	11,800
		£21,800
CAPITAL — R. BLACK		
Original balance	18,000	
Add profit	23,800	
	41,800	
Less drawings	20,000	£21,800

Note that the rent applicable to this year's operations is £2,400 (expense) whilst a total of £3,600 (cost) has actually been paid. Half of the second payment relates to the following year's operations so it is an asset (a prepayment, or unexpired cost) at 31 December. An opposite situation applies to the other expenses. £1,700 has been paid during the year but the expense incurred relating to the year is £1,900, the difference being a liability at the end of the year. The bad debt is an expense of the year because the £400 can no longer be regarded as an asset (a debtor) — its value has been lost.

Q.3f   Can the profit of £23,800 be regarded as an exact or completely objective figure?
Q.3g   The business started with £18,000 in the bank but finished with only £4,000, whilst at the same time making a profit of £23,800. Think of at least three reasons why profit or loss is not the same as increase or decrease in the bank balance.
Q.3h   To what extent would it be true to say that Robin Black was 'worth' £21,800?
Q.3i   On average, over the year, what mark-up has been added to cost to fix selling prices?

Tailpiece — Grieg Enterprises
In the introductory chapter we noted a range of accounting activities, including budgeting. Subsequently we have concentrated on the reporting of profits and financial position but, before ending the chapter, it may be interesting to see how the actual results of Grieg Enterprises' first year trading compared with John Grieg's budget. Budgeting is dealt with fully in a later chapter, but here we can use data already available to round off the illustration.

		Actual		*Budget*
Number of tables sold		820		900
		£		£
Sales revenue		16,400		18,000
Materials		9,320		10,800
		7,080		7,200
Commission	2,460		2,700	
Wages	1,200		1,200	
Rent	1,800		1,800	
Advertising	840		1,000	
Miscellaneous	450		300	
		6,750		7,000
		330		200

Alternatively:

	£	*£*
Sales revenue	16,400	18,000
Direct expenses (materials and commission)	11,780	13,500
Contribution	4,620	4,500
Other expenses	4,290	4,300
Net profit	330	200

Q.3j   Tell John Grieg how the business managed to make more profit than expected, though fewer tables were sold.

3.7   Additional questions

[1]
Alan Bate had one asset only, £800 in cash. He bought a second-hand motorbike for £600,

and spent £160 in reconditioning it. Having effectively done so, he advertised and sold it for £950, the cost of the advertisement being £10.

(a) Set out a statement showing his earnings (revenue), the total expenses, and the income (profit).
(b) Calculate what Bate is worth after the venture, and reconcile this with the amount he started with, and his profit.

[2]
At the beginning of March, a trader had £200 in the bank, but no other assets or liabilities. During March he bought goods on credit terms to the value of £560, and at 31 March had paid all but £80 of this. At 31 March there was a stock of unsold goods value £100. During March he sold goods for cash £220, and goods on credit terms for £380, of which £120 was still owing to him at 31 March. Other expenses paid during the month amounted to £40. (All money received had been paid into the bank, and all payments were by cheque.)

(a) Calculate the profit for March.
(b) Calculate the bank balance at 31 March.
(c) Set out the position of the business at 31 March in the form of a balance sheet.

[3]
Jane Ruskin started a part-time retail fruit business with a capital of £10,000, all in cash. During the period under review, the following transactions were completed:

Bought goods for cash	£7,000
Sold goods for cash	6,000
Sold goods on credit	3,000
Debtors paid in cash	2,400
Paid expenses from cash	800
Bought van for cash	4,000

At the end of the period there was no stock left.

Calculate the profit (or loss) for the period, and set out the balance sheet at the end of the period.

[4]
The position of T. Shaw's business at 31 December for three successive years was as follows:

	31 December 19X6 £	31 December 19X7 £	31 December 19X8 £
ASSETS			
Vehicle	10,000	9,000	8,000
Equipment	1,800	1,600	3,200
Stock	600	1,300	1,100
Debtors	400	500	700
Bank Balance	700	1,200	100
LIABILITIES			
Creditors	300	400	400

Throughout 19X7 and 19X8 Shaw withdrew £2,000 per month from the business.

Calculate the net profit for 19X7 and for 19X8.

[5]

(a) Describe in your own words the distinction between payments made by a business, and the expense of the business for a period.

Give two examples of payments which may not entirely be expenses of the period in which they were paid.

(b) Describe in your own words the distinction between receipts of a business and the revenue of a business for a period.

Give two examples of receipts which may not entirely be revenues of the period in which they were received.

[6]

For each of the following costs incurred by a business during its financial year ended March 19X7, decide how much is an expense of the year 19X6–19X7, and how much of 19X7–19X8.

	Cost 19X6–19X7 £	Expense 19X6–19X7 £	Expense 19X7–19X8 £
(a) Goods purchased Jan. 19X7 and all sold in May	4,000		
(b) Goods purchased Mar. 19X7 half of which sold before 31.3.X7, and the other half in April	2,000		
(c) Insurance premiums paid 1.1.X7, one year in advance	1,200		
(d) Coke for heating, bought Feb. 19X7, and mostly used by 31.3.X7	120		
(e) Supply of envelopes bought Mar. 19X7 and only part used by 31.3.X7	30		
(f) Rent for garages paid in Mar. 19X7 for the preceding quarter	250		
(g) Vehicle taxation paid Mar. 19X7	1,000		

[7]

The accounting period of D. Wilson (Electronics) Ltd ends on 31 December. Will each of the following sales be treated as revenue earned in 19X5 or 19X6?

(a) Goods despatched to A on 10 December 19X5. A sends his cheque in January 19X6.

(b) Goods despatched to B in November 19X5. B pays half of the account in December and the other half in January.

(c) C orders goods in December 19X5 and sends £10 deposit with his order. The goods (value £80) are despatched in January, and the balance outstanding paid in February.

[8]

On 1 January Tom Hill left his employment as a footwear repairer, to start in business on his own account. He had saved £4,000 and paid this into a business bank account as his capital. His transactions for the year are summarized as follows:

Equipment purchased during the year, £2,800. All this had been paid for except £400 still outstanding at 31 December.

Charges to customers for work done during the year, and received in cash, £23,400.

Charges to customers for work done on footwear still to be collected at 31 December, £1,200.

Leather and other materials purchased during the year, £4,200. Of this, £600 was still owing to the suppliers at 31 December. There was a stock of materials in the shop, value £400, at the year end.

Rent paid for the shop, £2,200. Another £300 was owing to the landlord in respect of the last few weeks of the year.

Amount withdrawn from business by Tom Hill for his own use, £15,000.

(a) Calculate the profit or loss for the year (ignore depreciation of equipment).
(b) Calculate the bank balance at 31 December.
(c) Set out the balance sheet at 31 December.

[9]

C. Bright started a business as a mobile potato merchant on 1 March 19X7. He opened a business bank account and paid in £2,000. He already had a van, and was to treat this as one of the business assets: the value at 1 March was £8,000. Bright's capital at 1 March was therefore £10,000.

The following is a summary of what happened during the following twelve months:

Potatoes bought at a cost of £27,200.
Owing to suppliers at 28 Feb. 19X8, £3,600.
Value of potatoes left in stock 28 Feb. 19X8, £1,500.
Potatoes sold for £45,100.
Debt from customer to be written off as irrecoverable £120.
Balance of debts owing from customers 28 Feb. 19X8, £2,800.
Van expenses paid for, £2,700.
Owing at 28 Feb. 19X8 for repairs to van £320.
Stationery, advertising and miscellaneous expenses paid for, £1,700.
Bright withdrew from business £13,000.
(Ignore depreciation of van.)

(a) Calculate the profit or loss for the year.
(b) Calculate the bank balance at 28 Feb. 19X8.
(c) Set out the balance sheet at 28 Feb. 19X8.
(d) If you were C. Bright, would you be satisfied with the results of the year's work?

[10]

Show, by completion of the columns (b) to (f) in the table opposite, how the position of this business changes as a result of the following transactions. (The starting position is given, and the first transaction has been completed as an example.)

(a) Bought equipment on credit terms for £220.
(b) Bought further stock of goods on credit terms for £130.
(c) Sold goods for £290 cash: they originally cost £200.
(d) Paid £20 cash for office expenses.
(e) Paid the equipment supplier the amount owing.
(f) Sold goods on credit terms for £110 (cost price £80).

After completing all the columns, show the calculation of profit for the period by summarizing the revenue earned and the expenses to be charged against it. (The resultant profit should of course agree with the profit figure in column (f).)

Transaction ⟶	£	(a)	(b)	(c)	(d)	(e)	(f)
ASSETS							
Equipment	—	220					
Vehicle	8,000	8,000					
Stock	480	480					
Debtors	—	—					
Bank/Cash	100	100					
	8,580	8,800					
Less							
LIABILITIES							
Creditors	—	220					
Net Assets	8,580	8,580					
Original capital	8,580	8,580					
Profit (loss)	—	—.					
	8,580	8,580					

[11]
Delete the inappropriate wording where an alternative is given in the following paragraph:

A balance sheet is a statement showing on the one hand the assets owned by the business/proprietor(s) at values based on their market value/cost, and on the other hand the sources from which the assets were derived. Such sources may include the capital provided by the proprietors, including profits retained in the business and outstanding debtors/creditors. The balance sheet can be represented by the equation

$$\text{Capital} \frac{\text{plus}}{\text{minus}} \text{Liabilities} = \text{Assets.}$$

The capital will be increased/decreased by profit earned in a period, and increased/decreased by the proprietor's personal drawings. Profit is measured by matching receipts of cash/revenues of a period against the expenses/payments of cash for the same period. For instance, the cost of goods included in the profit calculation will be related to those used/purchased during the period, and this amount will be deducted from the value of goods paid for/accepted by the customers. Costs incurred during the period but not yet treated as an expense will appear as liabilities/assets in the balance sheet at the end of the period.

[12]
At 31 December the following balances were extracted from the books of a trader:

	£	
Equipment	6,400	
Vehicle	5,600	
Capital	24,600	(balance as at beginning of year)
Drawings	7,000	(trader's withdrawals during year)
Opening stock (1 Jan.)	9,724	
Purchases	31,840	
Sales	47,816	
Rent, rates, insurance	1,852	
Admin. expenses	1,640	
Selling expenses	1,688	
Wages	5,296	
Debtors	3,720	
Creditors	2,290	
Bank overdraft	54	

(Note that the total of Assets and Expenses should equal the total of Liabilities and Revenue.)

Prepare the Profit and Loss account for the year and the Balance Sheet at the end of the year, taking into account the following:

(i) Stock was counted at 31 Dec. and valued at £12,720.
(ii) The total of the debtors' balances (£3,720) includes £90 owing from someone who will be unable to pay.
(iii) The amount for rent, rates and insurance includes £132 paid in advance for next year.

Chapter 4

Ledger Records

4.1 The form of the accounts

Up to this point we have concentrated on the elements of profit calculations and statements of financial position but have indicated that the information summarized in these statements is derived from records kept throughout the year. We now introduce the framework of the ledger records system.

A ledger is a set of accounts, and an account is a record of one particular aspect of the business as it is affected by the business transactions. These aspects can be classified, as we have already seen, into assets, liabilities (including capital), revenue and expenses. Accounts are therefore kept for each type of asset and liability, and each category of revenue and expense. How many accounts are kept will depend on the amount of detailed information the management want to have readily available: for instance, it might be decided to keep separate accounts for the expenses of heating, lighting and cleaning the factory; or alternatively the three could be grouped together in one account.

The ledger may be handwritten, prepared by an accounting machine or computerized. In the latter case records are maintained within the computer's memory store and printed out or visually displayed as and when required. To develop an understanding of the accounts system it is better for the time being to avoid the complexities of more sophisticated processing methods and concentrate on how (and why) entries are made in a manual or simple mechanized ledger where each account will have a separate page or card within a binder or filing tray.

An account, then, is a means of collecting together information about an aspect of the business. For instance, the account for Cash starts with the opening balance; receipts are added, and payments subtracted. Each asset and liability account shows in the same way the opening balance, and increases and decreases in that particular asset or liability. The balances carried forward at the end of the year in asset and liability accounts are the amounts to be summarized in the balance sheet. Each expense and revenue account shows the amount of that expense or revenue arising throughout the year; and the balances of these accounts at the end of the year will provide information for calculating the profit.

The conventional form of ledger account has two sides so that additions and deductions can be entered separately, rather than having to add and subtract in the same column. The sides are referred to as Debit (left-hand side of the account) and Credit (right-hand).

Here is a simple form of ledger account ruling:

Debit side   *Credit side*

Date	Details	£	Date	Details	£

4.2   Double entry and the accounting equation

The basis on which the ledger accounts are kept is that a debit entry in one account will be matched by a credit entry in some other account. Each event affects two aspects of the business and is recorded by debiting the account for one aspect and crediting the account for the other; hence the term 'double entry book-keeping'. For instance, if office equipment is bought for cash, one asset is being increased and another decreased: there will be a debit to the Office Equipment account and a credit to the Cash account.

We will look first at how this procedure applies to the different types of account and then consider the rationale of the system. Asset accounts and expense accounts are debited with increases to those assets or expenses and credited with decreases. Liability accounts (including capital for this purpose) and revenue accounts are credited with increases and debited with decreases. For example, paying wages from cash results in a debit to the Wages account (increasing an expense) and a credit to the Cash account (decreasing an asset). Selling goods on credit terms results in a debit to the customer's account (increasing an asset — a debtor) and a credit to the Sales account (increasing revenue).

Every transaction that you ever have to deal with must fit into this pattern and we can see that it is only a logical extension of what was discovered in the previous chapters. In Chapter 2 we referred to the balance sheet equation, one form of which was Assets = Liabilities + Capital. In Chapter 3 we saw that capital is increased by profit and also that Profit = Revenue − Expense. It follows that:

$$A = L + C + P$$
$$\text{or } A = L + C + (R - E)$$
$$\text{or } A + E = L + C + R$$

So any addition to one side of the equation must be balanced by an addition to the other side (or a deduction from the same side).

As an example of how this works here are a few transactions followed by the ledger accounts in which they have been recorded:

Jan.   1   J. Shaw commenced business, paying £1,000 as his capital into a business bank account.
     6   Purchased goods for £300, paying by cheque.
     9   Purchased goods on credit terms from V. Arthur, £200.
   15   Paid £150 by cheque to V. Arthur in part payment.
   20   Paid wages by cheque £60.

Capital A/c (J. Shaw)

		£
	Jan. 1 Cash	1,000

Cash at Bank A/c

	£			£
Jan. 1 Capital	1,000	Jan. 6 Purchases		300
		15 V. Arthur		150
		20 Wages		60

Purchases of Goods A/c

	£
Jan. 6 Cash	300
9 V. Arthur	200

V. Arthur A/c

	£		£
Jan. 15 Cash	150	Jan. 9 Purchases	200

Wages A/c

	£
Jan. 20 Cash	60

It can be seen from the above example that:

(a) The capital, which is the equivalent of a liability in the sense that it represents J. Shaw's claim on the business assets, has a credit balance of £1,000.
(b) Cash at bank, an asset, shows increases (receipts) of £1,000 and decreases (payments) of £510.
(c) Purchases of goods, an asset, shows that £500 of goods have been received.
(d) V. Arthur's account shows that there is a liability for £50 outstanding.
(e) Wages account shows that £60 has so far been incurred as an expense.

Q.4a Extending the above illustration, what entries would be needed for:

Jan. 22 Bought office equipment on credit terms from T. Abel Ltd, £360?
Jan. 24 Paid £200 for rent of the premises?

Summarizing the effect of entries on different types of account, we have:

	DEBIT	CREDIT
Assets	Increase	Decrease
Liabilities	Decrease	Increase
Expenses	Increase	(Decrease)
Revenue	(Decrease)	Increase

Fig. 4

The majority of entries in the Expense accounts will be debits: only when adjustments or transfers are required might there be anything to enter on the credit side. Similarly with Revenue accounts, the usual postings will be to the credit side. Another way of illustrating the inter-relationship of some typical ledger accounts is shown in *Fig. 5*.

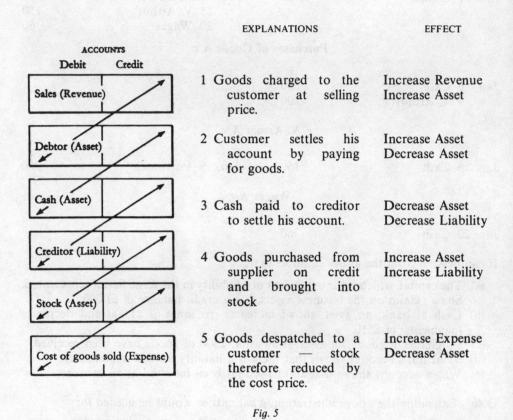

ACCOUNTS	EXPLANATIONS	EFFECT
Debit Credit		
Sales (Revenue)	1 Goods charged to the customer at selling price.	Increase Revenue Increase Asset
Debtor (Asset)	2 Customer settles his account by paying for goods.	Increase Asset Decrease Asset
Cash (Asset)	3 Cash paid to creditor to settle his account.	Decrease Asset Decrease Liability
Creditor (Liability)	4 Goods purchased from supplier on credit and brought into stock	Increase Asset Increase Liability
Stock (Asset)	5 Goods despatched to a customer — stock therefore reduced by the cost price.	Increase Expense Decrease Asset
Cost of goods sold (Expense)		

Fig. 5

Note that entry No. 5 is not always made at the time of sale because it may be difficult to identify the cost price of those particular goods. Adjusting the stock account at the end of a period has the same effect. If these were the only transactions that took place in an accounting period, the profit would be the difference between the balance of the one revenue account, and that of the one expense account.

4.3   Examples of ledger accounts

Here are some more detailed examples of how accounts may appear in a ledger.

Cash at the Bank A/c (8)

19X8		Ref.	£	p	19X8		Ref.	£	p
Mar. 1	Balance	b/f	136	10	Mar. 5	Wages	38	48	05
9	R. Bright	83	63	50	8	T. Williamson Ltd	74	37	80
10	Sales	26	109	22	12	Wages	38	46	20
19	Peters & Scott	190	235	70	19	Wages	38	53	45
25	Sales	26	83	68	24	Besstools Ltd	51	218	10
29	Hamblin & Co.	112	9	90	26	Electricity	42	20	25
					26	Wages	38	51	75
					31	Balance	c/d	162	50
			638	10				638	10
Apr. 1	Balance	b/f	162	50	Apr. 2	Wages	38	53	30
9	Sales	26	38	95					
	etc., etc.					etc., etc.			

Explanation: This is an account for one of the business assets — the cash held at the bank. Increases to the asset are on the left-hand side (debit), and decreases on the right-hand side (credit). The details shown refer to the sources of receipts and the reasons for payment, or names of payees. What goes in the reference column depends upon the system of entering accounts. It may refer to the document from which the entry was made, or to the number of the other account affected by the transaction. At 1 April the business had a balance of £162.50 at the bank.

Besstools Ltd A/c (51)

19X8		Ref.	£	p	19X8		Ref.	£	p
Mar. 24	Cash	8	218	10	Mar. 1	Balance	b/f	218	10
31	Balance	c/d	149	75	18	Goods	12	115	50
					24	Goods	12	9	45
					30	Goods	12	24	80
			367	85				367	85
Apr. 27	Cash	8	149	75	Apr. 1	Balance	b/f	149	75
					8	Goods	12	38	90
	etc., etc.					etc., etc.			

Explanation: This is an account for one of the business liabilities — a creditor supplying goods to the business. Increases in the liability are on the right-hand side (credit), and decreases on the left-hand side (debit). At 1 April the business owed £149.75 to Besstools Ltd.

Wages A/c (38)

19X8		Ref.	£	p	19X8		Ref.	£	p
Mar. 1	Balance	b/f	475	20	Mar. 31	Balance	c/d	674	65
5	Cash	8	48	05					
12	Cash	8	46	20					
19	Cash	8	53	45					
26	Cash	8	51	75					
			674	65				674	65
Apr. 1	Balance	b/f	674	65					
2	Cash	8	53	30					
	etc., etc.					etc., etc.			

Explanation: This is an account for one of the business expenses — wages. Increases to the expense are on the left-hand side (debit). In this example there are no decreases shown: these would only arise if adjustments or corrections were necessary. Up to 1 April £674.65 had been incurred in wages since the beginning of the accounting period.

This next example deals with the affairs of A. Booth in the first month of trading. Try making the ledger account entries yourself before looking at the answer which follows.

May 1 Booth opened a business bank account paying in £10,000 as capital
4 Bought goods on credit from Kay Ltd, £2,900
4 Bought goods and paid by cheque, £1,600
5 Withdrew £50 from the bank to keep as a cash balance
5 Paid £20 out of cash for miscellaneous expenses
7 Sold goods for cash £260 and paid this all into the bank account
11 Sold goods on credit terms to M. Wye, £80
11 Bought more goods from Kay Ltd, £420
14 Paid assistant's wages by cheque, £100
15 Sold goods on credit terms to C. Dee, £310
15 Paid miscellaneous expenses by cheque, £30
18 Sold goods on credit terms to M. Wye, £140
22 Sold goods for cash £490 and paid this all into the bank account
22 Paid miscellaneous expenses from cash, £10
26 Sent cheque for £2,000 to Kay Ltd
26 Sold goods on credit terms to C. Dee, £120
27 Bought shop fittings for £450, paying by cheque
29 Received cheque from C. Dee, £310
29 Paid wages by cheque, £120.

Before attempting this, notice that there are two small differences from the previous illustration. Some money is being kept in a cash box and so a separate Cash account will be needed in addition to the Bank account. Where sales are made, only the amount received or invoiced is known, so you cannot make any entries in respect of the cost price of the goods sold. We have already noted that it is usually difficult to make such entries for each individual sale, and we shall be explaining later what adjustments are required at the end of the period.

Ledger accounts for A. Booth's business

£   £

Capital (A. Booth)

				May	1	Bank	10,000

Purchases

May	4	Kay Ltd	2,900
	4	Bank	1,600
	11	Kay Ltd	420

Sales

				May	7	Bank	260
					11	M. Wye	80
					15	C. Dee	310
					18	M. Wye	140
					22	Bank	490
					26	C. Dee	120

Kay Ltd

May	26	Bank	2,000	May	4	Purchases	2,900
					11	Purchases	420

M. Wye

May	11	Sales	80
	18	Sales	140

C. Dee

May	15	Sales	310	May	29	Bank	310
	26	Sales	120				

Wages

May	14	Bank	100
	29	Bank	120

Miscellaneous Expenses

May	5	Cash	20
	15	Bank	30
	22	Cash	10

Bank

May	1	Capital	10,000	May	4	Purchases	1,600
	7	Sales	260		5	Cash	50
	22	Sales	490		14	Wages	100

		£				£
29	C. Dee	310	15	Misc. Expenses		30
			26	Kay Ltd		2,000
			27	Shop fittings		450
			29	Wages		120

Cash

May	5	Bank	50	May	5	Misc. Expenses	20
					22	Misc. Expenses	10

Shop Fittings

May 27	Bank	450

In this example we kept separate accounts for the cash held in the office and for the money at the bank. You may meet situations in which a two-column Cash account or Cash book is used to show both of them together but in separate columns. If A. Booth had kept a two-column Cash account, the first few entries would have appeared as follows:

Cash Account

		CASH	BANK				CASH	BANK
		£	£				£	£
May 1	Capital		10,000	May 4	Purchases			1,600
5	Bank	50		5	Cash			50
7	Sales		260	5	Misc. Expenses		20	

4.4   Balancing the accounts and the Trial Balance

Periodically, usually monthly, accounts with a number of entries will be balanced off, so that the balance at that point is represented as one figure, without having to repeatedly add both sides to find it. The three specimen accounts at the beginning of 4.3 were balanced in this way. If the debit side is greater than the credit side, there is a debit balance, and vice versa. The balance is then brought forward to the beginning of the next month, when transactions will continue to be entered in the account. For example, Kay Ltd account may appear as follows:

Kay Ltd

		£				£
May 26	Bank	2,000	May	4	Purchases	2,900
31	Balance	1,320	11	Purchases	420
		———				———
		3,320				3,320
		———				———
June 8	Bank	1,320	June 1	Balance	1,320
30	Balance	2,400	10	Purchases	2,400
		———				———
		3,720				3,720
		———				———
			July 1	Balance	2,400

Q.4b Describe the relationship between A. Booth and Kay Ltd at 1 July.

At any time, the total of the debit balances in the ledger should equal the credit balances. This is checked periodically, again probably monthly. The extraction of balances, to prove that total debits equal total credits, is called the Trial Balance. The trial balance for A. Booth's business at 31 May would be:

Trial Balance at 31 May

ACCOUNTS	BALANCES	
	Dr.	Cr.
	£	£
Capital		10,000
Purchases	4,920	
Sales		1,400
Kay Ltd		1,320
M. Wye	220	
C. Dee	120	
Wages	220	
Misc. Expenses	60	
Bank	6,710	
Cash	20	
Shop fittings	450	
	£12,720	£12,720

The purpose of the trial balance is merely to prove that each debit entry has had a corresponding credit entry. It does little else, and there are a number of types of error that may be made which will not be revealed by the trial balance. One example is where all reference to a transaction has been omitted entirely from the ledger, i.e. no debit or credit entry.

Similarly, if the same incorrect amount from one of the source documents, such as an invoice, is posted to both of the relevant accounts the trial balance will still balance. Again, there could be two errors which cancel each other out (compensating errors).

Q.4c One of the following situations is another example of a mistake arising in the ledger without affecting the balancing of the trial balance. Which one is it?

  (i) £10 cash discount deducted by a debtor credited to the Discounts Received account.
 (ii) £85.40 balance on K. Lee's account (a creditor) carried forward to the beginning of the next month as £8.54.
(iii) £60 for goods purchased on credit terms from G. Bee posted to the credit of B. Gee's account.

If there were no errors other than any arising from these situations by how much would a trial balance, extracted at the beginning of the new month, be out of balance?

Q.4d For each item in the trial balance of A. Booth's business, above, decide whether it is an asset, liability, expense or revenue to confirm the equation A + E = L + R (including capital as a liability).

Q.4e   The following are the account balances taken from the ledger of a business, C. Grant & Co. Decide whether each of them should be a debit or a credit balance, and enter in the appropriate column. If this is done correctly, the total debits should equal total credits. (Note that the accounts have been listed in random order: there is no significance about the sequence.)

ACCOUNT	BALANCE £	DEBIT £	CREDIT £
Cash in hand	36		
J. Small (debtor to C. Grant)	425		
Sale of goods	112,680		
Furniture and Fittings	3,000		
Wages and Salaries	42,840		
Capital — C. Grant	220,000		
Proprietor's drawings	18,529		
C. Large (creditor)	350		
Purchases of goods	79,600		
Vehicles	9,200		
Vehicle running expenses	1,390		
Land and buildings	159,400		
Bank balance	110		
Admin. expenses	18,500		
		£	£

Q.4f   We have been showing balances at the bank as debit balances in the accounts of a business. If you have your own personal bank account you will know that a favourable balance (from your point of view) is described as a credit balance. Can you explain why?

4.5   Ledger accounts at the end of the accounting period

At the end of an accounting period (usually the year end) expenses and revenues relevant to that period are transferred from their individual accounts into a Profit and Loss account — or it may be titled Trading and Profit and Loss account. The formally presented Profit and Loss account is generally a summarized version of the one in the ledger.

Before these transfers can be made, however, it will have to be decided to what extent the figures in the accounts are in fact relevant to that period, or whether any part should be carried forward as an asset or a liability into the next period. There may also be additional items to take into the calculation of profit which are not yet in the accounts. To illustrate these points, let us assume that we are to draw up a Trading and Profit and Loss account for A. Booth's business after the one month's trading.

First of all, we have already noted that the cost of goods sold (an expense) could not be readily identified each time a sale was made but that an end-of-period adjustment would be necessary. Of the total purchases, £4,920, some goods will have been sold and some still left in stock. (In your analysis in Q.4d the correct designation for Purchases should have been partly an expense and partly an asset.) To find the amount of the expense, stock in hand at the end of the period must be counted and valued — normally at cost price but we will consider this again in the next chapter. The cost of goods sold is then the purchases less the closing stock. Had there been any opening stock at the beginning of the period this would have been included (cost of goods sold = opening stock + purchases – closing stock). If we assume that the closing stock in this case was valued at £4,100 the cost of those goods sold during the period would, by deduction, be £820.

In closing off the ledger accounts the usual way of putting this into effect is to transfer the whole of the Purchases account to the Trading and Profit and Loss account as a debit but to credit, or deduct, the closing stock, the other side of that entry being to debit the amount as an asset to a Stock account. In this example the whole of the Sales account is a revenue of the period, so the first part of the profit calculation will appear in the ledger as follows:

Trading and Profit and Loss account for period ended 31 May 19X1

	£		£
Purchases	4,920	Sales	1,400
less Closing stock	4,100		
Cost of goods sold	820		
Gross profit	580		
	1,400		1,400

The Purchases and Sales accounts in the ledger will now have been closed off by transferring their totals to this account and a new account for Stock will appear with a debit balance of £4,100 representing the asset value at the end of the period. Notice that in the above account the £4,100 is in fact a credit but has been deducted from Purchases to enable the cost of goods sold figure to be shown more clearly.

Now the other expense items will be set against the gross profit to find the net profit. Let us assume that there is no adjustment necessary for the wages but that another £30 of miscellaneous expenses had been incurred but not yet paid for, and that there was also £150 rent owing. For the wages the total of £220 will be simply transferred to the Profit and Loss account and the Wages account closed off. For miscellaneous expenses £90 will be debited to the Profit and Loss account and credited to the Miscellaneous Expenses account, leaving a credit balance of £30 on that account representing the liability at the end of the period. Similarly, a Rent account will be opened, £150 credited and carried forward as a liability.

All the elements of the profit calculation will then have been brought together in the Trading and Profit and Loss account. The resulting net profit will be inserted on the debit side as the balancing figure — the excess of revenue (credits) over total expense (debits) — and to complete the double entry the net profit must then be credited to the Capital account, representing as it does an increase in the proprietor's interest. Now all the remaining balances on the ledger accounts are the assets and liabilities at the end of the period. They are carried forward in their respective accounts to form the opening balances for the next period and are also summarized in the Balance Sheet.

We now show how the ledger accounts would appear after all these adjustments and transfers have been made and the accounts balanced off.

Capital (A. Booth)

May 31	Balance	10,120	May 1	Bank	10,000
			31	Net profit	120
		10,120			10,120
			June 1	Balance	10,120

Purchases

May 4	Kay Ltd	2,900	May 31	P & L account	4,920
4	Bank	1,600			
11	Kay Ltd	420			
		4,920			4,920

Sales

May 31	P & L account	1,400	May 7	Bank	260
			11	M. Wye	80
			15	C. Dee	310
			18	M. Wye	140
			22	Bank	490
			26	C. Dee	120
		1,400			1,400

Kay Ltd

May 26	Bank	2,000	May 4	Purchases	2,900
31	Balance	1,320	11	Purchases	420
		3,320			3,320
			June 1	Balance	1,320

M. Wye

May 11	Sales	80	May 31	Balance	220
18	Sales	140			
		220			220
June 1	Balance	220			

C. Dee

May 15	Sales	310	May 29	Bank	310
26	Sales	120	31	Balance	120
		430			430
June 1	Balance	120			

Wages

May 14	Bank	100	May 31	P & L account		220
29	Bank	120				
		220				220

Miscellaneous Expenses

May 5	Cash	20	May 31	P & L account	90
15	Bank	30			
22	Cash	10			
31	Balance	30			
		90			90
			June 1	Balance	30

Rent

May 31	Balance	150	May 31	P & L account	150
			June 1	Balance	150

Bank

May 1	Capital	10,000	May 4	Purchases	1,600
7	Sales	260	5	Cash	50
22	Sales	490	14	Wages	100
29	C. Doo	310	15	Misc. Expenses	30
			26	Kay Ltd	2,000
			27	Shop fittings	450
			29	Wages	120
			31	Balance	6,710
		11,060			11,060
June 1	Balance	6,710			

Cash

May 5	Bank	50	May 5	Misc. Expenses	20
			22	Misc. Expenses	10
			31	Balance	20
		50			50
June 1	Balance	20			

Shop Fittings

May 27	Bank	450	May 31	Balance	450
June 1	Balance	450			

Stock

May 31	P & L account	4,100	May 31	Balance	4,100
June 1	Balance	4,100			

Trading and Profit and Loss account
for period ended 31 May 19X1

Purchases	4,920	Sales	1,400
less Closing stock	4,100		
	———		
Cost of goods sold	820		
Gross profit	580		
	———		———
	1,400		1,400
	———		———
Wages	220	Gross profit	580
Misc. Expenses	90		
Rent	150		
Net profit	120		
	———		———
	580		580
	———		———

The balances carried forward into the new period represent the assets and liabilities of the business and would be summarized in the balance sheet as shown below. Whilst the Trading and Profit and Loss account is technically part of the double entry system the Balance Sheet lists the balances outstanding but is not itself a ledger account.

Balance Sheet at 31 May 19X1

	£	£
Fixed Assets		
Shop fittings		450
Current Assets		
Stock	4,100	
Debtors	340	
Bank	6,710	
Cash	20	
	———	
	11,170	
	———	
Current Liabilities		
Trade creditors	1,320	
Accrued expenses	180	
	———	
	1,500	
	———	9,670
		———
Capital		10,120
		———

Remember that a Trading and Profit and Loss account and a Balance Sheet are usually prepared annually — we are using a monthly interval to illustrate the process with relatively few figures involved. To clarify the adjustment for closing stock let us continue for a further month, assuming:

	£
Sales for June	3,920
Purchases for June	2,610
Closing stock was counted at the end of June and valued at	4,358

The Stock account and the first part of the Trading and Profit and Loss account would appear as follows:

Stock

		£				£
June 1	Balance	4,100	June 30	P & L account		4,100
30	P & L account	4,358	30	Balance		4,358
		8,458				8,458
July 1	Balance	4,358				

Trading and Profit and Loss account
for period ended 30 June 19X1

Opening stock	4,100	Sales	3,920
Purchases	2,610		
	6,710		
less Closing stock	4,358		
Cost of goods sold	2,352		
Gross profit	1,568		
	3,920		3,920

Now here is one more example to illustrate the process of adjusting expense accounts so that the amount relating to the period concerned becomes part of the profit calculation irrespective of how much was actually paid in the same period. The following transactions were included in the first two years of trading for Gray & Co.

Rent of premises — £4,000 for six months, payable in advance on 1 April and 1 October. For the initial three months £2,000 was paid in January. From 1 April year 2 the rent was increased to £4,400 for six months.

Manager's bonus — calculated quarterly on the basis of sales and paid in the following month. Payments were — year 1, April £180, July £260, October £130 and in year 2, January £290, April £200, July £310, October £160. £330 was due in respect of the last quarter of year 2.

The accounts would appear as follows:

Rent

		£			£
Year 1			Year 1		
Jan.	Bank	2,000	Dec.	P & L account	8,000
April	Bank	4,000	Dec.	Balance	2,000
Oct.	Bank	4,000			
		10,000			10,000

Year 2			Year 2		
Jan.	Balance	2,000	Dec.	P & L account	8,600
April	Bank	4,400	Dec.	Balance	2,200
Oct.	Bank	4,400			
		10,800			10,800
Year 3					
Jan.	Balance	2,200			

(In the balance sheets at 31 December year 1 and year 2 the amount prepaid — £2,000 and £2,200, respectively — would be included as an asset. The charge of £8,600 for rent in year 2 represents three quarters of the year at £8,800 p.a. and one quarter at the old rate of £8,000 p.a.)

	£				£

Manager's Bonus

Year 1			Year 1		
April	Bank	180	Dec.	P & L account	860
July	Bank	260			
Oct.	Bank	130			
Dec.	Balance	290			
		860			860
Year 2			Year 2		
Jan.	Bank	290	Jan.	Balance	290
April	Bank	200	Dec.	P & L account	1,000
July	Bank	310			
Oct.	Bank	160			
Dec.	Balance	330			
		1,290			1,290
			Year 3		
			Jan.	Balance	330

(£290 would be included as a liability in the balance sheet at the end of year 1 because that amount had been earned by the manager in year 1 but was still outstanding. In January of year 2 the liability was cleared.)

Q.4g In the same set of accounts £80 was paid in October year 1 for maintenance of equipment. Further work was completed by the contractor in December year 1 but the invoice for £240 was not paid until February year 2. No other maintenance costs were incurred in year 2. Show the Maintenance of Equipment account for years 1 and 2.

4.6 Returns and discounts

It often happens that, after goods have been sold on credit terms, some of them may be returned for various reasons or an allowance for an over-charge may be made to the customer. The original entry debiting the customer and crediting Sales account will then need to be reversed in respect of the amount being allowed as a reduction of the bill. It is usual in these cases to open a separate account, called the Sales Returns account (or Returns Inwards account), instead of debiting the Sales account: by doing so the total value of returns and allowances can be more easily found. The amount allowed will therefore be debited to the Sales Returns account and credited to the customer's account. The document which goes to the customer to notify the allowance is called a credit note.

For example:

	£		£
		Sales	
		Feb. 10 F. Sharp	640

		Sales Returns	
Feb. 16 F. Sharp	130		

F. Sharp

	£		£
Feb. 10 Sales	640	Feb. 16 Returns	130
		Feb. 28 Balance	510
	640		640
Mar. 1 Balance	510	Mar. 27 Bank	510

At the end of the period the total of the sales returns (debit) will be deducted from the sales (credit) in the Trading account. Similarly any goods which the business returns to its suppliers, or allowances made, will be debited to the suppliers' accounts and credited to a Purchases Returns account (or Returns Outwards account). The total of this account will then be deducted from the purchases in the Trading account as shown below.

Trading account for year ended . . . .

	£	£		£	£
Opening stock		X	Sales	X	
Purchases	X		*less* Returns	X	X
less Returns	X	X			
		X			
Closing stock		X			
Cost of goods sold		X			
Gross profit		X			
		X			X

Another type of entry with which you may have to deal arises when *cash discount* for prompt payment is allowed or received. For instance, assume that B. Flatt is a debtor to our business for £200. He would normally be expected to settle the account within the next month or two but, if we wished to get the cash in quickly, we might offer an incentive, allowing him to deduct (say) 2½% cash discount for settlement within a short period of (say) 7 days. Acceptance of these terms would then mean that B. Flatt pays us £195 in full settlement of the outstanding debt — but we get it now rather than later. B. Flatt's account in our books would originally show a debit balance of £200. The £195 will be debited to Cash or Bank and credited to B. Flatt's account. However, this leaves a balance of £5 which cannot remain because all the debt has been settled. It represents an expense to us and must be transferred to the debit of a Discounts Allowed account, to be treated at the end of the year like all other expense accounts and charged against profits in the Profit and Loss account.

There is an opposite effect when we deduct cash discount in paying our creditors. This represents a gain and the transfer would be to the credit of a Discounts Received account.

Q.4h   We buy goods on credit terms from D. Major for £900 but are allowed £50 (confirmed by a credit note) for an agreed overcharge. Major then informs us that we can deduct 2% cash discount for settlement within 7 days and we accept. Show all the relevant accounts in our ledger.

You may also meet the term *trade discount*. Such a discount does not need any separate treatment in the ledger. It simply means that a supplier with a list of standard prices is prepared to make a deduction for certain customers or for supplying certain quantities. The net price (list price less trade discount) is the amount involved and it is this amount which is entered in the books.

4.7   Additional questions

[1]
Insert either 'Increase' or 'Decrease' in the spaces below, to show the effect of debit and credit postings on the balances of the accounts shown:

Accounts	Debit	Credit
Asset		
Capital		
Liabilities		
Expenses		
Revenue		

(Avoid referring to the similar table included in the chapter until you have completed the above.)

[2]
Against each of the following transactions has been shown the effect on Assets, Liabilities, Expenses or Revenue. Two of them are incorrect. Can you spot which ones and explain why they are incorrect?

	Transaction	*Effect*	
(a)	Bought goods for cash	Incr. A	Decr. A
(b)	Bought goods on credit terms	Incr. A	Incr. L
(c)	Sold goods for cash (ignore entry for cost of goods sold)	Incr. A	Incr. R
(d)	Sold goods on credit terms (ignore entry for cost of goods sold)	Decr. A	Incr. R
(e)	Paid wages from cash	Incr. E	Decr. A
(f)	Paid cheque to creditor	Decr. A	Decr. L
(g)	Received cheque from debtor	Incr. A	Decr. A
(h)	Borrowed money — to be repaid within 5 years	Incr. A	Incr. L
(i)	Bought office stationery on credit terms	Incr. E	Incr. L
(j)	Received cheque for refund of electricity charges overpaid	Incr. A	Incr. R

[3]

The following are a few of the accounts in the ledger of T. Wightman Ltd.

Copy the information given and balance off each of the accounts at 28 February. Then describe what each of the closing balances represents, and say what type of account it is (i.e. Asset, Liability, etc.).

(a)

Plant and Machinery A/c

		£		£
Feb.	1 Balance	6,000.00		
	27 T.L.N. Ltd	3,120.00		

(b)

Insurance A/c

		£		£
Feb.	1 Balance	80.20		
	24 Fire and Gen. Ins. Co.	130.10		

(c)

H. Dent Ltd A/c

		£			£
Feb.	1 Balance	136.63	Feb.	27 Cash	100.00
	28 Sales	624.27			

(d)

Peters & Williams Ltd A/c

		£			£
Feb.	21 Returns	103.20	Feb.	1 Balance	836.40
				20 Purchases	617.19
				28 Purchases	524.00

(e)

Bank A/c

		£			£
Feb.	1 Balance	1,308.68	Feb.	8 Petty Cash	60.00
	10 Debtors	3,109.42		13 Wages and N.I.	1,005.21
	18 Debtors	916.20			
	25 Sales	305.00		27 – do –	987.40
	27 Debtors	6,324.72		27 Creditors	4,822.48

(f)   **Sales A/c**

                                                              £
                                    Feb.   1 Balance   10,216.27
                                          28 Debtors   11,308.41

[4]
Open the appropriate accounts in T. Hall's ledger and enter the following transactions.
Balance off the accounts, and prepare a trial balance at the end of the month. (You can
either use a two-column Cash Book, with columns for Cash and Bank, or have separate
accounts for each.)

Mar. 3 Hall commenced business, paying £5,000 into a business bank account as his
         capital.
      4 Bought goods on credit terms from Shaw & Gregory Ltd, £635.25.
      5 Paid by cheque £32.15 for stationery (Office Expenses a/c).
      5 Paid by cheque £18.00 for insurance premium (Insurance a/c).
      8 Cashed a cheque for £50, and put the money into an office cash box.
      9 Paid £3.25 from cash for miscellaneous office expenses.
     12 Sales £36.80 — money received in cash.
     14 Sold goods on credit terms to C. White, £168.42.
     14 Paid wages from cash, £38.20.
     18 Sales £19.65 — money received in cash.
     20 Paid £30 cash into the bank account.
     21 Bought goods on credit terms from Shaw & Gregory Ltd, £180.15.
     24 Sales £149.10 — cheque received and paid into bank.
     25 Bought a second-hand delivery van for £2850.00, paying by cheque.
     28 Paid wages from cash, £36.80.
     28 Sold goods on credit terms to
             W. Turner   £83.42   and
             C. Longman   £162.14
     29 Sales £72.15 — money received in cash.
     29 Paid into bank all of the office cash except for £50.
     31 Received cheque from C. White for £160, the balance being allowed as cash
         discount.
     31 Sent cheque for £635.25 to Shaw & Gregory Ltd.

[5]
At the end of a month the trial balance does not balance, and a thorough check is made
of all the ledger postings. The errors shown below are discovered.

  (i) A sales invoice for £20 for goods supplied to R. Ball had been completely omitted
      from the books.
 (ii) A payment of £12 for stationery had been entered on the credit side of the Cash
      Book, and the credit side of the Stationery account.
(iii) In T. Waters account (a debtor), the debit side of the account had been undercast by
      £10 — there were no entries on the credit side.
 (iv) £16 paid for vehicle repairs had been posted to the Vehicles account.
  (v) Cash sales of £185 had been entered in the sales account as £155.
 (vi) The credit side of V. Walker's account (a creditor) totals £318 and the debit side
      £102. The balance has been entered in the trial balance as £218.
    (a) Which of the errors would not make any difference to the trial balance
        balancing — though still needing correction?

(b) Which would affect the balancing of the trial balance, and, when corrected, how much would be added to the debit side or credit side in each case?

(c) Assuming that all the errors have now been found, by how much was the trial balance out of balance in the first place?

[6]

Insert the title of the account and the amount to be debited and credited opposite the following business transactions over one week of trading:

	Account to be	
	Debited	Credited

(a) Cash paid into business bank account by proprietor, £4,000

(b) Bought goods for resale, £800, from J. Jones on credit terms

(c) Paid general rates, £200, on the business for six months in advance by cheque

(d) Paid J. Jones amount due less 2½% cash discount

(e) Sold goods to F. Beaver for £380 on credit terms

(f) Paid rent of premises for one week, £70 by cheque

(g) Paid wages, £80

[7]

At 1 January, A. Mann's balance sheet was as follows:

	£		£
CAPITAL	18,000	FIXED ASSETS	
CURRENT LIABILITIES		Vehicle	7,200
Creditors	1,600	Equipment	6,800
		CURRENT ASSETS	
		Stock	3,360
		Debtors	2,110
		Bank	130
	19,600		19,600

The Debtors and Creditors balances were made up as follows:

	£		£
DEBTORS		CREDITORS	
A. Dee	610	B.X. Ltd	1,150
T. Anderson	1,040	Wragg Supplies Ltd	450
P. Evans	460		
	2,110		1,600

Open accounts in the ledger for all of the above balances, and then post the following transactions which took place during January. Extract a Trial Balance at 31 January.

Credit sales	£
Jan. 6 A. Dee	350
12 B. Allsop	1,520
18 A. Dee	65
24 T. Anderson	1,632
25 P. Evans	2,100
28 T. Anderson	321

Credit purchases	£
Jan. 10 Wragg Supplies Ltd	3,750
18 B.X. Ltd	625

Payments into bank account	
Jan. 4 Cash sales	383
11 Cheques from A. Dee	610
and P. Evans	300
15 Cash sales	710
21 Cheques from T. Anderson	1,040
and B. Allsop	250

Payments from bank account	
Jan. 7 Wages	130
10 Repairs to vehicle	41
14 Wages	136
21 Wages	134
21 B.X. Ltd (£50 cash discount)	1,100
21 Wragg Supplies Ltd	300
28 Wages	140
28 Drawings — A. Mann	620

[8]
These are some of the ledger accounts of a business at the end of its trading year (31 December). Copy them into your ledger and close off the appropriate accounts to the Trading and Profit and Loss account. Complete the entries in the Capital account. Show how any figures derived from the information below would appear in the Balance Sheet.

Stock A/c

	£		£
Jan. 1 Balance	9,900		

(The closing stock at 31 December has now been counted, and valued at £12,420.)

Purchase A/c

Nov. 30 Balance	181,651	
Dec. 31 Creditors	13,122	

Sales A/c

	Nov. 30 Balance	223,526
	Dec. 31 Debtors	25,104

Wages A/c

Nov. 30	Balance	21,650
Dec. 31	Cash	2,205

Office Expenses A/c

Nov. 30	Balance	3,310
Dec. 31	Creditors	130
31	Cash	42

Rent and Rates A/c

Nov. 30	Balance	2,400

(A further £400 for the year is due but not yet paid at 31 December.)

Capital A/c

	Jan. 1 Balance	150,000

Drawings A/c

Nov. 30	Balance	12,815
Dec. 31	Cash	5,425

Vehicles A/c

Jan. 1	Balance	8,000

[9]

At 31 March, the end of the financial year, the following balances appeared in the books of a trader:

	Debit balance £	Credit balance £
Stock (opening balance)	16,000	
Purchases	79,600	
Sales		120,800
Goods returned to supplier, and allowances		900
Salaries and wages	13,800	
Rent, Rates, Insurance	6,100	
Miscellaneous expenses	3,700	
Advertising	700	
Capital		36,000
Drawings	12,500	
Equipment	19,000	
Debtors	9,800	
Creditors		6,900
Bank	3,400	
	£164,600	£164,600

(a) Open ledger accounts for each of these balances, and, taking into consideration the following adjustments, prepare the Trading and Profit and Loss account, and Balance Sheet. Close off the ledger accounts or bring down the balance, as appropriate. One or two extra ledger accounts may be necessary to deal with the adjustments. Adjustments required:

  (i) The closing stock was valued at £15,200.
  (ii) Rent, rates and insurance includes £300 paid in advance.
  (iii) A further £200 advertising expenditure has been incurred but not yet paid for.

(b) The trader thinks it would be useful to know the percentage of each of the following to the Sales figure — Gross Profit; each of the expenses; Net Profit. Calculate them for him.

[10]
The following trial balance, extracted from the books of a sole trader at the financial year end 31 December, does not balance because one or more of the ledger balances have been entered in the wrong column.

  (a) Identify and correct the error(s).
  (b) Then prepare the Trading and Profit and Loss account for the year to 31 December and a Balance Sheet at that date.
  (c) Show how the Stock account, the Rent account and the Capital account would appear in the ledger after completion of the final accounts.

Trial Balance at 31 December

	Dr £	Cr £
Capital account of proprietor		15,700
Opening stock	1,920	
Purchases	19,024	
Sales		39,211
Returns from customers	190	
Rent of premises	2,000	
Wages	6,026	
Office expenses		1,983
Cash discount allowed to debtors		320
Office equipment	13,530	
Debtors	2,124	
Creditors		1,117
Bank overdraft	125	
Cash in hand	36	
Proprietor's drawings	9,000	
	£53,975	£58,331

The closing stock was valued at £2,136.
Rent of premises for two months (£400) is outstanding at 31 December.

Chapter 5

Accounting for Assets

5.1 Introduction

The theme of this chapter is the accounting treatment of the main types of asset — we shall be looking at the principles involved and also at some practical aspects.

We have already seen that assets can be classed as fixed or current (refer back to Chapter 2, Section 2.5, if you are unsure about this distinction). A further division is into 'monetary' and 'non-monetary' items. The former includes money held either on the business premises or in an account at the bank (or other institution), together with sums owing from debtors — in other words, assets which are already in, or will soon be converted into, spendable money at the amounts stated. Non-monetary assets are held for 'physical' employment in the business either over a relatively long term (such as equipment) or as part of the operating cycle (stock).

$$
\begin{array}{lll}
\text{Non-monetary} & \left.\begin{array}{l}\text{Land and buildings} \\ \text{Plant and equipment} \\ \text{Vehicles}\end{array}\right] & \text{Fixed} \\
\text{assets} & & \text{assets} \\
& \left.\begin{array}{l}\text{Stock and work-in-progress} \\ \text{Debtors} \\ \text{Bank and cash}\end{array}\right] & \\
\text{Monetary assets} & & \text{Current} \\
& & \text{assets}
\end{array}
$$

What distinguishes monetary assets from non-monetary assets is more a matter of valuation than of timing. Stock might be turned into cash directly (cash sales) or indirectly (credit sales) over various intervals of time — for instance, in a supermarket the stock-to-cash cycle could be as short as a day or two whilst in other businesses it could be many months. Debtors often take one to two months to pay their debts but it may well be shorter or longer. The significant difference is that non-monetary items are valued on a cost to the business basis and have still to be processed through the trading operations, whilst monetary assets are already in realized and liquid form and their value can therefore be stated objectively in common currency without being dependent on future business activities.

Investments are another form of monetary asset and may be held on a short-term basis as a temporary use for surplus cash or on a long-term basis to secure a relationship with another organization. We shall not, however, be considering the treatment of investments in any detail in this introductory text.

It has been said that all non-monetary assets are in fact prepaid expenses, the thinking being that they will all eventually be used up in the course of business operations, their cost becoming an expense as and when this happens. Thus when an item of stock is sold its cost becomes an expense to be set against the revenue earned from the sale, and it is no longer an asset. Similarly, fixed assets do not last for ever, their cost becoming an expense over the period of their useful life by the process of depreciation.

5.2   Current assets: Monetary assets

From the points of view of record keeping and valuation, money in the bank or in a cash box is usually the easiest type of asset to deal with. It can be accounted for to the last penny with certainty. For the bank account there will be periodical confirmation of the transactions and latest balance in the form of bank statements, and these can be checked with the business's own records. Any differences are usually attributable to entries being made in the bank's records and in the business ledger on different dates, but a reconciliation can soon be made — this process is illustrated in Chapter 7. Similarly, keeping records of office cash presents no problems, though control and security aspects are obviously important. A simple system which helps to achieve control of office cash is also illustrated in Chapter 7.

For Debtors' balances the question of valuation has to be considered even though they are monetary assets. During the year, or at the year end, any amounts deemed to be irrecoverable should be written off as bad debts, but only after all reasonable steps to collect them have been taken. At the point where it has to be recognized that some or all of a debt is uncollectable that amount represents a loss (an expense) rather than an asset and must therefore be transferred from the debtor's account to a Bad Debts account for ultimate transfer to the Profit and Loss account. For instance:

D. Follter A/c

	£		£
June 30 Sales	195	Aug. 24 Bank	100
		Nov. 30 Bad debts	95
	195		195

Bad Debts A/c

	£		£
Nov. 30 D. Follter	95	Dec. 31 P & L account	95

After taking this action where necessary there will often still be some debtors' balances at the year end about which there is significant doubt but where the final act of writing off is not yet warranted. Whilst it may be difficult to quantify the element of doubt for specific debts it will perhaps be known from past experience that a certain percentage of debts outstanding at any time ultimately prove to be irrecoverable. In either case, to include all the debtors at the full amount would be stating the asset at more than it is expected to realize and not recognizing the fact that some loss has probably already taken place even though the amount involved is uncertain. This would be contrary to the principle of prudence already referred to. So whilst no further writing off of specific debts is appropriate there must be a reduction of the total Debtors figure in the Balance Sheet consistent with this element of doubt, with a consequent charge to the Profit and Loss account. Providing for a probable loss, of uncertain amount, in this way is often necessary in accounting, and is referred to as creating a provision.

Let us assume that the year-end balances of the debtors total £36,200 (after writing off all known bad debts) and the element of doubt is estimated at 2% (£724). The procedure is to debit the Profit and Loss account and credit a Provision for Doubtful Debts account with £724. In the Balance Sheet the provision will then be deducted from the Debtors total:

	£
Debtors	36,200
less Provision	724
	35,476

That overcomes the problem at the balance sheet date but what happens next year? The credit balance of the provision account is carried forward, and one method is to leave it unaltered until the next year end when a further review of outstanding Debtors takes place, again after writing off specific bad debts during the year — assume £650 in this case. If the remaining balances on debtors' accounts totalled £45,000 and the 2% uncertainty still seemed appropriate, the provision required at the second year end would be £900. Since £724 has already been provided, only a further £176 now needs charging to the Profit and Loss account. The Balance Sheet will then show:

	£
Debtors	45,000
less Provision	900
	44,100

The relevant accounts would then appear as follows:

Provision for Doubtful Debts

		£			£
Year 1	Balance	724	Year 1	Profit and Loss A/C	724
Year 2	Balance	900	Year 2	Balance	724
			2	Profit and Loss A/C	176
		900			900
			Year 3	Balance	900

Bad Debts

		£			£
Year 2	Various Debts	650	Year 2	Profit and Loss A/C	650

An alternative treatment, which may help you to see more clearly what is happening, is to keep only one account for both bad and doubtful debts. In the second year the actual bad debts of £650 would then be debited against the amount brought forward of

£724, leaving a credit balance of £74. To bring this up to the required closing provision, £826 would then be charged to Profit and Loss account in one sum (rather than in two sums, £650 and £176 as before).

The one account would appear as follows:

Bad and Doubtful Debts

		£			£
Year 1	Balance	724	Year 1	Profit and Loss A/C	724
		———			———
Year 2	Various Debtors	650	Year 2	Balance	724
2	Balance	900	2	Profit and Loss A/C	826
		———			———
		1,550			1,550
		———			———
			Year 3	Balance	900

Q.5a Assume that the provision account was maintained separately at £900 through the third year and that the debtors at the year end totalled £32,000, after writing off specific bad debts. In the light of the year's experience it was decided to adjust the provision to $2\frac{1}{2}\%$. What entries would need to be made? Show the ledger accounts.

Collecting outstanding debts as promptly as possible and the minimizing of losses through bad debts are important aspects of financial management in most organizations. Some assessment of creditworthiness of potential customers is usually applied, prevention being better than cure, but granting credit facilities is an incentive to do business and over-caution may result in loss of orders. There should be regular reviews of outstanding amounts, analysing the age of debts and taking the most appropriate action where there are signs of delay in payment. Usually statements of account are sent to debtors each month, summarizing transactions for that month and requesting payment of the balance. Reminders, letters or telephone calls may then be needed to follow up if there is no settlement in the normal period, which is often the month after the statement date. Whether legal action is finally taken depends on the amount involved, the costs of going to law and the likely outcome.

Q.5b Why is it so important for a business to collect debts as promptly as possible? Brown & Co. offers 2% cash discount for payment within seven days of delivery — otherwise the average collection period is about six weeks. Do you think the cash discount offer is justified?

5.3 Current assets: Stock

We have seen that the cost of goods sold is an expense to be set against the revenue earned from sales in calculating gross profit. It would be possible to record such expense as each item is sold, transferring the appropriate amount from a stock (asset) account to a cost of goods sold (expense) account. However, for most trading businesses this is impracticable and the more usual method is to calculate the amount in total for a period, as follows.

Value of stock at beginning of period
+ Stock purchased and received during the period
− Value of stock at end of period
= Cost of goods sold

Set out as a Trading Account, a typical gross profit calculation would appear as follows:

	£	£
Sales		30,000
Opening stock	5,000	
Purchases	24,000	
	29,000	
less Closing stock	9,000	
Cost of goods sold		20,000
Gross profit		10,000

(Other expenses would then be deducted to find the net profit.)

The amount of the expense and the resultant profit is thus dependent on how closing stock is valued.

Q.5c Note that the total cost of goods sold for a period calculated in this way may be more (but cannot be less) than the aggregate of the costs of all individual items sold during that period. You may like to speculate about reasons for this now, but we will return to the point again soon.

In practical terms the valuation of closing stock involves two stages — first finding the quantity of each item, then working out the value.

The quantity of stock on hand at the end of the accounting period (or at any other time) can be found in one or both of two ways. The proprietor, or one of his employees, will go round the premises and systematically count each item, entering the results on a stock sheet. The stock sheet might have been pre-prepared, with descriptions and locations, to speed the actual count. If it is the annual stocktaking, it should take place at the close of business on the last day of the accounting period, though for obvious reasons this is not always practicable. The alternative is to use the nearest available opportunity, perhaps the weekend, and to adjust the figures for purchases and sales occurring between the date of stocktaking and the year end. The other method of ascertaining the quantity of stock is to maintain continuous records for each item, adjusting the balance for each receipt and issue. This is clearly to be preferred if it is possible, because the management can then be in constant touch with the position of each item, and can achieve better control for purposes of knowing when to re-order and to avoid overstocking. Where this is done, the physical quantities must be checked with the stock records regularly, particularly the more significant items. Provided that such checks are adequate the closing stock quantities can be taken from the stock records.

Q.5d Consider the counting problems that a builders' merchant would have at the annual stocktaking.

The stock under consideration here is that of a trader, buying and selling goods in the same state — a wholesaler or retailer. The treatment of raw materials, work in progress and finished products of a manufacturer is dealt with in Chapter 11. Subject to an important qualification discussed below, the normal basis for valuing closing stock is the cost price originally paid for it. It would normally be wrong to show it at any higher valuation, because some element of profit would then be brought into account before the goods were sold. The two other points to be covered now are, first, the qualification to the cost price rule, and second, how the cost price is ascertained.

If there is any reason to believe that part of the stock held is now worth less to the business than its cost price, it should be included at the lower figure. For example, a business bought some items for £5 each, and expected to sell them for £8 each but because of a change in demand they had to be reduced to half-price, i.e. £4. A sale at the reduced price is reasonably certain. The valuation of the items still in stock at the year end would be £4 each. This is because there is an anticipated loss and the cause of it occurred in the accounting period under review. It may seem illogical that the accountant brings anticipated losses into a period of account whilst refusing to take notice of anticipated profits, but this is an example of the convention of *Prudence*. It is safer to provide for all likely losses in the period, but to disregard possible profits that have not yet been achieved. If there is an element of doubt, it is better to understate the profitability and position than to overstate them. All situations are not as clear-cut as in this example. For instance, it may be discovered that goods in stock have deteriorated in condition, or that their saleability is at risk for other reasons. If there is no ready means of determining an expected market value, it must be left to the responsible official to estimate the stock value, again applying the principle of prudence by erring, if anything, on the low side. Items of stock broken or 'mislaid' obviously cannot be included because the asset value has already been lost: they are an expense of the period. For example:

	£
Value of opening stock	300
Cost price of purchases	2,000
Items broken or pilfered	100
Value of closing stock	400

The total expense for the period is £1,900 (£300 + £2,000 − £400). This includes the cost of goods sold, £1,800, and the loss due to breakage, etc., £100.

Bearing in mind that the £400 closing stock value may be less than the original cost of those items you will see that there are two reasons here in answer to Q.5c. The basis of calculation is therefore the lower of cost or net realizable value, NRV being the estimated selling price less any further costs to be incurred before a sale can be effected. The reason is explained in Statement of Standard Accounting Practice No. 9 (see Chapter 6) as follows:

'The determination of profit for an accounting year requires the matching of costs with related revenues. The cost of unsold or unconsumed stocks and work in progress will have been incurred in the expectation of future revenue, and when this will not arise until a later year it is appropriate to carry forward this cost to be matched with the revenue when it arises; the applicable concept is the matching of cost and revenue in the year in which the revenue arises rather than in the year in which the cost is incurred. If there is no reasonable expectation of sufficient future revenue to cover cost incurred (e.g. as a result of deterioration, obsolescence or a change in demand), the irrecoverable cost should be charged to revenue in the year under review. Thus stocks and work in progress normally need to be stated at cost, or, if lower, at net realisable value.'

Q.5e   The closing stock in a warehouse has been counted and entered, with comments, on to a stock sheet as shown below. Calculate the total stock value.

Item	Quantity counted	Original cost (each) £	Expected S.P. (each) £	Notes	Stock Valuation £
a	300	4	7	10 damaged — will probably be thrown away	
b	120	3	5	all O.K.	
c	100	8	7	S.P. fallen due to change in demand	
d	500	10	15	all O.K.	
e	200	5	7	all O.K.	
f	40	3	4	20 are shop-soiled — will probably go for half price.	
					£

Having established that stock is valued at cost price (or net realizable value if that is lower) it remains to be considered how the cost price is found in practice. If continuous stock records are kept they might show prices as well as quantities, so that is one possibility. Alternatively, it may be necessary to refer back to suppliers' invoices. A problem that can arise in either case is in trying to identify specific items sold with those purchased, and this would affect the results if prices changed over a period — how such situations are resolved is dealt with in Chapter 11. For retailers there are particular difficulties if a large number of relatively small items are held. Many, including Marks & Spencer plc, calculate cost value by first listing selling prices and then deducting the normal gross profit margin.

Q.5f   Assume that products sold in a particular shop can be classified into three types according to the mark-up. For A items 25% is added to cost price when fixing selling prices, for B items it is $33\frac{1}{3}\%$ and for C items 50%. The retailer has counted the closing stock and valued it initially at selling price. The totals are, A items £3,650, B items £4,200 and C items £2,850. The B items figure includes £800 for goods already marked down to cost price (i.e. £800 is both the original cost and the revised expected selling price). What closing stock value should appear in the trading account and balance sheet?

5.4   Fixed assets

Some assets are purchased with the intention that they will be useful to the business over a relatively long period, providing the means by which its operations can be carried on. They have already been referred to as fixed assets and include such items as land and buildings, equipment, furniture or vehicles. Expenditure on fixed assets is sometimes termed Capital Expenditure, as distinct from Revenue Expenditure which is for the purchase of all other assets or services — those likely to be consumed or sold in the short term, for instance wages, rates, and goods for resale. Capital and Revenue Expenditure are terms derived from a method of accounting in vogue a century or so ago, and whilst not particularly apt nowadays, they are still in common usage. It would be more meaningful to talk about fixed and current expenditure. Whatever terms are used, the distinction is an important one. If expenditure is to be regarded as fixed, the asset acquired will be treated as a fixed asset, and its cost becomes an expense over several accounting periods by provisions for depreciation, as we shall soon be demonstrating. If it is not so regarded, the whole cost is usually an expense in one accounting period.

A computer costing £1,000, a motor lorry costing £10,000, a building site costing £100,000 are all fixed assets without any doubt. They should last for several years, and the aggregate expense needs apportioning over those years. Expenditure on stationery or petrol would clearly be classified as current expenditure. What of a stapling machine, however, which costs £5, and would be of service for many years; or some pallets costing £200 which may last for one, two or three years? Notice that it is simpler clerically to treat items as a current expense rather than to be involved in the calculation of annual depreciation charges. If the amount involved is relatively small, the convention of materiality would again apply. 'Relatively small' may mean £10 or less in one organization, or £500 or more in another, but the nature of the asset would also be taken into account in making a decision. It may be preferable to keep it on record as a fixed asset, rather than to have it charged immediately as an expense with the possibility of being forgotten about. If the anticipated useful life is relatively short and uncertain, the same basis for decision will apply. As was stated in Section 3.5, it is a question of whether strict compliance with the proper procedure for apportionment of expense will make any significant difference to the reporting of profits and position. Obviously in the case of the stapling machine it will not, whatever the size of the business, and no one would think of treating it as a fixed asset however long it lasted.

The cost of erecting a building, or installing new plant, is clearly fixed expenditure, but what is included in the cost of the building or plant? All of the costs necessarily incurred to bring the asset into a state of readiness for use or operation, are part of the fixed expenditure, and will be part of the asset's book value. This will therefore include site clearance, foundations, relevant legal charges, architects' fees, and other such costs.

During the asset's life, the costs of maintaining it in the same condition (e.g. pointing the building, servicing and repairing the plant) will be current expenditure, because they do not add to the asset's original capacity for usefulness. It is true that repairs and regular servicing often extend the useful life of an asset beyond what it might otherwise be, but this is not an argument for treating such costs as fixed expenditure. In estimating the life of the asset for depreciation purposes, adequate maintenance will be assumed. On the other hand, if anything is done which adds to its capacity, or otherwise makes it more useful to the business, the cost of the improvement would be treated as fixed expenditure.

Q.5g Would you expect each of the following to be classified as fixed expenditure or as current expenditure:

(a) cost of extension to factory buildings;

(b) cost of clearing the site prior to above extension;

(c) additional filing cabinets for sales office;
(d) painting and decorating boardroom;
(e) £360 spent on guards and other safety devices for machinery, as required by factory inspector;
(f) additional crockery for works canteen;
(g) cost of installing reconditioned engine in delivery van;
(h) wages paid to own workmen for installation of electrical wiring in new factory buildings?

It is usual to find only one ledger account for each type of fixed asset even though the balance represents several different items bought at various times. Supplementary records with details of each individual asset are likely to be kept — often termed a Plant Register (or Vehicles Register). There would be a card or sheet for each item showing depreciation calculations, tax allowances, maintenance history and any other information useful to management.

5.5   Fixed assets: Depreciation — principles and methods

Even a 'fixed' asset generally has a limited life, and can be expected to decline in its value to the business over a period of time. The factors involved in such a loss of value may be physical or economic. The chief physical cause is wear through usage. It may also deteriorate for other physical reasons, such as exposure to the elements. Proper maintenance and repair help to protract the useful life of some assets. Economic causes include:

(a) obsolescence — the asset itself, or the product it produces, being superseded by something newly available;
(b) inadequacy of the size or performance of the asset in an expanding business;
(c) change of policy, e.g. a decision to hire transport instead of using the business's own vehicle.

The decrease in the asset's future service potential arising through one or more of the above factors causes part or all the cost to become an expense, but this transition from asset to expense takes place gradually over the useful life of the asset. The problem is to apportion it as equitably as possible to the several accounting periods in which the asset is used. Over its whole life, the aggregate expense is the purchase cost less any proceeds of sale when the asset is taken out of service, though until this actually happens the length of the useful life, and the residual value, can only be estimated. The expense arising from the decreasing usefulness of a fixed asset is termed depreciation, and the accountant has to determine for each accounting period the appropriate amount to be deducted from the book value and shown as an expense. For example:

Early in year 1, XY Ltd bought a press for £20,000, and expected to have it in use for eight years, at the end of which time about £4,000 is anticipated from its sale. The total estimated expense in this case is therefore £16,000 and the company has to decide how much depreciation should be included as an expense in the profit calculation for year 1 and each subsequent year whilst the asset is still in use.

The most obvious and simple answer is to allocate an equal amount of the estimated depreciation, i.e. £2,000, to each of the eight years, and this method is in fact adopted by a large number of businesses. The purchase cost less the estimated terminal value is divided by the estimated number of years' life, to produce the annual depreciation charge. It is this amount which is then included as an expense in calculating the profit for each period, and which is deducted from the asset's book value. Determining the annual depreciation in this way is referred to as the Fixed-Instalment Method, or alternatively the Straight-Line Method. The reason for the latter name will be apparent from *Fig. 6*.

Notice that where the expected residual value is relatively small it is usually ignored in calculating depreciation.

Assuming that this is the only item of machinery, the balance sheet entry at the end of year 1 would be:

	£	£
FIXED ASSET		
Machinery (cost)	20,000	
less depreciation	2,000	18,000

It is important to understand that the asset's book value (or 'carrying value', as it is alternatively termed) at any stage is that part of the original cost that represents expected future benefits to the business, either in terms of operational use or from its eventual sale. The book value does not purport to be the saleable value at that date. For instance, profiling equipment costing £80,000 was designed for one particular purpose and expected to be fully operational for ten years. After two years at 10% per annum depreciation the book value would be £64,000, and this value in the balance sheet is justified, even though a sale at that time may produce only nominal scrap value. Future benefits equivalent to £64,000 are expected to accrue from using the equipment for the

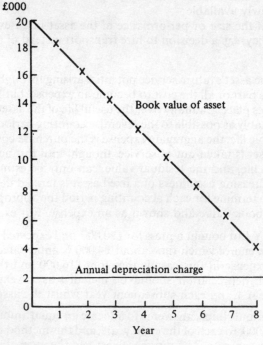

Fig. 6

remaining eight years. The reasoning relies on the assumption that the business will continue in existence for at least as long as the expected life of its operational assets, and this is referred to as the 'going-concern assumption'.

An alternative method of calculating the annual depreciation charge is the Reducing-Balance Method. A percentage is chosen which, when applied to the book value at each stage (the written-down value), will leave the approximate residual value expected at the end of the asset's useful life. Let us apply the reducing-balance method to the £20,000 press. The appropriate percentage can be found by a formula, and in this case is 18%. The amounts to be charged against profits each year and the resultant book values are shown below (*Fig. 7*) together with the corresponding figures based on the straight-line method for comparison.

Whilst the same overall result is achieved by this alternative method, the effect is obviously to charge higher proportions of the expense against the earlier years instead of equal annual instalments throughout. The argument for adopting the reducing-balance method is that with some assets, maintenance costs are likely to be light in the early years, increasing progressively throughout the asset's life. The aggregate expense of maintenance plus depreciation may therefore be more constant by using this method.

Q.5h In *Fig. 6* the straight-line method is shown graphically. Now draw the corresponding graph for the reducing-balance method, using the figures as in *Fig. 7* below.

	Reducing-Balance Method (18%)		Straight-line Method (10%)	
Year	Depreciation charge £	Written-down value £	Depreciation charge £	Written-down value £
1	3,600	16,400	2,000	18,000
2	2,952	13,448	2,000	16,000
3	2,421	11,027	2,000	14,000
4	1,985	9,042	2,000	12,000
5	1,627	7,415	2,000	10,000
6	1,335	6,080	2,000	8,000
7	1,094	4,986	2,000	6,000
8	898	4,088	2,000	4,000

Fig. 7

Q.5i The formula referred to above is:

$$\text{rate} = \left(1 - \sqrt[n]{\frac{R}{C}}\right)100\%$$

where n = number of years
R = residual value
C = original cost

If you wish to try out your mathematical aptitude work out the rate for the above example but with an estimated scrap value of £400 instead of £4,000.

There are other possible approaches to the calculation of depreciation in applying the principle that the overall expense should be apportioned as fairly as possible over the useful life of the fixed asset. For instance, if the expected total service potential could be expressed in units, such as flying hours for an aircraft or the number of productive operations for a machine, then measurement of actual performance for each year would be a good basis for apportionment.

5.6   Adjustment on disposal of an asset

Whichever method is used, the amount of the annual depreciation charge is decided by reference to one figure which is certain (the purchase price) and two estimates (the life and the residual value). Think again of the equipment purchased for £80,000 where the estimated life was 10 years and the expected residual value insignificant. Using the straight-line method the charge was £8,000 per annum, or 10% of the cost. What happens if actual experience is at variance with the estimates, as it usually is? For instance, towards the end of year 9 the production situation changes and, there being no further use for the equipment, it is sold for £800. Now depreciation of £64,000 has already been provided in the first eight years, leaving a book value of £16,000 at the start of year 9. Since only £800 is recovered in cash the remaining £15,200 of asset value must be written off in year 9. This sum represents the benefit from operating the equipment in that year and partly a correction for the underprovision in the first eight years. Year 9 is getting rather more than its fair share of depreciation charged against profits. Had the perfect crystal ball been available and the ultimate outcome predicted exactly from the outset, £8,800 would have been charged for each of nine years (= £79,200). However, absolute prescience is not a normal feature of business life, so annual provisions have to be made on the basis of the best estimates available and the balance of the net expense charged, or possibly credited, in the final year. Supposing that after the first four years, in which £32,000 (4 × £8,000) has been charged against profits, circumstances change and it becomes apparent that only three, rather than six, years of useful life remain. The appropriate action would then be to adjust the annual charge to £16,000 which would give a fairer matching of revenue and expense for those three years than if £10,000 was charged in years 5 and 6 with £28,000 in year 7.

This discussion illustrates one respect in which accounting is not an exact science. The determination of annual profit for a business holding a significant value of fixed assets depends on judgement about what will happen in the future. The overall net expense will find its way into the profit calculations, but the charge for any particular year may subsequently prove to have been an over- or underprovision. Most manufacturing companies are increasingly capital intensive, and depreciation as an element of profit calculation assumes greater importance.

A final related point in this section is the question of whether, having decided the annual depreciation rate, there should be an apportionment in the first year if the asset is purchased midway through the year, rather than at the beginning. If the equipment had been bought in May of year 1 instead of January, and the business decided that £8,000 was to be the annual depreciation charge, should £8,000, £4,000, or some more exact proportion, be treated as an expense of year 1? Thinking again about the expense over the whole life, it does not make any difference. If less is charged in the first year, the book value at the date of sale will be greater, and therefore the terminal adjustment will be different. However the £8,000 per annum was an attempt to estimate the annual expense arising from the use of the asset, and if it is in operation for only a part of the first year, the expense allocated to that year should in theory be only a proportion of the annual charge. It generally depends on the amounts involved as to whether apportionment is warranted, and to what degree of accuracy it is calculated. The convention of materiality is again applicable and there is also a need to be consistent in the treatment of similar items over the years. Some businesses make full provision in the first year irrespective of the date of purchase.

Q.5j   (i) T. Ltd bought a new delivery van for £16,000 on 27 February year 1. It was expected to be used for five years and then have a residual value of £4,000. Using the straight-line method what is the amount of annual depreciation to be charged? Express this also as a percentage of the cost.

(ii) Assume that the company's accounting year ends on 31 December and that a full year's depreciation was charged in year 1. Show the balance sheet entry on 31 December year 2 and explain what the book value of the asset represents.

(iii) T. Ltd sold the van for £6,000 in November year 4. What would be the total expense in respect of the van to be included in the profit calculation for year 4?

(iv) Now assume that only ten months' depreciation was charged in year 1. Calculate the expense for each of the four years. What is the difference from the original situation?

5.7   Effect of depreciation on resources of business

Imagine the improbable situation of a new business, with new fixed assets of £10,000, which are likely to last for ten years, but where no provision is made for depreciation. Imagine also that the proprietor withdraws all of the profit shown in his profit calculation. At the end of his year the position may be:

Abridged Profit Calculation		Abridged Balance Sheet	
	£		£
GROSS PROFIT	8,000	FIXED ASSETS	10,000
EXPENSES	5,000	NET CURRENT ASSETS	6,000
NET PROFIT	3,000	CAPITAL	£16,000
		(£16,000 + 3,000 − 3,000)	

If he maintained the same policy of withdrawing all the net profit throughout ten years, introduced no additional capital, bought no new fixed assets, nor sold any of the original ones, the balance sheet at the end of that time would still be the same as above. If the fixed assets had then to be discarded as worthless, it is apparent that his capital has really shrunk by £10,000, and he would have to inject a similar amount of additional capital (or borrow the money) to buy new fixed assets. Failure to provide depreciation on assets that are diminishing in value is just as bad as using money from the business bank account without recording it. This cautionary tale merely shows that by providing depreciation, the business is at least ensuring that an equivalent amount is retained rather than being withdrawn as part of the profit. If the straight-line method is used, the position at the end of the first year would be:

Abridged Profit Calculation		Abridged Balance Sheet	
	£		£
GROSS PROFIT	8,000	FIXED ASSETS	9,000
		(£10,000 – 1,000)	
EXPENSES	6,000	NET CURRENT ASSETS	7,000
(£5,000 + 1,000)			
NET PROFIT	£2,000	CAPITAL	£16,000
		(£16,000 + 2,000 – 2,000)	

Why, in this second case, has the amount of current assets increased by £1,000? Net profit is now only £2,000, and the proprietor has restricted his drawings to that amount, so an extra £1,000 has been left in the business. The £1,000 by which *expenses* have increased is not represented by an extra *payment* of £1,000. However, it is important to note that this does not necessarily mean the £1,000 will be in the bank and accumulating over the ten years to provide ready cash for replacement. Whilst the withdrawal of a corresponding amount has been precluded, and is still a part of the resources of the business, there may be other uses for it. For instance, if the scale of business is increasing, additional stock may be required, or the debtors may be higher, or additional fixed assets may be bought. There is no reason why the business should not set aside an equivalent amount each year, perhaps by investing it, so that the cash may be made available at the appropriate time, but of course if this is done, it cannot also be used for the other possible requirements instanced above.

One aspect of depreciation which will be developed later is the fact that even if the asset is to be replaced with its exact equivalent in size or capacity, the purchase price may have risen from the original amount. The depreciation provision would not therefore be adequate to ensure retention in the business of the amount required.

5.8   Depreciation in the ledger accounts

Using the profiling equipment example, in the ledger records there will be an account for Equipment with an opening debit balance of £80,000 at the time of purchase. At the end of each year a transfer will be made crediting the asset account and debiting the Depreciation account. In other words, the book value of the asset is being reduced by the depreciation charge which is now treated as an expense. As with other expenses, it will then be transferred to the Profit and Loss account, whilst the Balance Sheet entry will show the net book value. It is often found preferable to split the asset account into two parts, keeping one account to show the original cost of the asset (debit) and a separate account to record the accumulating provisions for depreciation (credit). Using the same example, the accounts at the end of year 3 would appear as follows:

Machinery account

Yr 3	£		£
Jan. 1 Balance b/fwd	80,000		

Provision for Depreciation account

		Yr 3	
		Jan. 1 Balance b/fwd	16,000
		Dec. 31 Depreciation a/c	8,000

Depreciation account

Yr 3		*Yr 3*	
Dec. 31 Prov. for Dep'n	8,000	Dec. 31 Profit & Loss a/c	8,000

The balances from the first two accounts would be carried forward to the next year and provide the figures for the balance sheet. Limited companies are required by the Companies Act to show the cost of fixed assets and the aggregate depreciation separately in their balance sheets.

Finally, we need to look at the entries on disposal of a fixed asset. Assume that a business buys three items of equipment at the beginning of year 1 at a total cost of £16,000. The depreciation rate used is $12\frac{1}{2}\%$ of cost per annum. At the beginning of year 4 one of the items which had originally cost £4,000 was sold for £2,350. The account balances at the beginning of year 4, but before the sale, would be:

Equipment account

Yr 4	£
Jan. 1 Balance b/fwd	16,000

Provision for Depreciation account

		Yr 4	£
		Jan. 1 Balance b/fwd	6,000

The book value of all the equipment is £10,000 and this includes £2,500 in respect of the item to be sold (i.e. £4,000 less £1,500 depreciation). For this item it now transpires that there has been an underprovision for the first three years of £150 or, in other words, there is a loss of £150 from the book value which must be treated as an expense. The ledger accounts would now show:

Equipment account

Yr 4	£	*Yr 4*	£
Jan. 1 Balance b/fwd	16,000	Jan. 1 Sale of equipment a/c	4,000

Provision for Depreciation account

Yr 4		*Yr 4*	£
Jan. 1 Sale of equipment a/c	1,500	Jan. 1 Balance b/fwd	6,000

Sale of Equipment account

Yr 4			*Yr 4*		£
Jan. 1	Equipment a/c	4,000	Jan. 1	Prov. for dep'n a/c	1,500
			1	Cash	2,350
			1	P & L a/c (loss)	150
		4,000			4,000

If a fixed asset sold for more than its book value the resultant gain, which arises because of previous overprovisions, would be credited to the Profit and Loss account. In either case, the 'loss' or 'gain' really represents the balancing adjustment of the depreciation charge.

5.9   Additional questions

[1]

In a retailer's balance sheet, money in the bank, stock held in the shop and the shop fittings are all shown as assets. Identify the main differences in the nature and valuation of these assets.

[2]

Joy started a sports equipment business a year ago and has so far traded only for cash. Some existing and potential customers have enquired about credit terms. Write a memorandum to Joy suggesting the points she needs to bear in mind and the procedures she should introduce.

[3]

After introducing credit terms Joy has noted that an account for goods supplied to The Village Wanderers FC in August, totalling £83.50, is still unpaid in October, though the terms of settlement were the month after delivery. Suggest what action should be taken and, if this includes writing to the club secretary, draft such a letter.

[4]

At 31 December 19X5 the balances in a company's books, and as shown in the balance sheet, included Debtors (total) £18,640 and Provision for Doubtful Debts £1,500. During the following year credit sales were made, totalling £83,240, the money received from Debtors totalled £76,390. Bad debts were written off during, or at the end of, the year amounting to £960. In respect of the remaining debtors it was thought that a provision of £1,800 was appropriate. Show the ledger accounts for Debtors, Bad Debts and Provision for Doubtful Debts and also the closing balance sheet entry.

[5]

	£
(a) The value of stock at the beginning of a period was	1,800
The purchase and receipt of goods for resale during the period was	27,600
The value of stock at the end of the period was	2,500
What was the expense of stock consumed?	

(b) If the stock at the end of the period had contained damaged items which were included and valued at £400 but which we now discover have an estimated saleable value of £200 only, what effect, if any, will this have on the expense of stock consumed? And what effect, if any, on the profit?

[6]
The expense of stock consumed during an accounting period is £13,740 and the stock value at the end of the period showed an increase of £1,450 over the stock value at the beginning. Compute the value of purchases for resale during the period.

[7]
From the following information prepare the Trading Account of L. Chambers & Son for the year to 31 December.

		£
Purchases of goods during the year		36,829
Stock at 1 January		9,587
Sales of goods during the year		49,108
Of the above sales, some were returned for various reasons, and the customers allowed credit		258
Stock at 31 December		10,342

[8]
A fire broke out in the warehouse of A.B. & Co. on 1 March, and destroyed all of the stock. To make the insurance claim, the value of the stock was needed, but there was no record of this. However, it was known that the stock at 1 January was £8,000, and that goods costing £7,000 had been purchased and received into stock during January and February. During the same period goods had been delivered from the warehouse at selling prices totalling £12,000. It was also known that the business added $33\frac{1}{3}\%$ to cost prices when fixing selling prices for all of the goods. What was the value of stock at 1 March?

[9]
The proprietor of a small engineering business finds he cannot take stock on 31 July because of factory holidays. Stock, therefore, was counted during a weekend in August, and afterwards valued at cost £9,580. Subsequent to 31 July and before stock was taken:

(i) goods were despatched and invoiced to customers at £1,460: these sales show a gross profit of £584,

(ii) goods received from and invoiced by suppliers since 31 July for £862 included spare parts worth £150 for the proprietor's motor boat.

Some stocks included and valued at cost in the stock sheets were obsolete, and the proprietor agreed with the auditor to value the items for balance sheet purposes at £80 below cost.

Prepare a statement showing the computation of the stock valuation at the end of the accounting year, 31 July.

[10]

The following is an extract from the stock sheets dated 31 December:

	Count- Units	Rate each	£	p	Comments on method of valuation
'A'	100				
'B'	50				
'C'	80				

Complete the stock sheet by valuing the items.

Additional data which may be needed:

'A' Most recent invoices show 80 were purchased on 14 November from Clayton & Co. for £168 plus £8 carriage charge; 30 came from XL Ltd on 20 December invoiced at £66 net.

'B' 80 from Jay & Co. cost £2 each less 5% cash discount for payment within seven days: prompt payment was made.

'C' These items were bought three years ago at £7 each. At the last year end they were all valued in stock at £5 each. Of the 80 currently in stock, 30 are unsaleable but have a scrap value of £5 the lot. There is an immediate 'fashion' market for the remainder at an estimated selling price of £7 each. However, this fashion sale will involve special packing and selling expenses of £1.20 each.

[11]

'Accountants seem to be inconsistent. If a business buys stock for £100 and expects to sell it later for £120 they would value the stock at £100, but if the expected sale price had dropped to £80 they would then value it at only £80. Why do accountants recognize probable losses before the time of sale but not probable profits?' Can you defend the accountants?

[12]

Explain in general terms what items would normally be included in the cost of erecting an office block which is to be treated as a fixed asset on completion.

[13]

The accountant was being questioned by a member of the works staff. 'That packaging equipment that cost us about ten thousand pounds a couple of years ago — I see it's now valued at £7,500 in the accounts. That can't be right. If we tried to sell it now, we should get virtually nothing for it'. How would you expect the accountant to reply?

[14]

A company recently purchased the following items for use in the office:

Item	Cost £	Est. life (years)	FA or E	Reason
Lever-arch files	8	4		
Typist's chair	115	10		
Typewriter	320	8		
Letter-opening machine	30	5		
Stationery — letterheads	180	2		
Ledger-posting machine	2,000	12		
Ledger trays (for above)	150	12		
Ledger cards (for above)	100	2		
Filing cabinet	130	10		
Security alarm system	2,400	20		
Pencils	5	1		

(a) Decide which items should be treated as Fixed Assets (FA) and which might be regarded as an expense in the year of acquisition (E).

(b) Give a reason for each decision.

[15]

Complete the missing information in the schedule. Assume straight-line method of depreciation.

	Cost (£)	Est. scrap value (£)	Net cost (£)	Est. life (years)	Annual Dep'n (£)	Annual rate per cent on cost (%)
(a)		100	900	4		
(b)	200	nil				20
(c)	1,600		1,200		120	
(d)	60,000			50	1,000	
(e)	1,000		1,000	1		

[16]

A lathe was bought on 1 January 19X0, the start of the financial year, for £20,000. The works engineer estimated a life of eight years with a final scrap value thought to be immaterial. Accordingly, $12\frac{1}{2}\%$ depreciation was charged in each of the next eight years.

(a) If the lathe is still being used for the whole of 19X8 discuss the effect on the Profit and Loss account and Balance Sheet. Could any action have been taken earlier to make the figures in the accounts more relevant?

(b) If the lathe had to be disposed of in December 19X5 for a scrap value of £800 what would be the charge against profits for 19X5? Explain what this represents.

[17]

A press was bought at the beginning of the accounting year on 1 January of year 1 for £32,000. The production engineer estimated a life of ten years and an ultimate saleable value of £2,000. The press became obsolete due to a significant change in production methods in December of year 5, and was sold for £9,000.

(a) Assume fixed-instalment method: calculate the depreciation rate on cost, and complete the schedule showing depreciation, book values and the adjustments necessary on disposal.

(b) Assume reducing-balance method: calculate the depreciation rate and complete the schedule showing depreciation, book values and the adjustments necessary on disposal.

(c) Compare the two methods of depreciation, and discuss the validity of each in the circumstances of this case.

	Fixed-Instalment Method ... % on cost			Reducing-Balance Method ... % on book value		
	Annual dep'n P & L a/c £	Cumu-lative dep'n £	Book value £	Annual dep'n P & L a/c £	Cumu-lative dep'n £	Book value £
1.1, year 1	—	—	32,000	—	—	32,000
31.12, year 1						
31.12, year 2						
31.12, year 3						
31.12, year 4						
31.12, year 5						

[18]
Robert Laing, a trader, has calculated his gross profit for the year to 30 September as £96,050. The other expenses to be set against this (other than depreciation) are:

	£
Wages	20,520
Vehicle running expenses	5,180
Miscellaneous office expenses	4,070
Advertising	1,300

The vehicles had a book value of £12,000 at the beginning of the year, and the office equipment £4,000. He depreciates these assets at 30% and 12½% respectively, using the reducing-balance method. There were no additions to the fixed assets during the year, nor were any sold.

(a) Calculate the Net Profit for the year by showing the remaining part of the Profit and Loss account.

(b) Show how the fixed assets would appear in the Balance Sheet.

[19]
At 31 December 19X7 the balance sheet for R. Lowe's business included the following items:

	£
FIXED ASSETS	
Vehicles (original cost £8,000)	4,800
Office equipment (original cost £3,000)	1,800
CURRENT ASSETS	
Stock of goods for re-sale	2,450
Rent and rates in advance	200
R. LOWE'S CAPITAL	11,800

(The other items have not been shown because you do not need the information for the purpose of this exercise.)

The following is a summary of the transactions which took place during 19X8:

	£
Goods sold	62,814
Goods purchased	36,305
Wages paid	9,851
Rent and Rates paid*	1,620
Miscellaneous expenses paid	1,804
Additional vehicle purchased during January	6,000
Lowe's personal drawings from the business	10,154

* (This includes £300 paid in advance for 19X9.)

At 31 December 19X8 the following additional balances were shown in the books:

	£
Bank balance	260
Cash in hand	30
Debtors	1,840
Creditors	2,500
Stock of goods for re-sale	3,220

The vehicles are depreciated by 20% of cost, and the office equipment by 10% of cost. Show the Profit and Loss account for 19X8 and the Balance Sheet at 31 December 19X8.

[20]

On 1 January of year 10 the fixed assets of a business were in the books as follows:

	Cost	Depreciation to date
	£	£
Equipment	36,000	14,400
Vehicles	15,800	9,480

Equipment is depreciated at 10% of cost and vehicles at 20% of cost. During year 10, transactions affecting the fixed assets were:

(a) Equipment originally costing £6,000 in year 6 was sold for £2,200.
(b) New equipment was purchased at a cost of £8,000. A further £200 had to be paid for the installation.
(c) A vehicle which cost £6,800 in year 7 was traded in against a new vehicle costing £7,400, the business having to pay another £5,200 in cash.

Make all the relevant entries in the ledger accounts and include the year 10 depreciation charge. Show the entries in the year 10 balance sheet. (Assume that the business charges a full year's depreciation in the year of purchase of all fixed assets.)

[21]

The following balances were extracted from the books of a sole trader at the 30 September year end.

(a) Enter the balances in the debit or credit column and check that the trial balance balances. (Do this by identifying the types of account and applying the rules explained in Section 4.2 rather than just referring to a previous trial balance.)

(b) Prepare the Trading and Profit and Loss account for the year to 30 September and a Balance Sheet at that date bearing in mind the effect of the notes shown after the trial balance.

(c) Show how each of the following accounts would appear in the ledger after completion of the final accounts: Capital account; Office expenses account; Equipment account (in this case depreciation can be credited directly to the asset account).

	Balance £	Dr £	Cr £
Cash in hand	48		
Bank balance	1,938		
Equipment (book value at beginning of year)	16,200		
Opening stock	2,982		
Purchases	81,204		
Purchase returns	182		
Sales	128,493		
Office expenses	6,933		
Advertising	1,168		
Wages	25,820		
Bad debts written off	102		
Debtors	18,120		
Creditors	12,840		
Capital	31,000		
Drawings	18,000		

Closing stock was valued at £8,346.

Included in the drawings is an amount of £120 which, after preparation of the trial balance, was found to be a payment for office expenses rather than a withdrawal by the proprietor.

Equipment is depreciated on the reducing balance basis at a rate of 20%.

A further £190 is owing for office expenses at the end of the year.

It was decided to make a provision for doubtful debts of £450 at the year end.

[22]

The main purpose of charging depreciation is to enable fixed assets to be replaced at the end of their useful lives. Examine this view very carefully, explaining the extent of your agreement or disagreement.

Chapter 6

Review of Concepts and Conventions and an Introduction to Interpretation

6.1 A matter of principle

We have already looked at the basis on which profit is measured, the financial position stated in a balance sheet and how all of this links with the ledger account system. Some fundamental accounting concepts were referred to as they became relevant, but it is now appropriate to summarize the underlying theoretical structure, whilst reviewing what has been learned so far.

The object of much academic research is to establish principles, theories or laws which make general statements about the detailed subject matter under investigation. The principles of magnetism in physics and the laws of supply and demand in economics are examples. These concise general statements may be applied to a wide range of practical problems and changing circumstances. This is the truth behind the paradox that 'there is nothing so practical as a sound theory'.

Unlike the laws of physics, chemistry and economics, the principles of accounting are not intended to help towards the *prediction* of future events. Accounting is itself a practical activity and the purpose of accounting theory is to examine the assumptions and ways of thinking which lie behind current accounting practice. Accounting theory seeks to make general statements about basic accounting concepts which are widely accepted by practitioners at a given time. Its function is therefore to provide a *rationale* for current accounting practice.

To avoid confusion with the idea of laws and principles in the natural sciences, writers on accounting theory often prefer the term 'postulates' instead of 'principles': it suggests a rather more tentative proposition of what may be taken for granted or assumed by practitioners. Alternatively, they are sometimes referred to as 'concepts' (ideas and assumptions fundamental to accounting practice) and 'conventions' (customary methods of working). The choice of generic term is not of any great consequence, particularly at this stage, but it is important that we understand the nature of these ideas and how they affect the practical work of the accountant. We shall look at the main ones under the headings of Concepts and Conventions.

6.2   Accounting concepts

Business entity

When introducing balance sheets in Chapter 2, one part of the definition emphasized that it was the financial position *of the business* which was being reported. This was reflected in the double-entry ledger account system, where the proprietor's account was shown on the credit side, thus recording the claim by the proprietor to a part of the business assets. Other people (creditors) may also have claims, and their accounts will show credit balances. The entity is the economic unit which controls the resources and carries on the business activity. This concept is a reminder that we are recording the events from the point of view of that unit (the business). The point of including it as a basic concept is that it limits and defines the scope of what is to be recorded.

When we deal with company accounts at a later stage, the separate identity of the business will be more apparent because it then conforms to the legal position: a limited company is recognized by law as a separate legal person, independent of the people who put capital into it. But with sole traders or partnerships, where the proprietor(s) are personally identified as legally responsible for the conduct of their businesses, the business entity concept still applies and the accounts are those of the business. Transactions which involve the proprietor(s) in a personal capacity only should not, therefore, have any part in the profit calculation or position statement. A person may, of course, run more than one business, and a separate set of books would then be kept for each.

Money measurement

This was also introduced in Chapter 2, as part of the balance sheet definition. It is a reminder of the fact that accounting reports deal only with aspects of the business which can be reduced to monetary terms. The many events and influences which affect the results or prospects of a business, but which are of a non-monetary nature (e.g. human relations, management expertise, goodwill, etc.) are outside the scope of accounting reports, and there is therefore a limit to what can be inferred from those reports. The other serious constraint of measurement in monetary units is that the unit is an unstable one: £1 today is a totally different unit from £1 of ten years ago: it will unfortunately buy far less. Despite this, the Assets column of a traditional balance sheet may add together £s invested in fixed assets (say) ten years ago, to the £s spent on buying stock perhaps last year, to the cash and debtors figures which are in today's £s, without making any distinction. The system rests on an assumption of stability which is clearly not justified by the facts. The problems which this raises are profound, and the attempts to overcome them will be referred to later. Sufficient for the moment that we are reminded of the limitations to the usefulness of accounting information which is reported in monetary units.

Cost

When goods or services are acquired by the business, the traditional basis for recording them is at historical cost — i.e. the amount actually paid, or agreed to be paid, for them. It is this historical cost which is then used for subsequent purposes within the records — for instance, if an item of stock is bought for £20, this is the amount which later becomes an expense in the calculation of profit when it is sold.

There could be different ways of assessing the real value to the business of goods or services, and such values may vary with time and circumstances. For instance, immediately after buying an item of stock for £20, the price at which similar items could be obtained may increase considerably; it might then be argued that the item we hold becomes worth more. By the Cost concept, however, this is ignored, and we stick to the historical cost as the measure of value in the books while it is an asset, and subsequently as the measure of the expense. Similarly, a piece of machinery is originally entered in the books at the cost of acquisition, and it is this amount which is apportioned as an expense in the following years of its useful life.

The argument for using the Cost basis is that it is the simplest and most objective way of dealing with transactions — the amount we agree to pay is a definite measure of the worth to the business at the time of acquisition. Its disadvantage is that the expenses reported in the Profit and Loss Account and the assets shown in the Balance Sheet may not reflect realistic up-to-date values, and could be misleading if decisions are taken on the basis of those reports. For instance, depreciation calculated at, say, 10% of the cost of a machine may not adequately represent the value of using that type of machine several years after the acquisition date, and the residual asset value in the Balance Sheet may also be misleading. This effect is often due to instability of monetary unit values, but might also arise from any other reason for re-assessing the economic value of a service or asset in the light of changing circumstances. Thus an alternative and much cheaper design of machine which will do the same job might subsequently have become available.

When prices are rising, profit measured on the historical cost basis will usually be overstated. This is because current revenues are being matched with past costs. The difference between the original cost of (say) a stock item and its replacement cost at the time of sale ought really to be held back and not regarded as part of profit which can be withdrawn by the proprietors — only by doing this can the business be sure of maintaining the operating capacity represented by the capital. For instance, £100 was invested in a business and all used to buy ten stock items at £10 each. At the end of the period they were all sold for £15 each. The historical cost profit is £50 and the proprietor may decide to withdraw that amount, maintaining his capital at £100. However, if the cost price had risen to £12.50 each at the time of sale the capital would then have been eroded in that it would buy only eight replacement items. From this point of view the profit should have been £25 rather than £50, leaving £125 in the capital account — enough to replace all ten items. This is a considerable problem, particularly when price changes are significant. We return to the discussion in Chapter 17.

Matching

This refers to the accepted basis for measuring profits and losses, which is the difference between the revenue earned in a period, and the expense which can be associated with that revenue. Other ways of reporting results could be devised, but the matching of revenue and associated expense is the one which has come to be universally adopted. When calculating profit at the end of a period, expenditure already incurred which relates to revenue which will be earned in a future period is carried forward as an asset: for example, stock, work in progress, prepayments, or the written-down value of fixed assets; but if all the benefit from the expenditure has already been extracted, there will be no carry-forward, and the expenditure will be part of the profit calculation for the period. In application this often raises practical difficulties, because judgments have to be made as to whether some expenditure should be written off as an expense, or carried forward as an asset on the strength of future expectations. The following extract from

Statement of Standard Accounting Practice No. 2 (Disclosure of accounting policies) makes this point:

> 'The main difficulty arises from the fact that many business transactions have financial effects spreading over a number of years. Decisions have to be made on the extent to which expenditure incurred in one year can reasonably be expected to produce benefits in the form of revenue in other years, and should therefore be carried forward, in whole or in part; that is, should be dealt with in the closing Balance Sheet, as distinct from being dealt with as an expense of the current year in the Profit and Loss Account, because the benefit has been exhausted in that year.'

Realization

This concept is closely related to the previous two: it refers to the point in time at which revenue is recognized, and therefore profit on the transaction brought into account. The method adopted by accountants is to recognize revenue when the goods or services concerned have been transferred to the customer, and an equivalent asset has either already been received, or the right to receive it has been established. This usually means that the customer has either paid cash in exchange for the goods, or has become a debtor for the amount shown on an invoice. When this happens, the revenue is brought into account, which usually means crediting the Sales account and debiting either Cash or Debtors, and in the same period the associated cost will be written off as an expense.

It could be argued that profit on a transaction accrues gradually as the work is done, or negotiations for the sale take place. For instance, a property repairer whose financial year ends on 31 December might have started a particular job in October but not have completed it and invoiced the charge to the customer until early in January. The invoice charge is £300, and the total expenses are £200, of which £150 was incurred up to the end of December. The normal accounting practice would be to carry forward £150 as an asset (Work in Progress) into the next year when the total expense of £200 will be set against the revenue of £300 to show a profit of £100 in that year. In other words, even though most of the profit has in fact been earned as a result of work done in the first year, we do not include it in the accounts until the revenue is recognized. There are some types of business situation in which the basis for revenue recognition has to be adapted to suit the circumstances. One of them is when goods are sold on hire-purchase terms.

Q.6a   Whilst you are not required to deal with hire-purchase transactions at this stage, can you see the reason why the normal basis for revenue recognition given above would be inappropriate?

Another example arises when a business undertakes long-term contracts. A contract may take several years and it would be unrealistic to wait for its completion before bringing any of the profit into account. It is usual in these cases for progress payments to be made to the contractor and for a proportion of the profit, after providing for contingencies, to be allocated to the periods of account whilst the contract is still in progress.

Going concern (continuity)

Assets are included in the Balance Sheet at the amounts they cost, or whatever proportion of that cost is still expected to yield useful benefits in the future. It is thus assumed that the business will continue in existence at least long enough to get the expected use from these assets. If this were not the case, a different view of asset valuation would have to be taken — one which had more reference to realizable values than to the carrying forward of unexpired proportions of cost.

6.3 Accounting conventions

Prudence

We have seen from the Realization concept that profits are not anticipated — they are brought into account for a normal trading transaction only when the sale is completed and there is a reasonable certainty of receiving payment. On the other hand, any losses which are thought to have arisen during the period will be provided for in that period even though their extent is not yet known with any certainty. There are many situations in which estimates of asset valuations have to be made on the basis of their expected future usefulness — for instance, items of stock purchased to meet a consumer demand which is now changing. Unfortunately there is no means of predicting exactly what will happen in the next accounting period, and expenditure has to be written off or carried forward as an asset on the strength of what is judged to be the most probable course of events. Where there is a range of options, the conventional treatment is to adopt a prudent approach providing for all likely losses or liabilities in the light of what information is available, but not anticipating any unrealized gains.

Materiality

Examples of Materiality have already been introduced in Sections 3.5 and 5.4. When deciding how to treat some items of expenditure, there are many instances where the amount involved is so relatively small that it would not make any significant difference to the result whether they were carried forward as assets, or written off as an expense. It is then usually appropriate to do the latter, even though there may be some small amount of benefit to be carried forward into the next period, because apportionment is not warranted. This particularly applies to small items of equipment, where it would be unnecessarily cumbersome to keep charging depreciation over a number of years. Materiality similarly relates to information disclosed in accounting reports. People using those reports should be made aware of all aspects which might influence their evaluation or decisions, so all information material enough for this purpose ought to be disclosed separately rather than being included with other figures.

Consistency

While still working within accepted accounting concepts, there is often scope for treating some items in different ways — for instance, we have just seen that at some point the accountant may decide to treat the purchase of small items of equipment as current expenditure, and would have to decide where to draw the line for this purpose. There are several other examples. The Consistency convention requires that similar items should be treated in the same manner from year to year; otherwise it would be difficult to make a proper comparison of the results. This does not mean that policy as regards the accounting treatment of particular items must always remain the same. For instance, there may be a very good reason for changing from a straight-line to a reducing balance basis for depreciation of some fixed assets in the belief that it will give a more appropriate allocation of the expense. If the effect in the year of change is material it should be disclosed in the annual accounting report.

6.4   Accounting standards

When introducing the concepts and conventions in Section 6.1, we noted that the point of having a conceptual framework is to provide a rationale for the way things are done in practice. That this framework has common acceptance means that when we look at the accounting results of a business, and perhaps use them as the basis for decisions, we can have confidence that they were produced in accordance with the concepts and conventions described. Even though there are severe limitations inherent in some of the concepts, we know of their existence and nature and can interpret the information accordingly. This still does not leave the users of accounting reports in an entirely satisfactory position because whilst working in accord with this framework of concepts there remains plenty of room for manoeuvre. For example, although asset values are based on cost there may be different views about what constitutes cost in some circumstances. When work in progress is carried forward at cost, to what extent should overheads be included as well as wages and materials? Similarly, different methods of charging depreciation can give different results though the concepts are still observed. There are many other examples. We could never reach a position where reported profits and asset values were absolutely exact and objective (not subject to variance according to individual opinion) because so much depends on judgment about what will happen in the future. However, an attempt to narrow the range of possibilities is being made by the Accounting Standards Committee representing the main professional bodies.

The Committee publishes from time to time Statements of Standard Accounting Practice setting out approved methods of accounting for certain types of transaction or circumstances. Professionally qualified accountants are expected to observe the standards or otherwise explain why they were not adhered to. Publication of the standards is preceded by 'exposure drafts' so that opinions can be taken into account before finalizing the statements. An example of an 'SSAP' is the one concerned with valuation of stocks and work in progress, and another deals with the treatment of taxation in company accounts. As your studies of accounting develop beyond this introductory stage you will need to be familiar with the provisions of the standards: they are being introduced here only to show that attempts to make accounting reports more meaningful are in progress.

6.5   Felix Holmes' business

Having summarized the underlying structure of concepts, assumptions and conventions, it may be useful to look at how they apply to the accounts of one particular business. This will also enable us to consolidate some other aspects of the first five chapters and provide a means of introducing the interpretation of accounts.

Felix Holmes has been in business as a small electrical wholesaler for some years. His financial position shown by the last balance sheet to be prepared was as follows:

Balance Sheet at 31 December 19X7

	£			£
CAPITAL	40,000	FIXED ASSETS		
CURRENT LIABILITIES				
Creditors	23,200	Equipment		4,000
		Vehicle		5,600
				9,600
		CURRENT ASSETS		
		Stock	18,000	
		Debtors	33,600	
		Bank	2,000	
				53,600
	63,200			63,200

He keeps proper accounting records, and at the end of 19X8 produces the following summary of information from them.

Trial Balance at 31 December 19X8

	Dr £	Cr £
Goods sold for cash		39,000
Goods sold on credit terms		246,000
Opening stock	18,000	
Purchases of goods	212,200	
Wages	24,850	
Heating, lighting and maintenance	1,720	
Vehicle running costs	6,800	
Administration and miscellaneous	6,030	
Rent, Rates and Insurance	7,960	
Equipment	4,000	
Vehicle	5,600	
Debtors	38,120	
Bank balance	7,320	
Creditors		27,100
F. Holmes — capital		40,000
F. Holmes drawings	19,500	
	£352,100	£352,100

This trial balance is a listing of the balances from the ledger accounts at the end of the year. A ledger account would be kept for each aspect for which separate information was required — in fact there would be more accounts than shown above because the debtors and creditors balances have been aggregated. They each represent one of the following:

Asset (e.g. Cash)
Liability or Capital (e.g. Creditors)
Expense (e.g. Vehicle running costs)
Revenue (e.g. Sales)

Some of the account balances will need adjusting at the end of the year. For instance, an account basically recording an expense may include some asset element if there is a prepayment, or a fixed asset account may need reducing by transfer to an expense in respect of the year's depreciation. Similarly, the opening stock and purchases represent an expense only to the extent that they have been used up and, for many businesses, this is not known until the year-end stock-taking: closing stock can then be brought into the books as an asset and the opening stock plus purchases correspondingly reduced to give the cost of goods sold figure.

In this case the sales represent the revenue earned in the period without any need for adjustment. The process of adjusting other accounts is to match expense (resources consumed) with the year's revenue. The assets carried forward to next year then represent either monetary assets such as cash and debtors, or other resources bought for use in the business where all or some proportion of their cost relates to future revenue.

We can now proceed to the adjustments that Holmes is having to make before he can calculate the profit, and draw up a new balance sheet. These are as follows:

(i) Holmes counted up the closing stock and valued it by reference to recent invoices. The most convenient time for taking stock happened to be two days before 31 December, and the total of the stock sheets on that date came to £20,220. In the following two days no further purchases were made but he noted that items costing £420 had been taken from stock.
(ii) Holmes uses the Reducing Balance method of depreciation, and is working on a percentage of 10% of the written-down value for equipment, and 30% of the written-down value for the vehicle.
(iii) A bonus to the employees as an extra reward for their efforts in 19X8 has been promised but not yet paid. The amount involved is £800.
(iv) The amount shown for Rent, Rates and Insurance includes £220 paid in advance for 19X9. There were no similar prepayments at the beginning of 19X8.

From this information the profit for 19X8 can be calculated and the new position stated at the end of that year. If possible, you should attempt to produce both of the statements before checking with the answers which follow.

Profit and Loss Account for year to 31 December 19X8

	£	£
SALES OF GOODS		285,000
COST OF GOODS SOLD:		
Opening stock + purchases	230,200	
less closing stock	19,800	210,400
GROSS PROFIT		74,600

	£	£
OTHER EXPENSES:		
Wages (including bonus)	25,650	
Vehicle costs	6,800	
Vehicle depreciation	1,680	
Equipment depreciation	400	
Heating, lighting and maintenance	1,720	
Administration and miscellaneous	6,030	
Rent, Rates and Insurance	7,740	50,020
NET PROFIT		24,580

Balance Sheet at 31 December 19X8

	£	£
FIXED ASSETS:		
Equipment		3,600
Vehicle		3,920
		7,520
CURRENT ASSETS:		
Stock	19,800	
Debtors and prepayments	38,340	
Cash at bank	7,320	
	65,460	
Less		
CURRENT LIABILITIES:		
Creditors	27,900	37,560
NET ASSETS EMPLOYED		45,080
PROPRIETOR'S CAPITAL:		
at 1 January 19X8		40,000
add net profit		24,580
		64,580
less drawings		19,500	45,080

6.6 Problems of profit measurement and valuation

Profit measurement

In the Felix Holmes example which we have just considered profit was arrived at by:

(i) matching business revenue for the period with related expense;
(ii) including revenue only when it was translated into cash or a legally enforceable debt;

(iii) determining expense on the basis of actual cost;
(iv) taking notice only of events measurable in money terms;
(v) assuming the business is a going concern;
(vi) applying the conventions of prudence, materiality and consistency where appropriate.

To what extent is £24,580 an accurate and indisputable measure of success in the year? Let us start with an unchallenged acceptance of the money measurement, realization and cost concepts. Some elements of the calculation are then quite certain, always assuming that the records have been properly kept. For instance, the invoiced value of goods sold and the amount paid for wages can be accounted for exactly. Other elements, however, may have been dependent on:

(a) the policy selected for treatment of those items, such as the method of stock valuation, the method of depreciation or the distinction between fixed and current expenditure in marginal cases, and
(b) judgment about future expectations, such as fixed asset lives, the net relizable value of stock where it is probably lower than original cost and whether a provision for doubtful debts was warranted.

The accounting standards previously referred to help to narrow the possible range of different methods of treatment (a) and give a rational and universally adopted basis for their selection whilst leaving room for choice about what is most appropriate to different circumstances. However, decisions about how much expenditure to charge as an expense in the year and how much to carry forward in asset values (b) is entirely a matter for commercial judgment. For Felix Holmes' business depreciation could have been charged at (say) 35% and 15%, respectively, on the vehicle and equipment (instead of 30% and 10%); a more cautious view in the valuation of some old stock could have reduced the total from £19,800 to (say) £17,000; and a more pessimistic opinion of the debtors' reliability may have prompted the creation of a provision for (say) £600. The original profit (£24,580) was no doubt calculated on a prudent basis but the revised amount of £20,700 reflects even greater prudence and only events after the year end will show which was nearer the mark. Whilst there is usually some degree of estimation in the profit calculation for any one year a self-correcting process operates over a longer period — for instance, any under- or overestimation of the depreciation· charge on a fixed asset will be adjusted when that asset is taken out of service. Profit-measurement problems mainly arise because the on-going life of an organization has to be broken up into annual periods for reporting purposes.

With Felix Holmes' business it would be difficult to imagine such problems making too great an impact on the annual profit figures because by the nature of the trading operations much of the expense to be set against revenue is reasonably certain. However, consider a manufacturing business where production is highly mechanized or automated (capital intensive) and the product life is hard to predict. Depreciation will represent a high proportion of total expense and could make very significant differences to the annual profit figures: so too could uncertainty in stock valuations. There might also be considerable development expenditure to design and test prospective new products. The company would have to decide the extent to which this may be carried forward for matching against revenue of future periods if and when the products were finally produced and sold — prudence could then be very difficult to apply and the accountant may play absolutely safe and charge all the development expenditure as an expense in the year in which it was incurred. At the other end of the spectrum of profit-measurement problems, think of a market trader selling fruit and vegetables from a rented stall. There are no fixed assets to depreciate, no stock-valuation problems, no development expenditure and probably no debtors to be doubtful about. The profit can be calculated to the last penny: it is derived from the bookkeeping process without any arbitrary allocations or estimates.

The implications of the money-measurement, realization and cost concepts have already been briefly referred to in Section 6.2 and it is sufficient here to remember that they may have a bearing on the evaluation of the year's results. For instance, more may have been achieved by Felix Holmes than is apparent from the profit figure if he devoted considerable effort in building up customer goodwill or if sales had been arranged but not quite finalized by the year end. On the other hand, in a period of rising prices, profits calculated on the historical cost basis tend to be overstated because in arriving at the expense for cost of goods sold and depreciation no allowance is made for the extra cost of replacing the stock or fixed assets. This can be a serious weakness of the traditional system when price changes are significant either because of high general inflation or for other reasons.

Valuation

All the above points are reflected in the balance sheet. It would be nice to think that the balance sheet gave a succinct statement of what the business is worth to the proprietor: this, however, is far from the truth, if by 'worth' we mean what he could sell the business for. The following are the main reasons:

(i)   The assets include an amount of cash, the value of which is beyond dispute, and the debtors, which will almost certainly realize the amount shown — had there been any doubt, an adjustment should have been made. Otherwise, the assets are included at the values originally paid, less any proportion already allocated as an expense — they are based on input (purchase) values rather than output (potential sales) values.

(ii) An underlying assumption is that the business is going to continue to function under the same proprietorship. This gives some point to the cost basis for asset values. The equipment shown as £3,600 may be worthless to anyone else, but the business is expecting it to be useful for some years to come, and is therefore justified in showing part of its cost as an asset.

(iii) Even if the business were to be sold, much would depend on whether it was as a going concern, or whether the assets were to be disposed of piecemeal. If sold as a going concern, the price to be paid would be negotiated, and would depend upon demand. If it was thought to be a thriving business, with continuing or increasing success potential, the price would reflect this element. The hidden asset which would thus be realized is termed 'goodwill'. There would be no point in attempting to value it as an asset whilst the business continues under the same proprietorship.

(iv) The fixed assets and stock were acquired at some date before 31 December 19X8. The value of money in real terms is subject to change, and for many years has been tending to fall. If the equipment was purchased four years ago for £5,500, its exact equivalent would now cost more than that. Whilst all asset values are expressed in pounds, the pound had different values when some of them were purchased.

(v)   Finally, the future success or failure of the business depends not only on the resources which can be objectively valued for balance sheet purposes but also on the human resources and on environmental factors. The balance sheet only deals with the financial position as it can be expressed in monetary terms.

6.7   Interpreting the results

This is a preliminary look at the way in which information about some aspects of the business can be gleaned from the statements. They may be seen and used for different reasons by people other than the management; for instance,

Inspector of Taxes — as the basis for tax assessment;
Bank Manager — when reviewing overdraft facilities;
Shareholders of a company — as part of the report of their directors' conduct of affairs.

Each will have regard to different factors, according to the nature of their interest. The management will view them as a convenient summary of performance and position, but will also have access to more detailed supporting information throughout the year as well as at the end of it. They should obviously not rely on the annual statements as the only financial barometer.

Q.6b   Before reading further, reconsider the Profit and Loss account and Balance Sheet in Section 6.5 from the point of view of Felix Holmes. Has it been a satisfactory year? Is the position at the end of it satisfactory?

Interpretation of accounts is developed in more detail in Chapter 17, but here are a few basic points which should help us to assess Holmes' performance. Each is qualified by the inadequacy of the information, but this is usually the case. Ratios extracted from the annual profit statement and balance sheet are general indicators only, the starting point for further enquiries. It must also be borne in mind that the statements are usually prepared and made available some time after the end of the year to which they refer.

(a) *Profitability.* Is £24,580 adequate? In the case of a sole trader it is important to note that 'profit' usually includes remuneration for the proprietor's own work in the business, so this makes all the difference in considering the adequacy. If we assume that Holmes' own services had a value equivalent to £16,000 (that is, he would have had to pay a manager £16,000 as an alternative to being personally involved), the true profit is £8,580. This has been earned by capital which at the end of the year was £45,080, giving a return of 19% (or 20% if based on average capital employed). This is better than he would probably have got from investing the same amount elsewhere but, in making such comparisons, notice that

   (i) if Holmes sold the business it might produce much more or much less than £45,080 for him to invest, for reasons already considered,
   (ii) a higher rate of return is expected from putting money into a business with all its attendant risks than from making a relatively safe investment,
   (iii) a proprietor may also have regard to criteria other than monetary returns when judging whether business life is sufficiently rewarding.

(b) *Retention of profit.* Another criterion is that he has made sufficient profit to leave a proportion of it in the business. This is generally desirable for at least three reasons:

(i) to allow for expansion;
(ii) to offset effects of inflation;
(iii) as a safety measure: next year may not be so successful.

Whether he has retained sufficient is open to question.

(c) *Gross profit*. The ratio of gross profit to sales is 26%:

$$\left(\frac{74,600 \times 100}{285,000}\right)$$

Holmes would check how this compared with last year, how it compared with the usual mark-up, and how it compared with figures for the trade, if they were available. Published statistics (see *Business Monitor SDA25*) give retail gross profit percentages and other useful figures for comparison. If his sales included types of goods yielding different rates of gross profit, the overall percentage would of course depend on the sales mix.

Q.6c If the gross profit to sales ratio last year was 30%, consider possible reasons why it has fallen.

(d) *Rate of stock-turn*. During the year the amount of business done (the turnover) was £285,000. The cost price of these sales was £210,400. The cost price of the average stock held during the year was £18,900, i.e.

$$\left(\frac{£18,000 + £19,800}{2}\right)$$

This means that the amount of business done represents approximately eleven times the average stock, (£210,400/£18,900) — or in other words, the rate of stock-turn was eleven times in the year. If the business had sold very large units each costing £18,900, and they always had one in stock, eleven units would have been sold during the year. In fact, the goods will be of varying size and values, and will be in stock for varying lengths of time, but *on average* stock is coming in and going out at the rate of eleven times per year. The average period in stock is therefore 52/11 weeks (about $4\frac{1}{2}$ weeks). Rate of stock-turn is a very significant indicator for a trader. If he can improve it, perhaps by better marketing or organization, his turnover and profits will increase without adding to the amount of money invested in stocks. How quickly stocks are disposed of may reflect policy as well as efficiency — perhaps a better rate of stock-turn could be achieved by a lower selling price, but in this case the overall effect on profits would have to be judged.

Q.6d Comment on the above method of finding the average stock held during the year.

(e) *Working capital*. This term refers to the net resources available for carrying on the day-to-day operations of the business and is found by deducting the current liabilities from the current assets (£37,560 in this example). The working capital ratio is the number of times the current assets exceed the current liabilities so at 31 December 19X8 it is 2.3 times — often expressed as 2.3:1. Having done this calculation it has to be admitted that not much can be read into the result by itself. It is a general indication only of the strength of the current resources and needs further analysis. A low ratio might indicate vulnerability but the ratio could also be too high if, for instance, the business carries more stock or cash than it really needs.

(f) *Liquidity.* An important element of the working capital position is whether the business can pay its way in the immediate future. However successful otherwise, difficulty in settling liabilities could cause a premature end to the venture. In this balance sheet there is £7,320 in the bank, and another £38,340 is likely to arrive there in the next month or so, giving £45,660 from which to pay current liabilities of £27,900 — a ratio of 1.6:1, which seems very safe. However, only by preparing estimates of receipts and payments for a few months in advance, will a satisfactory impression of the adequacy of cash be gained — Holmes may be planning to buy some new equipment.

Q.6e Compute the working capital and liquidity ratios for the previous year end.

There is much more to be said of interpretation of annual statements, but this has provided a start, and we shall be dealing with the topic more fully in Chapter 17. Whenever you now prepare or examine profit statements and balance sheets, attempt some basic interpretation on the above lines, but do not be too hasty in drawing conclusions.

6.8 Additional questions

[1]
A business has just bought for £180,000 a new machine which will probably continue to be of service for between ten and twenty years. Noting that the profits were exceptionally good the General Manager suggested to the Accountant that the machine be written off over four years. 'That should suit your ideas of prudence', he said. How would you expect the Accountant to respond, and why?

[2]
Joe Pinder is in business as a printer. He has been using very old premises for the last thirty years and it is expected that they will soon become the subject of a compulsory purchase order prior to redevelopment. The equipment he uses was purchased when he first started business. It cost £12,000 and has since been written off completely. It is very doubtful whether the equipment would survive being moved to any new premises. At his last year end the results and position were:

Profit and Loss account

	£		£
Rent	3,600	Gross profit	56,000
Wages	22,800		
Vehicle depreciation	800		
Light, heat and various			
other expenses	4,800		
Net profit	24,000		
	56,000		56,000

Balance Sheet

	£	£		£
Capital (at start)	8,000		Vehicle	3,200
add profit	24,000		Stock	2,800
			Debtors	3,100
	32,000		Bank balance	900
less drawings	24,000			
		8,000		
Creditors		2,000		
		10,000		10,000

Discuss the implications of the information given. How meaningful or realistic is the net profit figure and the position shown in the balance sheet? Consider this in the light of the functions of accounting reports and their effectiveness in serving these functions.

[3]
The following is the Profit and Loss account of a trading business:

	£	£
Sales		95,063
Opening stock	6,021	
Purchases	72,814	
	78,835	
less Closing stock	8,722	70,113
Gross profit		24,950
Wages	6,089	
Advertising	516	
Depreciation	1,210	
Office expenses	437	
Rent, rates and insurance	1,769	10,021
Net profit		£14,929

(a) In presenting this statement at the end of the year the accountant was asked why he had rounded off each item to the nearest pound, instead of including pence. He replied that in the first place it was easier to read in this form, and secondly that it would otherwise give an impression of absolute precision which was not warranted. What do you think he meant by the second part of the answer?

(b) Suggest how the measurement of profit in this example might have been affected by some of the accounting conventions.

[4]
Until now a particular business had always used the straight-line method of charging depreciation. A new accountant, after carefully investigating the position, thinks there is a very strong case for using the reducing balance method. 'But you can't change,' he was told 'because that would be against the convention of consistency.' What is your opinion?

[5]

In a company's balance sheet the assets are listed as follows:

	£
Buildings	23,800
Equipment	9,600
Stock of goods	10,300
Debtors	2,100
Balance at bank	800
	£46,600

A shareholder has asked you to explain what the total of the assets column represents. 'Does it mean that we have assets worth £46,600?' Give a full account of how balance sheet asset values are arrived at and state your views about the significance of the total.

[6]

Using the cost concept, current revenues are matched with historical costs. From what two points of view might this be a problem in a period of rising prices?

[7]

Outline three reasons why it would be difficult for a large company designing, manufacturing and selling engines for the aeronautical industry to arrive at an annual profit figure with any certainty. Compare or contrast this situation with that of a food supermarket.

[8]

Explain how the concepts of matching and cost apply to the provision of depreciation on a fixed asset. Use depreciation also to illustrate the conventions of prudence, materiality and consistency.

[9]

A company has just spent £30,000 on market research to investigate the potential sales for a new product being considered. Discuss the problems of applying the matching concept.

[10]

Consider the following statements and draw conclusions concerning the trading policies of the two organisations:

	Company 1	Company 2
	£	£
Sales	45,000	22,500
Cost of goods sold	30,000	13,500
Gross Profit	15,000	9,000
Expenses	9,000	5,000
Net Profit	6,000	4,000
Net Assets employed in companies	40,000	20,000

[11]
The following information relates to the first two years of a business:

	Year 1		Year 2	
	£000	£000	£000	£000
Sales		300		480
Opening stock	—		40	
Purchases	240		360	
	240		400	
less Closing stock	40		60	
Cost of goods sold		200		340
Gross profit		100		140
Other expenses		50		60
NET PROFIT		50		80
Capital at end of year		300		360

(a) For each of the two years, calculate:
    (i) Ratio of gross profit to sales.
    (ii) Rate of stock-turn.
    (iii) Ratio of net profit to capital employed.
(b) Compare the performance of the two years, and describe what you think
    has happened.

[12]
You have been asked for comments on the following balance sheet. What are the main
points you would make?

Balance Sheet at 31 December

CAPITAL	£	£	FIXED ASSETS	£	£
at 1 January	75,000		Buildings (at cost)		60,000
add Net Profit	6,000		Vehicle		
			Bal. at 1 Jan.	4,000	
	81,000		*less* depreciation	50	
less Drawings	9,000				3,950
		72,000	Equipment		
CURRENT LIABILITIES			Bal. at 1 Jan.	600	
Creditors and			*less* depreciation	20	
accruals		2,630			580
			CURRENT ASSETS		
			Stock		9,200
			Debtors and		
			prepayments		840
			Cash at bank		60
		£74,630			£74,630

[13]
Just when it looked as though business was picking up, Des Parrott found he was having difficulty in paying his creditors and went along to his friendly bank manager in the hope of arranging an overdraft. He took with him the following summary of the last two years' figures.

Profit and Loss accounts		Latest year £		Previous year £
Sales		200,000		180,000
Cost of goods sold		130,000		120,000
Gross Profit		70,000		60,000
Wages	30,000		26,000	
Expenses	11,000		8,000	
Depreciation	2,000		2,000	
		43,000		36,000
NET PROFIT		£27,000		£24,000

Balance Sheets		Latest year end £		Previous year end £
Fixed assets		48,000		40,000
Stock		50,000		30,000
Debtors		18,000		15,000
Bank balance				9,000
		£116,000		£94,000
Capital	84,000		80,000	
add profit	27,000		24,000	
	111,000		104,000	
less drawings	30,000		20,000	
		81,000		84,000
Loan		20,000		
Creditors		15,000		10,000
		£116,000		£94,000

Give your views as to why the position has deteriorated and list the points the bank manager would want to know more about.

[14]
Last year, Amy's trading results were as follows:

	£	£
Sales		36,000
Opening stock	4,800	
Purchases	24,000	
	28,800	
Closing stock	4,800	24,000
		12,000
Expenses		4,000
NET PROFIT		£8,000

This year, by spending £800 on advertising and reducing the selling prices to give 30% gross profit on sales, she found she could increase the rate of turnover of stock to seven times. The average stock remained the same and so did the other expenses. Calculate the new net profit.

[15]
Sam Whiting is considering buying a fish and chip business which he has seen advertised in the newspaper. The price asked is £6,000, which includes equipment valued at £3,000 (probable life, five years), the remainder being for goodwill. It is a lock-up rented shop; the rent, rates and insurance amount to £3,900 p.a. Whiting estimates that the electricity and gas will cost about £1,200 p.a. and he will need to employ a part-time assistant at £30 per week. He understands that the gross profit should be in the region of 40% of sales.

Whiting could find £4,000 capital and borrow the remainder at 10% p.a. interest. He thinks it would be worth his while to buy the business if he could earn a total of £15,000 p.a. to cover him for his own wages and a good return on the capital. Under the present ownership the shop opens eight times a week for fifty weeks in the year. Calculate how much on average he would need to take each time the shop was open in order to meet his target income.

[16]
Sam Whiting (see question 15 above) decided to buy the fish and chip business and he raised the purchase price as planned. At the end of the first year his takings were £60,000 and he had paid £37,800 for supplies with a further £700 owing. The rent, rates and insurance totalled £4,000 of which £200 is still owing, but he employed a paid part-time assistant for only half the time expected because his wife came to help out at other times. The electricity and gas cost £1,300 and he had to pay £100 for repairs to the equipment. He withdrew £13,600 from the business bank account for his own use during the year, and the loan interest was paid within the year.

Prepare the Profit and Loss Account for his first year and a Balance Sheet at the end of it. Compare the results with his budget and write a short report summarizing the reasons why he did better or worse than expected.

Chapter 7

Maintaining the Ledger Records

7.1 Methods of posting the ledger

The procedure for maintaining the ledger records and getting the details of the transactions into the accounts varies from business to business. In many cases it is wholly or partly mechanized or computerized. In this chapter we deal with aspects of ledger work in a basically manual system, but introduce principles applicable to any form of account-keeping.

A first principle is that no entry is made into the ledger accounts, whatever form they take, without there being some original record of the transaction. It may be an invoice, a payroll sheet, a cash register tally roll or cheque stub, but there must be some proper evidence of the source of the ledger entry. This is to ensure that only authenticated items find their way into the ledger, and also to allow reference back to the source document for further details, or for audit purposes. If the ledger clerk is allowed to make entries without such a prime record being maintained, errors (innocent or otherwise) will be inevitable. Some method of working must be adopted which precludes the possibility of documents for any transaction being created but not finding their way to the ledger clerk. This is often done by the serial numbering of documents.

For the more frequently recurring type of transaction the system will provide for collection of source material into batches, perhaps weekly or monthly, a batch then being posted to the ledger. This is clearly a more efficient way of working than to enter each item into the ledger as a transaction arises. Sales of goods on credit may be dealt with by retaining a copy of each sales invoice, and assembling the copies in weekly or monthly batches ready for posting. The total amount of the invoices in the batch, probably found by using an add/listing machine, can then be credited to the sales account as one figure, and each invoice total debited to the appropriate debtor's account. The business may, of course, want to analyse the sales into product groups, or some other classification, and this could be done by having separate ledger accounts, by having a sales account with analysis columns or by keeping subsidiary records of the analysis. Goods returned by customers, or allowances made to them for any other reason, would be the subject of credit notes. These are documents notifying the customer that his account has been credited, thus offsetting part of an earlier invoice. Copies of credit notes will also be posted periodically in batches.

Similarly, for purchases, the suppliers' invoices might be used as the posting media, the total of a batch being entered in the stock or purchases account, and each invoice

100

total credited to the suppliers' account. All the invoices may not refer to stock items, in which case they will need sorting according to the classification of expenditure involved, and posting to the debit of the appropriate accounts. A Purchases Analysis Book is sometimes used to facilitate this, rather than posting directly from the invoices. An example of this type of analysis is used in Chapter 10.

7.2   The Journal and correction of errors

In the merchants' books of a few centuries ago, all transactions were first described in a 'waste book'; then the names of the accounts and amounts to be debited and credited in respect of each transaction would be shown in a second book called the Journal. This was in effect an analysis of the elements of the transactions, and an instruction to post to the stated ledger accounts. The procedure was gradually streamlined, and the waste book dropped out of existence. Separate journals (or day books) were kept for each main type of transaction, for instance, a Sales Day Book for credit sales and a Purchases Day Book for credit purchases. The day books really amounted to lists of transactions in chronological order to facilitate posting. Since all the details are shown on copy sales invoices, or on suppliers' invoices, it is a duplication of effort to write them all again in a day book unless the book is to serve some subsidiary purpose such as analysis.

However, there is still usually a use for one type of journal. Some entries need to be made in the ledger which are not the result of one of the main types of transaction. Transfers and adjustments to accounts are necessary from time to time; for example, the writing off of a bad debt, or the correction of a previous posting error. The rule that these are properly documented is a very important one: there must be evidence of the reason for the entries, and there must also be an opportunity for them to be authorized before posting to the ledger. The journal, then, fulfils this purpose. Transactions of a non-routine nature, which would not be dealt with by a normal posting procedure, are entered first in the journal, stating the accounts and amounts to be posted, and the reason for the entries. Some responsible employee will vet the journal entries before they are entered into the ledger. Provided that the above purpose is achieved, the form of the journal is not important. The conventional form is used in *Fig. 8* to show two typical journal entries.

DATE	DETAILS	REF.	DR		CR	
			£	p	£	p
June 30	Bad Debts a/c		51	60		
	G. Wilkinson & Co.				35	50
	Simpson & Wills Ltd				16	10
	Account balances written off per					
	Board resolution 26/15. See					
	correspondence file					
June 30	T. C. Evans & Co. Ltd		43	90		
	T. Evans				43	90
	Correction of posting error from					
	May sales invoices					

Fig. 8

These items would then be posted to the appropriate ledger accounts, and cross-referenced.

Q.7a   In the previous year's accounts of a business, a debt of £24 owing from G. Steele was written off as a bad debt, and at the end of the year transferred as an expense to the Profit and Loss account. Now, in the current year, Steele has unexpectedly sent a cheque for £10. This has been entered in the cash book and posted to Steele's account. Show the journal entry for the other posting that will be necessary.

Q.7b   W. Irons was a debtor for £700. Since Irons was in financial difficulty it was agreed to accept some office furniture valued at this amount in complete settlement of his debt. Show the journal entry required.

Sometimes when a Trial Balance is extracted and does not balance it may not be possible to immediately locate and correct all of the errors contributing to the imbalance. In such cases a Suspense account might be opened with the amount of the difference between the two Trial Balance totals. With the insertion of this new account balance the totals will now agree but, of course, the Suspense account must be cleared as and when the errors are found.

For example, if the total of credit balances exceeded the total of debit balances by £820.68, a Suspense account with a debit balance for that amount might be created. Subsequently two errors are discovered:

  (i) a piece of equipment costing £4,900 had been posted from the Cash Book to the Equipment account as £4,000;
 (ii) goods purchased on credit terms from H. Hall for £79.32 had not been posted to Hall's account (though correctly included in the total posted to the Purchases account).

Correction of the first error would appear in the Journal as:

	Dr £ p	Cr £ p
Equipment a/c	900 00	
Suspense a/c		900 00
Correction of error in posting from C Bk p. 15		

Q.7c   Show the journal entry to correct the second error. Then show how the Suspense account would appear in the ledger.

7.3   Cash and bank accounts

The asset accounts for cash and bank are part of the basic framework of ledger accounts, but may be kept separately from the others. This is because there is often a separation of the responsibility for these assets and the records of them, from the rest of the ledger work. The cashier who is primarily responsible will keep a cash book in a form to suit the particular requirements of the business. Though it may be called a book, it still acts as a ledger account, and debit entries increasing the asset will always have to be credited to some other accounts, and vice versa. Frequently, only the record

Fig. 9

PETTY CASH BOOK

RECEIVED £ p	DATE		REF.	TOTAL PAID £ p	POSTAGE £ p	TRAVELLING EXPENSES £ p	OFFICE SUNDRIES £ p	CANTEEN SUNDRIES £ p
2 60	Jan. 1	Balance						
17 40	1	Cash book						
	Jan. 3	Postages	36	3 85	3 85			
	5	R. Hill, fares	37	1 05		1 05		
	5	Milk	38	1 75				1 75
	10	L. Watt, fares	39	90		90		
	18	Postage	40	1 50	1 50			
	18	Window cleaner	41	1 80			1 80	
	21	Post surcharge	42	10	10			
	25	Canteen	43	3 12				3 12
	30	Rail warrant	44	2 80		2 80		
				16 87	5 45	4 75	1 80	4 87
	31	Balance		3 13				
20 00				20 00				
3 13	Feb. 1	Balance						

(These four totals would be posted to the debit of the four accounts.)

of lodgements into bank, and withdrawals from bank, are kept in the main cash book. Payments in cash may be required only for comparatively trivial items, and an amount out of which they can be met is withdrawn from the bank, and handed to another clerk (Petty Cashier). The petty cashier records the receipt in a petty cash book (as a debit) and credits the payments made, for each of which there must be a proper receipt or voucher. The amount spent is reimbursed by the chief cashier to the petty cashier periodically, bringing the cash holding back to the original amount, called the 'imprest'. The petty cashier is responsible for this imprest, or advance, and, at any time, should be able to produce cash and receipts totalling to that amount. Like the main cash book, the petty cash book entries need posting to the appropriate ledger accounts, and analysis columns may be used to facilitate this where the payments are often for the same expenditure heading. An example of a petty cash book is shown in *Fig. 9* on p. 103.

Returning to the record of the bank lodgements and withdrawals, the balance of this can of course be checked periodically with statements from the bank. A bank statement is a copy of the customer's account in the books of the bank. If AB has an account at the Western Bank, and pays a cheque into it, AB will debit his cash book (an asset is being increased), and credit the account of the person from whom the cheque was received. The bank will receive the money, and credit in their books the account of the person who paid it in, i.e. AB. Thus, AB's account in the bank's ledger is credited with lodgements, and debited with withdrawals, the reverse of the asset account in his own books. Apart from this, however, the balances shown in each of the records at any date should in theory correspond. What happens in practice is that the same transaction may be recorded in the two records on different dates. For instance, if AB draws a cheque in favour of CD on 30 March, he will enter it into his cash book on that date. It may, however, be 1 April before CD receives it through the post, and a day or two later before it is cleared through the banking system. So the Western Bank may not record the transaction until, say, 3 April. Similarly, money paid into the bank on 31 March might not be credited to AB's account until the following day. If the two records are compared on 31 March, they would have to be reconciled for such items before proving that no errors had been made.

Q.7d AB has drawn cheques to the value of £230 at the end of March and sent them to the creditors concerned but they had not been cleared through the banking system by 31 March. AB's bank statement at 31 March shows a credit (favourable) balance of £150. What balance would you expect to find in AB's cash book?

Here is an example of a bank reconciliation.

CASH AT BANK A/c (in P. Wright's ledger)

			£				£
Jan.	1	Balance	165	Jan.	1	Tallis Ltd	53
	13	T. Sprakes	32		24	Spalding Supplies Co.	37
	20	R. Venner	57		27	T. & R. Baker	10
	31	M. Wild	28		31	Collins & Black	40
					31	Balance	142
			£282				£282

Statement of Account with
XY BANK LIMITED

P. Wright
16 Lord Street
Barston

Account No.
015374

Date	Particulars	Payments (Dr) £	Receipts (Cr) £	Balance £
Jan. 1	Balance			165
12	Tallis	53		112
13	Sprakes		32	144
20	Venner		57	201
31	Baker	10		191

Bank reconciliation statement at 31 January

	£	£
Balance as in Cash book		142
deduct amount paid in not yet credited		28
		114
add unpresented cheques	37	
	40	
		77
Balance as on Bank Statement		191

Some differences may initially arise because entries in the bank's records have not yet been included in the business ledger accounts. For example, a charge for interest or for its services may be made by the bank without prior notification, the customer's first knowledge of the charge being its appearance on the bank statement. The amount would have to be entered in the business cash book (or cash at bank account) to bring it up to date before completing the reconciliation statement. Similarly, by arrangement with the bank, amounts can be debited or credited directly to the customer's account and these will also need entering into the cash book if they have not already been posted.

Gray Ltd had a debit balance in the cash at bank account on 30 September of £1,632.56. The bank statement showed a credit balance of £3,086.24 on the same date. Reasons for the difference were identified as:

		£	p
Bank interest charged		28	42
Direct debit for payment of trade			
association subscription, not yet in			
business ledger		33	00
Unpresented cheques	Blake & Co.	1,483	24
	Wye Ltd	324	12
Money paid into bank but not yet credited		292	26

The first two items need to be entered in the cash at bank account and this should be done before preparing a reconciliation statement.

Cash at bank a/c

30 Sept	Balance	1,632.56	30 Sept	Bank interest	28.42
			30 Sept	Subscription	33.00
			30 Sept	Balance	1,571.14
		1,632.56			1,632.56

The revised balance can now be reconciled.

Bank reconciliation statement at 30 September

	£
Balance as in Cash book	1,571.14
deduct amount paid in not yet credited	292.26
	1,278.88
add unpresented cheques	1,807.36
Balance as on Bank Statement	3,086.24

7.4   Total accounts

It is obviously necessary to keep separate accounts for each of the individual debtors of the business. The number of such accounts may form a considerable proportion of all the accounts in the ledger, and for convenience they may be housed separately. One reason for doing this is to facilitate the division of clerical work on the ledger. What happens is that all of the debtors' accounts are kept separately in the Debtors Ledger, and one total debtors' account is substituted in the General Ledger, to show the position of the debtors as a whole. Whenever entries are made in the personal accounts in the debtors ledger, the total of the postings is also entered in the total debtors' account in the general ledger. Thus at any time it is easy to see the position of the debtors in total. It is also possible to agree the aggregate of balances in the personal accounts with the balance of the total account — a useful clerical check. Whenever it is necessary, subsidiary ledgers are created from the general ledger, and one total account substituted. There may be a separate creditors ledger with a total creditors account in the general ledger. Another application of this method may be to have separate accounts for each item of stock in a stock ledger, with one total stock account in the general ledger.

A diagram showing the interrelationship of the entries for a debtors ledger is shown in *Fig. 10*. Notice that the ledger accounts in the Debtors Ledger (Sales Ledger) are in a form slightly different from those we have used before. This format, allowing for the continuous 'up-dating' of the accounts is a typical feature of modern ledger systems. Only the debit side of the cash book is included for the purposes of the illustration. The receipts have been analysed into those affecting the Debtors Ledger, and into other receipts, so that a figure for entry into the total account can easily be ascertained. You will see that the total of the five individual debtors' accounts at 31 January, £38 (£5 + £10 + 0 + £3 + £20) equals the balance of the Debtors Ledger Total account.

As noted in Section 7.1, routine entries are processed in batches using copies of the original documents (or the documents themselves) as the posting media, or alternatively entering them first in some form of analysis book if a breakdown of the amounts was needed. Allowances to customers reducing earlier charges for returns or other reasons would be the subject of credit notes and copies of these would be posted in the same manner as the copy invoices above — but crediting the debtors and debiting a Sales Returns (or Allowances) account. Other adjustments, such as writing

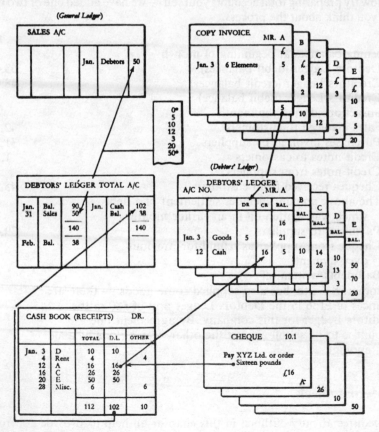

Fig. 10

off bad debts, would be posted to the individual debtors' accounts and to the total account from the journal.

In the books of Darby & Co. the creditors' accounts are kept in a separate ledger, with a Creditors Ledger Total account in the general ledger. The total of balances outstanding at 1 March was £6,320. During March the company received suppliers' invoices for £5,700 and credit notes from suppliers for £250. Cheques paid to suppliers during March totalled £5,980. The Creditors Ledger Total account for March would appear as follows:

Creditors Ledger Total Account

		£				£
March 31	Purchases Returns	250	March 1	Balance		6,320
31	Bank	5,980	31	Purchases		5,700
31	Balance	5,790				
		12,020				12,020
			April 1	Balance		5,790

Q.7e Now try preparing total accounts yourself — we have added one or two new items to make you think about the process.

	£
Opening balances at beginning of month	
Debtors Ledger (debit balances)	63,425
Creditors Ledger (credit balances)	48,914
Creditors Ledger (debit balance)	120
Transactions during the month	
Sales invoiced to customers	42,108
Purchases invoiced by suppliers	31,242
Credit notes to customers	1,314
Credit notes from suppliers	90
Cheques received from customers	45,275
The above amount includes settlement of a debt which was written off in an earlier month	260
Payments to suppliers	39,403
Cheque from supplier as refund for previous overpayment	120
Bad debts written off	138

A customer, XY Ltd, has also supplied some goods — there are balances of £136 in the Debtors Ledger and of £80 in the Creditors Ledger for this company. By agreement one amount is to be set off against the other (leaving one balance outstanding).

7.5 Internal check

The procedures already outlined in this chapter all help to provide control of data within the accounting system so that information extracted can be relied upon as being complete and accurate. A related feature of control, usually referred to as *internal check*, is the organization of the duties and responsibilities of the staff involved in such a way that the maximum possible independent confirmation of each part of the work is provided. For instance, the processing of data relating to credit sales passes through several different stages, including:

    collation of copy invoices,
    posting to the debtors' ledger,
    entering the total account as part of the general ledger work,
    receiving cash from debtors,
    making adjustments for allowances, etc.
    sending out statements, checking that the total of the individual account balances
        agrees with the total account balance
    following up overdue debts.

If one person was responsible for the whole of this work there would be scope for the fraudulent manipulation of the records and a greater risk of other clerical errors or omissions remaining undetected. So duties are separated in such a way as to reduce these dangers. For instance, the member of staff responsible for maintaining the debtors' ledger and sending out statements would not also be in charge of receiving cash from debtors and entering it in the cash book. In a small business there are obvious limitations to the extent to which this principle can be applied but there would have to be only one accounts clerk in a firm for it to have no relevance at all. In larger businesses or other organizations it is usual to have an *internal audit* function, independent of the accounting staff, where the main responsibility is to keep under review the various internal control and internal check procedures and test their operation.

Q.7f List the main stages in preparing the payroll and paying out wages and consider the opportunities for fraud if the internal check system is inadequate.

Q.7g At the end of April the Debtors Ledger Total Account (DLTA) in the general ledger of AB Ltd showed a balance of £18,687.40, but the listing of individual balances in the loose-leaf Debtors Ledger (DL) totalled £18,253.68. After a thorough check the following errors were discovered:

  (i) there was an addition error in one debtor's account, the debit side being undercast by £30.00;
 (ii) the total of the allowances (credit notes) for the month, £383.24, had not been entered in the DLTA;
(iii) a cheque for £138.91 received from a debtor was posted to the wrong side of the account in the DL;
 (iv) a copy sales invoice for CD & Co. was posted to the debit of CPD Ltd account in the DL;
  (v) the account for one debtor, with a balance of £324.80, had been 'temporarily' removed from the DL and was not included in the list of balances;
 (vi) a copy sales invoice for £68.50 had been completely omitted from the month's batch of copy invoices;
(vii) the cash book column for sums received from debtors was overcast by £100.00;
(viii) a copy sales invoice for £132.50 had been posted in the DL as £123.50;
 (ix) a balance of £64.50 for one debtor had been written off as a bad debt in the DL but there were no other entries.

(a) Tabulate the corrections to be made to the original figures using the following format and see if they can now be reconciled:

	DLTA balance		List of DL balances	
	+	−	+	−
(i)			30.00	

(b) Discuss which of the errors are the most serious from an internal check point of view and what action should be taken to improve the system.

7.6 Adapting the ledger records

The double-entry system of keeping accounts described in this and an earlier chapter provides a basic structure but not a straitjacket, and it may need adapting to satisfy the requirements of different situations. The examples of ledger records have been based on simple trading organizations, and variations appropriate to manufacturing businesses will be dealt with in Chapters 11 and 12. The criteria for judging the sort of basic system which we are now thinking of are:

(a) Does it produce reports which show a true and fair view of the performance and position of the business in accordance with accepted accounting principles, and are legal requirements satisfied?
(b) Does it provide information of the quality and detail most appropriate to management's needs for controlling the business affairs?

Continuing at this stage to think principally about organizations providing trading or other services, modifications to the basic pattern of accounts may arise because:

(a) It may be more difficult to determine what revenues and expenses are allocable to specific accounting periods than in previous examples. A car hire business, a dentist, a trader selling goods on hire purchase, and many others, would find that some different accounts were required to enable a proper profit calculation to be made.
(b) The basic accounts may not be sufficiently informative to provide a proper guide for management. So far, the accounts have led to the preparation of a Trading and Profit and Loss account, showing the results of the business as a whole. There may, however, be separate aspects of the business, such as a retailer having a number of branch shops, or a petrol station which also sells cars. The management should then want to know how each aspect contributes to the overall results, and the accounts must provide sufficient analysis for this purpose. Also, if the trader has part of his resources dispersed in different locations, there should be some means of controlling them by knowing from the books what the position ought to be at each point rather than just the total position.

The following example illustrates a simple adaptation aimed at making ledger accounts more informative.

Samuel Tilling

Samuel Tilling had for several years kept a fruit shop in which he and his wife served, with occasional part-time assistance. When the proprietor of the adjacent butcher's shop decided to retire and sell his business, Tilling was able to raise sufficient extra capital to take it over. It was continued as a butcher's shop, but the dividing wall was demolished, and one of the doors replaced by additional window space. A full-time butchery assistant was employed, and some economies were possible: for instance, the same van could be used for all deliveries.

It would be possible to aggregate all information in one set of accounts, i.e. all sales credited to one sales account, all purchases debited to one purchases account, etc. This would still satisfy the first criterion — that the profit of the one enlarged business could be properly calculated and the position reported. However, the accounts would not be very informative from the management point of view. It would be an advantage for Tilling to know the turnover of each section, and the gross profit contributed by each. This would enable him to observe the trends of business done by each of them, and also the separate ratios of gross profit to turnover, which would be quite different. To achieve this all that is necessary is for records of stock, purchases, and sales to be maintained separately, allowing interim and annual trading accounts to be produced for each section.

Purchases Account

	Fruit £	Meat £		Fruit £	Meat £
			Transfer to Trading A/c	108,000	170,200
	108,000	170,200		108,000	170,200

Sales Account

	Fruit £	Meat £		Fruit £	Meat £
Transfer to Trading A/c	120,000	200,000			
	120,000	200,000		120,000	200,000

Trading Account for Year to . . .

	Fruit £	Meat £		Fruit £	Meat £
Opening Stock	200	800	Sales	120,000	200,000
Purchases	108,000	170,200			
	108,200	171,000			
less Closing Stock	200	1,000			
Cost of goods sold	108,000	170,000			
Gross profit	12,000	30,000			
	£120,000	£200,000		£120,000	£200,000

Profit and Loss Account for Year to . . .

	£		£
Wages		Gross Profit — Fruit	12,000
Rent and rates		Gross Profit — Meat	30,000
Van expenses			
Lighting and heating			
Accountant's fees			
etc.			
etc.			
Net Profit			
	£42,000		£42,000

Cash taken in the shop from each of the sections would have to be kept separately until recorded and paid into bank. If credit customers were invoiced for both meat and fruit, the invoices would be analysed before posting to the sales account.

In this case it would be difficult to take the breakdown of profit much further, because most of the other expenses would now be common to both aspects, e.g. lighting and heating, delivery van, rates, accountants' fees, etc. But at least Tilling can assess whether each section is making a reasonable contribution to cover the common expenses and the required profit. If there was a clear division of duties it would be possible to take the analysis one step further by deducting the wages attributable to each section from gross profits.

7.7   Value added tax

Value added tax is a tax on the supply of goods or services which is eventually borne by the final consumer but is collected at each stage during production or distribution. As the name implies it is a tax on the increases in the value of items as they go through the various processes before reaching their ultimate usable state.

Let us take a simplified example to demonstrate how this works. A retailer sells furniture during a period for which the normal charge would be £2,000. VAT (presently at 15%) must be added so that the customers pay £2,300 and must bear the whole cost, including tax. The retailer has collected the £300 tax and is accountable to the revenue authorities for this amount but can first deduct any VAT paid on goods or services bought in during the same period. Assume that these cost £1,200 (net of tax) from the manufacturer, so £1,380 in total will have been paid and the £180 tax is set off against the £300, leaving the retailer to pay £120, which equals 15% of the value added (£2,000 – £1,200). Now the manufacturer having added £180 to the invoiced amount is accountable for this to the revenue authorities but can also deduct any VAT on goods or services purchased in the period. Assume that these are only in the form of timber bought from a forester for a total of £575 (£500 + VAT of £75). The manufacturer will therefore have to account to the revenue authorities for £105 (15% of £700 value added) and the forester will have to pay over the £75 assuming that there was no VAT on inputs of goods or services to set off against it. In summary:

Value added by forester (£500 − 0) at 15% = £ 75 tax paid by forester
Value added by manufacturer at 15%   =   105 tax paid by manufacturer
Value added by retailer at 15%   =   120 tax paid by retailer
Total value added at VAT rate of 15%   =   300 tax borne by customers

The accounting treatment in the books of a manufacturer or trader reflects this role as a collector of the tax and VAT should therefore not normally be included in income or expenditure. When the retailer sells the furniture for £2,300 only £2,000 of this will be credited to the sales account, the tax element going to the credit of a VAT account, whilst the debtors or cash account will be debited with the full invoice charge. Similarly £1,200 will be debited to the appropriate expense accounts, £180 to the VAT account and £1,380 credited to the suppliers account or to cash. This leaves the balance of £120 in the VAT account representing the liability to the revenue authorities.

There is a level of activity below which a trader would not be registered for VAT purposes and would not therefore be required to add VAT to the invoiced amounts. In such cases traders will still suffer value added tax on some of their inputs but cannot recover this from the revenue. The tax then becomes a part of their costs and will presumably be reflected in the prices charged.

Q.7h   A trader's transactions during a period included the following:

	£
Sold goods on credit	4,600
Bought new equipment on credit	2,760
Paid audit fees by cheque	690
Paid VAT to tax authority	160
Paid wages by cash	2,300
Bought stock items on credit	920

(a) The VAT account had a credit balance of £200 at the beginning of this period. Complete the account and say what the closing balance represents.
(b) For each of the first three items show by means of journal entries how the relevant accounts would be affected.

There are several other features of VAT which it is not appropriate to deal with here. This introduction will be sufficient to show the typical procedure and bookkeeping entries.

7.8 Additional questions

[1]
Consider each transaction below and indicate which account will be debited and which account will be credited:

		Debit	Credit
(a)	Cash introduced by proprietor		
(b)	Premises bought for cash		
(c)	Equipment bought on credit		
(d)	Goods for resale bought for cash		
(e)	Goods for resale bought on credit		
(f)	Paid wages and salaries		
(g)	Cash sales to customers		
(h)	Sales to customers on credit		

(i)   Cash drawings by proprietor
(j)   Goods taken by proprietor for private use
(k)   Proprietor brings his own car into the business
(l)   Unserviceable goods returned by credit customers
(m)   Cash received from credit customers in payment of
        debts
(n)   Cash paid to suppliers in payment for goods
        supplied previously on credit terms

[2]

Define in your own words what you understand by:

(a) a purchase invoice   (d) a sales invoice
(b) a cash register tally roll   (e) a statement from a supplier
(c) a credit note   (f) a cash receipt

[3]

During a week, very many invoices are received from suppliers of goods and services.
  Explain the steps you think necessary in order to sort, classify and ultimately make postings to the ledger accounts.

[4]

Enter the following transactions in the ledgers of James Dreb. Balance the accounts at the end of October, carrying down balances as appropriate.

Oct. 4   James Dreb paid £27,000 into a business bank account, and commenced
             trading.
Oct. 5   Bought equipment, £9,000, from H. Dane & Co. £4,000 was paid
             immediately, and the balance of £5,000 was to be paid on 3 Nov.
Oct. 6   Bought goods for resale, £700 from Axel Ltd: granted one week's credit.
             Cash sales during day, £300.
Oct. 8   Paid staff wages, £200 (in cash) after deducting £40 PAYE and £10
             National Insurance.
             Mr Dreb drew £400 cash out of business bank account for private
             purposes, and paid £20 for National Insurance (£10 deduction and £10
             contribution).
Oct. 13   Cash sales during day, £320.
Oct. 14   Paid Axel Ltd cheque for amount now due.
             Sales of £100 to Jones & Co. on weekly credit terms.
Oct. 15   Paid staff wages, £200 (in cash) after deducting £40 PAYE and £10
             National Insurance.
             Paid £20 for National Insurance.
Oct. 17   Paid three months rent for premises in advance, £400.
             Cash sales during day, £350.
Oct. 20   Bought goods for resale, £850 from Axel Ltd on one week's credit.
Oct. 22   Paid off wages, £200 (in cash) after deducting £40 PAYE and £10
             National Insurance.
             Paid £20 for National Insurance.
Oct. 24   Sales of £400 made to Norris Ltd: one month's credit allowed.
Oct. 25   Received cheque from F. Jones & Co. for amount due.
Oct. 28   Norris Ltd paid amount due.
Oct. 29   Paid staff wages, £200 (in cash) after deducting £40 PAYE and £10
             National Insurance.

Paid £20 for National Insurance.
Sundry expenses £150 paid by cheque.

At the end of October, balance the ledger accounts and prepare a trial balance. (Note that on October 8, the total cost of wages to be debited to the wages account is £260 made up of £250 gross wages and £10 employer's contribution for National Insurance. Of this, £220 is paid in cash and will be credited to the Cash account. The £40 tax deduction represents a liability to the Collector of Taxes and will be credited to that account. The wages for other weeks will be treated similarly. At some later date, usually the month end, the accumulated PAYE liability would be paid over to the Collector of Taxes.)

[5]
Roger East is a wholesaler and deals with a large number of retailers. He keeps a separate Debtors Ledger for the personal accounts of the retailers, and a Debtors Total account in the general ledger for control purposes. At 1 February the accounts showed the following balances:

	£
Debtors Total account (in General Ledger)	16,425
Personal accounts (in Debtors Ledger)	
C. Arthur	363
T. Beech & Co.	28
R. T. Bryant	135
A. Cooper Ltd	1,095
T. Cox	12
A. Daines & Son	249
other accounts*	14,543

(*We have shown these as one account to avoid making the exercise too lengthy.)

The following transactions took place during February. Open accounts with the above balances, and enter the transactions into them. Show the other accounts which would be affected in the General Ledger with the exception of the Cash Book — treat the list of cash and cheques received as an extract from the Cash Book. Balance off the personal accounts at the end of February and check that the aggregate of the balances in the Debtors Ledger is equal to the balance of the Debtors Total account.

	£
Credit sales during the month:	
C. Arthur	95
R. T. Bryant	208
A. Cooper Ltd	649
A. Daines & Son	84
other debtors	12,110
Cash or cheques received from debtors during the month:	
C. Arthur	363
T. Beech & Co.	28
R. T. Bryant	100
A. Cooper Ltd	958
A. Daines & Son	249
other debtors	13,782

Credit notes were sent during the month in respect of returns or allowances:

A. Cooper Ltd	84
other debtors	193

It was found that T. Cox was unable to pay the amount outstanding, and a decision was made to write off the balance of his account.

[6]

(a) The following is a summary of the transactions affecting the debtors and creditors of a business. Assume that total accounts are maintained in the general ledger, and show how these would appear. Balance them off at the end of the month.

	£
Balances at 1 March	
Debtors (total)	3,425
Creditors (total)	1,960
Credit sales during March	4,036
Credit purchases during March	1,845
Cash and cheques received from debtors	3,813
Cheques paid to creditors	1,890
Credit notes received from creditors for returns and allowances	103
Credit notes sent to Debtors for returns and allowances	90

(b) Explain the advantages of keeping total accounts for debtors and creditors.

[7]

At 30 September the balance of the bank account as shown in a trader's books was £83.24 overdrawn. The bank statement showed a different balance at that date, and the difference was found to result from:

	£
cheques drawn by the trader but unpresented at 30 Sept.	746.38
payments to the trader received directly into his bank account but not yet recorded in his own books	521.02

What was the balance on the bank statement?

[8]

The balance at 30 April shown by a statement received from the bank was £185.60 (credit). In the business books there was a debit bank balance of £136.20 at the same date. After making a detailed check, the following differences were discovered:

	£
cheques drawn and sent to suppliers during April, but unpresented at 30 April	94.25
cheques received from customer and paid into bank on 30 April but not credited in the bank's records until later	40.45
charges made by bank but not yet entered in cash book	4.40

(a) Explain why the £185.60 balance in the bank's records was a credit balance when it represented an asset of the business.

(b) Prepare a statement to reconcile the difference between the two records.

[9]
Using the documents shown below and on page 118, prepare a bank reconciliation statement at 15 November.

[10]
Adjustments need to be made to the ledger accounts of a business for the following reasons:
  (i) £36.24 received from a debtor, M. Walters & Co., has been incorrectly posted to Waterson Ltd account.
  (ii) £43 owing from R. Dupp has to be written off as a bad debt.
  (iii) A filing cabinet costing £85 has been charged to the Office Expenses account.
  (iv) The proprietor has taken goods purchased for stock to the value of £38.50 for his own personal use.
  (a) Make the journal entries necessary to record these adjustments, ready for posting to the ledger.
  (b) Explain why it would not be good practice to make the entries into the ledger directly without first showing them in the journal.

**Statement of Account with
Miday Bank Limited, Birmingham**

Sheet

14

D. Alan & Co.
Dirmingham

Account No.

123456

Date	Particular	Cheque No.	Payments	Receipts	Balance
			£	£	£
	Opening balance				233.20
5 Nov.		2996	21.50		211.70
8 Nov.	Sundries			153.35	365.05
8 Nov.		2997	5.75		359.30
9 Nov.	Consumer Assoc'n S/O		2.50		356.80
9 Nov.		2999	10.95		345.85
9 Nov.	Midland Ass. D/D		20.00		325.85
10 Nov.	Service charge		1.50		324.35
10 Nov.	Interest to date			.75	325.10
10 Nov.	Sundries			101.22	426.32
11 Nov.	Bank Giro credit			42.70	469.02
11 Nov.		3000	50.00		419.02
12 Nov.		2998	42.75		376.27

Cheques designated by Serial Numbers
S/O Standing Order   D/D Direct debit

Extract From Cash Book of D. Alan & Co.

Date	Details	£ p	Date	Details		£ p
1 Nov.	Balance b/d	233.20	2 Nov.	F. Jones	2994	14.25
1 Nov.	Cash sales	42.75	2 Nov.	Denton Ltd	2995	6.15
1 Nov.	Jennings &		2 Nov.	Foulkes	2996	21.50
	Co.	10.42	4 Nov.	Cash	2997	5.75
2 Nov.	W. Bagley	16.20	5 Nov.	Post Office	2998	42.75
2 Nov.	B. Maxfield	5.45	5 Nov.	Dunlop	2999	10.95
2 Nov.	C. Walter	17.22	9 Nov.	Cash	3000	50.00
3 Nov.	L. C. Lily'		10 Nov.	Schrader	3001	42.75
	& Co.	3.70	10 Nov.	T. I. Ltd	3002	27.00
3 Nov.	Adams &		10 Nov.	G.E.C.	3003	18.60
	Co.	27.00	10 Nov.	Sturdy Ltd	3004	5.20
4 Nov.	Cash sales	14.21	11 Nov.	Cash	3005	50.00
5 Nov.	Heffer Ltd	16.40				
5 Nov.	Cash sales	53.30	11 Nov.	Balance c/d		287.74
8 Nov.	Cash sales	17.82				
8 Nov.	K. Harris &					
	Co.	30.10				
8 Nov.	Giles & Co.	14.22				
9 Nov.	Payne Ltd	62.40				
9 Nov.	Cash sales	18.25				
		£582.64				£582.64
15 Nov.	Balance b/d	287.74				

[11]

(a) Prepare a petty cash book ruling with analysis columns. Decide what headings are appropriate after looking at the transactions in (b). Enter the opening balance at 1 March of £6.60.

(b) Enter the following transactions into the petty cash book. Total all the columns and carry forward the balance at 31 March.

2 March Received cheque to restore balance to imprest amount of £70.

2	Bought postage stamps £3.20.
6	Paid £12.16 for rail fares.
7	Paid 18p surcharge on a letter.
8	Paid £6.30 for office cleaning materials.
15	Bought postage stamps £5.70.
15	Paid £1.35 for bus fares.
19	Bought pencils and office sundries £2.80.
23	Paid £2.20 for registering letters.

25   Paid £8.80 to window cleaner.

28   Bought postage stamps £4.28.

30   Paid £13.10 for rail fares.

(c) Explain what happens to the totals of the analysis columns at the end of the month, and the relationship of the balance of petty cash to the rest of the double-entry system.

[12]
Describe the control features of a petty cash system and show how the principle of internal check applies.

[13]
You have been asked to audit the books of S. Wells Ltd at the year end (31 March). The proprietor has handed to you the ledger accounts together with a trial balance extracted from the general ledger which includes the following balances:

	£
Bank (debit)	377
Debtors Control A/c (total debtors)	22,210
Creditors Control A/c (total creditors)	11,425
Suspense A/c (debit)	155

The Suspense Account had been inserted as a temporary measure because the trial balance did not balance. Separate ledgers are kept for debtors and creditors personal accounts and the lists of balances at the end of the year total £22,290 and £11,200, respectively. The differences between these figures and the balances of the control accounts have not yet been traced. You are also given the bank statement for the last month of the year: this, together with a copy of the bank account in the general ledger, is shown below.

Bank Statement for March

Date	Details	Dr. £	Cr. £	Balance £
Mar. 1	Balance			1,436
3	Green Ltd		70	1,506
12	XL Garage	62		1,444
14	White & Co.		130	1,574
14	Long & Co.	210		1,364
20	Round Brothers	94		1,270
20	Black Ltd		110	1,380
28	Wages	1,123		257
30	Bank charges	22		235
30	Rent (standing order)	120		115
31	Grey & Son		280	395

Bank Account for March

			£				£
Mar.	1	Balance	1,374	Mar.	10	Long & Co.	210
	1	Green Ltd	70		14	Round Brothers	94
	10	White & Co.	130		26	Wages	1,123
	16	Black Ltd	110		30	Short Ltd	300
	25	Grey & Son	280				
	31	Cash paid in	140				

During the course of the audit you discover the following:

(i) The Debtors Control Account balance in the General Ledger has been undercast by £12.

(ii) The cheque received from Black Ltd in March was posted to the personal account as £100, though the Debtors Control Account was not affected by this error.

(iii) An invoice for goods supplied by Robinson & Co. Ltd (£136) had been posted to Robins & Sons Ltd account.

(iv) A refund of £20 received in respect of a previous overpayment of vehicle repair expenses had been debited to both the Cash Account and the Vehicle Repair Account.

(v) A copy invoice for goods sold in February (£242) has not been entered anywhere in the books.

(vi) An invoice for goods supplied by P. Peters Ltd for £30 has been correctly recorded in the purchase day book but was posted to the wrong side of the supplier's account in the Creditors Ledger.

(vii) When listing the balances in the Debtors Ledger an amount of £58 owing from a customer was included twice.

(viii) Returns to suppliers totalling £165 have been correctly entered in the Purchase Returns Account and in the supplier's personal accounts but no entry was made in the Creditors Control Account.

(ix) A debt of £300 owing from a customer was written off as a bad debt by the ledger clerk in January because it had been outstanding for a long time. The customer paid in full by cheque in February and this has been correctly posted. No correction of the January entry has been made.

(x) A payment of £86 for office expenses had been posted to the Office Expenses Account as £68.

(a) Update the Bank Account and prepare a reconciliation with the bank statement at 31 March.

(b) Rule the columns shown below and indicate the adjustments to be made to the General Ledger accounts and to the totals of the Debtors and Creditors Ledger balances arising from the items (i) to (x) above.

Item	Accounts in General Ledger				Debtors Ledger total of balances + or − £	Creditors Ledger total of balances + or − £
	To be debited	£	To be credited	£		

(c) Summarize the results of (b) together with any relevant effects of (a) to show whether the Suspense Account has been eliminated and whether the totals of the Debtors and Creditors Ledger balances now agree with the Debtors Control and Creditors Control Accounts in the General Ledger.

(d) Identify two of the items (i) to (x) which would cause particular concern to an auditor. Briefly give the reason and say how you would propose improving the internal control as a result.

Chapter 8

Incomplete Records and Accounts of Non-profit making Organizations

8.1 The incomplete records problem

Double-entry records are maintained by most businesses. They may be kept on the same lines as the ledger accounts outlined in earlier chapters, or they may form part of a more comprehensive and sophisticated system of data processing. However, there are some businesses which do not keep even the basic double-entry records to show their position and how it is affected by transactions. The reason is usually that the scale of operations is so small that account-keeping does not seem to be warranted: the proprietors might claim that they can mentally retain all the facts and figures they need, or can discover them on an *ad hoc* basis. That not all such claims are really justified is evidenced by the large number of bankruptcies where failure to keep adequate records is found to be a principal factor.

Our interest in the affairs of such organizations is not prompted by the possibility that your own employer might come into this category: rather it is because the exercise of trying to produce useful information from incomplete records may help to consolidate an understanding of some of the work we have done so far. Also, you could some time be called upon to unravel the financial affairs of a small business. If you work in the office of a public accountant, this is a distinct possibility. A part of the work in many professional offices is to prepare, as well as to audit, the accounts for clients with small businesses.

Incomplete records can cover a wide range of possibilities. At one extreme there may be absolutely no records at all, or it may be that attempts to keep them have not been wholly successful. Even though the proprietor has not produced much written evidence of his or her activities, some assistance may still be available in the form of bank statements, suppliers' invoices, etc. Each situation has to be dealt with on its merits. The important defect through failure to keep adequate day-to-day records is the absence of information for management decision and control purposes. All businesses need this, though admittedly for some it is less vital than for others. Though the accountant may be able to salvage from the situation sufficient figures to produce a set of final accounts, this is no substitute. The accountant should always make this apparent to clients whose records are inadequate, and advise them on ways of improving their systems.

This type of situation could not arise with a limited company. Section 221 of the Companies Act 1985 clearly states that accounting records must be kept and they must contain:

(1) entries from day to day of all sums of money received and expended by the company, and the matters in respect of which the receipt and expenditure takes place, and
(2) a record of the assets and liabilities of the company.

It should also be noted that traders registered for Value Added Tax must keep proper records of purchases and sales so that the tax element can be identified.

The sort of task which is involved in an incomplete records situation is illustrated by the following example.

> At the beginning of a year, T. L. Walker, who keeps no double-entry records at all, had a stock of goods with an estimated value of £500, and owed £340 to his trade creditors. Walker's bank statements were analysed, and a figure of £5,400 extracted for payment of suppliers' invoices during the year. At the end of the year the estimate of closing stock value was £400, and there were invoices awaiting payment totalling £520. What is the cost of goods sold during the year? (Try to work this out for yourself before referring to the answer.)

The answer appears to be:

	£
Balance of creditors at end of year	520
Payment of invoices	5,400
	5,920
Balance of creditors at beginning of year	340
Purchases during the year	5,580
Opening stock	500
Purchases	5,580
	6,080
Closing stock	400
Cost of goods sold	5,680

Q.8a   To what extent could this be regarded as a reliable calculation of the cost of goods sold for the year? Can you think of any questions you would want to ask if you were the accountant?

In most cases the solution has to be approached by reconstructing key ledger accounts in summary form, filling in the entries that are given or can be discovered and arriving at other figures by deduction.

For example, I. M. Green had a balance sheet as at 1 January showing the debtors as £1,060. Green kept inadequate records of sales but you are able to extract from the bank statements that £53,842 was received into the bank during the year from debtors. Green estimates that some debtors also paid him in cash — 'probably about £800 in total'. He remembers allowing one particular customer £150 cash discount for prompt payment of a large amount. There were also accounts totalling £900 which he knew were uncollectable and had to be abandoned. At 31 December Green thinks he is owed £1,200.

Q.8b   From your understanding of total accounts in the previous chapter you should be able to reconstruct the Debtors Total account in order to find the sales figure for the year. Having done this, in what respects is it open to question?

Sometimes you may find that the situation is confused by the fact that expenses or drawings have been paid out of cash takings before the balance is paid into the bank account. In the absence of proper records of such payments the accountant must rely on estimates. Again, reconstructing a summary cash account would be the only way of arriving at a figure for receipts from cash sales or cash received from debtors, as shown below.

Cash account

Opening balance (from last balance sheet)	Payments into bank (from bank statement)
Receipts from cash sales or debtors (derived)	Various expenses (estimated)
Withdrawn from bank (from bank statement)	Cash drawings (estimated)
	Closing balance (actual)

At least, in most cases, there will be bank statements available from which rather more reliable information can be gleaned, so a good starting point is often to prepare a summary of the bank account.

8.2   Incomplete records illustration

Frank Cox is a gentleman's hairdresser. He rents a lock-up shop, and employs one junior assistant. He does not keep any written records of earnings or expenses, except for a wages book. At the end of 19X8 the balance sheet extracted by his accountant was as follows:

Balance Sheet, 31 December 19X8

	£		£
Capital	1,520	Equipment	1,260
Trade creditors	120	Stock	180
Rent owing	20	Bank balance	220
	1,660		1,660

Bank statements and cheque stubs yield the following analysis:

	£
Balance at bank, 1 January 19X9	220
Lodgements during the year	4,346
	4,566

Cheques drawn for:

Suppliers' invoices	1,480	
Rent and insurances	2,470	
Electricity	380	
Bank charges	10	4,340
Balance at bank 31 December 19X9		226

Cox is also able to produce the following:

Wages record — all wages and contributions were paid by cash. Total during the year	£4,820
Invoices for payment at 31 December 19X9 (including one for repair of equipment, £36)	£114
Stock summary at 31 December 19X9	£208

Further enquiry revealed:

Cox had taken from cash for his own use (drawings) £300 per week throughout the year.

Goods used personally by Cox were estimated at a value of £30 for the year.

Payments by cash for sundry expenses were estimated at £190 for the year, and for purchase of goods, £70.

Included in the cheque payments to suppliers was an amount of £480 for new equipment.

Depreciation of equipment is to continue at 15% of the book value, including a full year's charge for the new items.

Rent outstanding at the year end is £60.

All the cash balance had been paid into bank at the year end.

From this information you should be able to complete his Profit and Loss Account for 19X9 and a Balance Sheet at 31 December 19X9. Again, don't refer to the following answer until you have made your own attempt. Pay particular attention to the setting out of your calculations: they should be comprehensible, as working papers, to anyone else.

The solution is as follows:

(a) *Calculation of value of goods purchased*

		£
Creditors at 31 December 19X9		114
Deduct repair item included		36
		78
Payments to creditors — through bank	1,480	
Deduct equipment included	480	
		1,000
		1,078
Creditors at 31 December 19X8		120

Goods purchased on credit	958
Goods purchased for cash	70
Total goods purchased	1,028
Deduct goods used personally	30
Total cost of goods purchased for business	998

(b) *Calculation of cash receipts*

Cash paid into bank		4,346
Payments out of cash:		
Wages	4,820	
Expenses	290	
Goods	70	
Cox's drawings (52 × £300)	15,600	
		20,780
Total cash receipts		25,126

(c) *Cox's drawings*

In cash	15,600
Goods	30
	15,630

Profit and Loss Account for 19X9

		£
Total business earnings (b) (charges for services, and sale of goods)		25,126
Goods in stock at 1 Jan.	180	
add Purchases (a)	998	
	1,178	
Goods in stock at 31 Dec.	208	
Goods used during the year	970	
Wages	4,820	
Rent and insurance (£60 + 2,470 − 20)	2,510	
Electricity	380	
Miscellaneous expenses	290	
Bank charges	10	
Repair of equipment	36	
Depreciation of equipment	261	
		9,277
NET PROFIT FOR YEAR		15,849

Balance Sheet at 31 December 19X9

	£		£
CAPITAL		EQUIPMENT (1,260 + 480)	1,740
at 1 Jan.	1,520	less DEPRECIATION	261
add Profit	15,849		
			1,479
	17,369	STOCK	208
less Drawings (c)	15,630	BANK BALANCE	226
at 31 Dec.	1,739		
TRADE CREDITORS	114		
RENT OWING	60		
	1,913		1,913

8.3   Deriving profit from position statements

As a last resort it would be possible to derive a figure for profit or loss by comparing the position at the beginning of the year with that at the end and taking into account estimates of drawings and further capital introduced. This is merely applying an understanding of the relationship of assets, liabilities, capital and profit introduced early in the book. You will remember that Assets − Liabilities = Capital and that Capital is increased by Profit. It could also be increased by the proprietor(s) investing more money in the business and will be decreased by Drawings.

As an illustration, no records of transactions have been kept by C. Lott. Most of Lott's dealings are in cash so the bank statements would not contribute significantly to a reconstruction of the accounts. You can discover the position at the beginning and end of the year as follows:

	1 January	31 December
	£	£
Bank balance	300	420
Cash in hand	1,060	200
Trade debtors	280	450
Trade creditors	1,400	980
Gas and electricity bills outstanding	250	520
Stock (estimated)	4,000	6,000
Equipment (estimated value)	8,000	9,000

Also, at the beginning of the year, Lott bought a second-hand van for £6,000 out of his personal bank account. This was to be regarded as a business asset and it seems reasonable to depreciate it over four years.

The position statements or balance sheets (sometimes known in these circumstances as 'statements of affairs') can be drawn up as follows:

	1 January	31 December
	£	£
Equipment	8,000	9,000
Van		4,500
Stock	4,000	6,000
Debtors	280	450
Bank balance	300	420
Cash in hand	1,060	200
	13,640	20,570
Creditors	1,650	1,500
Proprietor's interest (capital)	11,990	19,070

Q.8c Lott estimates the year's drawings as £18,000. The proprietor's interest has increased by £7,080 during the year, as shown above. Calculate the estimated profit for the year (remember that Lott introduced some new capital during the year).

8.4   Non-profit making organizations

So far, we have been dealing with organizations in business with the aim of making a profit. We have still to consider alternative forms of business ownership, partnerships and limited companies, where profits are also distributable to the proprietors. However, it is appropriate to note here that there are a variety of other organizations where the notion of profit or loss attributable to one or more proprietors does not arise. A wide range of clubs, societies and institutions will be accountable to their members without there being any personal ownership to be represented by capital accounts and without operating success being judged in terms of profitability. For a sports club, a community association, a charity, a body representing the interests of members of a trade or profession, or the many other forms of 'non-profit making' organizations the main financial aim will be to keep income more or less in balance with whatever expenditure is needed to fulfil the objectives of the organization in the short term and in the longer term.

In the simplest type of such organisations the only records likely to be kept are those for cash (and/or bank) receipts and payments. For example, the Much Ado Dramatic Society presents two productions annually, hiring the local church hall. The Society Treasurer will need to keep records of receipts for tickets sold and any other items of income. Payments will include such items as hire of costumes, scenery, rent of the hall, printing tickets and various sundry expenses. At the end of the year the Treasurer should report on the Society's finances at the annual meeting but all that will be necessary is a summary of the receipts and payments.

Much Ado Dramatic Society
Receipts and Payments account for year to 31 December 19X2

		£
Opening balance 1 January		80.50
Receipts		
Sale of tickets	295.60	
Refreshments profit	92.46	388.06
		468.56

Payments

Hire of Church hall	120.00	
Hire of costumes	65.00	
Printing, stationery, postage	94.25	
Sundries	18.72	
Donation to Church funds	80.00	377.97
Closing balance 31 December		£ 90.59

Q.8d   Can you think of any way in which this Receipts and Payments account could be made more informative for members?

Even at this simple level double entry records could still be kept and final accounts extracted in a similar way to the procedure we have followed previously but if all transactions are in cash and there are no significant other assets or liabilities there is little point. A Receipts and Payments account based on the cash book entries is adequate to convey to members the main elements of the year's transactions and what money the Society has in hand. If there were any material liabilities outstanding a note should be added so that members are aware that part of the closing balance is already committed.

8.5   Income and expenditure accounts

The above approach would not give an adequate representation of the year's financial transactions or closing position if there were significant assets and liabilities other than the cash balance. Also, as the nature of the transactions becomes more complex, the need for keeping full records of the effects of the transactions is more apparent. For most non-profit making organisations of any size an annual statement is needed which sets the revenues of the year against the expenses relating to those revenues together with a balance sheet showing the position of all the assets and liabilities. The principles we have been developing so far are also applicable to non-profit making organisations. The two main differences are that the excess of revenues over expenses cannot be regarded as 'profit' (or loss, if the other way round) and there is no capital attributable to individual proprietors. The balance of assets over liabilities at any point in time is regarded as an 'Accumulated Fund' representing the net resources available for future activities. Surpluses of revenues over expenses add to this fund, just as profit adds to capital in a sole trader's business but in this case there are no drawings. Depreciation of fixed assets is an item of expense as all items are now included on an accruals basis rather than just when money is received or paid.

The usual title given to the annual account is Income and Expenditure account. We have to adopt this title because it is in common usage but it is not really consistent with the recognised accounting terminology we have used so far. Revenue and Expense account would be more accurate. However, you should regard the Income and Expenditure account as being the equivalent of the Profit and Loss account. The surplus or deficit is the result of the year's operations after taking into account all relevant revenues and expenses whether or not they represent money actually received or paid within the year.

Here is an illustration. The Bagshot Tennis Club had the following assets and liabilities at the beginning of its year, 1 March 19X1.

	£
Pavilion (cost £6,000, less depreciation £2,400)	3,600
Sundry equipment (at valuation)	420
National Savings Investment account	2,000
Creditors for refreshments	18
Rents and insurance paid in advance	120
Members subscription for 19X1/2 received in advance	46
Bank balance	322
Cash in hand	24

Q.8e Calculate the Accumulated Fund at that date.

During the year to 28 February 19X2 the Cash and Bank book (in summary) showed the following receipts and payments.

	£		£
Opening balances	346	Refreshments	92
Subscriptions for 19X1/2	684	Rent and insurance	480
Subscriptions for 19X2/3	28	Postage and stationery	28
Interest on investment	180	New equipment	84
Dance and whist drives	254	Repairs to pavilion	116
Sale of refreshments	185	Repairs to fencing	86
Court hire	90	Annual affiliation fees	40
		National Savings account	300
		Sundries	46
		Closing balances (Bank £480	
		Cash £15)	495
	1,767		1,767

At end of the year rent and insurance has been prepaid by £140, the equipment is valued at £400, £30 is owing for refreshments and the pavilion is to be depreciated by 5% of cost. The Income and Expenditure account and Balance Sheet could be drawn up as shown below. Here, we have not given the calculations. You would need to do so in an examination. In this case you should check to see if you can confirm all the figures.

Bagshot Tennis Club
Income and Expenditure Account for year to 28 February 19X2

INCOME	£	£
Members' subscriptions		730
Dance and whist drives		254
Profit on sale of refreshments		81
Court hire		90
Interest on investment		180
		1,335

	£	£
EXPENDITURE		
Rent and insurance	460	
Postage and stationery	28	
Repairs to pavilion	116	
Repairs to fencing	86	
Affiliation fees	40	
Depreciation of pavilion	300	
Depreciation of equipment	104	
Sundries	46	
		1,180
SURPLUS FOR YEAR		
		155

Balance Sheet at 28 February 19X2

	£
ASSETS	
Pavilion	3,300
Equipment	400
Investment	2,300
Rent and insurance in advance	140
Bank balance	480
Cash in hand	15
	6,635
LIABILITIES	
Creditors	30
Members' subscriptions in advance	28
	58
ACCUMULATED FUND	
	6,577

You should have found that the Accumulated Fund is equal to the opening balance, £6,422 plus the year's surplus of £155. In presenting the financial statements at the annual meeting the Treasurer would probably show the previous year's figures for comparison. It is quite likely that the Treasurer will also prepare a budget of income and expenditure for the following year. This would provide more useful information when considering whether to make any change in the members' subscription, whether to increase fund-raising activities or any other decisions involving the finances for the coming year.

Some very much bigger organizations than the one in this illustration use income and expenditure accounts — in fact you will find the accounts for two large charities in Chapter 18 where we discuss further the way in which an organization's objectives and ownership (or membership) affect format and content of the annual accounts.

8.6   Additional questions

[1]

James Doe, a market trader, commenced business on 1 January. He maintains no double-entry records and very few written documents, although purchase invoices, cheque stubs, pay-in-slip counterfoils and bank statements are reasonably well preserved in a box-file.

An analysis of payments in the Bank Statements shows:

	£
Cheque paid to vendor of business (for goodwill £5,000; fittings £1,840; stocks £1,000)	7,840
Cheques paid to suppliers (goods for resale)	46,844
Cheques paid to City Treasurer — rates for year	1,680
Cheques paid for phone charges	1,300
Cheques paid to Midland Insurance — trade insurance	608
Bank charges and commission	60
Cheques cashed by James Doe (for assistant's wages £13,680, petty cash £2,800; living expenses £21,160)	37,640

An analysis of receipts in the Bank Statements shows:

Initial deposit by James Doe	9,040
Cheques received from credit customers	23,216
Cash sale receipts (all banked intact)	67,680

Verification disclosed that as at 31 December:

Cash sale receipts not yet banked	320
Credit customers cheques received but not yet banked	560
Cheques already sent to suppliers not yet cleared through bank statements	236
Stock of goods unsold at year end	1,140
Purchase invoices (for goods included in stock) not yet paid	1,236
Sales on credit already invoiced — remittances not yet received from customers	304

Various meetings with James Doe disclosed the following information:

(i) Incidental items paid out of petty cash, £32 per week.
(ii) Cash purchases (goods for resale) £1,088 — from petty cash.
(iii) Doe has taken goods from stock for personal consumption — estimated at £16 per week.
(iv) Depreciation at 10% per annum on cost of fittings is agreed.

Prepare, with appropriate working schedules:

(a) Reconciliation of the Bank Statement with the business cash account at 31 December; and
(b) Trading and Profit and Loss account for the year ended 31 December and a Balance Sheet at that date.

[2]

At the beginning of the year Mrs Shaw used part of her private savings of £20,000 to purchase a business, and for £18,000 she acquired tangible assets in a business as follows:

Fixed assets	£14,000
Stock	2,600
Debtors	1,400

The balance of her savings were paid into the business bank account.

Mrs Shaw kept no ledgers, but at the end of the first year, enquiries disclose:

1. All payments are by cheque, and receipts are banked intact.
2. She draws £100 per week in cash for private expenses, and also during the year goods from stock which are estimated to have cost £2,500.
3. The business bank statement at the year end shows a balance in hand of £3,150 but checking through counterfoils, it seems that cheques sent to suppliers, £190, have not been presented. Receipts not yet banked by Mrs Shaw amount to £140.
4. Sales invoices not paid at year end amount to £800.
5. Statements of account from suppliers at the year end total £2,820, but a scrutiny discloses:
   (a) £100 worth of goods shown on statements have not been received.
   (b) There is a calculation error in a supplier's invoice overcharging £20 for goods already received.
6. Business rent due for last week not yet paid, £200.
7. Stock counted and valued at year end £3,400.
8. The fixed assets are estimated to have a useful life of seven years.

Prepare a statement showing how much profit Mrs Shaw made during the year, and advise her on the financial position displayed at the year end. Show all necessary workings, and state any assumptions you make.

[3]

The financial position of Richard Evans' business at 30 September 19X8 was:

	£	£
Fixed assets (at cost October 19X6)		15,000
Stock at cost	14,580	
Trade debtors	12,600	
Bank	6,100	
	33,280	
Trade creditors	12,050	
Creditors for expenses	400	12,450
Net current assets		20,830
		£35,830
Financed by:		
Capital		£35,830

Mr Evans maintains an analysed cash book which, for the following year, shows:

	£
Receipts from trade customers	124,650
Cash sales receipts	142,170
Payments to trade suppliers	227,080
Cheque payments for general expenses	18,200
Wages and N.I. payments — assistants	22,700
Motor car bought for business	17,650
Withdrawn from bank for private purposes	20,000
Loan from T. Jones (July 19X9)	25,000

At 30 September 19X9, copy sales invoices awaiting payment by customers totalled £8,700. A scrutiny of general expenses showed insurance premiums £220 and vehicle licence £200 were paid in advance. Trade suppliers unpaid at year end £12,700. Creditors for expenses £1,650. Stock was counted on 5 October 19X9 and valued at £45,550. Since the close of business on 30 September sales amounting to £1,400 have been made (estimated to produce a 25% gross profit).

(a) Write up appropriate ledger accounts.
(b) Prepare Trading and Profit and Loss account for year ended 30 September 19X9 and balance sheet at that date, consistent with practice displayed in last year's statement.
(c) Comment on the annual performance of the business, the change in financial position, and any other matters worthy of note.

[4]
Let CB = value of creditors at beginning of the period.
CE = value of creditors at end of the period.
P = value of goods or services purchased on credit from suppliers during period.
M = payments to suppliers during period.

Using these symbols, devise the various equations representing:

(i) CE =
   Creditors at end
(ii) P =
   Goods purchased
(iii) M =
   Payments
(iv) CB =
   Creditors at
      beginning

Now using the following symbols:

DB = debtors at beginning of the period.
DE = debtors at end of the period.
S = value of goods sold on credit to customers during period.
R = remittances from customers during period.

derive the equations representing:

(i) DE =
   Debtors at end
(ii) S
   Credit sales   =
      during period
(iii) R
   Remittances   =
      during period
(iv) DR
   Debtors at   =
      beginning

[5]

Last year, you prepared from incomplete records the accounts of a local tradesman, Peter Wright. The final position was then:

Balance Sheet, 30 September, Year 3

	£
Van (cost £9,000)	5,400
Stock	11,400
Debtors	4,860
Prepaid insurance	240
Bank balance	1,590
	23,490
Trade creditors	2,490
Capital	£21,000

He has not acted on your suggestions to keep fuller records and has now approached you again to prepare the accounts up to 30 September, year 4.

The most reliable information available is a summary of the bank statements, which shows:

	£	
Balance on 1 October, year 3	1,590	
Cash paid in to bank	47,694	
Cheques from debtors	28,770	
	78,054	
Withdrawal by cheque:		
Proprietor's own drawings	6,000	
Purchase of goods	3,048	
New van (£10,800 less trade-in		
of old one £4,950)	5,850	
Rent, rates, insurance	3,720	
Office expenses	2,940	
Trade creditors	56,010	77,568
Balance at 30 September, year 4		£486

He sells goods on credit terms and for cash. Copies of sales invoices kept in an 'unpaid' file total £6,114 (at 30 September, year 4) but two of them, totalling £384, are so old that it is unlikely they will be paid — apparently unsuccessful attempts have already been made to recover these debts. Wright remembers that he allowed some customers discount for prompt payment and estimates the amount involved at £300.

There is £60 cash left in the office at 30 September, year 4. Wright uses the cash coming into the office to meet various payments before taking the remainder to his bank. Of these payments, the wages figure can be ascertained from a wages book as £14,160. Wright has also withdrawn 'an average of £300 cash each month' for his own use and has paid office expenses estimated at £480. He remembers that some debtors settled their accounts by cash and these amounts can be traced — they total £318.

Suppliers' invoices are kept in a box and stamped 'paid' when cheques are drawn. It appears that the total of goods purchased on credit during the year was £57,600, but some were returned and the records for these cannot be traced. It is noticed that some cheques sent to creditors near the end of the year, totalling £792, have not been presented by 30 September, year 4. The unpaid invoices for goods totalled £2,700 at 30 September, year 4.

It has been decided to provide for depreciation at 25% on the new van for the full year. Rates and insurance paid in advance at 30 September, year 4, amount to £660. The closing stock has been counted and valued at £12,360.

Prepare the Trading and Profit and Loss Account for the year to 30 September, year 4, and a Balance Sheet at that date. Show your calculations clearly.

[6]
You have been asked to prepare the final accounts of D. Wilks, a retailer who has not kept a full set of records. The position at the beginning of the year was:

	£	£
Fittings (cost £12,000)		7,600
Car (cost £4,800)		3,360
Stock		9,640
Debtors		7,420
Prepaid insurance		120
Bank balance		240
Cash balance		30
		28,410
Less		
Trade creditors	3,900	
Vehicle expenses accrued	60	3,960
		24,450

Goods are sold both on credit terms and for cash. Cash received in the shop was partly used for various payments before banking the remainder. It is estimated that these payments were:

	£
Wages	13,680
Petrol for vehicle	248
Creditors	600
Personal drawings	9,600

There was a cash balance on 31 December of £40. When there was insufficient cash for paying wages, cheques would be cashed at the bank.

A summary of the bank statements for the year shows:

	£
Opening balance 1 January	272
Cash paid into bank	21,204
Cheques from debtors	45,230
(debtors had settled their	
accounts by cheque only)	
	66,706

	£	£
Less		
Cash withdrawn for wages etc.	4,452	
Cheques to creditors	51,600	
Vehicle expenses	552	
Rates, insurance	1,520	
Advertising	420	
Miscellaneous expenses	1,256	
Personal drawings	700	60,500
Closing balance 31 December		£6,206

It appears that cheques sent to creditors totalling £520 were unpresented at the end of the year: the difference in the bank balances at 1 January was due to the same reason.

An amount of £184 owing from a debtor is to be written off as irrecoverable. Depreciation is to be charged for the year on the fittings at 10% of cost and on the car at 30% of the book value. The debtors and creditors balances at 31 December, year 4, were £8,600 and £3,640 respectively (before writing off the bad debt). During the year there were returns from credit customers of £440. Stock at 31 December, year 4, is valued at £6,848. Insurance has been prepaid by £200 and vehicle expenses are accrued £48 at the end of the year.

Prepare the Trading and Profit and Loss Account for the year to 31 December, year 4, and a Balance Sheet at that date. Show your workings clearly.

[7]

The Crown Bowls Club had been in existence for several years. A statement in the form of a Receipts and Payments account has always been presented at the annual general meeting. The most recent one is shown below.

Receipts and Payments Account for year to 30 October 19X5

	£		£
Bank balance 1 Nov 19X4	316	Rent paid	1,000
Visitors' fees	830	Refreshments	280
Members' subs	5,110	Wages	2,800
Whist drive proceeds	626	Equipment	1,600
Refreshments	310	Stationery, postage, etc.	450
Bequest from deceased member	500	Pavilion repairs	705
		Whist drive expenses	146
		Green maintenance	208
		Prizes	50
		Bank balance 30 Oct 19X5	453
	£7,692		£7,692

At the annual general meeting a member had observed 'We seem to be doing very well and should not need to increase our subscriptions for some time. We managed to pay £1,600 for new equipment and still finish with a higher bank balance.'

You have just been asked to take over as Treasurer of the Club.

(a) Assuming that it was decided to continue using a Receipts and Payments suggest how its form might be improved.

(b) What points do you think might have been made in response to the member's observation at the annual general meeting?

You decide that it would be better to produce an Income and Expenditure account and a Balance Sheet and that it would be a good idea to start by converting the last Receipts and Payments account so that there is fuller information for decisions and also a basis for comparison next year. Your investigations reveal that the pavilion is at least 30 years old and could not be expected to remain in useful service for much more than 4 years from October 19X5. £5,000 has been suggested as a valuation at 1 November 19X4. It was thought that there was equipment worth about £3,200 at 1 November 19X4 and also at that date rent had been paid in advance £200, members' subscriptions had been received in advance £160 and there was an unpaid invoice for pavilion repairs £135.

You also find that the members' subscriptions shown in the Receipts and Payments account include £60 arrears in respect of the previous year and £520 in advance for the year beginning 1 November 19X5. At 30 October 19X5 rent had been paid in advance £400, there was an outstanding invoice for pavilion repairs £560 and it was expected that members' subscriptions of £40 unpaid at that date would still be collected. A depreciation rate of 10% on the book value seems appropriate for the equipment.

(c) Prepare an Income and Expenditure account for the year ended 30 October 19X5 and a Balance Sheet at that date.

(d) Write a report summarising your comments about the Club's finances.

[8]

(a) Compare and contrast the Accumulated Fund balance in the Balance Sheet of a non-profit making organisation with the Capital account of a Sole Trader.

(b) Members of a Club have to pay a joining fee of £100, then an annual membership subscription of £20. How do you think the joining fee might be treated in the accounts of the Club?

(c) Where some members have not paid their annual subscriptions by the end of the year how do you think you should deal with the outstanding amounts?

(d) In addition to the annual Income and Expenditure account and Balance Sheet what further information on the finances of a non-profit making organisation do you think might be useful to present to members?

Chapter 9

Accounting for Different Forms of Organization

9.1 Introduction

The main development of accounting has been in the context of a sole trader — someone in business on his or her own account, providing all the capital and taking all the risks and rewards. This was the simplest way of introducing both concepts and methods. We continue with two other forms of business organization within the private sector, partnerships and limited companies, showing how ownership by more than one person affects the structure of accounting reports. Distinctions as regards ownership between public- and private-sector organizations and as regards objectives between those with a commercial orientation and those providing social or welfare services are then discussed and illustrated in Chapter 18.

Before proceeding with partnerships and companies it may be useful to recapitulate the significance of the profit figure to a sole trader as a basis for comparison with the other forms.

In Chapter 6 we looked at Felix Holmes' business, calculating the profit and setting out the period-end position. The calculation of the closing balance of capital in the balance sheet restates what would appear in the ledger accounts, as shown below.

Notice first of all that Holmes manages the business, and is also the sole owner. After payment of the trade creditors, he is the only person with a claim on the business assets. His drawings against profit during the year total £19,500, though it must be remembered that this presumably includes payment for his own work in the business, as discussed in Section 6.7. It was entirely his decision how much to take out. As it

	Drawings A/c		
	£		£
		19X8	
(Amounts withdrawn at		Dec. 31 Transfer to	
various dates, totalling . . .)	19,500	Capital A/c	19,500
	£19,500		£19,500

Capital A/c

19X8			19X8		
Dec. 31	Drawings	19,500	Jan. 1	Balance	40,000
31	Balance	45,080	Dec. 31	Net Profit	24,580
		£64,580			£64,580
			19X9		
			Jan. 1	Balance	45,080

happens, £5,080 of the year's profit was retained in the business, but he might have withdrawn £25,000 instead of £19,500, or as much as the bank situation would have permitted. The wisdom of retaining part of the year's profit has already been mentioned. Can you recollect the three reasons suggested earlier? However, the point now being made is that there is no restriction on drawings other than the availability of money in the bank; and it would be quite possible, however unfortunate or unwise, to finish the year with a reduced balance of capital. An alternative way of showing the information which at least makes the position clear, even though it would not help in times of difficulty, is to keep the original capital and the retained profits in separate accounts. Thus:

Capital	£40,000
Retained Profits	£5,080

In this way the trader could let the accounts reflect his policy decisions. Having decided what capital was necessary, he would be attempting to keep it intact, limiting withdrawals to the amount in the Retained Profits account. Over the years he may just have a general aim to retain profits, or it might be crystallized into more specific objectives. The purpose of keeping some profit back could be for expansion, that is, to enable additional resources to be employed, or it could be to offset reductions in the purchasing power of the £, particularly important when he comes to replace fixed assets. Additionally (or alternatively) his purpose may be as a hedge against less favourable trading conditions in subsequent years. If either or both of the first two reasons applied, it would be appropriate to make a transfer from the Retained Profits account into Capital, as an indication that he had no intention of withdrawing a corresponding amount out of the business. In this way the amount of the proprietor's interest would be split into two, that part regarded as necessary for the business on a long-term basis, and the other part representing the proportion of profits he feels justified in withdrawing if and when necessary. Having said all of this, it must be admitted that very few sole traders make any formal attempt to decide such policy and represent the distinction in the accounts, though most will be well aware of the significance of changes in the book value of their interest, and have a pretty shrewd idea as to the amount they should be keeping back. The reasons for raising the matter are twofold: first, it would be a decided step forward if many sole traders did consider the whole question of profit-retention policy more formally, though, of course, the weight of the argument depends somewhat on the amount of capital involved. Second, to understand the implications at this stage will provide a good foundation for examining the position of other organizations, particularly limited companies, where a distinction is obligatory.

Before leaving Felix Holmes consider how he could expand his business. One way is by continuing to retain part of the profits. He might also borrow money — from the bank or elsewhere. A further alternative is for someone else to introduce capital into the business, and become a partner.

9.2 Partnerships

Pooling financial resources is not the only motive for forming partnerships. The expertise of the partners may be complementary (e.g. solicitors specializing in their own branch of law), or a partnership could lead to more economic or convenient work arrangements (e.g. doctors). Generally it is open to any individuals collectively to form themselves into an unincorporated association (partnership), or alternatively to become incorporated as a limited company. In some professions, however, it is not desirable or even permissible to trade as an incorporated company.

When a partnership is formed, agreement will be reached on such important issues as the capital to be contributed by each partner, working arrangements and profit sharing. Providing there is no breach of the law, it is entirely up to the partners to negotiate their own arrangements. Capital may be contributed equally, or in any other mutually acceptable proportion that meets the situation. Profit-sharing ratios are again decided by agreement, and are not necessarily in the same proportion as capital contributions. There would usually be other factors to consider, such as the experience and reputation of each partner, the responsibility envisaged or the amount of time to be devoted to the business. The formula for determining profit appropriation may reflect any or all of these factors. Consider the following.

(a) *Allen and Brown* each contribute £5,000 capital to a partnership, and will be equally involved in all other respects. It is probable that they will share profits and losses equally.

(b) *Coles, Dawson and Edrich* form a partnership in which each has equal status and responsibility, and will devote more or less equal time and effort to the business affairs. Coles can contribute £12,000, Dawson £10,000 and Edrich £6,000 towards the total capital needed. Would it be equitable to share profits and losses in the ratio 6:5:3? Probably not, because capital resources represent only one of the factors influencing profitability. Since they are otherwise making equal contributions, the best arrangement may be to share profits (or losses) equally, after allowing for interest at a given rate on the capital sums to be charged against profits and credited to the individual partners. If a rate of 5% is chosen, and the profit to be shared is £32,000, the result would be:

	TOTAL £	C £	D £	E £
Interest on capital	1,400	600	500	300
Balance shared equally	30,600	10,200	10,200	10,200
	32,000	10,800	10,700	10,500

Here the capital is being treated as though it were a loan from the partners to the business, in order to adjust the final shares of each partner. There would have been little point in allowing interest on capital for Allen and Brown since it would not have affected the end result.

(c) *Freeman and Grant* form a partnership, Freeman providing most of the money, and Grant most of the effort. The capital contributions are £40,000 from Freeman and £10,000 from Grant. Grant is to work full time and be primarily responsible for the day-to-day conduct of affairs, but will consult Freeman on policy matters and more important decisions. Here again, the distribution of profit must be a matter for mutual arrangement. Interest on capital could be one element, and in this situation it may be decided that Grant should also have a fixed salary. After charging interest and salary, the balance of profit would then be shared in an agreed ratio, equally or otherwise. Whether or not partnership salaries enter into the profit-distribution formula depends on the circumstances. Where responsibility and duties of the partners is more or less equal, there would be little point, but differentials in seniority, experience and involvement require some adjustment, and this is often the best way of achieving it. If profits are shared without providing for partnership salaries first, this must be borne in mind in assessing the adequacy of total profit in relation to total capital employed.

Q.9a   Assuming that Freeman and Grant's agreement provides for interest on capital at 8%, a salary of £12,000 per annum for Grant, and the residual profit to be shared one-third:two-thirds, how would £37,000 profit be appropriated?

	Total £	Freeman £	Grant £
Interest			
Salary			
Balance of profit			

The agreed ratio for sharing profits would, of course, normally apply also in the event of a loss. What would happen if Freeman and Grant's profit had been insufficient to cover interest and salary, say, £13,000 instead of £37,000. As always with partnerships, reference must first be made to the agreement, to see if this situation is catered for. Generally the answer would be that interest and salary are still credited to the partners in full, and the residual loss is shared in the agreed ratio. Thus:

	Total £	Freeman £	Grant £
Interest	4,000	3,200	800
Salary	12,000		12,000
	16,000	3,200	12,800
Balance of loss	3,000	1,000	2,000
	13,000	2,200	10,800

The purpose of the Partnership Act 1890 is not to legislate for the conduct of partnership affairs, but to define where a partnership exists and to clarify the legal position where there is an element of doubt about the partners' intentions. Section 24 of the Act sets out the bases for deciding shares of profit where the partners have made no express or implied agreement to the contrary. For instance, if they have not come to any arrangement about interest on capital, and there is subsequently a dispute, by the terms of Section 24 no interest would be allowable. Similarly, partnership salaries could not be claimed in the absence of some evidence of agreement to the contrary. Where the profit-sharing ratio had not been specified in any way, the Act, if it had to be invoked, would require equal shares.

9.3   The partners' accounts

It is clearly essential to keep accounts which show separately the relationship of each partner with the firm as a whole. Moreover, for each partner, accounts showing the capital contribution and the share of the profit should be kept separately. With a sole proprietor, the desirability of keeping this distinction in evidence from a policy-making point of view has been referred to. With a partnership, it is more important. If one partner were to make withdrawals of capital it could jeopardize the position of the firm as a whole. Only by the provision of long-term finance can the business hold the resources of fixed assets and working capital necessary for its continued existence.

After the net profit calculation, the appropriation of the profit in the agreed manner will be shown in a further section of the Profit and Loss account. This section is sometimes referred to separately as the Appropriation account. The partners' shares are debited to the Appropriation account and credited to their individual accounts. If a proper distinction is made shares of profit are kept separately from capital, and another individual account, called the Current account, is used for this purpose. A credit in a partner's current account indicates the amount which could be withdrawn in respect of accrued profits, whereas a credit in the capital account, although also representing a claim by the partner on the business, is the amount contracted to be made available on a more permanent basis.

Cash drawings against profit are debited to the current account. Sometimes, where money has been withdrawn in anticipation of profits at intervals during the accounting period, the debits are assembled in a Drawings account, the aggregate being transferred to current account at the end of the period. The only merit of doing this, rather than debiting the current account direct, is that the latter will then show all the information in summarized form, i.e. the total drawings in one figure. If the total entitlement due to a partner at the end of the period has not been withdrawn, the remaining credit balance will be carried forward, and included with the liabilities in the balance sheet. This would normally be the case, because the profit calculation in respect of a period is not completed until some time afterwards, and the partners tend to keep within their estimates of the expected allocation. If it transpired that a current account was overdrawn, a debit balance would be carried forward to the next period, and shown in the balance sheet as a deduction either from other current account balances or from the capital of the partner concerned. It really represents an asset to the business, being the amount the partner should repay, or more probably have set against the share of profit in the subsequent period; but it is better to show the relationship between the business and its proprietors in one place. The foregoing can now be illustrated by a simple example.

Returning to Freeman and Grant (Section 9.2(c)), assume that at the beginning of a year the credit balances on their current accounts were £600 and £300 respectively. During the year to 31 December Freeman withdrew £10,400, and Grant £26,300, and the profit for the year was £37,000. The relevant accounts would be as follows:

Capital A/cs

		F	G				F	G
							£	£
				Jan.	1	Balance	40,000	10,000

Drawings A/cs

		F	G				F	G
(Amounts withdrawn at various dates, totalling . . .)		10,400	26,300	Dec. 31		Transfer to Current A/cs	10,400	26,300
		10,400	26,300				10,400	26,300

Current A/cs

		F	G				F	G
Dec. 31	Drawings	10,400	26,300	Jan.	1	Balance	600	300
31	Balances	400	800	Dec. 31		Interest	3,200	800
						Salary		12,000
						Profit	7,000	14,000
		10,800	27,100				10,800	27,100
				Jan.	1	Balance	400	800

Profit and Loss Account

		£			£
(Expenses)			(Gross Profit)		
NET PROFIT		37,000			
INTEREST	F	3,200	NET PROFIT		37,000
	G	800			
SALARY	G	12,000			
PROFIT	F	7,000			
	G	14,000			
		37,000			37,000

Extract from Balance Sheet at 31 December

		£
CAPITAL A/CS.		
	F	40,000
	G	10,000
CURRENT A/CS.		
	F	400
	G	800

In the above example, notice that the partnership salary of £12,000 due to Grant has been included as an appropriation of profit, rather than as an element of the profit calculation. This procedure can be justified because it represents part of the formula for appropriation of profit, and the £12,000 may be a measure of the differential in value of the two partners' services, rather than a realistic assessment of Grant's earning power. However, it is not a very strong argument, and how the salary is treated may depend on the partners' intentions as evidenced in their agreement. If a specific salary is to be payable to a partner on a regular monthly basis, and quite separately from his entitlement to profit, it could be recorded separately, and brought into the Profit and Loss account as an expense. Practice varies, but it should again be noted that before placing too much significance on the amount of net profit, the treatment of payment for services rendered by proprietors needs to be checked. A final point to be made here is that the partners should have a policy with regard to retention of profit. If they consider long-term retention necessary, the appropriate mutually agreed amount would be transferred from current accounts to capital accounts.

Q.9b   Reverting to Coles, Dawson and Edrich, assume that their current accounts had beginning of the year credit balances of £120, £20 and £70 respectively, and the drawings for the year were £10,890, £10,780 and £10,510 respectively. Their agreement is as in Section 9.2(b), and the year's profit is £32,000. Set out the Appropriation account and the Current accounts and show the balance sheet entries for the partners' interests.

9.4   Limited companies

The distinction between the sole trader and partnership form of organization and that of a company can be illustrated (see *Fig. 11*).

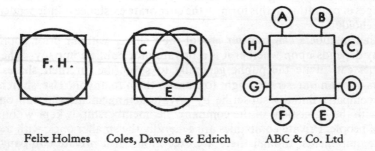

Felix Holmes   Coles, Dawson & Edrich   ABC & Co. Ltd

Fig. 11

Proprietors (people owning the business) are represented by circles, whilst the squares are the business organizations as legal entities. Only in the case of the limited company does the business have a legal personality of its own, distinct from that of the proprietors. If you conduct some transaction with Felix Holmes' business, you involve Felix Holmes personally, and he, as a legal person, can be held liable for any consequences, even though the amount of such liability may be in excess of the value of the business assets. Similarly, with a partnership, the partners are legally identified with the business they conduct, and have unlimited liability for its debts. For a sole proprietor and a partnership, management of the business is also the direct responsibility of the proprietors, whereas the shareholders of a company delegate management to a board of directors. The diagram represents the position of legal identity and of management, but for the sole proprietor and partnership it does not properly indicate the accounting position. Whatever the form of organization, the accounts are those of the business, as distinct from the owners, and in each case the owners are shown as having claims on the business assets for the amount of their interests (initial capital plus retained profits).

A limited company has a legal identity independent of the people who created it, or who currently hold shares of ownership. For instance, if shareholder E felt that the directors were defrauding him in some way he could bring an action against the company to obtain redress. The accounting treatment, therefore, corresponds with the legal entity position of a limited company. After the full amount payable for a share has been received by the company, the holder can have no further liability, whatever financial disaster may befall the company. Shareholders are not directly responsible for the management of the company's affairs, but appoint directors as their agents, directors fees for acting in this capacity being an expense of the business. In smaller companies, the principal shareholders are frequently also directors, but this does not affect their legal position. As shareholders, their liability is still limited, though in common with all directors, they have other statutory obligations arising from the Companies Acts, with penalties for non-compliance.

The total capital to be issued is split into units (shares), and shareholders (or members) agree to take and pay for a given number. £500,000 of share capital issued by a company may be in denominations of £1 shares (500,000); 10p shares (5,000,000); 50p shares (1,000,000); or any other unit that the company chooses. Shareholders expect to receive from the company a share of the annual profits, known as a dividend, and this is related to their individual holdings. A member of the company not wishing to continue holding some or all of the shares cannot just withdraw the money invested from the company, but may have them transferred to another person for a price to be agreed between the buyer and seller. The buyer then becomes a member. Such a transfer does not affect the functioning of the company, which is obviously one of the major advantages of operating in this form — the corporate existence is independent of that of the shareholders.

Whether members can transfer any of their shares without prior approval of the company depends upon whether it is a private or a public company. Whereas public companies can invite the public generally to subscribe for their shares, and their members have an unrestricted right to transfer them to anyone else, shareholders of a private company initially subscribe by private arrangement, and can only transfer shares with the agreement of the company: i.e. membership is kept within a selected group of people. Private companies are generally the smaller ones, with more modest capital requirements, though there are exceptions. If a private company wished to expand beyond the resources available by private arrangement, it would have to change its constitution to that required of a public company, and it could then apply to the Stock Exchange for its shares to be quoted and so made transferable without restriction. A public company must have PLC or plc at the end of its name, identifying it as a public limited company (for companies registered in Wales the Welsh equivalent of ccc is permitted), whilst private company names end with Ltd.

A requirement applicable to both public and private companies is that an annual return of certain information must be made to the Registrar of Companies, and to this is annexed a copy of the Profit and Loss Account and Balance Sheet for that year though the amount of detail to be given varies with the size of the company. It is then open to anyone to inspect this information, by application at the Company Registry (in Cardiff) or through one of the reporting agencies. Numerically, private companies are very much in the majority but, in terms of assets employed, the public companies are much more significant. A company like The British Petroleum Company plc with net assets to a book value of more than £10,000 million is the equivalent of several thousand private companies in terms of resources.

The division of share capital into units has already been referred to. The face value of the units is termed the Nominal (or Par) value; whilst the price at which shares are transferred from one person to another is the Market value. For those shares of public companies quoted on the Stock Exchange, there is a readily available indication of the price at which they can be bought or sold. Market prices fluctuate with changes in supply and demand, and these in turn are influenced by the apparent progress (or lack of it) the company is making, as well as by external factors affecting businesses as a whole, or that particular trade. Fluctuations in share prices do not have any immediate effect on the company itself, though they may reflect the upward or downward trend in its fortunes. Falling share prices, for instance, could create further loss of confidence, which in turn may exacerbate the downward trend.

If a company wished to make a further issue of shares, ranking equally with some already in circulation, the price they could ask is not restricted to the par value originally chosen. It will be influenced by an assessment of the potential demand for them. If shares of £1 par value each are offered for sale at £1.50, the extra 50p is referred to as the Premium. Premiums received by a company when issuing shares are recorded in the accounts separately from the Nominal value of the issue. The treatment of such items is dealt with later.

When two people enter into legal relationships, they are aware of each other's identity, or can make appropriate enquiries, if necessary by reference to Somerset House. For a company, which is an artificial person, there has to be a similar means of identification, and coupled with it, a specification of the powers with which it has been incorporated. This is the purpose of the Memorandum of Association, filed with the Registrar of Companies. It states the name, address, the capital which the company is authorized to issue, and the objects for which it has been formed. Also filed with the Registrar is a copy of the Articles of Association, setting out the internal regulations affecting shareholders and directors. As an appendix to the Companies Act 1985, there is a specimen set of articles designed for companies limited by shares, and referred to as Table A. Many companies adopt Table A with or without modifications, rather than draft their own. A company's Memorandum and Articles are both available for inspection at the Company Registry. The amount of authorized capital stated in the Memorandum is an estimate of the company's capital requirements, and issues must be kept within the amount stated, though it is a relatively straightforward procedure to get the authorized amount increased. Stamp duty is payable when capital is authorized, so a realistic amount would be included initially and increased as and when required.

9.5   Shares and Debentures

Preference shares

So far the company's capital has been referred to simply as consisting of shares. A company decides for itself what the terms of issue, and the rights of shareholders, are to be, and can issue two or more differing classes of share. Two general categories are Ordinary shares and Preference shares. Preference shares entitle the holder to a fixed rate of dividend each year, and this is specified in the name of the share (e.g. £1 6% Preference Shares). Preference dividend is allocated from profits in priority to appropriations to Ordinary shareholders. If profits only just covered Preference dividend, the Preference shareholders should still receive their full dividend, despite the fact that others get little or nothing. If profits available for distribution are insufficient to pay the Preference dividend, the dividend would generally be carried forward, and aggregated with the payment for the following year, or as soon as the profit situation allowed the accumulated arrears to be paid. Preference shares carrying this right are Cumulative Preference shares. Unless expressly referred to as non-cumulative, it can be assumed that they have cumulative rights. The other priority that generally attaches to Preference shares is for repayment of the capital sum in the event of the company being wound up, i.e. going out of existence. After payment of all prior debts (e.g. wages, taxes, creditors and loans) the Preference shareholders would be repaid the nominal value of their shares after which the Ordinary shareholders are entitled to what is left *pro rata*.

The dividend due to be paid out of profits each year is the given rate applied to the nominal value of the shares.

Q.9c   Thus, if AB held 100 £1 6% Preference shares in XYZ Ltd he should receive £6 per annum. This would be the return irrespective of the price AB paid for the shares. If he purchased them for £105, the dividend would be still £6.

In this latter situation, what percentage return would AB be getting on the amount he invested? (We shall be referring to this later as the 'yield'.)

A further feature of Preference shares is that they usually carry only restricted voting rights, or none at all.

Ordinary shares

Ordinary shareholders are usually entitled to the balance of the distributable profits after all prior claims have been met. This does not mean that all profits are necessarily distributed, with the Ordinary shareholders receiving what remains after payment of preference dividends. Most companies would wish to retain some of the profits in the business, but those that are retained add to the value of the business and it is the Ordinary shareholders who get any subsequent benefit. As we have already seen, in the event of the company being wound up, creditors and loans are first paid out of the proceeds; next the Preference shareholders get the par value of their holdings (or whatever other amount may have been agreed) and the balance is then distributable amongst the Ordinary shareholders. Apart from this remotely possible terminal benefit, if retentions are being made, the profitability of the company should increase, and the Ordinary shareholders benefit. Ordinary shareholders carry the real element of risk. In bad times their return may be little or nothing, whilst Preference shareholders are reasonably certain of their fixed amount. If the business prospers, however, it is the cause of the Ordinary shareholders only that is advanced. The term Equity is sometimes used to denote the class of shareholders (usually the Ordinary shares) taking the ultimate risk.

Ordinary shareholders would normally have one vote per share to be used in shareholders' meetings. Whilst this does not give them a say in the day-to-day conduct of affairs, at least the vote can be used in special meetings where fundamental policy changes are decided, or in the event of dissatisfaction with progress the constitution of the Board of Directors might be revised at the annual general meeting. At the annual general meeting the dividend to be paid on Ordinary shares is agreed, though this is generally a formality of confirming the rate recommended by the directors. By the terms of the Articles it would be possible for the members to reduce the proposed rate, but not to increase it. If dissatisfied, their only effective course of action is to express no confidence in the directors, and find new ones. For the members to be powerless to increase the rate of dividend may seem incongruous, but having entrusted their affairs to the directors, they must rely upon the Board to act in their best interest. The rate of dividend on Ordinary shares is usually expressed in pence per share.

The gap between market value and par value can be very much more pronounced with Ordinary shares than with Preference shares. Preference share market prices will generally fluctuate only to bring the fixed rate into line with the yield an investor can currently expect to earn on investments of similar type. The market price of Ordinary shares, however, responds to a variety of influences. As more profits are retained, the price should tend to rise because each share represents a proportion of the increasing net resources at the disposal of the company.

Q.9d   It would be a good idea to get the latest published accounts of one or two major companies and use them for reference as we discuss company accounts. For instance, at this stage, you might note the par value of the ordinary shares, then look at a national newspaper to see what the current market price is. How many ordinary shares have been issued by the company? Try multiplying this number by the market price per share to see what the market valuation of ordinary shareholders' interest is in total.

Other factors tending to raise or depress the market price will be trade and dividend prospects, the state of the economy generally, the international situation, and even a prospective change in government if subsequent legislation might be more or less favourable to shareholders' interests. Sometimes the rate of dividend declared on Ordinary shares may seem unduly high, but what concerns an investor is the yield he can get by investing his money in the company.

> If one hundred 25p Ordinary shares in XYZ Ltd are bought at £1 each, and the dividend rate is 10p per share (or 40% of par value), the yield on the investment is 10% (amount invested £100, dividend received £10).

Where a reasonable level of profitability can be confidently expected, the company may declare and pay an Interim dividend during the year and then a Final dividend at the end of the year.

Debentures

Another source of long-term funds for a company is the issue of Debentures. These are bonds acknowledging a loan to the company at a given rate of interest, and specifying the time of redemption, and other conditions. Debenture holders are therefore not members of the company, but creditors: they have no voting rights, except perhaps that they may be able to initiate some action in the event of the company's failure to pay interest. Debentures may be transferable in the same way as shares, and market prices can fluctuate as do those of Preference shares. In some cases, a specific asset, or all of the assets collectively, are charged as security for the loan. If the company was otherwise unable to repay the Debentures at the due date, these assets would have to be sold and the proceeds used for the redemption. Some larger companies in this country are able to offer unsecured Debentures. Their reputation is such that no security is necessary to make them an attractive investment.

The proceeds of the Debenture issue, like those of a share issue, provide finance for the company on a long-term basis. The difference is that the Debentures are evidence of money lent to the company rather than units of ownership. Interest on Debentures is an expense to be charged against profits. Payment does not depend upon the adequacy of profits and does not require to be sanctioned by the annual general meeting. Quite apart from the fact that assets may be specified as security, in the event of a company being wound up the Debenture holders would have priority over all shareholders. Therefore Debentures can generally be regarded as being a safer investment than Preference shares held in the same company which is likely to be reflected in the comparative yield. With both Preference shares and Debentures, the rate of dividend or interest to be fixed, and the other rights and conditions attaching to the securities, will, of course, depend on potential demand and what yield investors can get from similar securities. If a new issue of Debentures was offered at 5%, and $5\frac{1}{4}\%$ was the yield currently being achieved by comparable investments, the issue would have little chance of success unless some compensating advantage was included in the terms. This might be done by keeping the rate at 5% but issuing the Debentures at a discount, for instance, at 95 (£95 for £100 Debentures). The yield would then be $\frac{5}{95} \times 100 = 5.26\%$. Notice that the company's indebtedness to the Debenture holders is the par value, £100. Another way of increasing the attraction of an issue might be to specify that a premium will be paid on redemption.

9.6   Company Profit and Loss Accounts and Balance Sheets

In the ledger of a sole proprietor and of a partnership, separate personal accounts are maintained for each individual owner, and the balances are also shown separately in the Balance Sheet. In the ledger and Balance Sheet of a company, the par value of issued capital for each class of shares and debentures is included as an aggregate figure, though subsidiary records in the form of registers show the individual positions of each shareholder and debenture holder. Changes in holdings arising from transfers are recorded in the registers but do not affect the ledger accounts.

After the profit has been calculated, the recommendation of the directors for appropriation of profit will be shown in a further section of the Profit and Loss Account — as with a partnership. This may be referred to as an Appropriation account, though both the calculation and appropriation of profit is generally included under the single heading of Profit and Loss Account. Any unappropriated profit will remain as a credit balance in the Profit and Loss account, and appear in the balance sheet with the capital accounts. This is a similar position to the partners' current account balances if they are in credit. In the subsequent year, the credit balance of unappropriated profit will be accumulated with the balance of profit remaining in that year, and so on.

Recommended dividends are debited to the appropriation section of the Profit and Loss account, and credited to dividend accounts — one account for each class of shares. The Profit and Loss account and Balance Sheet have to be prepared and circulated to members in advance of the annual general meeting, and only after confirmation of the final dividend at that meeting can payments be made and the dividend accounts debited. Therefore the dividend accounts will have credit balances at the date of the Balance Sheet, and these appear as current liabilities. If interim dividends have been declared and paid during the year, they still represent an appropriation of profit (in anticipation) and will be included in the appropriation section of the Profit and Loss account, though no liability in respect of them will be outstanding at the year end, as in the case of the final dividends. The following example may help to clarify some of the points made.

FELLOWES & BRIGHT LTD

Balance Sheet at 31 December 19X1

	£	£
FIXED ASSETS		
Buildings		80,000
Plant and Equipment		190,000
		270,000
CURRENT ASSETS		
Stock	100,000	
Debtors	38,000	
Bank	2,000	
	140,000	
Less		
CURRENT LIABILITIES		
Creditors	22,000	
Proposed final dividend	18,000	
	40,000	
NET CURRENT ASSETS		100,000
TOTAL ASSETS LESS CURRENT LIABILITIES		370,000
Less		
8% Debentures 19X7–19X9*		40,000
NET ASSETS		£330,000
CAPITAL AND RESERVES		
20p Ordinary shares		300,000
Profit and Loss Account		30,000
		£330,000

* These dates indicate the period in which the debentures are redeemable.

The AGM was held in April 19X2 and the final dividend for 19X1 paid thereafter. In August 19X2 an interim dividend of 1p per share was declared and paid. For 19X2 a final dividend of 1.4p per share was recommended.

Profit and Loss Account for 19X2

	£		£
ADMIN. EXPENSES, ETC.	131,800	GROSS PROFIT	215,000
DEPRECIATION	18,000		
DIRECTORS' FEES	4,000		
DEBENTURE INTEREST	3,200		
NET PROFIT	58,000		
	£215,000		£215,000

	£		£
ORDINARY SHARE DIVIDEND:			
Interim	15,000	NET PROFIT	58,000
Final (proposed)	21,000	BALANCE FROM LAST YEAR	30,000
BALANCE C/FWD	52,000		
	£88,000		£88,000

Note that we shall be dealing later with the form of presentation, the Companies Act requirements, and the effect of taxation; but this example will serve to show how the main elements are treated. The relevant ledger accounts would appear as follows:

Ordinary share capital A/c

		Balance	300,000

8% Debenture A/c

		Balance	40,000

Ordinary Share Dividend A/c

19X2			19X2		
Apr.	Cash	18,000	Jan.	Balance	18,000
Aug.	Cash	15,000	Dec.	P & L a/c	36,000
Dec.	Balance	21,000			
		£36,000			£36,000
			1988		
			Jan.	Balance	21,000

Using hypothetical figures again for the other items, the closing Balance Sheet would be:

Balance Sheet at 31 December 19X2

	£	£
FIXED ASSETS		
Buildings		80,000
Plant and Equipment		200,000
		280,000
CURRENT ASSETS		
Stock	113,000	
Debtors	41,000	
Bank	3,000	
	157,000	
Less		
CURRENT LIABILITIES		
Creditors	24,000	
Proposed final dividend	21,000	
	45,000	
NET CURRENT ASSETS		112,000
TOTAL ASSETS LESS CURRENT LIABILITIES		392,000
Less		
8% Debentures 19X7–19X9		40,000
NET ASSETS		£352,000
CAPITAL AND RESERVES		
20p Ordinary shares		300,000
Profit and Loss account		52,000
		£352,000

It is important to understand what the Profit and Loss account balance represents. It is the accumulated amount of unappropriated profits retained in the business. If all the profits had been distributed this item would not be there and the assets would be £52,000 less in total. The amount retained is therefore being employed in the company amongst the various assets. In this respect 'Reserves', the generic term covering unappropriated profits and some other accounts you will meet later, is rather misleading if it suggests that a corresponding amount of money is being kept available to meet contingencies or future requirements. Whilst, of course, a company may wish to build up its bank account or make some temporary investment in preparation for a future commitment this does not affect the balance of the Profit and Loss account, which represents a source of total funds irrespective of how they are applied.

The Profit and Loss account balance will continue to increase in subsequent years if there are further unappropriated profits — in fact, for many companies you will find that the balance is greater than the amount of share capital. Refer to your own sets of published accounts to note the relative size of the reserves. The balance could decrease if there were losses or if dividends were declared at higher amounts than the net profit for any subsequent years. The amount of cash available constrains what dividends can be paid, but even if there were sufficient liquid resources dividends could not be declared in excess of the Profit and Loss account balance because this would then represent a repayment of capital, which is illegal except in certain specified circumstances. One other way in which the balance may be reduced is by capitalizing part of the reserves — transferring an amount to the share capital account — and we shall see how this is done in Chapter 16.

The balance sheet shows on the one hand the resources held by the business and on the other the sources from which they were derived, or who has a claim on them. This can be expressed diagrammatically, as in *Fig. 12*.

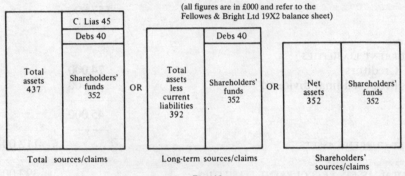

Fig. 12

The shareholders' 'claim' is a residual one. In the event of a winding-up the assets would be sold, liabilities paid off and whatever remained distributed to the shareholders. Thus, if the assets realized £370,000 on liquidation after settlement of current liabilities, £40,000 would go to the debenture holders and the balance distributed to shareholders at 22p per share, which is less than the book value of each share (£352,000/1,500,000). The book value of a share is an unreliable measure for all the reasons we discussed in Section 6.6 coupled with other factors that cause share prices (if a quoted company) to fluctuate. However, it is sometimes calculated for comparison with other values.

Q.9e From your sets of published accounts try to calculate the book value of an ordinary share. Remember to deduct the claims of any preference shareholders from the shareholders' funds total. Compare book value with market value. Can you suggest any reasons why there is such a difference?

It has already been mentioned that a company may issue shares at a premium. This would happen where shares of the same class are already in existence and commanding a market price above the par value. A further issue of similar shares, carrying the same dividend and voting rights, would therefore also command a price higher than par. The par value of the new shares is credited to the share capital account, and the premium to a share premium account. The share premium account therefore represents a part of the proceeds of the share issue. The only reason it is not included in the share capital account is that the latter is being maintained at par value. The premiums can be regarded as capital profits, and like retained revenue profits, the amount adds to the total claims of the ordinary shareholders. The major difference is that the share premium, because it is part of a share issue, cannot be used for dividend distribution, as can reserves which originate from profits. Money is raised by a share issue specifically to provide additional resources, and it would clearly be wrong to pay back part of the proceeds to the same or to other shareholders. A share premium account is a capital reserve whereas the balance of the profit and loss account is a revenue reserve.

9.7   Additional questions

[1]
    (a) List as many reasons as you can think of why businessmen may decide to join together to form a partnership rather than operate independently.
    (b) Why would you not expect to see a business name such as the following: 'Arnold & Baker Ltd, Accountants'?

[2]
Biggs and Hague have decided to form a partnership to run a retail drapery business. They wish to draw up a partnership agreement.

  List the main points which you think should be dealt with in the agreement.

[3]
Ellis, Vaughan and Ratcliffe have a partnership agreement under which profits and losses are shared in the ratio 3:2:1, subject to a guarantee that Ratcliffe's share shall not fall below £10,000.

  Show the Appropriation account for a year in which the net profit is £48,000.

[4]
Sellers, Lowe and Tye are negotiating to form a partnership. It is expected that they will contribute £100,000, £80,000 and £20,000, respectively. Two possible profit-sharing arrangements have been suggested, and the partners are trying to decide which they would prefer. They are:

    (a) Each partner to get 5% p.a. interest on capital. Lowe and Tye to have annual salaries of £5,000 and £15,000, respectively. Balance of profit or loss to be shared 2:2:1. Or:
    (b) Each partner to get 10% p.a. interest on capital. No partnership salaries. Balance of profit or loss to be shared 3:3:4.

It is difficult to estimate what the profits will be. They should not fall below £20,000, and it is unlikely that they will exceed £120,000 in the foreseeable future.

  Assume that you are advising Mr Tye. Summarize the information to help him decide which option he would prefer. (An important aspect of the question is the clarity with which you present the data.)

[5]
Craig and Benson are in partnership as estate agents, and share profits (or losses) in the ratio 3:2. The following are the ledger balances at 31 December:

Account	Debit balances £	Credit balances £
Furniture and equipment	24,000	
Vehicles	13,600	
Fees and commission		117,300
Advertising expenses	9,860	
Salaries	31,360	
Rent and rates	2,200	
Vehicle expenses	4,930	
Miscellaneous expenses	3,370	
Telephones	1,020	
Electricity	1,160	
Printing and stationery	2,050	
Accountant's fee	500	
Creditors (for stationery, advertising, etc.)		1,860
Debtors (fees outstanding)	2,480	
Bank balance	1,830	
Petty cash balance	180	
Capital account, Craig		20,000
Capital account, Benson		10,000
Current account, Craig		820
Current account, Benson		1,360
Drawings, Craig	30,700	
Drawings, Benson	22,100	
	£151,340	£151,340

Depreciation is charged on the furniture at 10% of the original cost (£32,000), and on the vehicles at 25% of the written-down value.

Prepare the Profit and Loss account to show the calculation of the profit or loss for the year and its appropriation. Prepare a Balance Sheet at 31 December. Also show how the current accounts and capital accounts for each partner would appear in the ledger.

[6]
Willis, Harper and Frost share profits and losses equally after allowing 6% interest on capital. The position of their personal accounts at 31 March (the end of their financial year) before making appropriations for that year is:

	Willis £	Harper £	Frost £
Capital accounts	16,000	12,000	11,000
Current accounts			
(all credit balances)	120	40	310
Drawings	12,270	12,420	12,300

The other balances in the books after extraction of the Profit and Loss account are:

	£
Net profit for year	36,900
Bank overdraft	142
Debtors and prepayments	632
Creditors and accruals	849
Freehold buildings	28,230
Furniture and equipment	11,034
Stock of materials	475

(a) Set out the appropriation of profits and the adjustments of current accounts in tabular form, as follows:

	Willis £	Harper £	Frost £	Total £
Interest on capital				
Balance of profits				
				36,900
Current a/cs opening balances				
Drawings				
Current a/cs closing balances				

(b) Prepare a balance sheet at 31 March.
(c) What seems to be the main problem facing the business, judging from these figures? Comment also on the position arising from the different balances of the current accounts. How does this affect the business?

[7]
Abel and Kane were partners in a hardware business. Abel took little part in the shop work but had provided most of the capital. The agreement was that they share profits and losses three-fifths for Abel and two-fifths for Kane after allowing interest on capital at 5% and an annual salary for Kane of £8,000. Abel had also loaned a further sum to the business and 10% per annum interest was allowed on this. The following is a list of balances at the end of a year's trading.

Balances at 31 March 19X4

	£	Dr	Cr
Sales for cash	133,950		
Sales on credit	46,310		
Opening stock	18,525		
Purchases	109,729		
Community tax	6,120		
Wages	29,207		

Discounts received	640
Heating and Lighting	1,852
Printing, advertising and miscellaneous	1,496
Interest on loan	650
Value added tax	300
Current accounts at 1 April 19X3 (owing to	
partners) — Abel	620
— Kane	230
Vehicle expenses	982
Insurance	631
Trade Debtors	3,462
Provision for doubtful debts	120
Trade Creditors	8,602
Shop Premises	120,000
Equipment	24,600
Vehicle	7,200
Loan from Abel	13,000
Bank balance (credit balance on bank	
statement)	593
Capital account — Abel	120,000
— Kane	30,000
Drawings — Abel	13,841
— Kane	14,884

At the end of the year it was realised that a debt of £102 from a customer should be written off and it was thought appropriate to increase the provision for doubtful debts to £200. An electricity bill for £186 was due for payment but insurance premiums had been paid in advance by £120. In February 19X4 a fire had destroyed some stock with an estimated value of £2,185: only £1,500 of this was recoverable from the insurance company and no entries had been made in the books at the year end. The stock at 31 March 19X4 was valued at £19,625. Depreciation is charged at 10% on the written down value of equipment and at 20% on the written down value of the vehicle.

(a) Enter the balances in the appropriate columns to make sure that the trial balance balances.
(b) Prepare the Profit and Loss account and Balance Sheet.
(c) Show how the partners' current accounts would appear in the ledger.

[8]
A company's balance sheet shows the following structure of capital employed:

	£
£1 ordinary shares	600,000
Unappropriated profits	450,000
6% £1 debentures	200,000
	£1,250,000

(a) What is the par value of the ordinary shares, and what is the net assets book value of each share?

(b) The market value of an ordinary share on the same date was £2.10. What factors might have caused this to be substantially different from the net assets book value?

(c) Would you expect the difference between the market value of the debentures and their par value to be as great as the difference between the market value and par value of the ordinary shares? Explain.

(d) If you bought some of these debentures for £1.20 each, what would the yield be?

(e) The ordinary shareholders have just had a dividend of 15p per share (15%). Explain why this is not such a generous return as it may at first seem.

(f) Why might ordinary shareholders generally expect to get a lower yield than debenture holders?

[9]

From the following balances of Bray & Sons Ltd at 31 December, prepare the final accounts and balance sheet:

	Dr £	Cr £
Gross profit		194,300
Admin. expenses, salaries, etc.	72,230	
Directors' fees	35,000	
Debenture interest	3,000	
Interim dividend	15,000	
Ordinary shares (20p each)		300,000
6% debentures		50,000
Balance of unappropriated profit at 1 Jan.		64,200
Land and buildings	244,000	
Plant and equipment	149,600	
Vehicles	22,000	
Bank balance	20,160	
Debtors and creditors	18,240	19,080
Stock on hand	48,350	
	£627,580	£627,580

The plant is to be depreciated by $12\frac{1}{2}\%$ of the original cost (£240,000) and the vehicles by 20% of the original cost (£40,000). It is proposed to pay a final dividend of 2p per share.

[10]

Contrast the position of Ordinary shareholders, Preference shareholders and Debenture holders as regards:

(a) Dividend or interest.
(b) Return of capital in the event of a winding up.
(c) Voting rights.

160   Accounting for different forms of organization

[11]

Balance Sheet of Gaystarr Ltd, 31 March, year 7

	£	£
SHARE CAPITAL AND RESERVES		
£1 ordinary shares		300,000
8% preference shares		50,000
Unappropriated profit		161,520
(balance of P & L a/c)		
7% DEBENTURES years 12–16		60,000
Total capital employed		£571,520
FIXED ASSETS		
Land and buildings		128,000
Plant and machinery		286,300
Vehicles		28,180
		442,480
CURRENT ASSETS		
Stock and work in progress	138,770	
Debtors and prepayments	32,060	
Bank and cash balances	8,140	
	178,970	
Less		
CURRENT LIABILITIES		
Creditors and accruals	24,930	
Proposed dividend	25,000	
	49,930	
Net current assets		129,040
Total net assets		£571,520

(a) Given that the Net Profit for the year was £63,260, and that the appropriations of profit were as follows:

Preference dividend	8%
Ordinary dividend — interim	6p per share
— final	7p per share

reconstruct the appropriation section of the Profit and Loss Account, and find the opening balance of unappropriated profit (i.e. at 1 April year 6).

(b) Show how the Ordinary Share Dividend account would appear in the ledger, assuming that the interim dividend was paid on 1 December year 7.

(c) If the company was wound up on the date of the balance sheet, and the net assets were sold for exactly the amount shown (£571,520), how much would the ordinary shareholders get back for each share held?

(d) If the company was wound up on the date of the balance sheet, and the net assets realized only £350,000, how much would the ordinary shareholders then get back for each share held?

(e) What do the dates shown after the 7% Debentures in the balance sheet indicate?

(f) A shareholder has asked you to explain what is meant by 'Reserves'. He wondered whether it was a sum saved up for future expansion or contingencies. Can you enlighten him?

[12]
The following balances were in the ledger of R. Venner & Bros. Ltd at 31 December 19X2.

	£		£
Sales	1,056,200	Purchases	885,250
Stock at 1 Jan. 19X2	126,030	Admin. expenses,	
Buildings (freehold)	320,000	salaries etc.	120,500
Fixtures and fittings	32,000	Audit fees	1,250
Vehicles	48,000	Directors' fees	12,000
Debtors	121,010	Advertising and selling	
Bank balance	4,970	expenses	36,390
Creditors	87,680	Profit and Loss bal.	63,520
£1 Ordinary shares	400,000		
5% Debentures	100,000		

(a) Prepare a Trial Balance from the above.

(b) Taking into account the following year-end adjustments, prepare the Trading and Profit and Loss account (including appropriations) for 19X2, and a Balance Sheet as at 31 December 19X2.

  (i) Closing stock was valued at £248,350.

  (ii) Depreciation is to be charged on book values — 10% on Fixtures and Fittings and 25% on Vehicles.

  (iii) Since the above balances were extracted it had been discovered that a cheque for £1,350 (included in the bank balance) was dishonoured by the drawer. It was very unlikely that the money would be recovered.

  (iv) £4,250 for salary increases and bonuses to the end of 19X2 had not been paid.

  (v) Interest on the debentures had not been paid.

  (vi) A first and final dividend of 9p per share was proposed.

(c) Given the following additional information about the company's position at 31 December 19X1 reconstruct the Balance Sheet at that date.
Debtors £96,160, Creditors £69,500, Bank balance £46,830.
The dividend for 19X1 was the same as for 19X2. Debenture interest for 19X1 had been paid within the year. No fixed assets had been bought or sold during 19X2.

(d) Using your answer to (c) and the following information from the 19X1 Trading and Profit and Loss account compare the performance and position of the company for the two years.

19X1 Sales £803,100; Gross Profit £237,540; Net Profit £81,160.

[13]

The accountant of a company is closing off the accounts at the end of the year (31 December 19X7) and preparing the Profit and Loss Account and Balance Sheet. Included in the ledger balances are:

	£
20p Ordinary shares	500,000
12% Debenture Stock	80,000
Retained Profits	314,000
Share premium account	28,000
Land and buildings (cost)	320,600
Equipment (cost)	136,000
Equipment (depreciation to date)	65,000
Provision for doubtful debts	2,100
Share issue expenses	14,000

Amongst the entries he has to make are the following:

(i) Several smaller items of equipment purchased during the year totalling £12,000 have been capitalized; it has now been decided that they should be treated as factory expenses.

(ii) Some equipment originally bought for £9,200 and with a book value of £4,000 at 1 January 19X7 was sold during the year for £6,200: the proceeds have been posted to the Sales account.

(iii) Depreciation on the equipment is to be charged at 20% of the book value.

(iv) Realizing that future replacement of equipment will cost much more than the original items it has been decided to set aside out of profits £60,000 in addition to the depreciation charge.

(v) The provision for doubtful debts is to be adjusted to £4,000.

(vi) The land and buildings have been revalued at £480,000 and it is decided to include this valuation in the accounts.

(vii) The share issue expenses were incurred during the year and are to be written off.

(viii) Interest on the debenture stock is now due for payment.

(ix) A final dividend of 3p per share is proposed.

(x) £10,000 is to be transferred to a Debenture redemption reserve account.

(a) Show by means of journal entries how each of the above items will be dealt with.

(b) Explain the difference between a charge against profits and an appropriation. Which of the above items would be appropriations of profit?

(c) Explain the difference between capital (fixed) expenditure and revenue (current) expenditure.

Chapter 10

Illustrating a Set of Accounts

10.1 T. C. Preece Ltd

Examples have been used in earlier chapters to illustrate particular aspects of accounting as they were discussed. The extended example in this chapter brings together much of the work done so far. It aims to give some concept of the operation of a set of accounts and also to recapitulate points previously made about the significance of the information and the principles upon which it is compiled. The answers to most parts of the example are given within the chapter, but you should try to do as much as possible before referring to them.

T. C. Preece Ltd is a small company selling office furniture and equipment. Tom Preece holds most of the shares; his wife and brother-in-law are the only other shareholders. The results for 19X5 and the year-end position are shown below.

Profit and Loss Account for 19X5

	£	£
NET SALES		736,240
COST OF GOODS SOLD		
Opening stock	85,720	
Purchases	559,890	
	645,610	
Closing stock	96,680	548,930
GROSS PROFIT		187,310
OTHER EXPENSES		
Salaries	70,060	
Commission	6,500	
Directors' fees	6,000	
Heating, lighting, etc.	3,360	
Rates and insurance	7,900	
Telephone, postage, etc.	930	

	£	£
Advertising	8,200	
Bank interest and charges	220	
Vehicle running expenses	7,300	
Vehicle depreciation	3,800	
Fixtures depreciation	1,000	
Buildings depreciation	2,400	
Bad debts written off	740	
Miscellaneous expenses	2,470	
		120,880
NET PROFIT BEFORE TAX		66,430
CORPORATION TAX (see Note 1 opposite)		25,750
NET PROFIT AFTER TAX		40,680
DIVIDENDS		
Interim	9,000	
Final (proposed)	18,000	
		27,000
PROFIT RETAINED		13,680
BALANCE BROUGHT FORWARD FROM LAST YEAR		41,240
BALANCE AS IN BALANCE SHEET		£54,920

Balance Sheet at 31 December 19X5

	Original cost £	Aggregate depreciation £	£
FIXED ASSETS (see Note 2 opposite)			
Freehold buildings	120,000	14,400	105,600
Fixtures	10,500	2,400	8,100
Vehicles	23,800	8,200	15,600
	154,300	25,000	129,300
CURRENT ASSETS			
Stock (at lower of cost or market value)		96,680	
Debtors and prepayments		98,770	
Petty Cash balance		50	
		195,500	

	£	£
Less		
CURRENT LIABILITIES		
Corporation tax (see Note 1 below)	25,750	
Bank overdraft	2,900	
Final dividend	18,000	
Trade creditors and accruals	73,230	
	119,880	
NET CURRENT ASSETS		75,620
		£204,920
ORDINARY SHARE CAPITAL, £1 SHARES		150,000
(AUTHORIZED AND ISSUED)		
RETAINED PROFITS		54,920
		£204,920

Note 1   Corporation Tax is dealt with in Chapter 16. At this stage all you need to know is that it is a tax assessed on the year's profits. It appears as a current liability, though payment will not be due for nine or more months after the balance sheet date.
Note 2   Fixed Assets — The figures in the right-hand column are the book values at 31 December 19X5. The original cost and the aggregate depreciation provided since the assets were bought are given as additional information. The 19X5 depreciation is included in the aggregate figure — for example, £4,400 of the vehicle depreciation must have been provided prior to 19X5, and the 19X5 charge makes this up to £8,200. Companies are required to give information about fixed assets in this way, and you will see below that this is facilitated by keeping separate ledger accounts.

Before proceeding to the next stage, look at the 19X5 statements and give an opinion on each of the following:

(a)   Does the profit seem reasonable?
(b)   Does the financial position at 31 December seem to be satisfactory?
(c)   Do you think the company is a long-established one?

10.2   The transactions

Rather than make the exercise unnecessarily long by entering all the year's transactions into the ledger accounts, we are assuming that the work for the first ten months has already been done. The balances up to 31 October are given, together with the transactions for the remainder of the year. Open accounts with balances as at 1 November, and then enter the transactions into them from the details given. Extract trial balances at the end of November and at the end of December.

Trial Balance at 31 October 19X6

LEDGER ACCOUNTS	Dr £	Cr £
Sales		677,300
Returns from customers, and allowances made to them	1,700	
Opening stock (1 Jan 19X6)	96,680	
Purchases	526,790	
Salaries (including employers' contributions)	62,830	
Commission	6,400	
Directors' fees	3,750	
Heating, lighting, etc.	3,040	
Rates and insurance	7,160	
Telephone, postage, etc.	665	
Advertising	9,070	
Bank interest and charges	50	
Vehicle running expenses	7,168	
Miscellaneous expenses	2,947	
Buildings (cost)	120,000	
Buildings — depreciation provision		14,400
Fixtures (cost)	11,800	
Fixtures — depreciation provision		2,400
Vehicles (cost)	23,800	
Vehicles — depreciation provision		8,200
Total debtors	98,070	
Bank	1,200	
Petty Cash	50	
Share capital		150,000
Retained profits		54,920
Corporation tax liability		25,750
Dividend (interim)	9,000	
Total creditors		58,700
Pension scheme		500
	992,170	992,170

The above accounts are in the General Ledger. In addition there are individual customers' personal accounts in the Debtors Ledger, and suppliers' personal accounts in the Creditors Ledger. The totals of the balances in these ledgers agree with the total Debtors and Creditors figures given. The company has approximately 70 'live' debtors' accounts (i.e. ones in which there are recent transactions), and approximately 15 live creditors' accounts. Again, in order to condense the exercise, only a few of each are included as named accounts, and the remainder are shown as 'other customers' and 'other suppliers'. The Debtors and Creditors balances at 31 October are made up as follows:

Debtors Balances		Creditors Balances	
	£		£
Anderson & Bayes Ltd	1,300	Adrian Advertising Co.	850
V. Andrews	610	Blake, Halley Ltd	3,630
T. Artist & Sons	3,030	Carson Supplies Ltd	7,420
Bevan Industries Ltd	950	Crowther & Wright	500
Other customers	92,180	Other suppliers	46,300
	98,070		58,700

TRANSACTIONS DURING NOVEMBER

(a) *Invoices received from suppliers of goods and services*
These have been analysed to facilitate posting to the ledger.

Date	Supplier	L fo.	Invoice total	Purchases of goods	Vehicle running expenses	Adver- tising	Misc.
			£	£	£	£	£
Nov. 3	Blake, Halley Ltd		940	940			
8	Carson Supplies Ltd		6,180	6,180			
16	Adrian Advertising		680			680	
24	Blake, Halley Ltd		1,610	1,610			
	Other suppliers during month		39,350	38,700	490		160
			48,760	47,430	490	680	160

(b)   *Invoices to customers for credit sales*

			£
Nov. 2	Bevan Industries Ltd		710
16	V. Andrews		140
29	V. Andrews		400
	Other customers during the month		67,890
			69,140

(c)   *Payments into bank account*

			£
Nov. 3	Proceeds of cash sales		110
12	do.		230
15	Cheque from V. Andrews		610
24	Cheque from Anderson & Bayes Ltd		1,300
29	Cheque from T. Artist & Sons		2,000
30	Proceeds of cash sales		190
	Cheques from other customers during the month		43,980

(d) *Payments from bank account*

		£
Nov. 19	Adrian Advertising	500
29	Blake, Halley Ltd	3,630
29	Carson Supplies Ltd	7,420
29	Crowther & Wright	500
30	Other suppliers during the month	29,420
30	Salaries and N.I. (see (e))	6,290
30	Collector of Taxes (see (e))	930
30	Petty cash (see (f))	30

(e) *Salaries for the month of November* (*summary of the payroll*)

	£	£
Gross pay		6,700
Deductions		
National Insurance	320	
Pension scheme	250	
PAYE	930	1,500
Net pay		5,200
Employers' contributions		
National Insurance	770	
Pension scheme	250	1,020

(f) *The Petty Cash book for November is shown.*   This need not be reproduced, but the total of each type of expense will have to be posted to the ledger, and the closing balance included in the trial balance.

RECEIPTS   PAYMENTS

		Total			Total	Telephone Postage	Vehicle expenses	Misc.
		£			£	£	£	£
Nov. 1	Balance	50	Nov. 5	Stamps	11	11		
			8	Window cleaning	3			3
			10	Gratuity	1			1
			10	Stamps	4	4		
			15	Petrol	5		5	
			20	Stamps	3	3		
			25	Sundries	3			3
30	Bank	30			30	18	5	7
			30	Balance	50			
		80			80			

(Extract Trial Balance at this stage. Locate and correct any errors before proceeding with the December transactions. Check also that the aggregate of the debtors and creditors account balances agree with the total accounts in the General Ledger.)

TRANSACTIONS DURING DECEMBER

(a) Invoices received from suppliers of goods and services

Date	Supplier	L Fo.	Invoice total	Purchases of goods	Vehicle running expenses	Heat and Light	Tele-phone	Rates
			£	£	£	£	£	£
Dec. 6	Blake, Halley Ltd		2,620	2,620				
8	Crowther & Wright		1,030	1,030				
15	Carson Supplies Ltd		4,730	4,730				
30	do.		1,390	1,390				
	Other suppliers during the month		50,780	46,340	640	470	280	3,050
			60,550	56,110	640	470	280	3,050

(b) *Invoices to customers for credit sales*

			£
Dec.	4	T. Artist & Sons	1,270
	18	Anderson & Bayes Ltd	930
		Other customers during month	71,050
			73,250

(c) *Credit note to customer for returns or allowances*

Dec.	8	Bevan Industries Ltd	£210

(d) *Payments into bank account*

			£
Dec.	4	Proceeds of cash sales	230
	8	Cheque from V. Andrews	140
	21	Cheque from T. Artist & Sons	1,030
	23	Proceeds of cash sales	820
		Cheques from other customers during the month	87,830

(e) *Payments from bank account*

			£
Dec.	3	Adrian Advertising Co.	1,030
	8	Bank charges	80
	22	Purchase of new vehicle	4,300
	28	Corporation tax	25,750
	28	Directors' fees	2,250
	29	Blake, Halley Ltd	940
	29	Carson Supplies Ltd	6,180
	31	Other suppliers during month	40,150
	31	Pension scheme	1,500
	31	Salaries and N.I. (see (f))	6,910
	31	Collector of Taxes (see (f))	980
	31	Petty cash	40

(f) *Salaries for the month of December* (*summary of payroll*)

	£	£
Gross pay		7,200
Deductions		
National Insurance	380	
Pension scheme	250	
PAYE	980	1,610
Net pay		5,590
Employers' contributions		
National Insurance	940	
Pension scheme	250	1,190

(g) *Petty Cash payments* (*summary of Petty Cash Book*)

		£
Telephone and postage		17
Vehicle expenses		7
Miscellaneous		16
(Reimbursed on 31 Dec.)		40

(Extract a Trial Balance at this stage. Locate and correct any errors before proceeding with the year-end work.)

10.3   Year-end adjustments

The accounts need adjustment in respect of the following points:

(a) Stocktaking. The most convenient time to take stock was on Sunday, 4 January (19X7). A list of all the items on the premises was made, and the value taken from suppliers' invoices. This gave a total of £103,630. On the previous day (Saturday, 3 January) goods with a cost price of £1,400 had been despatched to customers. Of the items listed, some had been used for demonstration purposes, and others were either damaged or shop-soiled. It was decided to reduce the stock value of these items by £4,200. In addition to the stock on the premises, some equipment was held by potential customers (on a trial basis) which had not been invoiced to them: the cost price involved was £2,700.

(b) Depreciation is charged on vehicles at 20% p.a. of the original cost, and on fixtures at 10% p.a. of the original cost.

(c) The new vehicle was purchased on 22 December for £10,000, £4,300 being paid by cheque and the balance of £5,700 being allowed for a vehicle traded-in as part exchange. The traded-in vehicle was bought in 19X4 for £9,000. A full year's depreciation is charged in the year of purchase of a vehicle, but none is charged in the year of sale. No adjustment for the trade-in had been made prior to 31 December.

(d) Commission is earned by some of the staff on the sales they initiate. At the end of December, £900 was owing in respect of commission earned during the year.

(e) Outstanding customers' accounts are followed up as necessary. At the end of the year, accounts totalling £800 were considerably overdue, despite reminders. It was not thought appropriate to write them off as bad debts at this stage, but since it was doubtful whether payment would be received a provision is to be made for this amount.

(f) Of the charges to the Rates and Insurance account, £1,850 related to 19X7.

(g) Corporation tax liability in respect of the 19X6 profit is estimated at £23,200, and a final dividend of 12p per share is proposed.

The Profit and Loss account for 19X6 and the Balance Sheet at 31 December 19X6 can now be completed. When you have done this, compare them with those for the previous year (set out in Section 10.1). Then prepare a report for presentation to the directors, with your comments on the performance and position.

10.4   Solution

Below you will find the Cash book, the trial balances, the final accounts and a report to the directors. You are urged to make a full attempt at the exercise before checking your figures.

CASH BOOK (BANK)

DR			Total Receipts	Debtors' Ledger	CR			Total Payments	Creditors' Ledger
Nov.	1	Balance	1,200		Nov.	19	Adrian Advtg Co.	500	500
	3	Sales	110			29	Blake, Halley Ltd	3,630	3,630
	12	Sales	230			29	Carson Supplies Ltd	7,420	7,420
	15	V. Andrews	610	610		29	Crowther & Wright	500	500
	24	Anderson & Bayes Ltd	1,300	1,300		30	Other Suppliers	29,420	29,420
	29	T. Artist & Sons	2,000	2,000		30	Salaries and N.I.	6,290	
	30	Sales	190			30	Collector of Taxes	930	
	30	Other customers	43,980	43,980		30	Petty Cash	30	
						30	Balance	900	
			49,620	47,890				49,620	41,470
Dec.	1	Balance	900		Dec.	3	Adrian Advtg Co.	1,030	1,030
	4	Sales	230			8	Bank charges	80	
	8	V. Andrews	140	140		22	Vehicle	4,300	
	21	T. Artist & Sons	1,030	1,030		28	Corporation Tax	25,750	
	23	Sales	820			28	Directors' fees	2,250	
	31	Other customers	87,830	87,830		29	Blake, Halley Ltd	940	940
						29	Carson Supplies Ltd	6,180	6,180
						31	Other suppliers	40,150	40,150
						31	Pension scheme	1,500	
						31	Salaries & N.I.	6,910	
						31	Collector of Taxes	980	
						31	Petty Cash	40	
						31	Balance	840	
			90,950	89,000				90,950	48,300·
19X7									
Jan.	1	Balance	840						

Trial balances

	30 Nov		31 Dec (before adjustments)	
	Dr £	Cr £	Dr £	Cr £
Cash at bank	900		840	
Petty cash	50		50	
Sales		746,970		821,270
Returns	1,700		1,910	
Stock	96,680		96,680	
Purchases	574,220		630,330	
Salaries	70,550		78,940	
Commission	6,400		6,400	
Directors' fees	3,750		6,000	
Heating and lighting	3,040		3,510	
Rates and Insurance	7,160		10,210	
Telephone and Postage	683		980	
Advertising	9,750		9,750	
Bank interest	50		130	
Vehicle running exps	7,663		8,310	
Miscellaneous exps	3,114		3,130	
Building/Depreciation	120,000	14,400	120,000	14,400
Fixtures/Depreciation	11,800	2,400	11,800	2,400
Vehicles/Depreciation	23,800	8,200	28,100	8,200
Total Debtors	119,320		103,360	
Total Creditors		65,990		78,240
Share Capital		150,000		150,000
Retained Profits		54,920		54,920
Corporation Tax		25,750		
Dividend	9,000		9,000	
Pension Scheme		1,000		
	1,069,630	1,069,630	1,129,430	1,129,430

Debtors at 31 Dec	£	Creditors at 31 Dec	£
Anderson & Bayes Ltd	930	Blake, Halley Ltd	4,230
V. Andrews	400	Carson Supplies Ltd	6,120
T. Artist & Sons	1,270	Crowther & Wright	1,030
Bevan Industries Ltd	1,450	Other suppliers	66,860
Other customers	99,310		
	103,360		78,240

Profit and Loss Account for 19X6

	£	£
NET SALES		819,360
COST OF GOODS SOLD		
Opening stock	96,680	
Purchases	630,330	
	727,010	
Closing stock	103,530	
		623,480
GROSS PROFIT		195,880
OTHER EXPENSES		
Salaries	78,940	
Commission	7,300	
Directors' fees	6,000	
Heating, lighting, etc.	3,510	
Rates and insurance	8,360	
Telephone, postage, etc.	980	
Advertising	9,750	
Bank interest and charges	130	
Vehicle running expenses	8,310	
Vehicle depreciation	4,760	
less gain on sale	300*	
	4,460	
Fixtures depreciation	1,180	
Buildings depreciation	2,400	
Doubtful debt provision	800	
Miscellaneous expenses	3,130	
		135,250
NET PROFIT BEFORE TAX		60,630
CORPORATION TAX		23,200
NET PROFIT AFTER TAX		37,430
DIVIDENDS		
Interim	9,000	
Final (proposed)	18,000	
		27,000
PROFIT RETAINED		10,430
BALANCE BROUGHT FORWARD FROM LAST YEAR		54,920
BALANCE AS IN BALANCE SHEET		65,350

*trade-in value £5,700 less book value £5,400

Balance Sheet at 31 December 19X6

	Original cost £	*Aggregate depreciation* £	£
FIXED ASSETS			
Freehold buildings	120,000	16,800	103,200
Fixtures	11,800	3,580	8,220
Vehicles	24,800	9,360	15,440
	156,600	29,740	126,860
CURRENT ASSETS			
Stock (at lower of cost or market value)		103,530	
Debtors and prepayments (less provision)		104,410	
Bank balance		840	
Petty Cash balance		50	
		208,830	
Less CURRENT LIABILITIES			
Corporation tax		23,200	
Final dividend		18,000	
Trade creditors and accruals		79,140	
		120,340	
NET CURRENT ASSETS			88,490
			215,350
ORDINARY SHARE CAPITAL, £1 SHARES			150,000
(AUTHORIZED AND ISSUED)			
RETAINED PROFITS			65,350
			215,350

REPORT TO THE DIRECTORS OF T. C. PREECE LTD
19X6 Annual Accounts

The following are the salient figures from the Profit and Loss Account for 19X6 and the Balance Sheet at 31 December 19X6 compared with the previous year.

	19X5 £	19X6 £	change £
SALES	736,240	819,360	+83,120 (+11%)
COST OF GOODS SOLD	548,930	623,480	+74,550 (+14%)
GROSS PROFIT	187,310	195,880	+ 8,570
EXPENSES	120,880	135,250	+14,370

NET PROFIT		66,430		60,630	− 5,800
TAX	25,750		23,200		
DIVIDEND	27,000	52,750	27,000	50,200	− 2,550
RETAINED		13,680		10,430	− 3,250
CASH AND BANK		−2,850		890	+ 3,740
STOCK		96,680		103,530	+ 6,850
DEBTORS		98,770		104,410	+ 5,640
		192,600		208,830	+16,230
CURRENT LIABILITIES		116,980		120,340	+ 3,360
WORKING CAPITAL		75,620		88,490	+12,870
FIXED ASSETS		129,300		126,860	− 2,440
CAPITAL EMPLOYED		204,920		215,350	+10,430

	19X5	19X6
GROSS PROFIT TO SALES	25.4%	23.9%
EXPENSES TO SALES	16.4%	16.5%
NET PROFIT TO SALES	9.0%	7.4%
NET PROFIT TO CAPITAL EMPLOYED	32%	28%
TURNOVER OF CAPITAL EMPLOYED	3.6 times	3.8 times
TURNOVER OF STOCK (COST OF GOODS SOLD/AVERAGE STOCK HOLDING)	6.0 times	6.2 times
LIQUIDITY RATIO (USING DEBTORS + BANK/CASH/CURRENT LIABILITIES)	0.80	0.88

Whilst sales revenue increased by 11% during the year the cost of goods sold rose by a proportionately greater amount, so the gross profit margin was reduced by $1\frac{1}{2}$%. This may be because increases in cost price were not adequately reflected in selling prices, possibly due to more competitive trading conditions, but it may also have resulted from changes in the mix of products sold or from other factors. It is impossible to judge without further data. A lower margin on higher sales may be good policy if it results in a higher net profit — that is, if relatively fixed expenses do not increase proportionately — but in this case the net profit is also reduced by $1\frac{1}{2}$% on sales. Wages and other expenses rose by over 10%, in total such increases more than offsetting the higher gross profit figure.

There was a small improvement in the intensity with which capital was employed, each £1 of capital generating £3.80 of sales against £3.60 last year, but this only slightly offset the effect of the lower net profit margin resulting in a reduction in the return on capital employed from 32% to 28%:

$$(9\% \times 3.6 = 32\%)$$
$$(7.4\% \times 3.8 = 28\%)$$

In judging the adequacy of a 28% return on capital it has to be remembered that this was before tax (= 17% after tax) and that the profit must provide not only a reasonable return to the shareholders but also funds for expansion and to offset higher costs when assets are replaced. If the cost prices of stock items and fixed assets are rising, a business needs more capital to maintain the same capacity. In this context the proportion of the available profit distributed as dividend (72%) could be rather high but information on the financial implications of future plans would be needed before commenting further on the distribution and retention policy.

The balance-sheet position appears to be reasonably sound. The fact that debtors and cash do not quite cover the current liabilities is presumably not a real problem — the ratio has improved over the year and the liabilities figure includes taxation which will not become due for at least nine months. Only by preparing a cash budget for the next few months can the liquidity situation be properly appraised. It is interesting to see how additional funds resulting from the year's profit were utilized. This is a summary of the source and uses.

	£	£
Net profit for the year		60,630
add back depreciation because this		
did not involve any expenditure		8,040
Funds generated from operations		68,670
Used for:		
Payment of taxation	25,750	
Payment of dividends	27,000	
Purchase of new fixed assets,		
less proceeds of sale	5,600	
Increase in working capital		
items: Stock	6,850	
Debtors	5,640	
Creditors	(5,910)	
		6,580
		64,930
Increase in bank balance		£3,740

In conclusion, whilst some aspects can only be evaluated in the light of additional information, it seems that the most serious concern is the reduction in net profit despite the higher turnover. This needs investigating and any possible action taken to ensure that the trend does not continue.

10.5   Additional question

With only one month to go to the year end (30 June), a trial balance was extracted from the books of Extralite Ltd lighting equipment wholesalers:

Trial Balance, 31 May

	Dr £	Cr £
Ordinary share capital (25p shares)		150,000
Profit and Loss account balance		68,700

	£	£
Freehold buildings (at cost)	120,000	
Furniture and equipment (at cost)	27,000	
Depreciation provision — furniture and equipment		9,000
Vehicles (at cost)	16,000	
Depreciation provision — vehicles		7,000
Stock on hand at beginning of year	68,650	
Debtors Ledger balances	90,200	
Creditors Ledger balances		43,830
Bank	24,010	
Sales		667,340
Purchases	486,150	
Salaries and wages	61,080	
Directors' fees	10,000	
Rates and insurance	13,100	
Vehicle running expenses	8,520	
Advertising and publicity	2,000	
Lighting and heating	6,190	
Miscellaneous expenses	5,470	
Interim dividend	7,500	
	£945,870	£945,870

The Debtors and Creditors balances at 31 May were:

Debtors	£	Creditors	£
A. C. Bright	3,300	I.E.A. Ltd	21,080
Croxton & Sons	1,950	Litemakers Ltd	18,100
T. L. Farmer Ltd	15,850	T. & K. Perry Ltd	4,650
Friend & Heywood Ltd	28,010		
L. Knowles	1,280		
Mander & Ross	21,280		
T. Silverman	9,500		
A. Todd Ltd	9,030		
	£90,200		£43,830

During June the following transactions took place:

£

CREDIT SALES:

June	8	T. L. Farmer Ltd	13,150
	10	A. C. Bright	960
	10	Mander & Ross	8,460
	19	T. L. Farmer Ltd	3,040
	22	Friend & Heywood Ltd	36,280
	29	T. Silverman	7,520
	29	Mander & Ross	13,630

£

CREDIT PURCHASES

		£
June 10	Litemakers Ltd	28,600
21	I.E.A. Ltd	13,420
29	I.E.A. Ltd	22,180

RECEIPTS (paid into bank on same days)

		£
June 5	L. Knowles	580
5	T. L. Farmer Ltd	15,850
8	A. C. Bright	3,300
29	Friend & Heywood Ltd	22,000
29	Mander & Ross	21,280
30	T. Silverman	5,000
30	A. Todd Ltd	9,030
30	Croxton & Sons	1,950

PAYMENTS (by cheque)

		£
June 2	I.E.A. Ltd	13,600
2	Wages	480
9	Wages	510
12	Petrol and oil	230
16	Wages	480
16	Miscellaneous expenses	230
23	Wages	500
29	T. & K. Perry Ltd	4,650
29	I.E.A. Ltd	7,480
30	Litemakers Ltd	18,100
30	Wages	610
30	Petrol and oil	280
30	Miscellaneous expenses	520
30	Salaries	2,800

Adjustments to be made at the year end are as follows:

(i) Apart from the balances owing to suppliers of goods, the following amounts were outstanding:

	£
Electricity account	600
Maintenance and repair of vehicles	390
Advertising	1,100
Audit fees	1,000
Directors' fees	10,000

(ii) Insurance had been paid in advance to the extent of £1,300.

(iii) The cheque received from Knowles on 5 June represented the final payment from his estate in bankruptcy: the balance of his account must therefore be written off.

(iv) Depreciation is to be charged on the Furniture and Equipment at 10% of original cost, and on the Vehicles at 20% of original cost.

(v) Stock in the warehouse was counted on Sunday 2 July, and valued at £68,300. Some goods had been despatched on 1 July; the cost price of these goods was £1,800. During June, goods value (cost price) £1,400 had been sent to a customer on a sale-or-return basis, and by 30 June had not been invoiced to them.

(vi) Corporation tax is estimated to be £30,000, and other appropriations proposed are:

a final dividend of 2.5p per share.

Open ledger accounts at 1 June, and post the June transactions. Then make the year-end adjustments, and prepare the final accounts and balance sheet.

Chapter 11

Accounting in Manufacturing Businesses

11.1 Production systems

An accounting system should reflect the reality of the production process in financial terms. The accounts of a manufacturer will therefore differ in form and content from those of a trader. This chapter introduces some of the problems of preparing accounts for a manufacturing business, particularly the questions of stock valuation and departmental analysis. It is a bridge to the discussion of cost and management accounting in the subsequent chapters.

The basic techniques of accounting can be applied to any type of business. Indeed, as accounting is essentially concerned with the reporting of economic information, these techniques are relevant outside the business world as we normally understand it, and can be applied to any economic unit. The private citizen may keep personal accounts on his home computer or even on the back of an envelope, and non-profit-making organizations such as sports clubs or students' associations need to prepare financial reports of their activities and position if their affairs are to be managed efficiently. In studying the flows between the various sectors of the economy as a whole, attempts are made to present the information in 'national income accounts'. The success or failure of government economic policies is to a large extent dependent on the accuracy of these national income accounts.

We have already seen, in Chapter 9, how different forms of organization require special treatment within the basic accounting framework. This discussion concentrated our attention on the legal structure of the business unit — sole proprietor, partnership or limited company. Another approach is to look at the type of activity undertaken by the organization. If we consider the full range of business enterprise from the street trader to a multinational corporation such as Unilever, we are struck by the wide variation in size, production processes and complexity. Obviously, the accounts of a farmer, a chemical works and a bank will have to be prepared in different forms if they are to provide meaningful information. All three must know how they stand financially, and what profit is being earned; so profit and loss accounts and balance sheets, based on the general principles already discussed, have to be prepared. However, the three businesses operate different systems of production, and so, before reaching the profit and loss account stage, different accounts are needed to show how the profit is generated.

The principle throughout is quite simple. A set of accounts needs to mirror the reality of the production system in financial terms, as far as this is possible within the existing techniques and conventions of accountancy. Before looking at the accounting implications of the principle, it may be helpful to look more closely at the wide variety of production systems found in modern business. It is perhaps worth reminding ourselves at this point that to the economist, any activity which creates 'utility' is productive, and so we must beware of equating 'production' with 'manufacturing', and also of thinking of a clerk and anyone else who is not actually engaged in making a saleable product as being 'non-productive'. Extracting, transforming, assembling, designing, transporting, storing, financing, advising and repairing are but a few of many activities carried on within different production systems.

Q.11a   Describe the following production systems by listing the inputs, production processes, and outputs, of the businesses:

> a dairy farmer;
> a building contractor;
> an architect;
> a stone quarry;
> an international airline;
> an insurance company;
> a steel works.

11.2   Manufacturing businesses

Although in previous chapters reference has been made to other types of business venture, most of our attention has been directed to the trader. This is a fairly simple productive system because, unlike the manufacturer, the trader does not transform the goods physically. A retailer's 'inputs' are goods which he buys from a wholesaler or a manufacturer, and his 'outputs' are sales to the public. The productive processes consist of storing, 'breaking bulk' and possibly giving other services such as advice and transport.

In earlier chapters we have seen how the production system of a trader is described in accounting terms. The trading account shows quite clearly what is happening. He starts the period with stocks of goods for resale, and throughout the period adds to these stocks by purchases from manufacturers or wholesalers. By subtracting the cost value of closing stocks, the cost of the goods actually sold can be deduced. This is then compared with the value of all sales during the period, whether for cash or on credit, and the difference is the gross profit. Other expenses (or inputs to the productive process) such as salaries, heating and lighting are charged to the profit and loss account.

A manufacturer has a rather more complex production system. Raw materials are transformed physically, often in a number of stages, and the finished goods are sold to retailers, wholesalers or direct to consumers. It may be best to approach the general problem of factory accounting by looking at an imaginary company in the furniture industry, which confines its activities to making two models of bookcase. The following diagram (*Fig. 13* on p. 183) gives a simplified view of the production system. It shows both the physical flow of production, and the additional costs incurred at each stage. Value is added as work progresses in the same way as a snowball increases in size as it is rolled downhill.

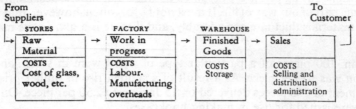

Fig. 13

We have seen how a trader must adjust for changes in stock values when preparing his annual accounts. The same is true of the manufacturer. He has opening stocks of finished goods in the warehouse; goods are continually coming in from the factory; and all these goods will be available for sale. When preparing the Trading Account at the end of the period, any closing stocks of finished goods must be valued and deducted from the total cost of goods available for sale, to find the cost of goods sold. At the end of the period there will also be stocks of wood, etc., in the raw materials store, as well as partly completed bookcases in the factory. The accounts must reflect the different stages of production, and show stock values at each stage. Using our bookcase factory again, let us look a little more closely at some of the accounting problems involved.

11.3   The valuation of raw materials

Wood, glass and metal parts are being purchased throughout the accounting period. When they are needed, the storekeeper issues them to the factory. So far as the accounts are concerned, these raw materials are charged to production at cost, i.e. what was paid to the supplier; and the closing stock is also valued at cost. In the next chapter the significance of this procedure will be more apparent when the problem of finding the material cost of products is discussed. The general principle of valuation — 'lower of cost or net realizable value' — applies to raw materials as well as finished stock. For instance, when stock is taken, it may be found that for various reasons some materials are no longer usable on either of the current models: their cost cannot therefore be the correct valuation, and the scrap value (if any) must be substituted.

A more difficult valuation problem arises when the prices of raw materials have changed during the accounting period. If prices are constant, there is no difficulty in deciding the raw materials 'cost'. If prices change, there may be a range of possible 'costs' for us to choose from when valuing the stock at the end of the period. The accounting difficulty arises because it is usually impossible or inconvenient to link an issue from store with a specific purchase of the material so as to give an 'actual' cost. Materials are coming in and out all the time, and so some accounting assumption has to be used to value issues to the factory.

There are three possibilities:

(1) to assume that issues were made from stock at the earliest possible price: this is the 'common sense' assumption that the first item of stock in is the first out (FIFO);

(2) to assume that issues were made at the latest possible price (last in, first out, or LIFO);

(3) to value at an average price.

The implications of these three methods of stock valuation can best be shown in a simple example. Rising prices are assumed because, since the 1930s, inflation seems to have become part of our way of life. It must not be forgotten, however, that the prices of some raw materials fluctuate considerably, and if there is a glut in the market, prices will fall.

On 1 Jan. 100 pieces of a particular type of wood were in stock, and the stock valuation was £2 per piece. As a result of a sudden rise in timber prices, the next consignment of 200 pieces delivered on 15 Jan. cost £2.50 per piece. On 20 Jan. 100 pieces were issued for use in making bookcases.

The following is a typical form of account for showing movements of materials.

		RECEIPTS			ISSUES			BALANCE		
DATE	DETAILS	Quantity	Price £	Value £	Quantity	Price £	Value £	Quantity	Price £	Value £
Jan. 1	Opening stock							100	2	200
15	Purchases	200	2.50	500				300	—	700
20	Issue to work in progress				100			200		

What are we to put in the price and value columns for the issue on 20 Jan., and how should the closing balance be valued?

Taking the FIFO assumption first, the issue on 20 Jan. would have been the whole of the opening stock at 1 Jan. and so production would have been charged £200, which was the book value of that stock. To make the account balance, closing stock on 31 Jan. would be valued at £500.

Under LIFO, the assumption is that the issue was made from the 200 pieces bought on 15 Jan. The price of that consignment was £2.50 and so the issue on 20 Jan. would be valued at £250 with the implication that the closing stock was worth £450.

In summary:

		FIFO	LIFO
		£	£
Jan. 20	Issue to work in progress	200	250
31	Value of closing stock	500	450

Putting the case more generally, we may say that in a period of rising prices, FIFO will charge less to current production than LIFO, but that FIFO would show a correspondingly higher closing stock. If prices are falling, the situation is the mirror image of that under inflation; FIFO will charge more to current production than LIFO.

FIFO is more common than LIFO in practice, probably because the assumption accords with common-sense ideas about how stock should be issued. Another method in general use is to value issues on the weighted average of stock prices in the accounting period. For instance, in the month of January there were two prices, £2 and

£2.50. The simple average would be £2.25 but this gives both prices the same weighting. Clearly, £2.50 should be given twice as much weighting as £2 because twice as much material was in stock at that price. The weighted average can be calculated by dividing the quantity in stock (300) into its total value (£700):

$$\frac{£700}{300} = 2.333$$

Production would be charged with $100 \times £2.333 = £233$. The closing stock would be $200 \times £2.333 = £467$.

Q.11b The following table carries on from the previous example and shows stocks and issues of the same material for February.

		RECEIPTS			ISSUES			BALANCE		
DATE	DETAILS	Quantity	Price £	Value £	Quantity	Price £	Value £	Quantity	Price £	Value £
Feb. 1	Opening stock							200		
2	Purchases	200	2.50					400		
4	Issues to W.I.P.				100			300		
10	Purchases	200	2.75					500		
16	Issues to W.I.P.				300			200		

Complete the table, assuming (a) FIFO, (b) LIFO and (c) weighted average methods of valuation. *Note:* You will not need to use the price column in all cases. The values for the opening balance are carried forward from the January calculations above.

Two general conclusions must be drawn from this discussion. The first is that the cost of material issued from stores and the consequent valuation of stocks is not wholly a matter of objective fact. It depends in part on the particular method of pricing issues that the accountant chooses to adopt. Different methods give different answers. The second point is that these difficulties become less serious if the same method is used consistently in all accounting periods. If a change in the basis of valuation is introduced, the effect on profit caused by the change should be isolated and shown separately.

11.4   Accounting for raw materials

Apart from these problems of valuation, the accountant has the practical problem of keeping an accurate record of all these comings and goings. If there was a large quantity of low-priced items, such as screws, the weighted average would be the most practical method. Where high-cost items can be linked with an individual job, the actual purchase price of the unit would be charged to work in progress. If a standard costing system is in operation materials would be charged at standard price. Most businesses carrying stocks of any kind would be advised to use a computer system for controlling stock and accounting for material issues.

The foundation of any accounting system is the quality of the basic data recording the transactions which have taken place. As a check on the accuracy of the materials accounting system, the total value of materials issued may be calculated in an alternative way, using the following formula:

> Opening stock of raw materials
> + Purchases of raw materials
> − Closing stock of raw materials
> = Value of materials issued

From a practical point of view, the validity of the calculation depends heavily on the accuracy of the physical stocktaking. In Chapter 5 the stocktaking procedures of a trader were discussed. In a factory, the task of counting the thousands of individual items can be formidable. This check may be made periodically as when a group of clerks descends on the stores at the Balance Sheet date in an attempt to verify the physical stock with the stores records. An alternative to this 'day of judgement' approach is to have a small group of specialist stocktaking clerks making random checks continuously throughout the year. From a number of points of view, this method has much to commend it, the principal one being that serious discrepancies can be investigated immediately. The method of annual stocktaking is rather like shutting the stable door after the horse has bolted.

Q.11c   On 31 March 19X1 Bookcases Ltd valued their stocks of wood, glass, metal parts and other raw materials at £37,800. During the year, invoices for raw materials purchased were received for £201,600. Goods-received notes had been signed to indicate that these goods had actually been received into stores, except for goods to the value of £2,100 which had been returned to the supplier as not being up to specification. On 31 March 19X2 another stocktaking put the value of raw materials at £48,500. The firm has a costing system for materials, which involves the production control section making out requisitions charged to either Model 1 or Model 2. The stores must issue materials only against such a requisition, and the information from these documents is used to adjust the stores records. The total value of the requisitions was £174,870. The company uses the FIFO system of pricing issues.

(a) What discrepancy is brought to light?
(b) Assume that you have been asked by the management of Bookcases Ltd to investigate. List the possible explanations for this discrepancy and make some recommendations about how it could be avoided in future.

11.5   Work in progress

As the raw materials are issued to the factory, they go through a number of production processes. If we look round the factory at any one point in time, we might see bookcases in various stages of completion, from pieces of wood which have just come from the stores, to bookcases which are virtually complete apart from final inspection or packaging. At the beginning and end of the accounting period, therefore, there is a certain amount of 'work in progress'. If we want to find out the value of the finished goods produced in the period, we must recognize the fact that production is a continuing process and adjust for work-in-progress stocks in the same way that we allowed for stock movements in raw materials. The calculation will be as follows:

Opening Stock W.I.P. + Manufacturing costs incurred during the period
− Closing stocks W.I.P. − Factory cost of finished goods.

The above formula raises two important questions:

(a) What should be included in manufacturing costs?
(b) How do we value W.I.P.?

(a) Manufacturing costs

As the raw materials come from the stores, workers are engaged in a series of operations such as cutting, planing and sanding the wood, making grooves for the glass doors, jointing and assembling the sections, fixing the back, finishing, inspection and packaging. It is relatively easy to link the cost of raw materials and the wages of workers on the production line with a particular model of bookcase. Exactly how this can be done will be touched upon in the next chapter on costing techniques. At this stage, however, it will be enough to say that raw materials, production-line wages and any other costs which can be linked directly with a particular product, are called direct costs, and their total is called *prime cost*.

On the other hand, there are many costs which cannot easily be linked with products, but which must be accounted for to arrive at the total cost of manufacture. These are called indirect manufacturing costs, and their total, *manufacturing overhead*. Some workers such as the storekeepers, the inspectors and the production supervisors, although essential for the smooth running of the factory, will probably be treated as indirect labour. Some materials, such as glue, sandpaper and oil, are issued generally, and so must be linked with the factory as a whole, as must depreciation, fire insurance, heating, lighting and power for the machines. Rates will probably be payable for the company as a whole, and so only that portion which relates to the factory should be included as a manufacturing cost. In the factory a number of general-purpose machines, such as bandsaws, sanding machines and planing machines, are in use. The cost of repairs, maintenance and the depreciation of these machines must be included. The cost of some small tools such as portable drills and screwdrivers is charged in total as they are issued to the factory. All these and any other manufacturing overheads would be classified in a way which would be likely to give the most useful information to management.

(b) Valuation of work in progress

As the work progresses through the factory, value is added at each stage. Direct and indirect costs are incurred as the raw materials are gradually transformed into finished bookcases. As we have seen at the annual stocktaking, an attempt has to be made to value all the partly finished work in the factory. The principle is simple: only the direct and indirect manufacturing costs which have been incurred *up to and including that stage* will be included in the valuation. For example, the direct labour cost of completing a Model 2 Bookcase is £10. At the date of stocktaking, there is a partly completed Model 2 bookcase on which £7.50 has been incurred in direct wages, and which contains materials to the value of £25 at that stage. It has been estimated beforehand that total manufacturing overhead for the year will be £140,000 and that total direct wages will be £70,000.

Q.11d Value the above item of work in progress, assuming that manufacturing overhead is absorbed into the product proportionally with direct labour.

At stocktaking there will be many items of work in progress at various stages of manufacture, and so the application of the general principle may prove complicated in practice. Each item of work in progress will have to be valued separately.

11.6   Finished goods

In valuing finished goods, only the cost of manufacture (prime cost + manufacturing overhead) will be included, assuming that this is lower than what the goods are likely to fetch when sold. Selling and administration costs will be charged to the profit and loss account in the usual way. It might be argued that some 'selling expenses', such as the cost of market research, are incurred before the bookcases are made and should therefore be included in the finished stock valuation. After all, the wise businessman makes what he is fairly sure he can sell, rather than tries to sell what he happens to have made. The accountant, however, takes a more conservative view, and so selling costs are usually written off in the period in which they are incurred, and not carried forward in the finished stock valuation.

11.7   Manufacturing accounts

Having discussed in some detail the physical and accounting aspects of the manufacturing process, the traditional form of presenting the accounts of a manufacturer's total operations should present no difficulty. Notice how the costs of manufacture are accumulated at the appropriate stages, and how the stock adjustments for raw materials and work in progress are made.

BOOKCASES LTD

Manufacturing Account for the year ended 31 March 19X2

	£	£	£
Stock of Raw Materials, 31 March 19X1		37,800	
Purchases	201,600		
less Purchases returns	2,100		
		199,500	
		237,300	
less Stock of raw materials, 31 March 19X2		48,500	
Raw Materials Issued			188,800
Direct wages			76,200
			265,000

PRIME COST OF MANUFACTURE

Manufacturing overhead:	£
Indirect wages	21,600
Indirect materials	15,000
Tools	3,900
Maintenance, repairs	21,700
Power, light, heat (factory)	16,800
Rates (factory)	7,000
Insurance (factory)	2,600
Depreciation of factory buildings	10,000
Depreciation of machinery	32,000
Total manufacturing overhead	130,600
TOTAL MANUFACTURING COSTS INCURRED	395,600
add Valuation of work in progress, 31 Mar. 19X1	26,500
	422,100
less Valuation of work in progress, 31 Mar. 19X2	55,700
COST OF FINISHED GOODS MANUFACTURED	£366,400

The next stage is to prepare the Trading account for Bookcases Ltd. This follows exactly the same principles as for a trader, the only difference being that instead of 'Purchases', the equivalent entry will be for 'Cost of finished goods manufactured'. In our example the total accumulated cost in the Manufacturing account (£366,400) will be debited to the Trading account.

Trading Account

	£		£
Stock of finished goods, 31 March 19X1	69,800	SALES	598,600
add			
Cost of finished goods manufactured	366,400		
Goods available for sale	436,200		
less			
Stock of finished goods, 31 March 19X2	92,700		
COST OF GOODS SOLD	343,500		
GROSS PROFIT	255,100		
	598,600		598,600

Q.11e Assume that production of bookcases in the year ending 31 March 19X2 had been 50% higher than it actually was. Look carefully at the elements of prime cost and manufacturing overhead, and suggest which costs would have:

(a) remained about the same;
(b) increased about 50%;
(c) increased, but not as much as 50%.

We shall be returning to this classification later on in the book, when we consider the question of cost behaviour. The distinction between fixed, variable and semi-variable costs is essential when presenting information to guide management decisions.

The reader will be familiar with the next stage: the preparation of the Profit and Loss account starting with the gross profit derived from the Trading account.

Q.11f Complete the Profit and Loss account of Bookcases Ltd given the following information:

Selling expenses	£21,500
Administration expenses	£26,800

Interest on £100,000 8% debentures has to be paid. £78,000 is the estimate of corporation tax liability for the year.

The opening balance of the Profit and Loss account	£21,300

It is proposed to pay a dividend of 25p per share on the ordinary share capital of £300,000 (£1 shares).

11.8   From manufacturing accounts to cost accounting

The accounts of Bookcases Ltd which we have prepared state the results of the business as a whole. For some purposes, such as satisfying the Inland Revenue for tax assessment, this is quite adequate. On the other hand, the management may well require more information if it is to conduct its affairs efficiently. An obvious weakness in the present form of the accounts is that there is no analysis of the relative profitability of the two models produced. One way in which this can be done in this simple example is to apply the technique of departmental accounting discussed in Chapter 7.

Q.11g Re-draft the Manufacturing and Trading accounts of Bookcases Ltd to show the relative profitability of the two models. From internal records, the following information is provided:

	Model 1	Model 2	Total
	£	£	£
Raw materials issued to the factory	69,700	119,100	188,800
Direct wages	36,300	39,900	76,200
Increase in W.I.P. during the year	13,200	16,000	29,200
Stocks of finished bookcases, 31 March 19X1	33,600	36,200	69,800
Stocks of finished bookcases, 31 March 19X2	55,200	37,500	92,700
Sales	216,500	382,100	598,600

Manufacturing overhead is apportioned between the two models on the basis of prime cost (raw materials issued + direct wages). It is not practicable to apportion selling and administration expenses.

This method may be satisfactory for the simple type of factory which we have been using as our example throughout this chapter, although even here it is obvious that detailed internal records will be needed to show, for example, how materials and direct labour are to be charged to products. If we think of a more complex organization making thousands of different products in several divisions and factories and departments within each factory, more sophisticated techniques must be used. These techniques are referred to as Cost Accounting, and they will be the subject of the next two chapters. In Chapter 12 we shall give a brief outline of the methods used to find what products have cost in the past. Chapters 13 and 14 are more forward looking in that they deal with the accounting techniques used in planning and control.

It will be clear that the main objective of these techniques is to provide information for management to take decisions more efficiently. The presentation of accounting information with this purpose in mind is called Management Accounting. In Chapter 15 we shall look at some of the ways in which the accountant can help management solve some specific problems apart from cost finding and cost control. Management Accounting is therefore a wider field than Cost Accounting and, although the terms are often used loosely, it is usual to limit Cost Accounting to those techniques which are principally concerned with the accumulation and analysis of past and future costs.

11.9   Additional questions

[1]

Find the value of work in progress on 31 January given the following information:

	£
Stock of finished goods 31 Jan.	400
Stock of finished goods 1 Jan.	600
Cost of goods sold during January	6,000
Stock of work in progress 1 Jan.	500
Material issued to work in progress during January	2,000
Labour cost incurred in January	3,800
Factory overhead absorbed in January	1,500

[2]

(a) Prepare a stock record card in the format:

	Received			Issued			Balance		
	Quantity	Rate	Amount	Quantity	Rate	Amount	Quantity	Rate	Amount
		£	£		£	£		£	£
1 Jan.	—	—	—	—	—	—	500	1.00	500

Using the FIFO basis of issue and valuation, record the following items and balance the stock record card after each transaction:

Castings received	Castings issued
2 Jan. 500 at £1.20 each	5 Jan. 600
8 Jan. 500 at £1.10 each	10 Jan. 600
15 Jan. 500 at £1.20 each	18 Jan. 600
22 Jan. 500 at £1.10 each	25 Jan. 600

Stock at 1 January is shown on the card.

(b) Using the LIFO basis of issue and valuation, re-present the stock record card.
(c) Comment on the two methods of stock valuation.

[3]

The records of the stores department of the XYZ Manufacturing Co. for the month of April show the following transactions for a particular raw material used by the company:

Balance, 1 April	600 lb at £3.00 per lb
Purchase, 9 April	3,800 lb at £3.50 per lb
Issue, 12 April	1,000 lb
Issue, 13 April	2,000 lb
Purchase, 20 April	1,000 lb at £3.25 per lb
Issue, 25 April	1,200 lb

(a) Calculate the value of the stock of the raw material on 30 April under each of the following cost flow assumptions:

(i) FIFO
(ii) LIFO
(iii) Simple average cost
(iv) Weighted average cost
(v) At a standard cost of £3.00 which was fixed on 1 January.

(b) An analysis of purchase invoices for the previous three months reveals the following prices paid for the material

During Jan.	£2.80,	£3.20,	£3.60,	per lb
During Feb.	£3.90,	£4.00,	£2.70,	per lb
During Mar.	£2.90,	£3.00,	£3.20,	per lb

There are no special discounts for quantity allowed, and no marked seasonal variation in price of the material.

Comment on the validity of the various methods of stock valuation used in (a) in the light of the additional information given.

[4]

The estimated factory cost of a product is as follows:

Direct materials	£2.50 per unit (1 lb)
Direct labour	£1.50 per unit
Factory overhead	150% of Direct labour

(a) From the following information complete a Manufacturing account:

	£	
Purchase of raw materials	4,500	1,500 lb
Opening stock of raw materials	500	200 lb
Closing stock of raw materials		400 lb
Factory wages (direct)	2,100	
Factory wages (indirect)	1,300	
Power	400	
Factory sundry expenses	600	
Depreciation of plant	100	
Rates (50% Factory)	100	

1,100 complete units are produced during June, and a further 100 units are 50% complete at the end of the month. There was no work in progress at the beginning of the month. The FIFO method of pricing materials issues is used, and the estimated factory cost is the basis for valuing work in progress.

(b) Revise the original estimated factory cost for the product in the light of the information in the accounts you have just prepared.

[5]

(a) Arundel Ltd manufactures and retails its own products. Production is carried out in a separate building. Proper material stocks are maintained at cost, and Work in Progress is physically counted and valued (at prime cost, i.e. material plus operators' wages) each accounting year end.

Prepare a Manufacturing statement from the following information:

		£
Wages to: Operators		276,500
Supervision		26,000
Maintenance		20,100
Power		37,200
Machinery repairs		11,500
Factory expenses		28,420
Depreciation — machinery		27,000
Material purchased and received during year		341,460
Stocks 1 January:	Materials	51,400
	W.I.P.	18,920
Stocks 31 December:	Materials	36,560
	W.I.P.	16,440

The finished goods manufactured during the year are transferred to the retailing department at factory cost.

(b) The retailing department of Arundel Ltd receives finished goods from the manufacturing department, and sells to the retail trade on monthly credit terms.

Prepare a Trading Statement from the following information:

	£
Stocks in warehouse: 1 January	nil
31 December	56,000
Distribution expenses	45,100
Sales on credit during year	1,136,150

(c) Prepare the Profit and Loss Statement of Arundel Ltd for the year ended 31 December using the following additional information:

	£
Rates, water, rents, maintenance	32,000
Lighting, heating	9,200
Insurances	8,400
General expenses	5,000
Depreciation — office equipment	4,800
Advertising and printing	6,250
Motor car expenses, travelling	26,000
Debenture interest payable (gross)	2,800
Professional fees	3,600
Corporation tax — based on current year's profits	35,000
Administrative wages and insurances, etc.	116,000
Pension fund contributions	10,000

(d) Having now completed the Manufacturing, Trading and Profit and Loss Statements for Arundel Ltd consider the following supplementary question:

If the policy of the Arundel management was to transfer the finished goods from the manufacturing department to the retailing department at a value in excess of factory cost

(i) What effect, if any, would this policy have on the profit shown in the accounts you have prepared?

(ii) Would the closing stock valuation in the Trading account differ from £56,000? Explain.

(iii) Would any further adjustment need to be considered? For example is there any element of profit not realized?

(iv) What reason(s) can you think of which would cause management to consider transferring the finished goods at a value higher than factory cost?

[6]

The Highlow Co. was formed to make a single product, and the following information relates to the first three years of its existence:

	Year 1	Year 2	Year 3
Variable costs per unit	£12	£13	£14
Selling price per unit	£20	£20	£22
Sales (units)	10,000	13,000	9,000
Production (units)	12,000	14,000	8,000
Total Fixed Costs	£60,000	£60,000	£65,000

Prepare statements for each of the three years assuming that stock is valued on basis of variable costs incurred, and the FIFO method of stock valuation is used.

[7]
Frank Jones, a retail trader, sells electrical goods, hardware and crockery.

Transactions during the week ended 31 January were:

	£
Bought goods for resale	7,020
Salaries — specialist departmental staff	600
Wages — general assistants	700
Establishment expenses and depreciation	580
Sales during the week	10,040

The Stock on 1 January was £1,500 and at the close of business on 31 January was £1,480.

(i) Prepare a Trading and Profit and Loss Statement for the week and insert appropriate Gross Profit, Expenses and Net Profit percentages.
(ii) Do you consider the week's results satisfactory? Give your reasons.
(iii) What additional data will you need in order to present Mr Jones with a more information management statement?

An analysis of stock values, at cost, on 1 January showed:

	£
Electrical goods	400
Hardware	800
Crockery	300
	£1,500

A FIFO basis of valuation is used. Prices have remained stable for many months.

Purchases during January were:

	£
Electrical goods	2,700
Hardware	2,520
Crockery	1,800
	£7,020

and Sales were:

	£
Electrical goods	3,460
Hardware	3,660
Crockery	2,920
	£10,040

At the close of business on 31 January stock, again valued at cost on FIFO basis, was:

	£
Electrical Goods	500
Hardware	780
Crockery	200
	£1,480

Specialist staff salaries were equally distributed over the three departments but other expenses were not apportioned.

(i)   Prepare a Trading and Profit and Loss Statement showing profit made on each selling line and insert appropriate percentages.
(ii) Which selling line would you advise Mr Jones to concentrate on in order to maximize his profit? Explain.
(iii) Are there any other factors Mr Jones should consider before committing himself on your advice in (ii)?

[8]
(a) If a company maintains a perpetual inventory control system, is it also necessary to have an annual inventory?
(b) 'The control of materials must meet two opposing management needs.' Discuss.

[9]
The following information relates to a company which uses the FIFO method of stock valuation:

	Units	Value £
Opening stock at 1 March	6,000	6,000
Purchases:		
March	8,000	9,600
May	12,000	15,000
August	10,000	12,500
November	5,000	6,500

Closing Stock at 29 December was valued at £8,000.

Calculate the Cost of Goods Sold using the LIFO method, stating any assumption you make.

[10]
The Income Statements of the Excelsior Manufacturing Co. over a five year period are as follows:

	£000				
	Year 1	Year 2	Year 3	Year 4	Year 5
SALES	£	£	£	£	£
Home	1,300	1,210	1,250	1,300	1,300
Overseas	3,100	4,040	4,950	5,710	6,930
	4,400	5,250	6,200	7,010	8,230

	Year 1 £	Year 2 £	£000 Year 3 £	Year 4 £	Year 5 £
COST OF GOODS SOLD					
Direct Materials	750	800	900	1,200	1,500
Direct Labour	1,200	1,300	1,500	1,600	1,800
Manufacturing Overheads	1,200	1,500	1,750	1,900	2,500
	3,150	3,600	4,150	4,700	5,800
Gross Profit	1,250	1,650	2,050	2,310	2,430
NON-MANUFACTURING OVERHEADS					
Marketing	300	400	500	550	550
Research & Development	300	500	700	850	900
Administrative	150	200	250	250	250
Depreciation	50	70	80	80	130
	800	1,170	1,530	1,730	1,830
Net Profit before Tax	450	480	520	580	600
Index of Retail Prices	100	110	120	135	145

(a) Show the breakdown of £1 sales between profit and the major constituents of cost in years 1 and 5 in the form of pie charts.
(b) Show the detail of sales and net profit for the five-year period in graph form.
(c) Express the gross profit and net profit figures for the five years at year 1 prices.
(d) Comment on the performance of the company over the five-year period indicating any significant trends.

[11]
Describe the 'production system' of a large retailer with a number of branches. Take a particular company such as Marks and Spencer or Sainsburys as an example and try to answer the following questions:

Who supplies the merchandise?
How is the merchandise distributed to branches?
What types of merchandise are stocked?
What additional services are provided to customers (e.g. credit, transport, advice)?

How would the rate of turnover $\left[\dfrac{\text{annual sales}}{\text{average stock}} \right]$ compare with other types of retaile

How would you compare the profitability of branches?

Your answer should include a flow diagram of the production system.

Chapter 12
Cost Finding

12.1 Introduction

If the financial accounts present a total picture of the firm's costs the cost accounts analyse those costs by linking them to the production process. Materials, labour and other costs are allocated and apportioned to the jobs, processes, services or other units produced. The Cost Accountant accounts for cost. This chapter outlines the basic principles of Cost Accounting and shows how they may be applied to a variety of production processes from jobbing manufacture to the provision of public services.

Historically, cost accounting grew out of the desire of manufacturers to find out the true cost of their products and to check that selling prices covered expense and provided an adequate profit. During the eighteenth century, manufacturing in factories emerged as a more efficient method of organization than the traditional 'domestic system' of putting out work to be done in the workers' own homes. These factories were not large by modern standards, but raised entirely fresh problems of management to the new breed of entrepreneurs that brought them into existence. Pollard's fascinating study of the Industrial Revolution in Great Britain gives many illustrations to show that these early factory owners appreciated the need to analyse costs. For instance, Josiah Wedgwood, the great innovator in the pottery industry, admitted in 1776 that he had been 'puzzling his brain all the last week to find out proper data and methods of calculating the expenses of manufacture, sale and loss, etc., to be laid upon each article of manufacture, but without success'.[1]

However, as Pollard points out, this failure to evolve adequate costing techniques in the early Industrial Revolution was not, by itself, critical to business success or failure. At that time, selling prices tended to be so far above total costs, no matter how calculated, that almost any pricing policy was bound to show a surplus, at least among the leaders in their industries.[2] Today, business organization is more complex, and profit margins are generally smaller. An adequate system of cost finding is therefore necessary if the modern business is to keep track of its activities. Cost accounting developed, mainly in this century, when fierce international competition forced businessmen to look carefully at costs and trim their profit margins.

[1] Pollard, S., *The Genesis of Modern Management*, London, Edward Arnold, 1965, p. 225.
[2] *Op. cit.*, p. 245.

Before looking in detail at techniques, there are three preliminary points which may help to put the subject in perspective.

(1) A system of cost finding is only capable of providing information after the event. For this reason it is sometimes called 'historical costing'. There is an old saying to the effect that 'an estimate is an opinion, but a cost is a fact'. As we shall see, it is somewhat ambitious to describe as 'fact' a product cost which is based on a number of arbitrary assumptions about stock valuations, overhead apportionments and the like. None the less, the saying does emphasize the point that product costs are in the nature of *post mortem* reports.

(2) Cost-finding techniques attempt to account for all costs of the organization. If the management of British Leyland wish to know the 'cost' of a Metro they must include not only the obvious costs of raw materials, component parts and the wages of workers on the assembly line, but also a proportion of those indirect costs which may seem rather remote from the business of actually making the car. Take, for instance, the wages of the commissionaire at the factory gate. This is an example of a 'common cost' incurred for the benefit of the company as a whole rather than for one particular model of car. A 'true cost' of the Metro must, however, include a proportion of his wages. If the system tries to account for *all* costs, direct and indirect, fixed and variable, we sometimes refer to it as 'absorption costing'. Although useful for some purposes, absorption costing may be positively misleading if the results are to be used to guide some management actions. In Chapter 15 we shall return to this point when we introduce Marginal Costing as an alternative method of presenting information to management. For the present we shall ignore the important distinction between fixed and variable costs.

(3) The final point is one of terminology. Accountants and economists use the word 'cost' in different ways. The economist is particularly concerned with 'opportunity cost' — the value of the alternative forgone by following a given line of action. The opportunity cost of buying a video recorder may be the holiday abroad that we have to do without to pay for it. Although accounting systems do not usually record opportunity costs, businessmen should bear the economic concept in mind if they are to take rational decisions. Could the existing plant be made to produce an alternative range of products? Could the capital invested in the business earn a higher yield if invested elsewhere?

12.2   The elements of cost

It is beyond the scope of this book to study in detail the many forms, recording systems and procedures used in actual cost-finding systems; indeed, no one book could give a complete survey of all the methods in use. The installation of any data-processing system, particularly one concerned with costing information, is very much a practical matter, and textbook systems cannot be transferred without modification to actual business situations. Does the system rely on clerical effort; or has the business a computer? Is the production system basically assembling, processing, jobbing, or a combination of these? Who is to originate the basic records? What degree of accuracy is required? How quickly is the information needed?

By answering these and many other questions, the cost accountant has the creative task of applying the basic principles of costing to the productive system of the business.

No matter how sophisticated the cost accounts may look on paper, they will be useless if they do not rest on the foundation of a practical system of data collection. For instance, if material requisitions are made out on a bench in the machine shop by supervisors who do not fully understand the departmental, stores and product codes, and have no particular interest in the mechanics of the costing system, it is unlikely that the materials accounting system will provide much information of value to management. The solution may be to train the supervisors, or let the production control section originate the requisitions, or both.

From the point of view of recording and analysing the costs of a business, it is convenient to classify them into three elements: materials, labour and other costs. Many writers refer to this third element as 'expense', but it would be rather confusing to adopt this terminology, as earlier in the book we have agreed to use the word 'expense' to mean any expired cost. Words may mean what we want them to mean, but it would indeed be an Alice-in-Wonderland situation if we changed their meaning half way through the argument. Diagrammatically:

Elements of Cost		
materials	labour	other costs

Let us now look at each of these elements of cost in turn, indicating briefly some of the general problems of data collection associated with them.

Materials

A wide variety of commodities, ranging from raw materials and component parts to stationery and consumable stores, will be ordered by the business. The purchasing department will initiate these orders on receiving information about requirements from the production control section, stores or direct from departments. The management of material stock levels involves striking the right balance between having too much capital tied up in stocks which are not immediately required and running the risk of production grinding to a halt because essential supplies are out of stock.

When is a commodity not a material in the costing sense? A useful test is to ask whether the commodity is received into a store before it is issued. Most commodities will go through a store, but coke may be delivered direct to the boiler-house, and some components may be ordered direct to a job in progress without going through stores. In both cases, these would be treated as 'other costs' rather than materials.

The issue of material, whether it is to be directly incorporated in the finished product or is an indirect material, such as lubricant for the machines, is usually against a requisition. This document provides the authority for stores to issue the material and is also the basic record of the materials accounting system. Not all factories will use requisitions, however: for instance, in a process industry, such as chemicals, 'issues' from a storage tank or vat may be metered to show actual usage. The problems of valuing materials issues were discussed in the preceding chapter.

Labour

Any remuneration to the employees of the business, whether it be called wages, salaries, bonuses or commission, is part of the labour cost. The test is whether the payment appears on the firm's payroll. For instance, the fee paid to an outside adviser, such as an architect or solicitor, would come under the heading of 'other costs'. So would travelling expenses, and similar payments which are not part of an employee's remuneration. Under the PAYE system of income tax deduction, the workers will receive their remuneration net. So far as the firm's costs are concerned, it is the gross amount which must be accounted for, as the employer is merely acting as a tax collector for the Inland Revenue.

If a worker's wage, or part of his wages, can be linked with a particular production or process, this would be a direct labour cost. Unfortunately this is not always practicable, even for production workers. Identification of wage with job is easiest under a straight piece-rate system. Here, workers are paid according to what they produce, and there is a fixed rate of remuneration for each job. If workers are paid on a time basis, or even under one of the more ingenious systems of 'payment by results', more detailed records have to be kept of how workers spend their time. Only then can a fair proportion of wages be charged to individual jobs.

There is growing disillusionment with piece rates and payment by results in general. Such systems are often unduly complicated, easily 'fiddled', and based on an obsolete view of the role of management in a modern business. Measured day rates, job evaluation and merit rating are more satisfactory techniques for motivating workers and getting rid of the piece-rate jungle. Unfortunately, from the cost accountant's point of view, the introduction of these techniques often makes it more difficult to identify wages paid to the worker with particular jobs.

Another factor making the identification of direct labour cost more difficult is the growth of automation. In an automated factory, for instance, few, if any, workers are directly employed on the assembly line. The main tasks will be to maintain the automated system, avoid breakdowns and ensure that quality is assured. It is rarely possible to link these activities to specific units of production. In both manufacturing and service industries there has been a tendency to employ a higher proportion of 'indirect workers' such as administrators, financial staff and computer personnel.

From a data collection point of view, the problem is to account for all the time spend by the employee in earning his remuneration. A common method in use is to have a time-sheet for each worker, recording all time spent on his 'direct' and 'indirect' activities, and charging the relevant job or department with the labour cost of the time elapsed.

Other costs

This is a residual classification. It includes the cost of services which outsiders render to the business. It may be possible to link some of these services to work in progress, and so treat it as a direct cost. For instance, a particular stage of the manufacturing process may be subcontracted. When the subcontractor sends his invoice the cost can be charged direct to the job. However, this situation is unusual. Most services, such as insurance, electricity and the local authority's services as listed on the back of the rate-demand note, can only be treated as overheads.

Apart from services by outsiders, we must also include as a cost the depreciation charge on fixed assets. In a manufacturing business, depreciation of plant and machinery, factory buildings, etc., is usually charged as an indirect manufacturing cost, as fixed assets are rarely installed for the benefit of one particular cost unit.

12.3   Prime cost and overhead

As indicated in the section on labour costs it is often impractical to draw a distinction between 'direct' and 'indirect' labour costs in automated production systems. Wherever possible, however, management will try to relate as many costs as possible to specific units of production. This will help in estimating product costs and controlling the production system.

Whether a particular cost is treated as direct or indirect depends on practical considerations. Raw materials and 'production labour' can usually be linked with a product, but this is not always possible, particularly with labour. It is conceivable that Bookcases Ltd makes its two models in separate factories. In this, rather unlikely, situation almost all materials, all labour, including supervision, inspection, etc., and many other costs could be charged direct to Model 1 or Model 2. Even in this case it is possible that management would like to know the cost of each batch of bookcases made in the factories. The batch rather than the model would now be the cost unit, and costs such as supervision, depreciation and power would have to be treated as indirect.

We have already introduced the terms Prime Cost and Overhead in discussing the total manufacturing account.

Prime Cost = *Direct* materials, labour and other costs
Overhead = *Indirect* materials, labour and other costs

Diagrammatically:

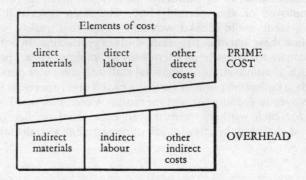

Overhead can itself be subdivided into manufacturing, selling and administration overhead.

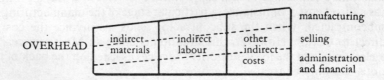

Q.12a   What is the most likely classification of the following costs? Complete the table.

COST	ELEMENT	PRIME COST OR OVERHEAD
Raw materials	material	Prime Cost
Oil for machinery	material	Manufacturing O/H
Salesmen's commission	labour	Selling O/H
Depreciation of office machinery	other cost	Administration O/H
Cost clerks' salaries		
Stationery used in the Sales Office		
Extra allowance for overtime work — factory workers		
Interest on bank overdraft		
Fire insurance		
Fee to advertising agency		
Depreciation on cars used by salesmen		
Directors' fees		
Electricity account		
Subcontractor's charge for work on a production job		
Employer's National Insurance contribution		

Note that in some cases it may be necessary to apportion a cost between different types of overhead.

12.4   Cost finding in action — job costing

The simplest type of costing system is used in production systems where it is possible to identify jobs as they progress through the system and where it is important to find the cost of each separate job. The motor-car repair garage is an obvious example. Each job is different and it is important to record the parts and labour used on each job so that the customer may be charged correctly. Building, civil engineering, printing and ship building are typical jobbing industries. Such businesses may vary considerably in size (from a small bespoke tailor to a heavy electrical engineering company) and type of activity (a management consultant is providing a 'jobbing' service for his clients). Some businesses may undertake jobbing work in addition to making for stock. For instance Bookcases Ltd, in addition to the two standard models made for stock, may also take on special contract work for equipping libraries. In jobbing production systems the job or contract is the obvious 'cost unit'. Total costs must be allocated or apportioned to the individual jobs in hand (see the diagram on p. 205).

Custom Yachts Ltd make and equip luxury yachts, each one being designed to meet the special requirements of the customer. The company will have up to four 'jobs' on hand at any one moment. Each job is given a number, and direct costs will be charged to that code. For instance, if steel is issued from stores to Job No. 1, information on the requisition will allow the accounting entries to be made. Materials Account will be credited with the value of the material, and Work in Progress Account debited. There will, however, be separate records for each individual job, and the Work in Progress Account will be merely a total account of the individual jobs. The treatment is similar to the total accounts for debtors and creditors, discussed in Chapter 7.

CUSTOM YACHTS LTD

Total Work in Progress Account

	£		£
Opening balance	250,000	Finished boats	212,000
Direct materials	160,000	Closing balance	353,000
Direct wages	70,000		
Direct expense	15,000		
Manufacturing overhead	70,000		
	565,000		565,000
Opening balance next period	353,000		

This total statement of work in progress is analysed as follows:

CUSTOM YACHTS LTD

Job Analysis

	Total £000	Job 1	Job 2	Job 3	Job 4		Total £000	Job 1	Job 2	Job 3	Job 4
Opening balance	250	13	150	40	47	Finished boats	212	—	222	—	—
Direct materials	160	50	30	25	55	Closing balance	353	116	—	85	152
Direct wages	70	20	15	10	25						
Direct expenses	15	13	12	—	—						
Manufacturing overhead	70	20	15	10	25						
	565	116	222	85	152		565	116	222	85	152
Opening balance next period	353	116	—	85	152						

This analysis shows in detail the position with regard to the four boats which have been under construction during the year. Job No. 2 is complete and its accumulated cost of £222,000 is transferred to the finished goods account. As work is still continuing on the other three jobs, these balances carry forward to the next period.

There will be total accounts and related detailed records for creditors and finished goods, and these will be kept on the same principle as the work in progress records described above. The diagram on p. 206 shows the complete system.

Manufacturing overhead

The system of data collection will enable direct costs to be charged to the job. In the case of manufacturing overhead, this is by definition an impossible task. However, it is usually possible to charge these overheads to a department or other suitable 'cost centre'. These cost centres will be either 'production' departments, such as the fabrication shop, or 'service' departments, such as the drawing office. The stages by

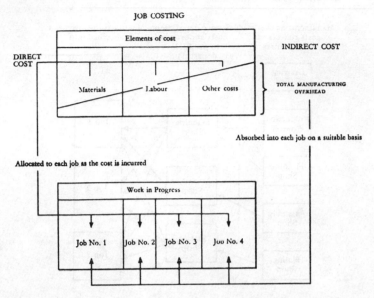

COST FINDING

which manufacturing overhead is collected and absorbed into the various jobs in progress may be summarized as follows:

(1) Manufacturing overhead is collected under 'cost centre' codes.
(2) The total of 'service' cost centres is apportioned on a suitable basis to 'production' cost centres; e.g. the total cost of the works canteen may be apportioned to production departments on the basis of the number of workers in each production department.
(3) The enlarged overhead cost of the production departments is absorbed by jobs on some suitable basis. The method chosen is bound to be arbitrary, but should give some indication of the usage of overhead services by jobs. Separate absorption rates would need to be calculated for each production department.

In Section 11.5, Bookcases Ltd used the direct labour cost method of absorbing manufacturing overhead into work in progress. Estimates were made of total manufacturing overhead for the year (£140,000) and the total direct wages for the year (£70,000). Dividing one by the other gives an absorption rate of 200%. Each job passing through that part of the factory will be charged this rate. Custom Yachts Ltd also uses the direct labour cost method for absorbing manufacturing overhead but in this case the absorption rate is 100%. Other methods in use relate overhead to direct labour hours, prime cost or to machine usage. The method chosen will depend to a large extent on whether the business is capital intensive or labour intensive. For instance, in a shirt factory, overhead might be recovered as a percentage of the standard production time. In a paper mill, products might be charged overhead according to their usage of plant.

The following diagram shows the stages of costing for manufacturing overheads in a business making three products. There are three production departments and two service departments (the Drawing Office and the Production Control Department).

COSTING FOR MANUFACTURING OVERHEAD

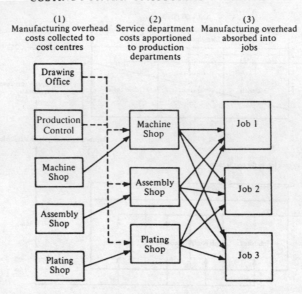

The following table shows how the costing system operates in practice:

Manufacturing Overhead Costs	Total	Production Departments			Service Departments	
		Machine Shop	Assembly Shop	Plating Shop	Drawing Office	Production Control Office
Indirect Material	2,000	500	500	500	200	300
Indirect Labour	4,000	600	700	700	1,500	500
Indirect Expenses	3,600	500	500	600	1,000	1,000
	9,600	1,600	1,700	1,800	2,700	1,800
Service Departments: Production control		400	900	400	100	−1,800
Drawing office		1,600	1,100	100	−2,800	—
Total manufacturing overheads	9,600	3,600	3,700	2,300	—	—
Direct Labour cost	6,500	2,100	2,200	2,200		
Overhead rate as a % or direct labour costs		171%	168%	105%		

Each of the three jobs would be charged for overheads at the appropriate rate depending on the time taken by the job in each of the three production departments. It is assumed in this calculation that the drawing office does not do any work for the production control office.

JOB COSTING SYSTEM

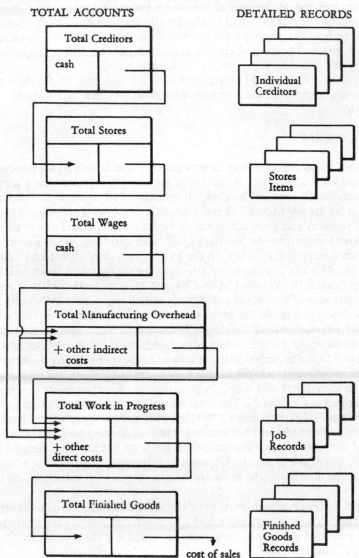

TOTAL ACCOUNTS   DETAILED RECORDS

In spite of the ingenuity of these procedures, there are three important qualifications which force us to treat the final result with caution.

(1) The choice of a basis for apportionment is a matter of opinion, not an exact science. Cost accountants may differ about which method to apply in a particular situation. The greater the proportion of overhead to prime costs, the more do product costs reflect these accounting assumptions rather than recorded fact.

(2) In any period the overhead actually 'absorbed' will be based on an estimate of total overhead costs and production likely to be achieved. Custom Yachts Ltd decided to recover manufacturing overhead at a rate of 100% of direct labour cost. In arriving at this rate, estimates must be made of total overhead likely to be

incurred, the number of hours likely to be worked and expected rates of pay. Only at the end of the period will it be known whether these estimates are realistic and the rate sufficient to absorb all overhead in product costs. The most likely result is that overhead will be over- or under-recovered. The validity of any current 'product costs' is therefore dependent on the skill of the accountant in making his estimate of the correct absorption rate.

(3) The system outlined takes no account of cost behaviour, i.e. the extent to which overheads vary with production. Marginal costing attempts to meet this objection.

12.5   Unit costing

The job is the obvious cost unit in all cases where individual orders are produced to the customer's special requirements. A variant of job costing is found where items are not produced individually but in batches; Bookcases Ltd receive an order from a department store for 500 Model 143 bookcases. This model was designed specially for sale to large retailers and each batch has to be treated separately as customers have slightly different requirements for packaging and labelling. This particular order becomes batch number 13. As work on the batch progresses, direct and indirect costs are charged to 143/13 as in job costing, dividing the total cost of batch 143/13 by 500.

When introducing Bookcases Ltd in Chapter 11 it was inferred that most of the factory's output was of two standard models which were mass produced for stock. When operating in this mode the appropriate cost unit would be neither a job nor a batch but the average cost of making a bookcase. Let us assume that there is an assembly line devoted to the continuous production of Bookcase Model 1. All materials issued to the assembly line and labour and expenses directly incurred on the assembly line are charged to Model 1. Factory overhead is absorbed on a direct labour cost basis. Raw material and work in progress stock adjustments are made in the manner described in Chapter 11. The total manufacturing cost of the assembly line for the accounting period is then divided by the number of bookcases completed to obtain an average unit cost of Model 1 bookcases for the accounting period. Unit cost systems are installed in mass-production industries such as baking and electric light bulb manufacture, where the production system is relatively simple and it is not thought necessary to account for costs at intermediate stages of production, as in process industries.

This type of costing is also important in service industries such as banking, retailing or insurance and in public services such as education and health care. In these cases the unit would be defined in terms of the service provided, e.g. the cost of clearing a cheque or providing a hospital bed.

The principles involved may be illustrated by looking at unit costs in the education service. So far as primary education is concerned, unit-cost calculations are similar to those adopted in the bookcase example. Total costs of providing primary school education in an authority would be divided by the number of primary school children enrolled to give a unit cost per pupil. Although the children, teachers and parents may not welcome the comparison, from a costing point of view a primary school child is as much a standard unit as the bookcase in our earlier example.

Q.12b   The following table compares the unit cost of teaching a primary school child in Barsetshire with the average cost per primary school pupil for all English counties in a particular financial year.

Cost per Primary School Pupil

	Barsetshire £	All English counties £
Teachers	483	461
Other employees	91	70
Premises	104	92
Books, Equipment and Materials	33	21
Other Supplies and Services	2	2
Home to School Transport	6	9
Other costs	10	7
Total Gross Expenditure	729	662
Income	2	3
Total Net Expenditure	727	659

The primary school pupil–teacher ratio in Barsetshire is 20.9:1 compared with an average of 23.2:1 for English counties as a whole.

Does the relatively high unit cost of educating a primary school child in Barsetshire necessarily mean that the education service in Barsetshire is 'inefficient'? Give reasons for your answer.

The calculation of unit costs in further and higher education is more complicated. Whereas almost all primary school children attend full time for three terms, a student in further or higher education may be enrolled on a full-time, sandwich, part-time day, evening, block release or short course. Before working out unit costs we must convert total student enrolments into *equivalent units* — the 'full-time equivalent' student is the obvious choice in this case. For official purposes the following conversion factors are currently in use for calculating full-time equivalent students on 'advanced' courses:

Full-time student   = 1
Sandwich-course student = 0.9
Part-time student   = 0.4
Evening only   = 0.2

Q.12c Suggest a formula for calculating the full-time equivalent of the total students in a college enrolled on a short course. Such courses vary in length from a half-day course with three hours' tuition to a two-week intensive course with 70 hours' tuition. On average, full-time students follow classes for 20 hours per week. Because of the extra preparation required a 50% allowance is given for students on short courses as compared with other students.

Apart from variations in mode of attendance, there are other important differences between students which need to be accounted for if our unit-cost calculations are to have any validity. Although all students may be equal, some cost more than others! An engineering student is taught for more hours a week, uses more materials and equipment and requires more space than an accountancy student. Consider the following table which is based on an official report on the costs of polytechnics.

POLYTECHNIC COSTS PER STUDENT

	Poly A £	Poly B £	Poly C £	Poly D £	Poly E £	Poly F £
Academic staff	1,537	1,332	1,419	1,311	1,392	1,715
Non-teaching staff	634	317	738	372	441	787
Premises & Grounds	376	303	450	227	276	438
Supplies & Services	237	173	339	273	254	235
Transport	81	33	55	65	27	48
Establishment expenses	91	114	110	103	81	149
Miscellaneous	16	2	7	1	2	15
TOTAL EXPENDITURE	2,972	2,274	3,118	2,352	2,473	3,387
Student numbers Full-time Equivalents	6,557	6,958	5,215	4,077	3,069	6,033

Although the student numbers are expressed as full-time equivalents using the conversion factors mentioned above, the table makes no allowances for the different mix of subject disciplines at the six institutions. The cost of teaching a student at Polytechnic B is almost two-thirds that of his counterpart at Polytechnic F. However, before making valid comparisons, we would need to have more information about the proportion of students studying various subjects at these institutions. Polytechnic B, for instance, may have a high proportion of students on humanities and social science courses, where a relatively low unit cost would be expected. In order to compensate for these differences subject-weighting factors have been officially agreed for each major group of academic disciplines. If a student on a humanities course is taken as base with a cost weighting of 1.0, a student on an applied science course (which requires expensively equipped laboratories with technician support) is given a cost weighting of 1.7. Students on music, drama and visual arts courses have a weighting of 1.8 to compensate for the individual and small group teaching which is necessary in these subjects. The unit costing system for higher education, therefore, must define equivalent units which take account of both changes in the mode of attendance and the subject studied.

This extended discussion of the problems of costing in the education service illustrates the critical importance of defining valid equivalents in any unit-costing system. In many service industries there is the added problem of choosing the most appropriate unit. Manufactured output is invariably defined in physical terms — loaves of bread, tonnes of steel or barrels of beer — and certain services may also be defined as discrete units of production — a cheque cleared or an insurance policy processed. However, many services are provided continuously over a period of time, and in these cases a compound unit of measurement is required — a kilowatt hour of electricity, education of a student for a year, passenger mile or tonne mile in railway costing.

Q.12d Suggest the most appropriate cost unit in the following organizations. Discuss any particular problems which may arise in defining equivalent units:

(a) a general hospital with maternity, surgical, intensive care, casualty and geriatric wards

(b) a hotel in central London
(c) The National Coal Board
(d) a public library service

12.6 Process costing

The method of unit costing described in the previous section is appropriate where goods are produced or services are provided through relatively simple production systems. Because modern methods of production are often more complex, it is important to analyse these systems to account for what is happening at the various stages of production. In the case of assembly industries such as motor-car or television-set manufacture, a system of 'multiple costing' is commonly used. The value added at the various sub-assembly stages is gradually accumulated until the final assembly stage in order to build up the cost of the finished product.

A similar technique of building up the total cost through stages is used in process costing. In industries such as brewing, food manufacture and chemicals, raw materials pass through a series of processes before they are transformed into a saleable product. At each state, direct labour, overhead and possibly other material costs will be incurred.

Diagrammatically:

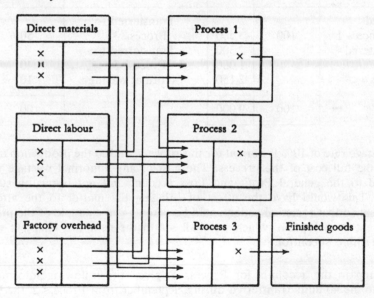

A column for units produced would appear alongside the value column so that a unit cost can be easily calculated. It is as important to define equivalent units in process costing as in simple unit-costing systems. The above system of accounts is appropriate for simple consecutive processes. Process costing systems may also be designed for more complex situations such as the following:

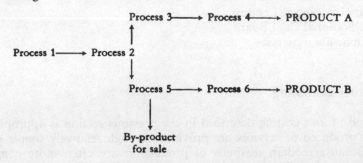

Clearly, the main accounting difficulty is in dividing the cost of Process 2 between Processes 3 and 5. This would be done on the basis of technical information about the proportion of Process 2 output used in Processes 3 and 5. The by-product arising from Process 5 is of relatively minor importance and so the proceeds from the sale of the by-product, less any expenses incurred in making it saleable, will be credited to Process 5.

Let us assume that the accounts for Process 2 are as follows:

PROCESS 2 — SEPTEMBER

	Units produced	£		· Units produced	£
Transferred from Process 1	100	3,500	Transferred to Process 3	50	5,000
Direct material		2,300	Transferred to Process 5	40	4,000
Direct labour		1,050			
Overheads		2,150	Normal wastage	10	
	100	9,000		100	9,000

The wastage rate of 10% is normal for this process, and so the production of 90 units will bear the full cost of the process. The cost of any abnormal wastage would be transferred to the general Profit and Loss account and not borne by subsequent processes. This would have the effect of bringing the matter to the attention of management so that remedial action could be taken — an example of the principle of 'management by exception' which we shall see in the next two chapters which are concerned with cost control.

Q.12e   Prepare the accounts for Process 5, given the following information. In addition to the 40 units transferred during September from Process 2, the following costs are allocated to Process 5 during the month:

	£
Direct materials	350
Direct labour	1,300
Overhead	1,710

The sale of Process 5 by-products realized £386, and £44 was incurred in preparing these by-products for sale. Ten per cent of the input is lost in process, and this is considered to be a normal rate of wastage. In addition, two units on which an estimated £184 had been spent were scrapped because of a plant failure.

What is the cumulative unit cost of Process 5 output?

12.7   Integrated accounts

Historically, cost accounting grew separately from traditional financial accounting. The Cost Accountant was in charge of a separate 'Cost Office' usually close to the works. Some of his information came from the Financial Accountant, but most of the detail would come from the shop floor, the stores and the factory managers. The cost accounts which he prepared were self-contained and not part of the financial accounts.

Even today some firms have two separate accounting systems side-by-side. The financial accounts are concerned with total results, and the cost accounts with detailed analysis of these results. Clearly there must be a certain amount of overlapping, not to mention conflicting assumptions and data between the two systems. It is therefore necessary to prepare a statement 'reconciling' the results of the two sets of accounts. The bank reconciliation statement is an analogous exercise.

Such a situation is far from satisfactory: it ought to be possible to treat all accounting information in the business as a unified whole. However, it was not until the introduction of punched-card accounting systems that it became feasible to install fully integrated systems. Later, with the development of computer data-processing, integrated systems became commonplace, at least in large organizations. The advent of mini and micro computers and the use of standard packages for such tasks as payroll accounting has now made it possible for small businesses to use the power of the computer to handle the detailed transactions behind the totals of such accounts as the Wages Account and the Work in Progress Account. Total accounts for presentation in traditional form are available at the same time as a detailed analysis for costing purposes.

12.8   Conclusion

In describing the mechanics of cost-finding systems we have been constantly reminded that the subjective opinions of the accountant play an important part in the process. Bases of overhead apportionment and absorption and methods of stock valuation are just two examples. This is not to say that these systems are worthless. In any human activity value judgments have to be made, and the cost accountant, by virtue of his professional training and knowledge of the business, ought to be in the strongest position to make judgments about such matters as stock valuation. The main point to remember is that costs are not objective fact. Managers and others who use cost reports ought to be aware of the assumptions and limitations of this information.

Suppose the cost accountant tells the production manager that the cost of making the Widget Mark II in January was 6.453p. This sounds most impressive, but before accepting it as the final word on the subject the manager should find out:

(1) the accounting assumptions behind the cost;
(2) whether the system of data collection is reliable.

He should then remember that this information relates to the past. What's done cannot be undone. As a manager he is concerned with the present and future rather than with the past. The cost tells him nothing about the efficiency of his operations. Perhaps the Widget ought to have been produced for 4p in January. In other words, the manager needs additional information to help him to plan and control costs. This will be the subject of the next two chapters.

12.9   Additional questions

[1]

'A sound costing system should match the production system which it attempts to describe.' Discuss and illustrate with reference the following production systems:

    (a) a brickworks
    (b) a jobbing printer
    (c) a restaurant
    (d) a brewery
    (e) an advertising agency
    (f) a computer manufacturer.

[2]

What factors would be considered in determining the optimum level of stocks of component parts in a stores serving a mass-production assembly line?

[3]

Cost finding and control is as important in the professional office as it is in a manufacturing business.

    List the main items of expense likely to occur in a professional accountant's office, and then discuss the requirements of a suitable costing system.

[4]

What production is required during the current week to clear the orders received during the week, and also the outstanding orders brought forward from the previous week?

	Product 1 Quantity	Product 2 Quantity
Stocks at beginning of week	102	407
Outstanding orders brought forward	120	350
Orders received during week	310	708
Minimum stocks to be carried	80	300

[5]

The following information relates to the total materials transactions for the XYZ Manufacturing Co. for the month of February. Show the entries in the appropriate total accounts.

    (1) Materials ordered by purchasing department, £12,000.
    (2) Goods received notes issued for materials value £11,000.
    (3) Materials returned to suppliers, £500.
    (4) Paid suppliers £10,000 after deducting £500 cash discount.
    (5) Materials issued to production departments, £8,500.
    (6) Faulty material returned to stores from the assembly line, £400.
    (7) Requisitions for indirect materials, £1,500.

[6]

As works manager you ask the cost accountant for information about the cost of a particular component XYZ, as you believe that it may be cheaper to buy from a supplier than manufacture in the works. The cost accountant prepares the following table:

Cost of Component XYZ

	Jan. Year 1	Jan. Year 2
Direct materials	3.459p	4.526p
Direct labour	5.617p	7.245p
Factory overhead 200% of direct labour	11.234p	14.490p
Total cost of manufacture	20.310p	26.261p

(a) Comment on the value of the information provided.
(b) List the main accounting assumptions that have had to be taken in arriving at the production costs.

[7]

In an integrated system of accounts (job costing) which accounts would be debited and credited as a result of each of the following:

(i) Raw materials bought on credit terms
(ii) Wages paid in cash
(iii) Raw materials issued to production
(iv) Wages apportioned partly to production and partly to factory overheads
(v) Payment of creditors' accounts
(vi) Jobs completed and transferred to finished goods stock
(vii) Electricity account received — relates partly to factory and partly to administration
(viii) Materials from stores used in factory but not chargeable to specific jobs
(ix) Goods sold to customers on credit terms (two entries required)
(x) Raw materials scrapped due to deterioration
(xi) Cash received from debtors
(xii) Factory overheads apportioned to specific jobs
(xiii) Bad debts written off
(xiv) Materials returned to supplier because of poor quality
(xv) Sub-contract work completed

[8]

The following information relates to the production department of a factory.

Budgeted overhead costs for the year	£250,000
Budgeted labour costs for the year:	
100,000 hours unskilled labour	£2.50 per hour
100,000 hours skilled labour	£3.75 per hour

(a) Calculate the following alternative overhead absorption rates:
  (i) labour cost rate;
  (ii) labour hour rate.
(b) Apply the two rates to Job 25 which requires 20 hours of unskilled labour and 10 hours of skilled labour.

(c) In what circumstances would the labour cost rate be more appropriate than the labour hour rate or vice versa?

(d) When would it be more appropriate to use a machine hour rate than either of the above labour rates?

[9]

(a) Calculate overhead absorption rates based on
   (i) machine hours
   (ii) labour cost
   (iii) labour hours

from the following information extracted from a departmental budget for the year ending 31 December.

Total hours of machine utilization	10,000
Budgeted fixed overhead	£38,000
Budgeted variable overhead	£10 per labour hour
Budgeted labour hours	25,000 (£100,000 cost)

(b) Calculate the total cost of the following job using each of the above methods.

Job No. XYZ

Direct labour (150 hours)	£600
Direct materials	£700
Machine hours	100

(c) What considerations would the accountant have in mind when choosing one of the above rates?

[10]

A small factory has three departments, *X*, *Y* and *Z*. The cost accountant has decided to apportion each item of overhead to these three departments on the most appropriate basis and then to absorb these overheads into production as a percentage of direct labour. The following information is provided for April:

	Department X	Department Y	Department Z
Direct labour	£1,200	£2,400	£1,800
Direct materials issued	£3,500	£4,500	£4,000
Number of direct workers	3	10	6
Plant value	£5,000	£3,000	£10,000
Area	500 sq ft	750 sq ft	750 sq ft

Overhead costs April

	£
Heating and lighting	600
Employers liability insurance	180
Supervision	1,400
Store-keeping costs	240
Depreciation of plant	900
Canteen costs	600
Fire insurance	100
Rent and rates	400
Personnel Department costs	800

Calculate the departmental absorption rates for April.

[11]

In a particular factory, workers are paid on a piece-rate basis, but there is a guaranteed basic rate of £2 per hour for all time spent on production work. An overtime premium of 50% of time rate is allowed. Time spent on maintenance and setting up is allowed at 125% of basic rate.

The following data relate to G. Brown in a particular week:

	Piece-rate allowance
	£
Jobs completed: Job 213	12.50
Job 615	13.90
Job 814	12.20
Job 731	16.80
Time spent on production jobs	37 hours

Job 213 was completed in 4 hours overtime.
3 hours were spent on maintenance and setting up.
$1\frac{1}{2}$ hours were lost due to machine breakdown (time rate allowed).

(a) Compute G. Brown's total wages.
(b) Suggest how the various items of cost would be treated in the cost accounts.

[12]

Using the figures below, compute a cost, and indicate the matters you would consider in setting a selling price for Order 123 received today.

		£
Estimated materials		150

	Hours	Rate
Labour — Operators	40	£2.50
— Assembly	7	£2.30
— Packing	2	£2.00
Machine time	30 hours	

Analysis of departmental activity and overheads

Department	Machine	Assembly	Packing
Overheads last year	£20,000	£8,000	£4,000
Overheads budget this year	£22,000	£9,000	£5,000
Labour hours last year	10,000	8,000	4,000
Labour hours budget this year	9,000	10,000	4,000
Machine hours last year	9,000		
Machine hours budgeted this year	10,000		

[13]

In a certain process 100 units of input value £1,300 were introduced from the previous process. Process costs incurred for the month are as follows:

Materials £700.
Direct labour £300.
Overhead is absorbed at a composite rate of £2 per unit throughput plus 50% of the labour cost incurred on the process.
80 units are completed during the month and only one-half of the wastage is considered a normal process loss. It is the practice of the

company to credit the cost of abnormal wastage to the Process Account.

It is assumed that costs are incurred pro rata over the 100 units of input and that the cost of normal wastage is a charge against current production.

(a) Prepare the Process Account.
(b) How would the charge for abnormal wastage be treated in the accounts?

[14]
Factory overhead today constitutes a much larger proportion of total manufacturing costs than in the past, and this trend is expected to continue. Why?

[15]
A company wishes to develop departmental overhead rates for product costing. The company has prepared the following budgeted overhead for the coming year based upon normal capacity.

Department	Budgeted overhead £
Building and land	149,000
Cafeteria	84,000
Personnel	28,000
Power	200,000
Material stores	345,000
Pension scheme	155,000
Maintenance	280,000

In order to determine departmental overhead allocation rates, service department overhead must be allocated to the two production departments F and G. You are given the following information:

	Dept F	Dept G
Direct labour hours	12,000	18,000
Number of employees	50	70
Square feet of space	25,000	10,000
Machine hours	5,000	3,000
Material used (last year)	£800,000	£350,000
Direct labour cost	£230,000	£320,000

(a) Allocate the service department budgeted costs to the production departments.
(b) Compute departmental overhead allocation rates based upon direct labour hours.

[16]
'Accuracy is required in cost accounting, but only to a degree.' Discuss.

[17]
An employee is paid £5 per hour but the cost of employment is far higher than that for the company concerned. Explain.

[18]

The following information relates to the operation of a major airline.

	Longhaul Services	Shorthaul Services	Total Scheduled	Total Charter	Total Airline
TRAFFIC					
Available tonne km (ATK) (m)	5,474	1,225	6,699	495	7,194
Revenue tonne km (RTK) (m)	4,549	695	4,244	406	4,650
Overall load factor (%)	64.8	56.7	63.4	81.9	64.6
Passengers carried (000)	3,739	10,467	14,206	2,035	16,241
Revenue passenger km (m)	26,855	7,351	34,206	4,410	38,616
Available seat km (m)	41,730	11,656	53,386	5,311	58,697
Passenger load factor (%)	64.4	63.1	64.1	83.0	65.8
Mail tonne km (000)	136,975	17,799	154,774	—	154,774
Freight tonne km (000)	919,483	48,149	967,632	—	967,632

COSTS AND REVENUE	pence
Operating expenditure per ATK	27.0
Revenue per RTK	49.6
Revenue per passenger km	5.55

(a) Explain the significance of the overall load factor and the passenger load factor in evaluating the airline's performance. Why should the load factors on charter flights be higher than on scheduled flights?

(b) It is reported that the breakeven passenger load factor is 54.8%. Comment on the significance of this information in the light of the airline's actual performance.

(c) Why is operating expenditure related to ATK whereas revenue is related to RTK?

(d) ATK per employee has risen from 106,300 in 1975 to 199,300 in 1984. Revenue per RTK has risen from 21.1p in 1975 to 49.6p in 1984. Comment on the value of these two measures of the airline's performance.

[19]

The British Railways Board publishes a number of performance indicators, of which the following is a selection relating entirely to passenger business.

SAMPLE RAILWAYS PERFORMANCE INDICATORS YEARS 1980–1983

Passenger Business		Year 1	Year 2	Year 3	Year 4
Receipts per passenger mile	pence	6.04	6.08	5.76	6.12
Passenger miles per loaded train mile (average train load)	no.	97	95	96	97
Train service (operating) expenses per train mile	index	100	106	110	107
Train service (maintenance) expenses per train mile	index	100	104	115	102
Terminal expenses per train mile	index	100	106	121	117
Percentage of trains arriving within 5 min of booked time	%	89	90	88	90
Percentage of trains cancelled	%	1.4	1.1	1.3	1.0

Note: Monetary items have been converted to current price levels using the following deflators: Year 1 = 80.4; Year 2 = 88.6; Year 3 = 94.3; Year 4 = 100.

(1) What do you think would be the effect on each of the above indicators if the British Railways Board (with the Government's agreement) decided on the following policies. (Treat each decision separately.)
   (a) Reduce fares by 10%.
   (b) Close down the least economic 10% of the railway system.
   (c) Reduce manning levels by 10% throughout the service.
(2) Suggest appropriate performance indicators for freight business.

Chapter 13

Planning and Control: Standard Costing

13.1 Planning and control

The Management Accountant does not only record costs which have already been incurred. He looks to the future by expressing the plans of the business in financial terms and providing cost control information. The techniques of budgetary control and standard costing have been developed to help him in this forward-looking role. This chapter introduces standard costing and Chapter 14 examines the role of budgets as control devices in business organizations and public authorities.

Planning

All activities, from running a church bazaar to managing the economy, need planning. The more complex the activity, the greater is the need for a carefully-thought-out plan. Modern technology creates a need for more planning at national and company levels.[1] For instance, compared with the first motor cars, the modern mass-produced models need years of planning by a variety of specialist 'technocrats'. Designers try to translate the public's requirements, as indicated by market research, into a production model. Prototypes are tested and, if satisfactory, production engineers design the special-purpose tools needed for mass production. Materials requirements have to be planned in advance, and where possible the purchasing department will make long-term contracts. Labour requirements will be shown in a manpower plan, which may indicate the need for recruitment and training, if shortages of particular skills are likely in the future. Marketing has to be planned from the initial market research to advertising, selling and distributing the completed model. The accountant is concerned with planning finance and assessing the profitability of the whole project.

As a first step in the planning process, long-range objectives must be set for the company. This process should raise fundamental questions about future development. What kind of business should the company be in? What share of the market is possible? What rates of profitability and growth should be achieved? How important are 'non-economic objectives' such as creating a favourable company image? The choice of objectives will be based on a close study of the present economic, social and political

[1] See Galbraith, J. K., The New Industrial State, Hamish Hamilton, 1967.

environment, and an assessment of future trends. For instance, as a result of such a survey, the management of a cigarette manufacturing company may conclude that the total market for cigarettes is stagnating. What is the company to do in order to meet its long-term growth and profitability objectives? Should it adopt an aggressive marketing policy aimed at capturing a higher share of the cigarette market? Should it develop new products, such as cigars, which appear to be a faster-growing sector of the total tobacco market? Should it try to sell its products in new markets, e.g. an export sales campaign? Should it diversify into products such as potato crisps or soft drinks, which can be marketed through the same outlets as cigarettes? Should it move into something completely different, such as the 'leisure industry' if a higher rate of return on investment could be achieved by this strategy? In a rapidly changing world, companies must constantly ask themselves the basic question, 'What business are we in?'

After strategic planning for the company's long-term future, the organization structure and information system must be planned to meet the changing administrative needs of this strategy. How much independence should be given to the product divisions of a multiproduct company? How much information should they report to head office? Finally, the day-to-day operations of the company need to be planned. Production, marketing, financing, manning, purchasing and all the other activities of the modern business, need to be coordinated into an operating plan. When expressed in financial terms, this operating plan becomes a budgetary control system.

Q.13a   Select a business organization with which you are familiar: it may be the firm where you are employed or a well-known company such as Marks & Spencer or Jaguar.

What have been the main changes in the product range of the business over the last five years? Who are the company's main competitors? Are there any general economic, political, technological or social trends which might affect the business? Do you think the business should change its current policies by adopting such strategies as product diversification or market development?

Control

Having set company objectives, and prepared strategic, administrative and operating plans, management must make sure that the plans are either carried out, or altered in the light of changed circumstances. This is the function of control. However, it would be wrong to consider planning and control as separate activities. It is better to think of them as two aspects of the continuous process of management.

The concept of control is not confined to management. The science of cybernetics tries to discover general principles of control behind mechanical, biological, social and other systems. It is relatively easy to understand the working of a mechanical control system. A room thermostat, for instance, keeps the air between two predetermined temperatures. A thermometer measures the temperature and control is exercised by switching the current to the heater on or off, depending on which limit is reached.

More generally, we may show the working of a system by the diagram on p. 223 on p. 223 Think again of the thermostat, and see how its operation can be explained by using the loop sequence of the diagram. Management processes are not so straightforward. A business is a social system as well as a technical system, and human behaviour is not as easy to measure and control as the performance of a machine. An added complication is that a business is not a closed, static system like a thermostat, but an open system

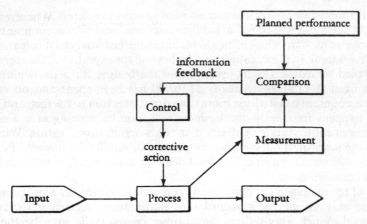

reacting to and dealing with its economic, social, legal and political environment. This environment is constantly changing, and the firm's plans must change with it.

The accountant's role

So far, we have discussed planning and control in general terms. What part has the accountant to play in this process? In one sense he is concerned with the whole, because all plans have financial implications, and nearly all the firm's activities will incur costs which must be accounted for. In practice his main concern will be with four of the activities shown in the loop diagram:

(1) the financial implications of *plans*;
(2) the *measurement* of cost of the firm's activities;
(3) the *comparison* of actual costs with planned costs;
(4) the *feedback of information* to management about significant deviations from plans, in financial terms.

There are therefore two ways in which it may be said that the accountant has a limited specialist role in planning and control. In the first place, the planning activities of the business are not simply accounting exercises. The formulation of the manpower plan, for instance, relies mainly on the application of specialized personnel management techniques. The accountant will need to be involved in any discussion of the financial implications of the plan, but many key concepts, such as the quality of labour skills and state of labour relations, cannot be expressed in financial terms. Performance is often measured in non-financial terms, e.g. by calculating rates of labour turnover, and taking the 'stock' of various skills to see if they match planned requirements. Accounting information must be used in deciding whether the manpower plan has been achieved, but it is not the only source of control information. Similar observations could be made about research and development plans, marketing plans, strategic plans and administrative plans.

The second important limitation of the accountant's role is that he usually stops short of taking the necessary action to achieve practical control. His task is to present information to management in such a form that action may be taken to correct deviations from plan. The principle of 'management by exception' means that only differences between planned and actual costs (variances) need to be spotlighted. If everything is running smoothly, there is no need to report in detail. Wherever possible, causes for the deviation will be indicated (variance analysis). The accountant's reports will therefore give as many clues as possible, but in the last analysis it is management's job to put things right. In many cases it will be beyond the expertise of the accountant to suggest detailed remedies. Let us assume that the budget for a particular research project was fixed at £150,000. Already £170,000 has been spent and no results are visible. The accountant can do little more than draw attention to the fact, and point out that if this happens frequently, the business will soon be running at a loss. He has alerted management to a state of affairs that needs urgent investigation. What should they do? Write the project off, continue as planned or modify the project? Perhaps the original £150,000 was unrealistic. The final decision will depend on technical as much as financial considerations.

The role of the management accountant is therefore somewhat ambiguous. In one company he may be merely a recorder of information, reporting variances, but powerless to do much about them. In another company he may be the effective controller, with power to initiate special investigations, and cooperating with management in deciding what action is necessary to correct variances. The practical contribution of the management accountant will depend on his status in the organization, his own personal qualities as a communicator and diplomat, and the extent to which the company is 'cost conscious'.

In discussing the process of control, it was suggested that measured performance should be compared with a plan, and any variances fed back as information to management. So far as accounting for the company's current operations is concerned, Budgetary Control and Standard Costing meet these requirements. This chapter and Chapter 14 will therefore be concerned with these techniques. A company may use both, or it may be sufficient to have one without the other. In any event, actual cost is compared with budgeted or standard cost, and the resulting variances are analysed to guide management in the action to be taken.

Before looking at these in detail, let us briefly consider the position of a business without either technique in effective operation. Control requires comparison of actual costs with some yardstick. Other possible yardsticks in the absence of budgets or standard costs are:

(1) actual costs in previous accounting periods; and
(2) the actual costs of other firms in the same industry.

(1) Historical costing

In the previous chapter we mentioned the limitations of historical costing as a method of control. A table of product costs over a period of time gives a certain amount of information for control purposes. It may show seasonal trends, relative changes between the various elements of cost and the general cost trend.

However, it is essential to exercise great caution in interpreting such historical cost information. The wrong conclusions may be drawn. Costs may be increasing, but is this due to inefficiency, or increasing prices outside the firm's control? One month's results could be compared with last month's or with the figures for the same month last year, but it may be that the firm was grossly inefficient throughout the entire period. Historical accounting will never give this sort of information. Even steady or declining unit cost figures may disguise inefficiencies. Perhaps productivity ought to be increasing to bring unit cost down even further.

(2) Uniform cost systems

In some industries a trade association may ask its members to supply cost information on a uniform basis. After analysis, the results are published, and each participating firm can compare its own costs with others in the industry. This can obviously be useful control information for a management wishing to know if it is keeping up with its competitors in technical and management efficiency.

As with historical costing, uniform cost systems need to be interpreted with care. Are the firms making comparable products? Do the firms prepare their accounts on standardized lines, and do they make similar assumptions about such matters as the valuation of stocks and fixed assets? In the last analysis there is no substitute for financial planning through budgets and standard costs if the company is to exercise effective control.

13.2 Standard costing

Budgetary Control is the application of the general principles of planning and control to the whole organization and its various departments and activities. Standard Costing applies the concept of control by variance analysis to products, processes and other cost units. For a manufactured product, a 'standard cost' would be prepared, which would state what the product 'ought' to cost in direct materials, direct labour and factory overhead. Actual costs, as produced by the cost-finding system, would be compared with this standard to produce a variance. The total variance is analysed to give some indication of the reasons for the difference.

To illustrate the working of a standard costing system we shall study the operations of a small manufacturing firm, returning to the case in the next chapter to build up a budgetary control system for the firm.

Some years ago Bill Robinson set up a successful 'Do It Yourself' shop, but later felt that the DIY boom was over. He looked around for some outlet for his business capacities and saw that mail order sales were likely to expand rapidly and yield a higher rate of profit than his shop. He saw that there was a demand for a simple type of self-assembly coffee table and he thought that by producing a standard model and by selling direct to the public through mail order, his product could be sold at a bargain price. However, he realizes that success in this new venture will depend on his ability to plan and control his manufacturing costs. He therefore decides to install a simple standard costing system.

His starting point must be the technical details of making the tables. What are the standard material, labour and overhead costs per table? What variances can be calculated? Can corrective action be taken if an unfavourable variance is reported? As total standard cost is the sum of its parts, we shall look at direct material, direct labour, and manufacturing overhead, in turn.

Materials

The material cost of the coffee table depends on two things: (a) the quantity of timber required, and (b) the price of timber. The accountant will have to study drawings, materials specifications and other technical data, to fix the standard quantity. The purchasing section will have information on price trends, and so the standard price can be fixed.

$$\text{Standard Material Cost} = \text{Standard Quantity} \times \text{Standard Price}$$

As an illustration, let us take the table top only. This is designed to be made of solid pine, and a study of the drawings indicates that 6,000 cubic centimetres is a fair standard quantity. The standard price of pine is estimated as £1.25 per 1,000 cc. The standard material cost may be calculated as follows:

$$\begin{array}{ccc} \text{Standard Quantity} \times \text{Standard Price} = \text{Standard Material Cost} \\ 6 \qquad\qquad \times \qquad £1.25 \qquad = \qquad £7.50 \end{array}$$

Let us assume that the actual quantity of pine used on a particular occasion was 7,000 cc, and the price paid was £1.50 per 1,000 cc.

$$\begin{array}{ccc} \text{Actual Quantity} \times \text{Actual Price} = \text{Actual Material Cost} \\ 7 \qquad\qquad \times \qquad £1.50 \qquad = \qquad £10.50 \end{array}$$

The difference between the Actual Material Cost and the Standard Material Cost is the Total Material Variance.

$$\begin{array}{ccc} \text{Actual Material Cost} - \text{Standard Material Cost} = \text{Material Variance} \\ £10.50 \qquad\qquad - \qquad £7.50 \qquad\qquad = \qquad £3 \end{array}$$

The analysis of the total material variance should become clear if material costs are represented diagrammatically (below) as areas formed by multiplying prices by quantities. The total area is the actual material cost, the unshaded area is the standard material cost, and the total shaded area is the materials variance.

To what extent is the materials variance due to the price increase, and to what extent has it been caused by the increased usage of wood? By separating this total variance into a materials price variance and a materials usage variance it is possible to give the correct weighting to each of these causes. The diagram shows the principle on which the calculations are based.

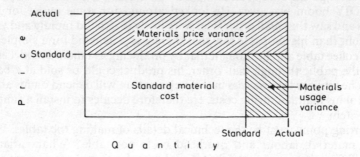

$$\begin{array}{ccc} (\text{Actual Price} - \text{Standard Price}) \times \text{Actual Quantity} = \text{Materials Price Variance} \\ (£1.50 - £1.25) \qquad\qquad \times \qquad 7 \qquad = \qquad £1.75 \end{array}$$

$$\begin{array}{ccc} (\text{Actual Quantity} - \text{Standard Quantity}) \times \text{Standard Price} = \text{Materials Usage Variance} \\ (7 - 6) \qquad\qquad \times \qquad £1.25 \qquad\qquad £1.25 \end{array}$$

The materials variance for the table top of £3 is therefore made up of a price variance of £1.75 and a usage variance of £1.25. In this example, both price and usage variances are 'unfavourable'. It is possible for a favourable variance to arise in certain circumstances. The formula is still applicable, but for a favourable variance the calculation will give a negative result.

Q.13b Assuming the same standard information about the table top as above, calculate (a) materials variance, (b) materials price variance, (c) materials usage variance, if the actual price is £1.20 per 1,000 cc, and the actual quantity used in 8,000 cc.

Having done our calculations, we must now analyse any variances which seem significant enough to warrant investigation. Is an unfavourable price variance the result of poor buying, such as failure to secure a quantity discount; or is it due to 'uncontrollable' factors such as general inflation? Whatever the reason, it is obvious that in a large factory with specialist departments, the price variance is uncontrollable so far as the production manager is concerned. It is the purchasing manager who will be asked for an explanation. As unfavourable usage variance may arise from a host of possible causes, from faulty materials, inadequate training and poor workmanship, to the system of remuneration which may stress quantity to the detriment of quality. The variance report acts like a warning light. Control can only be exercised if we know the specific causes of the variance. Usually this will mean collecting more detailed information about material usage from scrap reports and discussions with supervisors and inspectors.

The final stage in the control cycle is to take effective action to correct any weaknesses. Should a quality control be introduced? Is operator training adequate? Are quality standards unnecessarily high? If management information is not followed by management action, the whole exercise is a waste of time and money.

Labour

Standards for labour cost are prepared on the same principles as materials standards. The standard time required to complete the job will be fixed on the basis of work study data. The standard rate for the appropriate grade of labour will probably be set by a national or local trade union agreement. Standard labour cost is simply standard rate times standard time. Variances may arise because there has been a change in the wage rate, or a difference in the time taken to complete the job.

Bill Robinson's Production Cost Budget (on p. 241) contains enough information to fix a standard labour cost for a coffee table. The standard time is 1 hour, and the standard labour cost rate is £7.50 per hour. The standard labour cost of a coffee table is therefore £7.50.

The method of calculating labour variances is similar to that used when calculating materials variances.

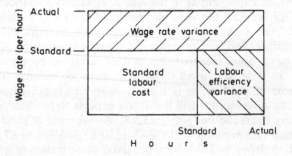

Again the diagram assumes that both variances are unfavourable. More generally the two variances may be calculated by formulae.

(Actual Rate – Standard Rate) × Actual Hours = Wage Rate Variance

(Actual Hours – Standard Hours) × Standard Rate = Labour Efficiency Variance

The observant reader may have wondered why the shaded section in the top right-hand corner of the diagram should be assigned entirely to the wage rate variance rather than the labour efficiency variance. [A similar question arises in the case of materials variances.] The answer is that this is how most accountants actually do the calculations even though in theory an alternative approach might be equally valid. This question is beyond the scope of an introductory textbook but it illustrates the point that the choice of accounting techniques is often the subject of debate.

Q.13c Bill Robinson has budgeted to make 400 tables in May. This production is achieved in 425 hours. A new national wage agreement with the trade union increases the hourly rate to £8 per hour during May. Calculate the appropriate labour variances for May assuming that the workers are paid by the hour. What action can/should Bill Robinson take?

Q.13d The table on p. 229 was prepared from the time sheets of workers in the machine shop of an engineering works for a particular week after an unfavourable labour efficiency variance of £510 was reported for that week. Complete the labour efficiency report and explain the significance of the efficiency and productivity percentages. Comment on the report, and suggest any action which should be taken to reduce the variance in future weeks. Dennis was engaged on 28 June, and is learning the job by working alongside Smith, an experienced worker.

Manufacturing overhead

In the case of materials and labour, we saw that variances could be analysed into price (rate) and efficiency (usage). The case of overheads is rather more complex. Overhead prices such as insurance, rates, rent and the electricity tariff, may change and so give an overhead price variance. This could happen whether the overheads are fixed or variable.

Manufacturing overhead services such as power, consumable materials and tools will vary with production. They may be used efficiently or wasted, and management needs some control indicator similar to the labour efficiency variance or the materials usage variance. This is called the variable overhead efficiency variance.

In the case of fixed manufacturing overhead, such as rent, factory and rates, depreciation of buildings and factory insurance, there is no question of 'efficient usage'. These expenses have been incurred no matter what is produced, and factory management can do little to control them. The main worry with fixed overhead is whether the volume of production is high enough to absorb these expenses at a reasonable rate. For most months Bill Robinson expects to produce 500 tables with a fixed manufacturing overhead budget of £3,500. At this rate of production the fixed overhead absorption rate per table will therefore be £3,500/500 or £7. During August, however, production drops to 350 tables, but fixed manufacturing overhead remains the same. If the fixed overhead rate had been fixed at £7 per table there would be an underrecovery of fixed overheads of £1,050 in respect of August's production as only £2,450 (350 × £7) would be recovered compared with £3,500 incurred.

LABOUR EFFICIENCY REPORT

WEEK ENDING JULY 6

Name	(1) Total hours	(2) Total productive hours	(3) Production (in standard hours*)	(3)/(2) ×100 Efficiency %	(3)/(1) ×100 Productivity %	(1)–(2) Non-productive time	Analysis of non-productive time
Brown, B. L.	38	34	30			4	Waiting for material
Cooke, G. K.	40	36	32			4	Waiting for material
Dennis, L.	36	30	12			6	Rectification and training
Gale, P.	38	32	28			6	Waiting for work
Jones, L. W.	42	34	32			8	Waiting for work, and waiting for materials
Lomax, A.	40	34	28			6	Maintenance work
Smith, P. H.	38	32	26			6	Waiting for work; instructing
Wilson, G.	36	32	30			4	Waiting for materials
Total	308	264	218			44	

* E.g. the standard labour content of production.

Speaking more generally, we may say that whenever the business is running below planned production capacity, the absorption rate for fixed overhead will increase. In a standard costing system, this will show as an unfavourable 'volume variance'. So far as production management is concerned, this is 'uncontrollable' but it is, of course, a major responsibility of the marketing department to make sure that the factory is working as near full capacity as possible.

At this stage it may be convenient to summarize the main variances which have been introduced. The (C) or (U) after each variance shows whether it would be considered controllable or uncontrollable by the production manager in a typical manufacturing company.

VARIANCES ARISING FROM

	Price changes	Efficiency changes	Capacity changes
Materials	Materials price variance (U)	Materials usage variance (C)	—
Labour	Wage rate variance (U)	Labour efficiency variance (C)	—
Variable overhead	Variable overhead price variance (U)	Overhead efficiency variance (C)	—
Fixed overhead	Fixed overhead price variance (U)	—	Volume variance (U)

MANUFACTURING OVERHEAD   VARIANCE REPORT   MACHINE SHOP, WEEK 16

Actual activity attained...75%

	Budget at 100% capacity	Budget adjusted for 75% capacity	Actual cost	Variance analysis		
				Total	Efficiency	Price
	£ £	£ £	£	£	£	£
Indirect labour:						
clerical	260	260	285	25	—	25
inspection	190	170	180	10	10	—
supervision	120	120	145	25	—	25
maintenance	160	120	110	F 10	F 10	—
labouring	240	180	180	—	F 15	15
other	120	100	130	30	30	—
Total indirect labour	1,090	950	1,030	80	15	65
National Insurance	110	90	90	—	—	—
Overtime allowance	180	30	60	30	30	—
Fuel and oil	240	180	210	30	10	20
Electricity	130	110	120	10	F 20	30
Consumable stores	180	135	210	75	80	F 5
Tools	200	150	180	30	30	—
Depreciation	300	250	250	—	—	—
TOTAL	2,430	1,895	2,150	255	145	110

It is not appropriate in an introductory text to show how the overhead variances are calculated. The reader is referred to the standard works on cost accountancy for details, but s/he should be warned that there is no one system which commands universal acceptance. The main thing is to understand the significance of reported variances, and to know what action could be taken to correct adverse trends.

Flexible budgeting is a popular and convenient method of reporting overhead variances to production management. Let us assume that the factory is working at 75% capacity. There will be an unfavourable volume variance, but this is hardly the responsibility of the production manager. However, the low capacity also means that standards for variable overheads are unrealistic if they were fixed on the assumption that 100% capacity would be attained. The sensible thing would be to adjust or 'flex' the standards for variable overheads in accordance with the level of activity actually reached. The difference between actual overhead costs and this adjusted standard could then be analysed into efficiency and price variances.

The example of a Manufacturing Overhead Variance Report on p. 230 shows one possible way of reporting variance information to management by means of a flexible budget.

Q.13e List the items of cost in the above example under the headings of (a) variable costs, (b) semi-variable costs, (c) fixed costs. Account for the cost behaviour of overtime allowances. As manager of the machine shop, what action would you take on receiving this report?

There is a danger when setting up a system of standard costing to concentrate attention on the variance calculations. Variances are not ends in themselves. They have value to the organization only if managers study variance reports and ask why the variances occurred and, if unfavourable, decide what corrective action should be taken.

If a variance report is to be an effective guide for management action it must therefore satisfy certain criteria. Variances should be identified quickly and reported as frequently as possible (in some cases daily) to the manager responsible for the costs incurred. Reports should be objective and easily understood by the recipients. The system must be flexible and responsive to changes in the environment. Above all, any control system must be acceptable as reasonable and realistic within the organization. As we shall see in the next chapter, the benefits claimed for standard costing and budgetary control in achieving more effective coordination within the organization may be offset by their adverse effect on motivation unless the system is carefully designed.

13.3   Additional questions

[1]
An extract from the standard cost card of the product showed:

Standards	Material A	Material B
Standard material allowance per *unit*	1 lb	2 lb
Standard material price per *lb*	10p	5p

The material actually used in production was:

	Material A		Material B	
	lb	£	lb	£
January	6,400	670	12,200	600
February	7,800	780	13,800	700
March	8,000	820	15,600	790

Units actually produced during:

January	6,000 units
February	7,000 „
March	8,000 „

Calculate the material price and the material usage variances for each type of material for each month.

[2]
The standard costs of the products of XYZ Manufacturing Co. incorporate labour rates for workers in the assembly department based on an old payment system under which workers were paid varying rates based on length of service, foremen's reports, etc. With the agreement of the trade union it has now been decided that all workers on the assembly line will be paid a fixed rate of £144 for a 36-hour week.

The following labour variance report is presented to the manager of the assembly department for the week ending 19 July. All workers have worked the full 36 hours in that week.

Employee	Wage Rate Variance unfavourable	Labour efficiency variance	
		favourable	unfavourable
	£	£	£
D. Hume	32	24	—
T. Hobbes	16	—	24
W. James	16	20	—
G. Berkeley	8	—	48
G. E. Moore	—	—	52
J. S. Mill	32	12	—

You are required:
  (a) To calculate the standard rate per hour which has been used in the above calculation for each individual worker.
  (b) To calculate the output of each worker assuming that the standard time for one unit of production is one hour.
  (c) To comment on the situation disclosed by the report.

[3]
The prime cost standards established for the production of an engineering component were:

Direct labour	2 hours at £5 per hour
Raw materials	1 lb at £2.5 per lb

The production for January was 150 units and the actual results recorded were:

Direct labour   290 hours for £1,595
Raw materials   165 lb for £396

(a) Prepare a cost statement showing the prime cost variances for January.
(b) Suggest possible explanations for the variances and any action which could be taken by the works manager on receiving the variance report.

[4]

The works manager in a company working a three-shift system is considering the following direct labour performances for week ended 4 November, which showed:

Shift Times	Foreman	Production in Units	Actual hours	Labour Costs* £
0600–1400	Mr X	1,800	920	3,500
1400–2200	Mr Y	2,000	980	4,100
2200–0600	Mr Z	1,600	840	3,400

* excluding any shift-working bonuses

The standard performance is 30 minutes per unit. The standard direct wages £4 per hour.

Calculate appropriate variances and comment on each shift performance. Calculate to nearest £1.

[5]

The Nadir Manufacturing Co. has serious adverse variances in each of the following categories for the month of March:

(a) Variable Overhead price variance
(b) Overhead efficiency variance
(c) Volume variance
(d) Materials Usage variance

Suggest two possible reasons in each case, and say what action the Managing Director could take to deal with the situation.

[6]

R. Maxfield Ltd makes and sells a standard-type container and the following data are presented to you:

	Budget			Actual		
	Qty	Each	£	Qty	Each	£
Sales	1,000	4.00	4,000	1,200	4.10	4,920
Less						
Material		1.00	1,000			1,220
Labour	1,000	0.50	500	1,200		580
Variable o/hds		0.40	400			500
	1,000	1.90	1,900	1,200		2,300
Contribution			2,100			2,620
Fixed o/hds			1,700			1,800
NET PROFIT			£ 400			£ 820

(a) Prepare a report showing clearly the reasons for the variation between the budgeted and the actual net profit.
(b) If you think that there are limitations in the information you have supplied, what other information would you wish to show and what additional data would you need to provide it?

[7]

What social, economic, and political considerations would have to be taken into account when preparing budgets for the following organization at the present time:

(a) a car manufacturer;
(b) a pharaceutical company;
(c) a hospital;
(d) British Rail.

[8]

The following data are extracted from the purchasing and production records of a manufacturing company:

Purchasing records showed 1,500 lb of raw material bought in accordance with the works order — actual cost £750.
Production records showed that the 1,500 lb of raw material (above) had been used in making 120 units of the product.

The standards set for the product were:

Raw material — weight allowance 10 lb per unit
Standard price — 40p per lb.

(a) Prepare a statement of material variances showing price and usage, using the data given above.

On further investigation it is discovered that two purchase orders were placed for the material in question as follows:

Order 1 — 1,200 lb (the standard allowance for 120 units) at 45p per lb
Order 2 — 300 lb on the authority of an 'urgent excess requisition' from the works at 70p per lb

(b) Reconsider your previous variance analysis (in (a) above), recompute if you think appropriate, and explain why.
(c) How would you avoid any misplaced criticism of personnel arising from the variance analysis you have produced?

[9]

As production manager of a general engineering works you are presented with the following analysis of results for the machine shop.

Machine Shop: June
£

Standard Direct Material Cost	20,000
Standard Direct Labour Cost	12,500
	32,500

Variances from Standard

	Adverse £	Favourable £	
Direct Labour			
Rate of Pay	250		
Idle Time	1,500		
Efficiency		1,000	
Direct Material			
Price		3,000	
Usage	2,500		
	4,250	4,000	250
Actual Cost of Direct Material and Labour		32,750	

Required:
(a) Briefly explain the meaning of the variances.
(b) The machine shop supervisor says that there are no problems in his department because 'we are only £250 over our budget'. Do you agree?

[10]
The production of Chemico passes through three separate processes. At each of these stages material is added and labour and overhead costs are incurred.

Work in process at the beginning of Period 1 consists of 4,000 input units which had passed through the first process, the cost at that point being £90,000. During Period 1 additional material costing £50,000 was added and labour costs of £30,000 were incurred. Process Overhead is charged at the rate of 80% of process labour costs. 3,000 units were fully complete at the end of Period 1 and it was estimated that 500 units were 50% incomplete in respect of additional material, labour and overhead. The remainder of the units (estimated to be 25% completed in Process 2) were scrapped due to a breakdown of the plant. This loss is to be treated as an abnormal wastage.

Write up Process 2 Account for Period 1 showing clearly the cost to be transferred to Process 3, the treatment of the scrapped units and the value of the work in process at the end of the period.

[11]

The following table reports the results for March of the Blanko product division of the Universal Manufacturing Group:

	£
Standard profit for the period	60,000
Variances (unfavourable in brackets).	

	£
Sales margin	4,000
Sales quantity	3,000
Materials usage	4,000
Factory overhead:	(8,000)
Expenditure	(3,000)
Volume/capacity	15,000
Selling overhead:	
Volume	4,000
Expenditure — fixed	(1,000)
Expenditure — variable	(500)

Total Variances	17,500
Actual profit for the period	£77,500

Explain the significance of this report. Is any action needed by management? Note: some of the variances are not referred to in the text — you should be able to infer their significance from the names of the variances.

Chapter 14

Planning and Control: Budgetary Control

14.1 Introduction

Enough has been said already to emphasize the need for planning and control if a business organization is to achieve its objectives. Public-sector organizations such as hospitals or local authorities have equally pressing problems of coordination. All organizations, whether public or private, must resolve the basic economic problem of allocating scarce means to competing ends in an efficient manner. Although this chapter is primarily concerned with planning and control in profit-orientated organizations, Section 14.4 considers the importance of budgets in public-sector accounting.

Budgetary control is an attempt to coordinate the operations of an organization by expressing operational plans in financial terms. We have already referred to the important distinction between strategic and operational planning. Strategic planning raises such long-term issues as deciding 'what business will we be in in five years from now?' and requires an analysis of the actual and potential threats and opportunities which should influence long-term plans. Let us assume that forecasts have been made of the company's potential markets and a long-term strategy has been laid down. The next task is to coordinate plans for the next accounting period to make sure that current operational plans are consistent with long-term strategic objectives.

Budgets provide such a comprehensive plan, integrating all the organization's current operations. In business planning systems the end result will be a 'master budget' which summarizes the planned profit for the period and shows the projected balance-sheet positions at the end of the period. To reach this goal, functional budgets will need to be prepared for each of the major operating activities, such as sales, production and purchasing. These in turn may be subdivided into departmental budgets in whatever detail is needed for control of the company's operations. Each of these individual budgets must be compatible with the others. It is no use budgeting for the production of 1,000 motor cars per week if the skilled labour is not available to make them, or if sales are likely to be only 750 per week.

Budgets are related to the organization of the company, so that each manager's budget reflects his responsibilities. It is essential that managers should cooperate in the preparation of budgets, and agree that budgets set attainable goals. Technical data on which budgets are based will come from the departments. The accountant or budget officer will express these plans in financial terms. Coordination is often achieved through a budget committee consisting of senior managers, to make sure that budgets are compatible and realistic. Budgets are not mere accounting exercises, but the means by which the organization's policies are expressed, coordinated and controlled. Profit planning and resource budgeting are the two main purposes of budgetary control. Although it is convenient to examine each group of budgets separately, it should be remembered that both form part of a coordinated system.

14.2   Budgets for profit planning

The preparation of individual budgets should follow a logical sequence. The starting point is determined by the company's 'limiting factor', or the major factor constraining future growth. Most companies can manufacture all that can be sold, and so the sales budget is the logical starting point. In some cases, productive capacity may be the limiting factor; in others, shortage of skilled labour. If, as in the years following 1945, certain materials are in short supply, the materials budget should be prepared first.

The diagram on p. 239 shows a typical system of budgets for profit planning, assuming that sales are the limiting factor. As budgets are prepared, new limiting factors may become apparent. For instance, the production budget may imply a labour force well above current manpower forecasts. This new bottleneck means that production and sales plans will have to be scaled down, or that a new manpower plan is needed. If the final results are to be realistic, all inconsistencies between budgets will have to be removed.

Budgetary control is a system of responsibility accounting. A budget will be prepared to plan all the activity controlled by each individual manager. Actual results will be compared with budgets and the resulting variances should indicate any corrective action necessary to make sure that a budget proves to be unrealistic in practice. A company with substantial export markets might find that a sudden change in the exchange rate or a crisis in the Middle East has a dramatic effect on their business prospects. Existing plans and budgets are now worse than useless. A budget provides a useful guide for management action; it should not become a straitjacket.

In Chapter 13 we introduced Bill Robinson and his coffee tables. The following sections develop this case history to illustrate a simple budgetary control system for profit and resource planning. The case illustrates the close link between standard costing and budgetary control systems in practice. Bill Robinson's production budget, for instance, is prepared by multiplying total budgeted production of coffee tables by the standard cost of one coffee table. The calculation of overhead variances presupposed a budget for the workshop and an estimate of his total production capacity. The case study indicates the sequence which should be followed in the budget planning cycle. The reader should compare the details of the case with the various relationships shown in the diagram on p. 239 and consider at each stage what additional complications would arise in a larger multiproduct company.

Sales budget

In April 19X5 Bill Robinson sold his Do It Yourself business and opened a small workshop. In the first eight months, 3,000 tables were sold and he felt optimistic about the future. During 19X6 he intends to consolidate his success with the coffee table, but in 19X7 he will bring out new products to add to the range, using the same marketing

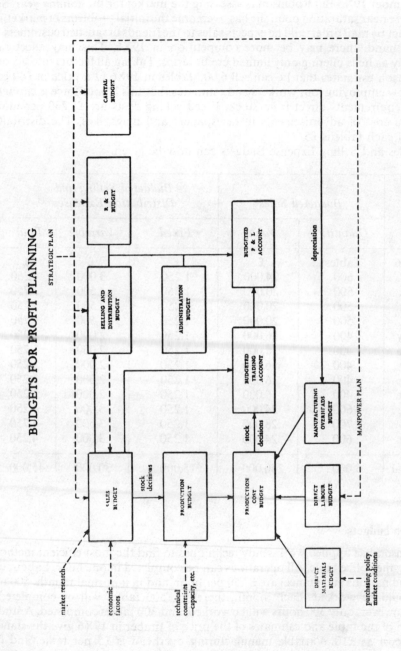

BUDGETS FOR PROFIT PLANNING

techniques. This will mean extending the workshop and buying new machinery, but this investment can wait until later.

In December 19X5 Bill Robinson is assessing the market for the coming year. Sales are nowhere near saturation point; he has overcome the initial problems of marketing a new product by mail order; and he expects sales to the friends of satisfied customers. On the other hand, there may be more competition in 19X6. This may affect sales, particularly as he is offering only limited credit terms. Taking all factors into account, Bill Robinson estimates that he can sell 6,000 tables in 19X6 at a price of £40 each.

He is now employing four workers and estimates that this labour force is enough to meet all requirements direct from stock. Fixed selling costs are £1,250 per month, mainly the cost of advertisements in newspapers and magazines. The distribution expense of each table is £5.

The Sales and Selling Expense Budgets can now be given.

| | Budgeted Sales | | Budgeted Selling and Distribution Expenses | | |
	Quantity	Value	Fixed	Variable	Total
19X6	Tables	£	£	£	£
Jan.	600	24,000	1,250	3,000	4,250
Feb.	500	20,000	1,250	2,500	3,750
Mar.	500	20,000	1,250	2,500	3,750
Apr.	500	20,000	1,250	2,500	3,750
May	400	16,000	1,250	2,000	3,250
June	400	16,000	1,250	2,000	3,250
July	400	16,000	1,250	2,000	3,250
Aug.	400	16,000	1,250	2,000	3,250
Sept.	400	16,000	1,250	2,000	3,250
Oct.	600	24,000	1,250	3,000	4,250
Nov.	700	28,000	1,250	3,500	4,750
Dec.	600	24,000	1,250	3,000	4,250
Total	6,000	240,000	15,000	30,000	45,000

Production budgets

Bill Robinson has applied work-study techniques to find the most efficient method of producing the coffee table. All operations can be completed in one hour. Labour costs (wages and national insurance) are £7.50 per hour, and in a normal month, 500 man-hours would be worked. Each month, therefore, 500 tables will be completed. In August, however, only 300 hours will be worked, and 300 tables completed. A study of the design of the table and estimates of the price of timber in 19X6 give the standard material cost as £10. Variable manufacturing overhead is £5 per table, and fixed manufacturing overhead including depreciation of machines, is estimated at £42,000 for the full year.

The Production and Production Cost Budgets may now be prepared. On 1 January there were 500 completed tables in stock.

19X6	Production budget	Tables available for sale	Sales budget	Budgeted closing stock	Production Cost Budget				
					Materials	Labour	Variable manufacturing overhead	Fixed manufacturing overhead	Total
	tables	tables	tables	tables	£	£	£	£	£
Opening stock	500								
Jan.	500	1,000	600	400	5,000	3,750	2,500	3,500	14,750
Feb.	500	900	500	400	5,000	3,750	2,500	3,500	14,750
Mar.	500	900	500	400	5,000	3,750	2,500	3,500	14,750
Apr.	500	900	500	400	5,000	3,750	2,500	3,500	14,750
May	500	900	400	500	5,000	3,750	2,500	3,500	14,750
June	500	1,000	400	600	5,000	3,750	2,500	3,500	14,750
July	500	1,100	400	700	5,000	3,750	2,500	3,500	14,750
Aug.	300	1,000	400	600	3,000	2,250	1,500	3,500	10,250
Sept.	500	1,100	400	700	5,000	3,750	2,500	3,500	14,750
Oct.	500	1,200	600	600	5,000	3,750	2,500	3,500	14,750
Nov.	500	1,100	700	400	5,000	3,750	2,500	3,500	14,750
Dec.	500	900	600	300	5,000	3,750	2,500	3,500	14,750
Total	5,800		6,000		58,000	43,500	29,000	42,000	172,500

Finally the totals of the separate budgets are brought together to give a budgeted profit for the year. Administration expenses are expected to be incurred at a rate of £1,000 per month for the full year. There are no separate research and development expenses. Only variable production costs are included in the valuation of stock.

Budgeted Trading and Profit and Loss Account
for the year ending 31 December 19X6

	£	£
Budgeted Sales		240,000
Opening stock of tables, 500 at £22.50	11,250	
add Budgeted production cost	172,500	
	183,750	
less Closing stock of tables, 300 at £22.50	6,750	177,000
BUDGETED GROSS PROFIT		63,000
Budgeted selling and distribution expense	45,000	
Budgeted administration expense	12,000	57,000
BUDGETED NET PROFIT		6,000

14.3   Resource budgets

Apart from planning for profit, a system of budgets will also plan the availability of materials, men, machinery and money. This is the function of resource budgets. The materials cost budget and the labour cost budget have been introduced as part of the profit-planning exercise. Management is concerned not only that materials and labour are used efficiently, but that these resources are available in the right place and at the right time. For instance, the preparation of the labour cost budget may warn the personnel manager of possible future shortage of certain skills.

Plans for the acquisition of plant and machinery, land and buildings, motor vehicles and other fixed assets, are coordinated in a 'Capital Budget'. By definition, these assets will yield up their value to the company over a period longer than one year. Capital budgets will therefore be prepared for several years in advance; decisions about investment in new projects will be closely linked to the long-range strategic plan. The techniques used for evaluating projects will be discussed in the next chapter. As businesses become more and more 'capital intensive', the subject of capital budgeting is increasing in importance.

A business has two major financial goals — profitability and liquidity. Many businesses have failed, not necessarily because they were unprofitable, but because they ran short of working capital. A 'cash budget' shows the implications of the company's plans on its liquid position. Possible shortages of cash are indicated, and the accountant can plan finance to meet the situation. For instance, if the shortage is merely a temporary embarrassment, a bank overdraft may be arranged. If the shortage is more permanent, long-term finance, such as fresh capital through a 'rights' issue, may be needed. The final possibility is that the budget might warn management that the company is in danger of over-trading, and that it would be prudent to cut back its planned rate of expansion. Cash has become the new limiting factor, and all other plans must be adjusted accordingly.

The cash budget is usually prepared on a monthly basis. As all economic activity has cash implications at some stage, the cash budget, like the profit budget, will draw on all the other budgets. The form will depend on the 'liquidity cycle' of the business. For instance, a retail grocer buying his supplies from a 'cash and carry' wholesaler has the following simple liquidity cycle:

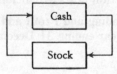

On the other hand, a manufacturer buying stock and selling the finished goods on credit will have the following more complex cycle:

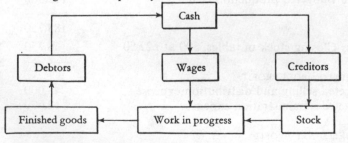

The debtors position may be deduced from the sales budget, and the creditors position from the materials budget and other budgets implying the ordering of goods and services on credit. The cash position is also affected by taxation, dividends and similar appropriations of profit, and also by plans to introduce fresh capital. The main components of the cash budget are shown in the following diagram:

THE CASH BUDGET

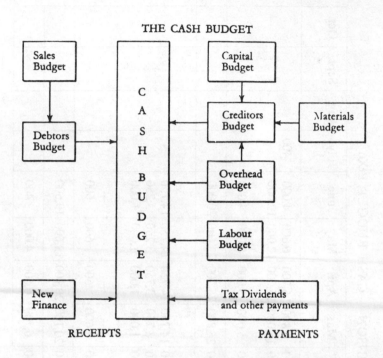

RECEIPTS   PAYMENTS

The Cash Budget of Bill Robinson for 19X6 may now be prepared, given this additional information.

Seventy-five per cent of sales are for cash. The remaining 25% settle their accounts on average one month after sale. Materials are bought one month before planned usage. One month's credit is given by suppliers. All other costs are paid during the month for which they are budgeted.

Towards the end of the year he proposes to build an extension to the workshop. Payments for this work will be £3,000 in November 19X6 and £5,000 in December 19X6. Bill Robinson draws out £600 per month for his own use. Taxation will be payable in equal instalments of £2,500 in January 19X6 and July 19X6. The opening cash position on 1 January 19X6 was £5,000.

Q.14a Bill Robinson's Cash Budget for the first six months of 19X6 is shown on p. 244. Complete the Cash Budget for the rest of the year. Comment on Bill Robinson's liquidity during the year. What action needs to be taken in the light of this cash budget? As a result of your recommendations it will be necessary to re-draft the Sales, Production and Profit budgets presented earlier in the chapter.

BILL ROBINSON — CASH BUDGET, 19X6

	Jan.	Feb.	Mar.	Apr.	May	June	July	Aug.	Sept.	Oct.	Nov.	Dec.
RECEIPTS												
Opening cash	5,000	5,000	6,800	6,700	6,600	4,000	400					
Cash sales, 75% current month	18,000	15,000	15,000	15,000	12,000	12,000						
Receipts from debtors, 25% of previous month	*6,000	6,000	5,000	5,000	5,000	4,000						
TOTAL	29,000	26,900	26,800	26,700	23,600	20,000						
PAYMENTS												
Production costs	14,750	14,750	14,750	14,750	14,750	14,750						
Selling and distribution expense	4,250	3,750	3,750	3,750	3,250	3,250						
Administration expense	1,000	1,000	1,000	1,000	1,000	1,000						
Taxation	2,500	—	—	—	—	—						
Capital budget	—	—	—	—	—	—						
Drawings	600	600	600	600	600	600						
TOTAL	23,100	20,100	20,100	20,100	19,600	19,600						
BALANCE	5,900	6,800	6,700	6,600	4,000	400						

* assumed.

14.4   Budgets in the public sector

Although the discussion so far has been confined to budgeting in business organizations, the concept of control through budgets has particular significance in the public
service. For instance, the annual presentation by the Chancellor of the Exchequer to the
House of Commons of his estimates of British government revenue, expenditure and
borrowing for the next fiscal year is traditionally called 'The Budget'. This section
introduces some of the special problems of budgeting in the public sector by examining
the annual budget for a local authority service.

There are many similarities between public-service budgeting procedures and
budgetary control systems in large business enterprises. In both cases, objectives have
to be set, inconsistencies between sectional plans resolved and forecasts made about
future trends in an uncertain environment. The essential function of budgeting remains
the same: to express complex interrelated plans in the common language of finance.

In one respect, however, there is an important difference. In a private business the
various activities of the organization — marketing, production, personnel, research,
etc. — are all interdependent in the sense that the net effect of all these activities should
be profit for the company as a whole. In place of the overriding profit motive of the
business corporation, public sector objectives are strongly influenced by political
considerations. Planned expenditure in the public service will therefore reflect the
priorities of the party in power, subject to statutory obligations to provide services and
other constraints. A government's freedom of action to reduce defence spending may be
limited by treaty obligations, for instance.

Q.14b   Consider the following summary of Central Government expenditure plans.

Public Expenditure Programme

Planned Changes

	Last year estimated outturn £m	Current year plans £m	Change cash (%)	Change* real terms (%)
Defence	15,716	17,031	+8.4	+3.2
Overseas services and aid	2,294	2,283	−0.5	−5.2
Agriculture, fisheries, food and forestry	2,087	2,048	−1.9	−6.5
Trade, industry, energy and employment	6,080	5,609	−7.7	−12.1
Arts and libraries	624	599	−4.0	−8.6
Transport	4,560	4,372	−4.1	−8.7
Housing	2,760	2,496	−9.6	−13.9
Other environmental services	3,787	3,451	−8.9	−13.2
Law, order and protective services	4,681	4,901	+4.7	−0.3
Education and Science	13,356	13,052	−2.3	−6.9
Health and personal social services	14,688	15,421	+5.0	0.0

* An average inflation rate of 5% is assumed.

Planned Changes

	Last year estimated outturn £m	Current year plans £m	Change cash (%)	Change* real terms (%)
Social security	35,324	37,207	+5.3	+0.3
Other public services	1,666	1,788	+7.3	+2.2
Common services	950	1,105	+16.3	+10.7
Scotland	6,767	6,863	+1.4	−3.4
Wales	2,587	2,585	−0.1	−4.8
N. Ireland	3,799	4,032	+6.1	+1.1
Total without adjustments	121,726	124,843	+2.6	−1.8
Planning total after adjustments	120,328	126,353	+5.0	0.0

* An average inflation rate of 5% is assumed.

(1) On the basis of the above table, what would you consider were the main priorities for government expenditure in this financial year?
(2) What will be the main external influences and constraints determining levels of expenditure on each of the following services:
Defence;   Social Services;   Education
(3) What are the arguments for and against this method of setting 'cash limits' on government spending plans?

Setting expenditure targets in the public service is a complex process. The spending plans of the various departments must be assembled and political priorities agreed between and within programmes. Possible sources of revenue will be reviewed but the politicians will need to take account of public pressure to reduce public expenditure as well as pressures from the spending departments to increase it. The final 'package' will attempt to match these conflicting demands with the available resources.

Because public service budgets are, in effect, the financial reflection of political priorities, it is not easy to change allocations between services during the financial year. A business is in a stronger position to react quickly to external changes. For instance, it may become appropriate to spend more on advertising and less on production than was allowed in the budget if market conditions suddenly become difficult. It would be more difficult for central government to make major changes in its spending plans between different services without risking a political row.

Similar considerations apply in local government. A County Council must determine precisely what it intends to spend on the various services such as education, police and social services which it provides. Central government provides finance through the annual Rate Support Grant but the balance must be made up from the rates levied on private and business property occupiers in the county and charges for services. When the budget for a particular service has been fixed, the officers responsible for managing that service must keep within it, otherwise the revenue and expenditure sides of the authority's revenue budget will be out of balance. The County Librarian, for instance, would not be allowed to spend more than the budgeted allocation for the library service. Local Authorities hold reserves to meet unforeseen contingencies but any significant overspending in the course of the financial year would have to be met by rate increases next year. This would be most unpopular with the rate payers, and the councillors in power are anxious to be re-elected!

Let us now see how the budget for a local government service is drawn up in practice. The following table shows the agreed estimates for the libraries service in Barsetshire for Financial Year 3. The budget has been agreed by the Leisure Services Committee, together with the budgets for other leisure services such as youth work, support for sport and the arts and the cost of leisure centres and country parks. The total allocation to leisure services is a policy decision to be determined by the full County Council in the light of competing claims from all County Council services. Barsetshire will be forced to make a number of 'cuts' in its services for Financial Year 3. Rate Support Grant from central government has been reduced and the Local Authority wishes to avoid a large increase in the rates.

BARSETSHIRE COUNTY COUNCIL
ANNUAL BUDGET, FINANCIAL YEAR 3

Leisure Services Committee: Library

	Actual Year 1 £000	Actual Year 2 £000	Policy Variations Year 3 £000	Inflation Allowance Year 3 £000	Budget Year 3 £000
Expenditure					
Employees					
Professional and					
Clerical	3,200	3,510	20	175	3,705
Other	405	550	2	28	580
Premises	550	640	—	25	665
Supplies and Services					
Book Fund	1,730	2,080	(−)150	75	2,005
Records and Cassettes	60	65	(−)5	2	62
Other	170	155	(−)5	5	155
Transport	120	150	(−)10	5	145
Establishment Expenses	210	240	—	10	250
Debt charges	550	650	20	—	670
	6,995	8,040	(−)128	325	8,237
Income from fees,					
charges and trading	400	450	10	10	470
	6,595	7,590	(−)138	315	7,787

Note: The 'policy variations' column shows planned real changes in the services provided as compared with the current year (year 2). An inflation allowance is then added to give a cash limited budget for year 3.

Statistics

	Year 1	Year 2	Year 3 (estimate)
Employees	530	560	570
Book Stock (000s)	2,400	2,500	2,500
Book purchases (000s)	250	280	260
Book issues (000s)	13,500	13,100	13,200
Total hours opening per week	2,600	2,700	2,800

Q.14c Comment on the main trends in Barsetshire's library service provision over the three-year period shown. How has the local authority decided to apply the 'cuts' in the library service? What will be the likely long-term effect on the service provided?

14.5 Budgets and motivation

Many studies by behavioural scientists have been highly critical of some budgetary control and standard costing systems. The objection is basically that budgets presuppose a rigid, bureaucratic type of organization, and an over-simple view of motivation.

Modern writers on organization are moving away from the classical approach, which emphasizes formal relationships, organization charts and job descriptions. In a rapidly changing environment, businesses may have to change policies and organization as opportunities arise. Budgets may be a brake to progress if they are not used flexibly. The situation sometimes arises where a manager feels that he must spend up to the budget limit, otherwise the allowance will be cut back next period. Where this happens, budgets are encouraging inefficiency rather than controlling it.

It is rather naïve to assume that as soon as an unfavourable variance is reported to a manager, he will try to put things right. Motivation is complex and too often accountants have concentrated on the setting of budgets and calculation of variances rather than the way in which the variance information is actually used by managers. For instance, is it better, psychologically, to set tight standards based on an unattainable ideal, or to set attainable standards which incorporate a reasonable margin for error?

The moral of these researches is not that budgets are a waste of time, if not positively harmful. It is rather that budgets relate to people, and if the accountant sees them merely as exercises in arithmetic, he should not be surprised if things go wrong. Perhaps in the future, budgetary control and similar topics will be as much the concern of psychologists and sociologists as accountants.

14.6 Additional questions

[1]
Prepare a materials purchase budget (in kgs only) for the three months January, February and March.

(1) Estimated sales of finished product:

Jan.	6,000	units
Feb.	7,000	,,
Mar.	8,000	,,
April	6,600	,,
May	8,400	,,

(2) Stocking policy is to maintain a sufficient quantity of finished goods at the month end to exactly satisfy the estimated sales for the following month. This is and has been adhered to, and it is confirmed that 6,000 units were in stock on 1 January.

(3) The standard cost card for the product shows the standard material constant *per unit* to be:

Standard Quantity Material A — 1 kg
,,   ,,   ,,   B — 2 kg

Stocking policy is to maintain a sufficient quantity of raw materials on hand at the end of each month to meet half of the production requirements for the following month. This policy is always adhered to.

[2]

From the following forecasted information, prepare a budget for an activity of 1,000 units.

Activity in units	600	900	1,200	1,500
	£	£	£	£
Direct labour	150	225	300	375
Indirect labour	218	227	236	245
Raw materials	120	180	240	300
Rent and Rates	200	200	200	200
Salaries	400	450	500	500

Using the budget for 1,000 units, express as a rate per unit:

(a) the variable overhead recovery rate;
(b) the fixed overhead recovery rate.

[3]

On the basis of past records the following budgets have been prepared by the Flexico Manufacturing Co. to represent the extremes of high and low volume of production likely to be encountered by the company.

	Production at 4,000 units	Production at 8,000 units
	£	£
Materials	8,000	16,000
Labour	5,000	10,000
Power	1,800	2,600
Repairs	2,000	3,000
Supervision	1,000	1,800
Rates and Rent	600	600
Indirect materials	1,200	2,000

Supervision is a 'step' function. A new supervisor has to be employed for every 2,000 units produced. Other semivariable expenses are incurred evenly over the production range. Power is charged on the basis of a flat fixed charge plus a variable charge based on kilowatt hours used over a minimum consumption which is expected to be reached at 6,000 units of production.

Prepare a set of flexible budgets to cover the following levels of production:

4,000;   5,000;   6,000;   7,000;   8,000 units.

[4]
B.C. Ltd makes and sells three products:

	PRODUCT 1	PRODUCT 2	PRODUCT 3
Sales estimate for year to			
31 December	20,000 units	10,000 units	5,000 units
Standards for year to			
31 December	Per unit	Per unit	Per unit
	£	£	£
Direct material	0.50	0.60	0.70
Direct wages	0.20	0.40	0.50
Variable other costs	0.20	0.40	0.50
Allocated fixed costs	0.20	0.35	0.40
	(£4,000)	(£3,500)	(£2,000)
Net profit	0.10	0.25	0.20
Selling Price	£1.20	£2.00	£2.30

The Marketing Manager considers that additional press advertising would stimulate demand as follows:

	Additional Advertising £	Additional Sales units
On Product 1	2,000	8,000
„ „ 2	2,500	10,000
„ „ 3	2,600	7,000

Prepare statement(s) for Board consideration setting out the effects of the Marketing Manager's proposals and comment on the policy and the figures supplied.

[5]
The management of Duswell Ltd plan to increase production and sales during the next year as follows:

	UNITS Prod.	Sales		UNITS Prod.	Sales
Jan.	1,000	800	July	1,500	1,600
Feb.	1,200	1,000	Aug.	1,600	1,600
Mar.	1,200	1,200	Sept.	1,600	1,700
April	1,400	1,300	Oct.	1,800	1,900
May	1,500	1,400	Nov.	2,000	2,000
June	1,500	1,600	Dec.	2,000	2,000

The selling price should remain constant at £10 per unit, the expansion resulting most from increased advertising. Payments to the advertising agents are likely to be £1,000 in January, £1,500 in April, £1,800 in July and £2,400 in October.

Raw materials cost £4 per unit. Payment is made to suppliers one month after delivery, and the materials are held in stock for an average of one month before issue to production. Wages and other variable expenses cost £3 per unit. Salaries and other administrative and production expenses are expected to be £1,600 per month for the first five months and then £2,000 per month.

New production equipment has been ordered at a cost of £6,000. This should be delivered in March and the agreement is to pay for it by three equal instalments in April, May and June. Dividend payments of £600 are due in April.

All goods are sold on credit terms and the average interval before payment is two months. Sales during the previous November and December were 700 and 800 units respectively.

The bank balance at 1 January was £7,500.

(a) Prepare a cash budget for the year. What overdraft facilities would the company be seeking?
(b) Assuming depreciation for the year was £5,000, calculate the estimated profit for the year. Can you reconcile the reduction in the bank balance during the year with the profit?

[6]

(a) 'My budget makes my task easier. It would be different if it were imposed without consultation. In that case the job would be very tough.'
(b) 'Personally I prefer a management not to set standards. A good foreman ought to take care of that himself. If I am responsible for a job, I must see to it that my people perform as efficiently as possible.'
(c) 'I have the experience that my budget is cut by 10% (by the accountant). Therefore if I've made a realistic budget, I increase it by 10%.'
(d) 'It is useful that we as managers of different departments learn to speak the same language.'

The above are statements by managers who were involved in budgetary control systems. They are taken from interviews conducted by Hofstede and his co-workers as part of a survey of budgetary control systems in five Dutch companies. Discuss the implications of each statement for the accountant who is responsible for setting up a budgetary control system.

(See G. H. Hofstede, *The Game of Budget Control*, Tavistock, 1968.)

[7]

The following statements by managers interviewed in the Hofstede study relate to the problem of whether to set tight (unattainable) or slack (attainable) standards in a control system.

Discuss the views expressed and say to what extent they are reconcilable.

'I think negative variances have more impact than positive ones.'
'If we've made it we're all happy.'

'Standards imperceptibly penetrate into one's mind.'
'Standards are like traffic signs, they prevent accidents.'
'We tell the fellows it's a matter of honour to attain standard time.'
'I'd be happier if the system was just a tiny bit looser.'

(op. cit., pp. 150–151.)

[8]

In recent years behavioural scientists and writers on organization theory have levied criticism against budgetary control and standard costing systems, particularly in that they restrict a worker's motivation and achievements. Why is this so?

[9]

At a budget committee meeting the subject of manufacturing wages is under discussion and the accountant agrees that the best system of wages control is one that results in the lowest costs. It is therefore preferable to set labour performance standards which are difficult (even impossible) to attain. By so doing, he argues, the operator is forced to produce an actual performance better than he would if the standard set was easily attainable.

Do you think that the accountant is correct in his assumption? Discuss.

[10]

Kipps & Co. are retailers who are commencing business on 1 July. The owners will start the business from premises valued at £30,000 and cash to a value of £18,000. Fittings worth £10,000 will be purchased, to be paid for in two equal instalments of £5,000 on the last day of August and September, respectively. From July, £1,500 per month will be withdrawn in cash as salary for the owners.

The sales forecast is as follows:

August	September	October	November	December
£6,000	£7,500	£12,000	£27,000	£60,000

Sales are on one month's credit; however, it is anticipated that 40% of debtors will delay payment for one month beyond the due date. Gross profit is $33\frac{1}{3}\%$ of sales value.
Forecast purchases are:

July	August	September	October	November	December
£5,000	£8,000	£15,000	£18,000	£27,000	£8,000

— all purchases are paid for in the month after purchase.
Expenses are £1,000 for July and thereafter 12% of monthly sales.
Depreciation for the first half year of trading will be £625.

(a) Provide an estimate of the net profit for the first half-year's business.
(b) Prepare a cash forecast for the half year, commenting on your results and recommending any action you think appropriate.

[11]

Oxfam is a charity carrying on the following principal activities:

(i) Donations collection — via regular contributors and special fund-raising campaigns.
(ii) Commercial activities — a retail shop and mail-order organization trading in donated goods, Third-World craft products and cards.

(iii) Improvement projects — one-off capital investment schemes for individual communities, e.g. well construction.
(iv) Long-term assistance — regular support for specific individuals/communities.
(v) Disaster relief.
(vi) Administration.

Suggest a system of management which would assist in the planning and control of Oxfam's various activities and help it attain its basic objectives.

[12]
Bloggs Plc, manufactures and sells three products whose standard material costs and selling price are as follows:

	PRODUCTS		
	A	B	C
	£	£	£
Selling Price	80	86	170
Materials			
Component X (£5 each)	10	10	15
Component Y (£3 each)	9	9	15

The sales of each product for January and February are expected to be as follows:

	A	B	C
	(units)	(units)	(units)
Jan.	40,000	35,000	20,000
Feb.	50,000	40,000	25,000

It is company policy to maintain stocks of finished goods at 10% of expected sales for the following month. It is also policy to maintain stocks of components X and Y at 5% of expected usage for the following month.
Prepare the following budgets for the month of January for Bloggs Plc.

(1) Sales (in quantities and value).
(2) Production (quantities only).
(3) Material usage (quantities only).
(4) Materials purchases (in quantities and value).

Chapter 15

Accounting Information and Decision Taking

15.1 Introduction

Managers must take decisions and accounts need to be presented in such a way that wise choices are more likely to be taken. Marginal costing, breakeven analysis, differential costing and project appraisal are techniques which focus on this need for sound information for decision taking.

Apart from planning and controlling costs, the other main contribution of the management accountant is to provide information to help management take decisions. What prices should be charged for the company's products? Should the company buy an expensive item of equipment? Is it cheaper to send a consignment by road or by rail? Should a new factory be opened, and if so, where? Should a component be manufactured by the company or bought outside? Some of these decisions are of major strategic importance; others are fairly routine operating decisions. In all cases, accurate, up-to-date accounting information, presented in a meaningful way, is the first step to rational decision taking.

Before looking in detail at the contribution of the management accountant in the decision taking process, it is important to appreciate three important limitations on his role in practice.

(1) Decisions look to the future; accounting systems are usually better at describing what has happened in the past. Even information about past costs may not be available in an ideal form to assist decision taking. In the world of classical economics, it is assumed that a firm strives to maximize its profit by continuing production until marginal cost equals marginal revenue. In the large multiproduct firm, no accounting system possible could tell management the precise point at which profit is maximized. The best that can be achieved in practice is a 'satisfactory' level of profit. The future is uncertain, and many decisions must be taken by weighing the balance of probabilities, rather than by applying a neat accounting formula which gives a clear-cut answer. For instance, in deciding how much of the cost of a machine to charge as depreciation expense in an accounting period, estimates must be made about the machine's future life and residual value. It needs a very brave engineer to say dogmatically that a particular lathe has a working life of eight years. He might feel that the most likely term was eight years,

but there was a 20% probability that the machine would be used for ten years, and a 20% probability that it would become obsolete after six years. Accounting information sometimes looks more certain than it is. It is often more honest to use the mathematical language of probabilities to describe a business situation.

(2) Traditional accounting techniques may not give the best solution if the problem is complex. If management has a straight choice of sending a consignment by rail or by road, it is relatively easy to assess the financial implications of these two alternatives. If, on the other hand, the problem is to find the most efficient distribution system from an infinite number of possibilities, mathematical techniques such as linear programming using the transportation model are required.

There is a growing tendency to express complex business problems in terms of mathematics. This approach is called Operational Research, and a number of techniques with such delightful names as 'the Monte Carlo method', 'Queueing Theory' and 'Dynamic Programming' have been developed to solve standard business problems. What is the optimum number of check-out points in a supermarket? What is the best mix of a range of products, each with a different profit margin and production constraints? It is beyond the scope of this book to discuss these techniques, but the management accountant of the future will have to be familiar with them if he is to retain his position as chief adviser on management decisions.

(3) The third limitation applies to Operational Research as much as the more traditional management accounting techniques which are the subject of this chapter. It is impossible to express the human aspect of decisions in either accounting or mathematical terms. Accounts only record transactions which are capable of easy measurement in financial terms. Thus a balance sheet will give values for fixed and current assets, but not for customer relations, technical know-how or the stock of managerial skills.

Many decisions to be taken by management involve more than a calculation of economic advantages. Let us assume that there is a proposal to install an automated assembly line in a factory. The project is first evaluated financially, and it appears that considerable savings could be achieved over the present method. Before any final decision is made, there are many other factors which need to be considered. What is the probable effect on labour relations? How will any redundancies be handled? Is it possible to recruit the skilled labour for programming and maintaining the automated plant? What consultation with the unions is necessary? What is the best timing for the proposed change? It is obvious that in some cases, human factors are more important, and require greater management skill than financial analysis.

The main areas of decision taking which have been selected for discussion are:

(1) Decisions requiring an understanding of the distinction between fixed and variable costs. This way of looking at costs is called, in this country, Marginal Costing, because it focuses attention on changes in costs and revenue at the margin.
(2) Decisions involving a choice between alternative courses of action. This requires the calculation of differential costs.
(3) The appraisal of projects which may have a life-span of several years.

15.2   Marginal costing

As we have seen in previous chapters, costs show a variety of patterns of behaviour as production increases. Some costs, such as rent and rates, are a function of time, and so are fixed in the current accounting period. The rate bill will be the same whether the factory is working at full capacity or whether nothing is produced at all. At the other extreme, the wages of a direct worker paid by piece rate will vary proportionally with production. If the piece rate is £1.50 per unit, the wage costs will be £150 for 100 units of production, £300 for 200 units of production, and so on. Graphically, these two extreme cases may be shown as follows:

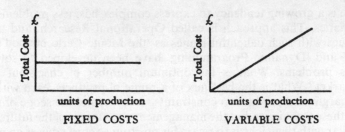

FIXED COSTS   VARIABLE COSTS

Q.15a How would you classify the charge for depreciation of machinery (a) if calculated on the straight line method, or (b) if calculated on the basis of the number of hours worked by the machinery?

In practice, many costs do not fall neatly into the two categories, e.g. the rental of a telephone includes a fixed element (quarterly charge) and a variable element based on use. The use of the telephone will tend to vary with production, so the cost curve will look like this:

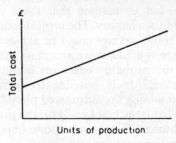

TELEPHONE RENTAL.

Q.15b Draw the cost curve for the salaries of supervisors. For the first 100 units of production, one supervisor is employed at £8,500 p.a. For production levels from 101 units to 200 units, an additional supervisor is engaged at the same salary, and so on for every additional 100 units up to the capacity of the plant, which is 1,000 units.

It will be seen from these two examples of semi-variable costs that they can be analysed into fixed and variable components. For the rest of this section, therefore, we shall make the assumption that the total costs of the business can be split into a fixed element and a variable element.

An example will show the importance of looking at costs in this way when decisions are to be taken. A firm makes four products, and the cost-finding system provides the following information.

PRODUCT COSTS FOR DECEMBER, ABSORPTION COSTING

PRODUCTS (COST IN £)

	A	B	C	D	TOTAL
Direct materials	380	310	670	490	1,850
Direct labour	420	340	580	520	1,860
Variable overheads	380	360	390	450	1,580
Fixed overheads	300	290	410	380	1,380
Total costs	1,480	1,300	2,050	1,840	6,670
Sales	1,440	1,380	2,590	2,510	7,920
Profit or (Loss)	(40)	80	540	670	1,250

The firm uses an absorption costing system whereby all overheads costs, fixed and variable, are apportioned to the four products. It appears that Product A is making a loss, but the firm would be most unwise to drop it from the range if it could not expand production of the other products to fill the gap. Such action would save the variable costs of manufacturing Product A, but the fixed costs of £300 have still to be met. The remaining three products would now show an increase in cost, because they would each bear a proportion of the fixed costs apportioned to Product A. The effect would be to reduce the firm's total profits from £1,250 to £990. Check this by re-drafting the table for Products B, C and D only. Spread the fixed costs charged to Product A equally between the other three products. Product B now makes a loss. What would be the effect on total profit if Product B is now discontinued?

If cost information is not to be misleading, it should be presented in an alternative form when this type of decision is to be taken. Absorption costing involves the apportionment of fixed overheads between products on some arbitrary basis. In fact these costs are borne by the company as a whole, and it is better to show this state of affairs in the cost report. With a *marginal cost* presentation, a 'contribution' to fixed overhead and profit is worked out for each product. It is normally sound policy to continue making any product whose variable costs are less than sales revenue, always assuming that it is not possible to substitute production which would yield a larger contribution. The following table represents the same cost information for the four products in marginal costing form. It will be seen immediately that each product makes a contribution to fixed costs and overheads.

PRODUCTION COSTS FOR DECEMBER. MARGINAL COSTING

PRODUCTS (COST IN £)

	A	B	C	D	TOTAL
Direct materials	380	310	670	490	1,850
Direct labour	420	340	580	520	1,860
Variable overhead	380	360	390	450	1,580
Total variable costs	1,180	1,010	1,640	1,460	5,290
Sales	1,440	1,380	2,590	2,510	7,920
Contribution to fixed costs and profit	260	370	950	1,050	2,630
Total fixed overheads					1,380
Profit					1,250

Q.15c Explain why British Rail run holiday excursion trains at reduced rates.

The marginal costing approach is not limited to showing the contribution of different products to fixed overhead and profit. We shall discuss three other major applications: pricing policy, breakeven analysis and differential costs.

15.3   Pricing policy

Economic theory tells that, apart from the limiting case of perfect competition, a firm has a range of possible choices about price. A low price will mean a high quantity demanded, and any increase in price restricts the quantity sold depending on the elasticity of demand for the product. Naturally a firm will try to fix a price which gives maximum contribution to fixed overhead and profit.

In the long term, prices must cover all costs for the firm, including fixed costs. This is sometimes known as full-cost pricing. In practice, many firms try to achieve this by adding percentages to estimated prime cost or direct labour to cover total overhead costs and provide a margin for profit. Consider the following cost statement, for example:

	£
Direct materials	5.60
Direct labour	3.60
Overheads 200% on direct labour cost	7.20
TOTAL COST	16.40
Profit margin (25% of total cost)	4.10
SELLING PRICE	20.50

There are a number of situations where the businessman has to look more carefully at the prices he is quoting to customers than is apparent from the above calculation. Let us suppose that the business has spare capacity, and wishes to use these resources to break into a highly competitive export market. What is the lowest price that can be quoted to make it worth while undertaking the business? In the example given above, the businessman would have to analyse overheads into their fixed and variable elements, e.g.

	£
Direct materials	5.60
Direct labour	3.60
Variable overhead	4.20
	13.40

Any price over £13.40 would yield a contribution, and so it would be worthwhile undertaking the business rather than rejecting it. In general terms it may be stated that where there is surplus capacity, the highest price above total variable cost (marginal cost) should be accepted, other things being equal. Fixed costs can be ignored because they will be incurred whatever decision the firm takes about this new business.

15.4   Breakeven analysis

A breakeven chart gives a visual presentation of the relationship between profit and volume. We have already seen how the behaviour of fixed and variable costs can be shown by cost lines. The total cost line will be found by adding together the fixed and variable cost lines.

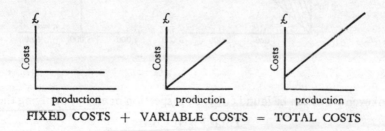

FIXED COSTS + VARIABLE COSTS = TOTAL COSTS

The sales revenue line will start at the origin, but should be steeper than the variable cost curve, because the rate at which revenue is earned must be greater than the rate at which variable costs are incurred if any contribution is to be made to fixed costs and profit.

The breakeven chart is produced by superimposing the Sales Revenue line on the Total Cost line.

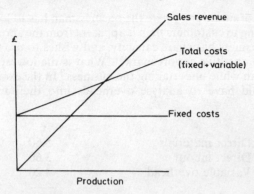

Example

Grasscut Ltd produces electrical lawn mowers of a standard design at a variable cost of £18 each. The fixed costs of the factory are £60,000 a year, and the lawn mowers sell to wholesalers at £36 each. The capacity of the factory is 5,000 lawn mowers.

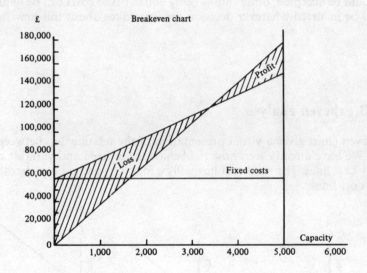

The breakeven point can be found either by inspection or else by applying the formula

$$\text{Breakeven point} = \frac{\text{Total Fixed Costs}}{\text{Selling price per unit} - \text{Variable costs per unit}}$$

$$= \frac{60,000}{36 - 18} = 3,333 \text{ units}$$

This is equivalent to $66\frac{2}{3}\%$ capacity. For any level of production below 3,333 units, the firm will be operating at a loss. As production increases beyond the breakeven point, the rate of profit earned will increase. At full capacity of 5,000 units, the total profit will be £30,000.

Breakeven analysis can assist management in two main ways:

(1) It is important to know the general relationship between fixed and variable costs. For instance, a steel works would have a high proportion of fixed costs, whereas a shirt manufacturer's costs would be mainly variable.

BREAK-EVEN CHARTS FOR TWO BUSINESSES

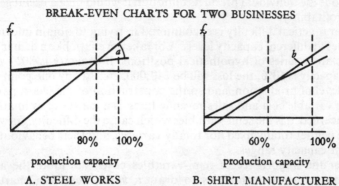

production capacity	production capacity
A. STEEL WORKS	B. SHIRT MANUFACTURER

The angles of incidence *a* and *b* in the diagrams above show the rate at which profit is earned beyond the breakeven point. Pricing policy in a firm with a high angle of incidence needs to be fairly flexible. A relatively low price will cover variable costs and make some contribution to fixed costs but in the long term total costs must be covered if the firm is to remain in business. The other key piece of information shown by these charts is the capacity level at which the firm breaks even. In the two charts shown, the steel works is clearly in a more vulnerable position. Management effort must be concentrated on making sure that the works is running as near full capacity as possible.

(2) Breakeven charts can show the effect of different management decisions on the firm's profitability. We have seen that profit could be increased (or loss reduced) by operating at a higher capacity. There are, however, other policies that the firm could follow to improve profitability. It could increase selling prices, decrease variable costs per unit, or decrease total fixed costs.

Q.15d Grasscut Ltd is considering three possible policy alternatives:

(1) Increase wholesale selling price to £40 per lawn mower. Sales would be reduced to 4,000 lawn mowers as a result of this policy.
(2) A cost saving campaign to reduce costs to £15 per unit. Budgeted sales: 5,000 lawn mowers.
(3) Fixed costs are reduced to £45,000. Budgeted sales: 5,000 lawn mowers.

Which course of action should Grasscut Ltd adopt?

15.5 Limitations of breakeven charts

Breakeven analysis shows vividly the critical relationship between profit and volume. There are unfortunately a number of practical and theoretical difficulties in using the technique.

(1) The example of the lawn mower factory assumes a business making a single product. In the multi-product firm it is not so easy to draw breakeven charts for each

individual product. Fixed costs are incurred mainly for the business as a whole. If an attempt is made to apportion these costs to products, we find ourselves back to the arbitrary apportionments of absorption costing. A composite breakeven chart for all the firm's activities would not provide information to enable managers to take decisions about the individual products although it would give a useful general view of the firm's profitability.

(2) Another practical difficulty is encountered in trying to obtain information about costs and sales at different capacity levels. A breakeven chart, like a demand curve, is an attempt to state a series of hypothetical positions. If capacity is 80%, profit will be £20,000. If capacity is 50%, the loss will be £40,000, etc. At any one point in time there is only one level of production, and so the construction of the chart, particularly the slopes of the variable cost and sales revenue lines, is a matter of estimation. So far as costs are concerned, it is the semi-variables which cause the difficulty. As we saw earlier, the costs are neither totally fixed nor totally variable, and their behaviour may change over different capacity ranges.

The higher the importance of semi-variables costs, the more the accountant is dependent on statistical techniques to draw a valid breakeven chart. From past information it may be possible to prepare a scatter diagram showing the relationships between production costs and capacity. As the information relates to past experience, it is important to make sure that the figures are comparable. For instance, past cost experience should be adjusted to present-day values by the use of index numbers.

A statistical technique known as regression analysis may be used to derive a total cost curve from a mass of empirical data. Let us assume that we have collected cost information about supervision costs in a factory over a number of years. We make the assumption that this is a semi-variable cost which can be expressed in the form $T = F + Vq$, where T = Total Cost; F = Total Fixed Costs; V = Variable costs per unit; q = quantity produced.

The historical cost data must first be transformed into current costs by applying an appropriate series of index numbers. The current cost data can now be plotted on a 'scatter diagram' to show all the relationships between supervision costs and production capacity which have been experienced over the period.

By using a technique of linear regression analysis known as the 'least squares' method, it is possible to give values to F and V and so draw a straight line which gives the best fit to the points on the scatter diagram.

(3) Finally the economist would raise a number of theoretical objections to breakeven analysis as generally practised by the accountant. Traditional economic

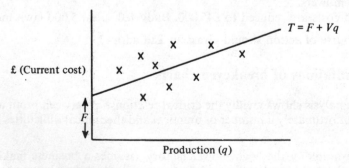

Regression line for supervision costs

theory describes the position of a firm operating under market conditions of 'imperfect competition' in the following way:

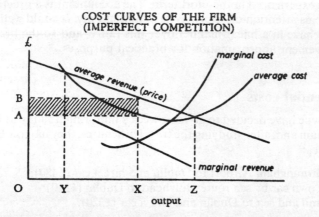

COST CURVES OF THE FIRM
(IMPERFECT COMPETITION)

It will be noticed that there are two breakeven points, Y and Z. Any level of production between these points is profitable, but X is the optimum. At this point, marginal cost is equal to marginal revenue. Profit is at its maximum and is calculated by multiplying the quantity produced by the difference between average revenue and average total costs at that point (the shaded area or AB × OX).

The differing assumptions of the accountant are evident if his breakeven chart is re-drafted in terms of marginal cost and marginal revenue. Instead of showing total costs and revenues, the following chart gives the same information expressed as increments to total cost and total revenue caused by the last unit of production.

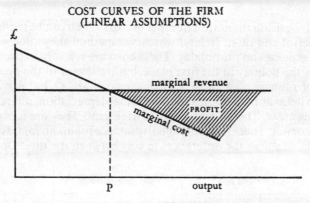

COST CURVES OF THE FIRM
(LINEAR ASSUMPTIONS)

There is only one breakeven point, P, and apparently the optimum level of production is infinity. This strange result occurs because the accountant has assumed that both costs and revenue behave in a *linear* fashion. The economist believes that sooner or later diminishing returns will set in, and therefore the marginal cost curve will turn upwards. He may also discard the assumption of perfect competition implicit in the breakeven chart. Sooner or later the price will have to be lowered if increased production is to be sold.

Are these two views of the nature of costs irreconcilable? Fortunately the difficulty is more apparent than real, and arises because the economist and the accountant are looking at cost behaviour from different standpoints. The economist is trying to provide a complete theory of the firm, and so his attention is focused on the two limiting cases of very low capacity and an artificial level of overcapacity where diminishing returns must be experienced in the short term. The accountant is a practical man, and so concentrates his attention on likely levels of output only. It could well be that costs and revenues behave in a linear manner over this range, and so the breakeven chart provides a convenient approximation for practical purposes.

15.6   Differential costs

A man and his wife have decided to go for a week's motoring holiday in Ireland. They live in Birmingham and, after studying the travel brochures, they narrow their choice to three possibilities:

(1)   Fly from Birmingham Airport to Dublin and hire a car (£480);
(2)   Take their own car by sea route Holyhead to Dublin (£210);
(3)   Travel by rail and sea to Dublin and hire a car (£320).

The tour operator quotes the figures in brackets as the prices of a package deal for two persons in the high season. They also obtain the following information from a motoring organization about the running costs of their car.

Estimated running costs: 1300 cc engine

Petrol and Oil	10.6p per mile
Wear and Tear (tyres, service, repairs and replacements)	6.3p per mile
Total Variable Costs	16.9p per mile

In reaching their decision there are a number of costs which can be ignored. They will have to pay for petrol and oil in Ireland whichever method they choose. The same is true of incidental expenses on the holiday. These costs are relevant in deciding whether they should go on the holiday in the first place, but irrelevant to the present decision. The fixed costs of running a car with a 1300 cc engine are £2,100 per annum. This figure covers such items as road tax, insurance, annual depreciation, interest on capital, garage and parking costs. These fixed costs are irrelevant. They are incurred whether they go on holiday or not. There is no additional insurance premium for travel in Ireland.

The following table shows the differences in cost between the three options:

	(1) Air and hire			(2) Sea with own car			(3) Sea and hire		
	Mileage	Rate	Cost	Mileage	Rate	Cost	Mileage	Rate	Cost
			£			£			£
Basic cost			480			210			300
Taxis to and from airport or station			40						20
Travel to and from ship				300	16.9p	51			
Wear and tear of car in Ireland				1000	6.3p	63			
			520			324			320

The differential cost of flying and hiring a car is much higher than the other two options and, on the face of it, they would reject this alternative. The differential costs of options (2) and (3) are virtually identical and the choice between these two would depend on non-economic factors. What if their own car broke down on holiday (option (2))? Perhaps it would be better to hire a car and have more peace of mind. On the other hand, it may be more convenient to take their own car if they wish to take bulky items such as fishing tackle or golf clubs. Other non-economic factors may persuade them to reconsider option (1) in spite of the higher differential cost. They may feel that a bad sea crossing would spoil the start of the holiday. Perhaps the additional cost is less important to them than the amount of travelling time saved. Decisions are not always made purely on economic considerations, and this applies to major business decisions as well as this simple holiday choice. However, it is important to set out clearly those differential costs which are quantifiable before non-economic factors are taken into account.

Going back to the table of differential costs, it will be seen that there are two basic criteria for the inclusion of any item.

(1) Is it a *future* cost? The fixed costs relating to their own care are irrelevant because they were incurred in the past. They are committed costs or sunk costs, and nothing to be decided now will alter that fact. The same reasoning applies to depreciation charges on equipment bought in the past. The whole cost of the equipment is a sunk cost. The depreciation charge is simply an accounting device to apportion this sunk cost between different accounting periods. It should not affect future decisions.

(2) Is it a *differential* cost? Costs common to all decisions are excluded; differences only are shown.

If marginal costing is defined as a costing technique which brings out the distinction between fixed and variable costs, it will be seen that differential costing is a broader concept. Admittedly most fixed costs are sunk costs, but not all variable costs are relevant differential costs. For instance, in the example there are two variable cost rates for running the car. The 16.9p rate is relevant in England, and the 6.3p rate in Ireland.

In looking at the various short-term decisions, such as whether to buy or lease a machine, whether a manufacturer should buy a component outside or make it in the factory, it is better to apply the tests of relevance already given. Is it a future cost? Is it a differential cost? Preconceived notions about whether an item of cost is fixed or variable may well prove misleading when trying to identify relevant differences in cost at the margin.

Q.15e   There is a proposal to install a new power press in an engineering works. You are given the following information:

	Old Power Press	New Power Press
Cost	£10,000	£12,000
Depreciation written off	£7,000	
Expected future life	4 years	10 years
Material	£1.50 per unit	£1.50 per unit
Production capacity per annum	2,000 units	2,400 units

	Old Power Press	New Power Press
Labour cost	£85 per week	£85 per week
Power	£300 per annum	£500 per annum
Consumable stores	£500 per annum	£600 per annum
Maintenance	£600 per annum	£300 per annum

Both presses would be in operation for 52 weeks in the year. Prepare a table showing the differential costs per unit of production on the new press as compared with the old press. What action should be taken in the light of this cost comparison and any other information which you consider to be relevant? Ignore interest and investment grants. *Hint*: remember that the cost of the old press and the depreciation written off are sunk costs.

15.7   Project appraisal

In the power press example above, the decision was based on a simple calculation of differential costs. There is, however, an additional complication in this type of problem compared with some of the short-term decisions that have been mentioned. The choice between making or buying out, or between rail or road transport, is a choice between current alternatives. Capital projects such as purchasing new machinery or building a new factory will only generate profit in the future. Time is an additional dimension in the appraisal of these projects.

Investment in capital projects involves a high initial cost which, it is hoped, will be justified by increased income over a period of time. There are two important aspects of this situation. In the first place the accountant may have to look into the distant future to estimate these returns. Uncertainties about the state of the market, the life of the machine and technological innovation will blur the decision. The other consideration is that different projects will have different patterns of cash flow over time. We shall look at these two issues of risk and cash flow in turn.

Risk

It is impossible for a decision maker to be able to predict the results of his actions with complete certainty. In practice a manager must operate under conditions of uncertainty (where the probability of different possible outcomes is unknown) or risk (where it is possible to assign probabilities to these outcomes).

Let us assume that an electronics company wishes to invest a substantial sum of money in a research and development project in solid state devices. It is notoriously difficult to predict the cost of a research and development programme, particularly in a field of high technology. When the research manager was first asked, his initial guess was that this project would cost £300,000 in total. Further consideration of all the factors enabled the research manager to refine this statement and express his prediction in probabilistic form:

There is a 30% chance that the project will cost £500,000.
There is a 60% chance that the project will cost £300,000.
There is a 10% chance that the project will cost £200,000.

By weighting each of the three outcomes by their respective probabilities, we may calculate the Expected Monetary Value (EMV) of the cost of this proposal:

$$EMV = (0.3 \times 500,000) + (0.6 \times 300,000) + (0.1 \times 200,000) = £350,000$$

In spite of all the difficulties involved in assigning realistic probabilities to each outcome, the EMV (£350,000) is likely to be a more satisfactory guide than the original guess (£300,000) when making a decision about whether to start the programme.

The subject of risk analysis is more complex than this example would suggest. For instance, the attitude of the decision maker in the above example would be different if it was estimated that the business would incur unacceptably heavy losses if the project were to cost £500,000 *and* if the subsequent sales of the product during the next two years were 50% below budget (there is a 20% probability of this happening). The probability of both these outcomes occurring together is 0.2×0.3 or 0.06. The company may decide that even a 6% chance of financial disaster is not worth taking.

Cash flow

The importance of recognizing differences in the pattern of cash flows between different projects may be illustrated by applying three common methods of appraisal in turn to the facts of a simple example.

The production manager of an engineering works needs a new lathe to cope with future expansion of production. Technical considerations narrow the choice to between two models, each costing £10,000. The increase in Sales Revenue is likely to be the same whichever machine is installed, but past experience shows that maintenance and other costs of running the machines will show different patterns. The table shows the production manager's estimate of the most likely pattern. Both machines are likely to be obsolete at the end of the six years.

ESTIMATED NET CASH FLOWS

	Lathe A			Lathe B		
	Gross Revenue	Running Expenses	Net Cash Flow	Gross Revenue	Running Expenses	Net Cash Flow
	£	£	£	£	£	£
Year 1	10,000	5,000	5,000	10,000	7,000	3,000
Year 2	10,000	6,000	4,000	10,000	7,000	3,000
Year 3	10,000	7,000	3,000	10,000	7,000	3,000
Year 4	10,000	8,000	2,000	10,000	7,000	3,000
Year 5	10,000	8,000	2,000	10,000	7,000	3,000
Year 6	10,000	9,000	1,000	10,000	7,000	3,000

Before introducing the methods of appraisal, there are three preliminary points which can be dealt with quickly.

(1) The problem is to 'rank' the two projects in order of merit. Rather different considerations apply if the accountant is 'screening' projects. For instance, it may be policy to allow all projects with a likely average return of over 15% on outlay.

Obviously in this instance only one machine will be bought, even though they might both satisfy the firm's screening criterion as individual projects.

(2)   As alternatives are being ranked, it is only necessary to include differential costs. In this simple example the initial outlay of £10,000 is the same in both cases, and so can be ignored in the calculations. If the residual values of the machines is the same at the end of six years, this can also be ignored. The annual charge for depreciation will not be included in the calculation because it is a notional charge against profits of a proportion of the initial outlay. It is not a cash flow.

(3)   In practice, technical considerations such as reliability, quality and the availability of spares, are of crucial importance in appraising any capital project. These points will have been thoroughly discussed before the accountant is called in to advise on the financial implications. Even then, his estimates of future cash flows will depend heavily on the technical information supplied by the experts.

Three methods of appraisal to be discussed are (1) Rate of Return on initial outlay, (2) Payback, and (3) Net Present Value.

(1) Rate of Return

The total estimated cash flow over the life of the project is divided by the estimated life of the project. The result is expressed as a percentage of the initial outlay. For example,

LATHE A   Average annual cash flows

$$= £\frac{5,000+4,000+3,000+2,000+2,000+1,000}{6}$$

$$= £\frac{17,000}{6}$$

$$= £2,833$$

Rate of return on initial outlay

$$= \frac{2,833}{10,000} = 28.3\%$$

LATHE B   Average annual cash flows

$$= £3,000$$

Rate of return on initial outlay

$$= \frac{3,000}{10,000} \times 100\% = 30\%$$

By this method, Lathe B would be chosen. Cash flows throughout the whole life of the project are included in the calculation, but no weighting is given to flows which occur in the early years.

(2) The Payback method

How soon is the original outlay recouped by income? At the end of year 3 the cumulative position is as follows:

	Cumulative net cash flows	
	Lathe A	Lathe B
	£	£
End of year 1	5,000	3,000
End of year 2	9,000	6,000
End of year 3	12,000	9,000

If Lathe A is installed the initial outlay will be recovered before the end of year 3. The outlay on Lathe B will only be completely recovered during year 4. Lathe A would be chosen as the payback period is shorter.

This method gives due weight to the early years and stresses the importance of a rapid cash turnover, but goes to the opposite extreme of ignoring all cash flows after payback.

(3) Net Present Value (NPV)

A sound method of appraisal must avoid the biases of both Rate of Return and Payback by giving each annual cash flow an appropriate weighting. This can be achieved by using an appropriate rate of interest to discount these future cash flows.

There are many techniques within the broad heading of Discounted Cash Flow (DCF). The Net Present Value method is shown here because it is the easiest method to understand and apply in practice. The merits and demerits of NPV and other methods such as Internal Rate of Return, and Sinking Fund Rate of Return, are hotly debated by the specialists. The interested reader is referred to the accountancy journals for the latest state of the debate.

The principle behind NPV is quite simple. I would rather have £100 now than in a year's time. If a rate of discount (equivalent to the interest rate likely to be earned if the money were invested) is assumed, this preference for present cash rather than future cash can be expressed more accurately. For instance, at an 8% rate of discount, £10 in one year's time is equivalent to £9.26 today; £10 in two years' time is equivalent to £8.57 today. Putting this another way, £9.26 invested today at 8% would be worth £10 in one year's time and £8.57 invested today at 8%, would be worth £10 in two years' time. Diagramatically:

PRESENT VALUE OF £10 AT VARIOUS DATES

Rate of discount 8%

Present Value	Today	One year from today	2 years from today	3 years from today	4 years from today	etc.
£10.00 ←		£10	£10	£10	£10	£10
9.26 ←						
8.57 ←						
7.94 ←						
7.35 ←						

Tables are published which show the present value of £1, assuming different rates of discount. An extract from such a table is given over the page.

Present Value of £1.00 $(1+r)^{-n}$

No. of years from the present	6%	10%
1	0.9434	0.9091
2	0.8900	0.8264
3	0.8396	0.7513
4	0.7921	0.6830
5	0.7473	0.6209
6	0.7050	0.5645

For instance, if the estimated net cash flow from a project is £200 per annum for five years, the *discounted* cash flow at 10% rate of discount would be calculated as follows:

Year	Net cash flow £	Discount factor	Discounted cash flow £
1	200	0.9091	181.82
2	200	0.8264	165.28
3	200	0.7513	150.26
4	200	0.6830	136.60
5	200	0.6209	124.18
	£1,000		£758.14

The net present value of the project is £758.14. If the company is 'screening' projects, the present proposal would pass the test if its initial cost is less than £758.

The appropriate discount factor may be applied to the cash flows in the example. Ten per cent is assumed to be a suitable rate of interest for this type of project. The discounted cash flow likely to arise from installing Lathe A could be compared with the equivalent flows from installing Lathe B. As the following table shows, it is possible to arrive at the same answer by the shorter route of discounting differential costs only. The question to be asked is therefore, 'What is the net present value of the differential gains and losses from installing Lathe A rather than Lathe B?'

Year	Estimated net cash flows from installing Lathe A	Estimated net cash flows from installing Lathe B	Differential gains (+) and losses (−) from installing Lathe A rather than Lathe B	Discount factor 10%	Net present value of differential costs
	£	£	£		£
1	5,000	3,000	+2,000	0.9091	+1,818
2	4,000	3,000	+1,000	0.8264	+ 826
3	3,000	3,000	nil	0.7513	—
4	2,000	3,000	−1,000	0.6830	− 683
5	2,000	3,000	−1,000	0.6209	− 621
6	1,000	3,000	−2,000	0.5645	−1,129
Total			−1,000		+ 211

The total net present value of the differential costs is positive (+£211). On these assumptions, therefore, Lathe A would be bought.

Q.15f   Assume that there is a sharp fall in interest rates. Recalculate the example, using 6% as your discount factor. Which lathe would be bought?

In spite of some technical problems (such as choosing a suitable rate of interest in NPV) and the practical difficulty of trying to look into the future, there is no doubt that Discounted Cash Flow techniques give due weight to the time dimension in project appraisal. They are preferable to the rather crude approach of such techniques as rate of return and payback.

There are also a number of practical reasons why accountants should be prepared to spend time applying the more sophisticated approach of DCF, at least for major projects. In a time of relatively high interest rates, the time pattern of cash flows is of crucial importance. Government policies to stimulate capital investment through investment grants or taxation allowances need to be taken into account before decisions are made. Finally there is the most important point of all. Modern technology is capital intensive. Business success depends to an increasing extent on skill and judgement in evaluating high-cost projects. These proposals will originate with research scientists, engineers and other technical experts. The accountant's contribution is to prepare information about alternative proposals, so that any decision taken will at least be financially sound.

15.8   Additional questions

[1]
Accountants may adopt the Total Absorption Cost Method or the Marginal Cost Method when considering the apportionment of fixed overheads.

   (a)   Explain these two methods and discuss the implications consequent upon using each of them.
   (b)   Prepare a statement showing the effect of each method using the figures below:

	Standards per unit £
Variable costs	
Material	4.00
Labour	2.00
Fixed factory overheads	0.50

Fixed factory overheads were forecast at £18,000 p.a. at the beginning of the year when the annual budgeted production was set at 12,000 units.

Selling price was constant at £14 per unit.

The actual figures for the year turned out to be:

	£
Materials	39,000
Labour	21,000
Variable factory overheads	5,600
Fixed factory overheads	18,900

Actual production during the year was 10,000 units of which 8,000 were sold and delivered to customers.

(Your lecturer may suggest a suitable layout.)

[2]

The policy of Forbes Ltd is to establish selling prices by adding 25% to Total Absorption Cost. The company currently produces a single product (X) and forecasts:

	Per unit £	*Total for year* £
Direct materials and direct expenses	1.75	175,000
Direct labour (1½ hours)	0.75	75,000
Fixed overheads		150,000
Net profit		100,000
SALES (100,000 units)	5.00	£500,000

Machine time amounting to 1 hour is spent on each unit of product X. The directors believe they have developed another profitable product (Y) and decide to manufacture both products.

The selling price of product Y is set in accordance with normal practice, i.e. Total Absorption Cost plus 25%.

Specifications and operation schedules shown product Y is estimated to cost:

	Per unit £
Direct materials and direct expenses	3.00
Direct labour (2 hours)	1.00

Machine time per unit of product Y is 1½ hours.

The total available labour hours for the year will remain at 150,000 hours and machine hours at 100,000 hours. It will not be possible to increase these labour and machine hours during the year.

(a) Prepare an operating statement showing the unit and total costs of products X and Y, the selling prices in accordance with company policy and the profit made on each product and in total.
Comment on the company policy of setting selling prices.

(b) Assume that the production and sales for the year are forecast as follows:

Product X	60,000 units
and Product Y	20,000 units

Prepare a forecast operating statement for the year using this information.

(c) And now a more difficult part of the problem — assuming that a minimum quantity of product X of 40,000 units and product Y of 16,000 units must be produced to satisfy standing contracts calculate the total quantity of each product which should be produced and sold in order to maximize the forecast annual profit.

[3]
The Rodeo Co. manufactures a single product, and for the current accounting year the following information is available:

Current selling price	£5 per unit
Budgeted sales volume	20,000 units
Budgeted fixed costs	£1.80 per unit
Budgeted variable costs	£2.20 per unit

The management is not satisfied with the current rate of return on capital invested, and wishes to increase profit margins. On the basis of market research the Sales Manager produces the following forecast of the likely effect of possible changes in selling price on total demand:

Selling price	Sales volume
£4 per unit	29,000
£4.50 per unit	25,000
£5 per unit	20,000
£5.50 per unit	17,000
£6 per unit	15,000

At the same time the Sales Manager advises that by spending £6,000 on an advertising campaign all these forecasts of sales volume could be increased by 10%.
Advise the management on the best possible course of action to adopt.

[4]
(a) A company makes and sells a single product, which has the following characteristics:

Selling price per unit	= £5
Variable cost per unit	= £3
Total fixed cost	= £12,000 (up to a maximum output of 10,000 units p.a.)

Compute the breakeven point of the product in terms of sales value.

(b) An increase in output beyond 10,000 units per annum will cause the total fixed costs to increase to a level of £24,000 per annum (maximum output now increased to 20,000 units per annum). Assuming that selling price per unit, and variable cost per unit, remain unaltered, compute:

the new breakeven point in terms of units.

(c) If the selling price is reduced by 8%, what quantity will have to be sold in order to produce the same net profit as in (b)(ii) above?

[5]
Your company is considering two alternative projects which will require capital outlays of £85,000 and £120,000, respectively, at the beginning of the first year. Estimated cash inflows after tax arising from each project are as follows:

	Project A £	Project B £
1st year	20,000	30,000
2nd year	30,000	45,000
3rd year	30,000	45,000
4th year	25,000	40,000
5th year	20,000	
	£125,000	£160,000

Assume that the cash flow occurs at end of year.

You are required to determine which is the more profitable of the two projects, using a 10% discount rate.

[6]
A supplier of component parts has sent in a quotation of 46p for Part No. 613 which at the moment is manufactured in XYZ Company's own machine shop. An analysis of the cost information for the current accounting period reveals the following:

	Unit cost of Part No. 613 p
Direct material	20.0
Direct labour	10.0
Power	4.0
Depreciation on machinery	4.0
Consumable stores	2.0
Supervision and inspection	4.0
Rates and space charges	1.5
Other variable costs	3.5
Other fixed costs	3.0
	52.0

It is estimated that half of the depreciation charge is due to wear and tear, and half is due to the passage of time. Supervision and Inspection is a semi-variable cost.

The supplier's quotation is a firm price for the next twelve months. The XYZ Company expects that its own raw material prices will rise by 10% during that time and there is a strong possibility that there will be a 10% increase in labour rates for both direct and indirect workers.

If Part No. 613 were supplied from outside, the machine shop would be free to produce Part No. 619 instead. This component takes the same length of time to produce as Part No. 613, and it is estimated that it would make a contribution of 1.0p per unit.

Should the quotation from the supplier be accepted?

[7]
A firm has the choice of buying either Machine X or Machine Y to manufacture Widgets Mark II. Both machines can be used only for Widgets Mark II, and as they are both capable of a similar rate of output the decision is to be taken on financial grounds alone.

The firm's engineer has made the following estimates:

	Machine X	Machine Y
Life	3 years	6 years
Price	£1,000	£2,000
Operating cost	£	£
1st year	200	100
2nd year	400	200
3rd year	500	300
4th year		400
5th year		500
6th year		600
Scrap value	300	200

Which machine would be chosen,

(a) assuming that the firm is to cease production of Widgets Mark II at the end of year 3; and
(b) assuming that the firm is to make Widgets Mark II for the next six years.

Assume a discount rate of 10%.

There is a fair degree of certainty about the level of operating costs in the next six years, but there is a strong possibility that the price of machinery will have risen by 20% in three years' time.

[8]
Two companies, A Ltd and B Ltd, both manufacture and sell a similar product. A Ltd is labour intensive whereas B Ltd is capital intensive.

	A Ltd	B Ltd
Variable costs per unit:	£	£
Materials and components	2.00	2.00
Labour	3.00	0.70
Fixed factory expenses and depreciation		
p.a.	£20,000	£300,000
Production capacity (units)	10,000	100,000
Selling price per unit	£8.50	£8.50

(a) Prepare breakeven graphs for each company and read off the following:

(i) Breakeven points in units and in sales revenue.
(ii) Margin of safety.
(iii) Angle of incidence.

    (b) Check the breakeven points for each company by calculating them arithmetically.

        Submit your workings.

    (c)

        (i) Assuming the total demand for the product is 110,000 units, read from the graphs the profit made by each company.

        (ii) If the total demand falls to 100,000 units then, theoretically, what unit selling price should B Ltd fix in order to maintain its full capacity working?

    (d) Now assume another change in the circumstances. Each company produces at full capacity. Total sales were 71,500 units, and stocks at the year end in A Ltd were 3,500 units and in B Ltd 35,000 units.

Stocks in each company at the beginning of the year were not significant.

What value would you place on the year end stock if:

        (i) Each company had deliberately overproduced to meet a demand expected to increase following an intensive advertising campaign in the new year?

        (ii) The sales during the current year were depressed due to national economic conditions which are likely to continue for a further two years?

        (iii) Sales during the current year were depressed due to imports of a cheaper foreign product which performs similarly and is preferred by some areas of the market?

[9]

In Chapter 11 (question 7) you presented accounting statements and advice to Frank Jones concerning the maximization of his profits. Refer to these statements.

Now incorporate the following information supplied by Mr Jones:

Floor space devoted to:	
Electrical goods is	20%
Hardware goods is	40%
Crockery goods is	40%
	100%

Do you wish to change your advice to Mr Jones now that you have this additional information?

Explain why and re-draft appropriate accounting statements.

[10]

A newspaper group controls four newspapers and the following information illustrates the group's position:

	Grantham Record	Nottingham Daily	Leicester Echo	Derby News
	£	£	£	£
Sales	40,000	80,000	60,000	20,000
Materials	11,000	12,000	11,000	8,000
Labour	17,500	22,000	19,000	12,500
Factory overheads	4,000	8,000	6,000	2,000
Editorial staff	4,500	9,000	13,500	1,000
Local staff costs	3,500	8,000	17,000	1,000
	40,500	59,000	66,500	24,500
Profit (Loss)	(500)	21,000	(6,500)	(4,500)

NOTES
1. All the papers are printed in the Nottingham factory, and the factory overheads charge represents each newspaper's share of the total factory overheads.
2. The editorial staff and local staff costs relate exclusively to each newspaper and these people would be made redundant should their newspaper be discontinued.
3. There is a proposal before the board that only the *Nottingham Daily* should continue to be published as it is the only profitable paper. However, it has been estimated that if the *Derby News* were to be closed, £4,000 of advertising could be transferred to the *Leicester Echo*.
4. No savings would be made in the Nottingham factory if any one of the newspapers was still required to be printed there.

(a) Re-draft the original data in a form which enables management to see more accurately the position of each paper.
(b) State, with reasons,
 (i) the effect of the proposal before the board;
 (ii) the optimum policy based upon the information given.

[11]
A company, currently operating at 80% capacity, has the following Profit and Loss Account:

	£	£
Sales		320,000
Costs:		
Direct materials	100,000	
Direct labour	40,000	
Variable overheads	20,000	
Fixed overheads	130,000	290,000
Profit		30,000

It has just received an offer of an overseas order that would require the use of half the factory's capacity. The order, which must be taken in full or rejected completely, must be supplied at prices 10% below current home prices.

Management are in a dilemma. They can either:

(a) reject the order and carry on with home sales only as currently;
(b) accept the order, split capacity equally between overseas and home sales, and turn away excess home demand; or
(c) increase factory capacity so they can accept the export order and maintain the present home sales level by:
  (i) buying machinery that will increase factory capacity by 10% and fixed costs by £20,000; and
  (ii) working overtime at time and a half to meet balance of required capacity.

What course of action would you advise management to take?

[12]

A company is considering replacing a sound but somewhat old-fashioned machine by a more up-to-date special-purpose one. Unfortunately in five years' time the work done on these types of machines will end.

The following data are given:

	Existing Machine (£)	New Machine (£)
Book value	24,000	—
Resale value now	10,000	—
Purchase price	40,000	30,000
Residual value in 5 years	4,000	5,000
Annual cash running costs	9,000	8,000
Annual receipts from		
production	15,000	16,000

Depreciation on the existing machine is to be charged in the accounts at one fifth of (book value minus residual value in five years). Depreciation on the new machine would be one-fifth of (purchase price minus residual value in five years).

(a) Calculate the effect on the income statement of the company
  (i) if the existing machine is retained for the next five years,
  (ii) and then if the new machine replaces the existing machine for the next five years.
(b) Calculate the effect on the net cash flow of the firm in (a)(i) and (ii) above.

(c) Which of these calculations is more useful to management in making this decision.

[13]

The current costs of a product manufactured by the Dombey Co. are:

	Unit Cost
	£
Direct Labour	6
Direct Material	6
Variable Overhead	3
Fixed Overhead	5
	£20

The product is at present manufactured on a machine which can be expected to last ten more years, but which has no salvage or trade-in value.

A new machine to produce the same product would cost £100,000, and manufacturing costs would be:

	Unit Cost
	£
Direct Labour	4
Direct Material	6
Variable Overhead	2
Fixed Overhead	6
	£18

The fixed overhead costs comprise allocations of central service department costs and depreciation of machinery.

The new machine has an expected life of ten years.

It is expected that demand for the product will be 10,000 units each year at a selling price of £30 per unit. It is anticipated that the product can be marketed for ten years, after which it will be obsolete.

The appropriate time discount rate of the company is 10% per annum.

(a) Should the company buy the new machine?
(b) Assume the product could be purchased from an outside supplier at a price of £14 per unit. Do you consider the company should make or buy the product?
(c) Discuss briefly the principles and assumptions on which your conclusions for (a) and (b) are based. What other factors should be taken into consideration before a final decision is made?

[14]
Mr and Mrs Jones own a boarding house in Brighton. During the twenty-week season average occupancy is 20 guests per week at an average charge of £100 per person per week.

They have estimated their costs to be as follows:

	Costs for 1 week in season	Annual costs (excluding proportion for owner residence)
	£	£
Food	300	
Assistance with cooking and cleaning	150	
Laundry	20	
Heat and light	50	
Depreciation of furniture and equipment		1,000
Rates		1,000
Telephone, advertising and other expenses		3,000
	520	5,000

(a) Prepare a budgeted Profit and Loss account for the year based on the above data.
(b) Estimate the average number of guests per week in season required to break even.
(c) Mr and Mrs Jones are considering opening out of season for 32 weeks in cooperation with a local language school. What policy should they adopt when agreeing a charge for these guests with the language school?

[15]
Jack Bloggs, a redundant car worker, has agreed to renovate a dilapidated car for his neighbour. They agreed that he would charge 'full cost' for the work, which would take about 90 hours of his spare time, spread over a six-week period.

The other information available is as follows:

(a) Certain spare parts which he intends to use for the job cost him £18 last year, but would cost £26 to replace now. If he does not use them for this job, he expects to be able to use them in the near future on other jobs.
(b) Other materials and components would have to be purchased at a cost of £35.
(c) The work will be carried out in Jack's garage which he rents on a long lease for £5.00 per week.
(d) Equipment to be used cost £250 three years ago and has an expected life of six years. Wear and tear on this job is expected to be negligible.
(e) In addition to the above equipment, Jack will have to hire a hoist and some special tools at a total cost of £20.
(f) A car radio which was purchased last year for £27 could be sold second-hand for about £20, but Jack has agreed to fit it into his neighbour's car as part of the renovation work since he has no other use for it.
(g) Ordering parts and making various other arrangements connected with the job will involve a number of telephone calls amounting to 100 units. Jack's last telephone bill showed the following details:

	£
Quarterly rental:	15
Call units charged: 750 at 2p:	15
Total cost for the quarter	£30

(h) Jack was paid £3 per hour in his previous job.

Calculate the relevant 'full cost' which Jack should charge his neighbour, explaining your treatment of each of the above items.

Chapter 16

Limited Companies — Further Aspects

16.1 The Companies Acts

In this chapter we return to the topic of limited companies' accounts, introduced in Chapter 9. Some further considerations are now dealt with, particularly with the aim of helping you to comprehend company accounts in their published form.

There is little legal control over sole proprietors' businesses; they are relatively free to conduct their business affairs wisely or foolishly, according to their abilities. Admittedly creditors could suffer by their incompetence but it is a calculated risk — they are dealing with individuals and must assess their personal reliability and status. Similarly with a partnership, there are no specific legal constraints. The Partnership Act 1890 merely helps us to recognize when a partnership exists and to stipulate what rights and obligations between the partners will be implied if they have not otherwise agreed. If people go into a business and retain full personal liability for its debts, it is principally their own interests that are advanced or jeopardized according to their conduct of the business.

The situation with a limited company is very different. Even if it is a small private company managed by the principal shareholders, their liability is limited, and creditors or other claimants have no legal recourse beyond the assets of the company. The creditors of a larger public company are in a similar position, but additionally the shareholders also need some measure of protection for they have invested money in an organization in which they can exercise little effective control. Since the privilege of limited liability was first introduced in the mid-nineteenth century, there has been a succession of Companies Acts aiming to ensure that all reasonable protection and information is given to persons having dealings with companies. As the size, influence and membership of companies has progressively increased and as loopholes in the legislation have been exploited, so the codifying statutes have grown more extensive.

The Companies Act 1985 consolidated the relevant law up to that date and is the main source of reference, though subsequent developments will continue to require additional legislation. Many of the legislative changes in recent years arose from the need to harmonize our law with that of other member states of the European Community. EC 'directives' have to be incorporated into the separate laws of member countries within a specified time. Further extensions or modifications of company legislation can be expected for this reason.

You will have to study the statutory accounting provisions in some depth if you proceed with more advanced accounting courses but, within the scope of this book, it is sufficient to introduce what the 1985 Act has to say about accounting principles and the disclosure of accounting information. Only an overview is given here to show the general scope and purpose of the legislation.

16.2   Accounting requirements — principles

The paramount requirement for the form and content of company accounts is that the Balance Sheet must give a true and fair view of the state of affairs at the end of the financial year and the Profit and Loss account a true and fair view of the profit or loss for the financial year. This is referred to as the true and fair 'override' in that compliance with detailed regulations could still be insufficient if a true and fair view was not given — the spirit of the law transcends the letter.

But what is a true and fair view? It would be impossible to give a comprehensive definition and the Act does not attempt one, partly because the concept has to be seen in the context of the differing circumstances of individual companies and partly because it should not be frozen in time — opinions about truth and fairness can change according to evolving ideas of what constitutes good practice. It is a matter for the courts to decide in the event of a dispute, though judicial intervention is rarely necessary. Generally speaking, the true and fair concept means that accounting information must be adequate in both quantity and quality to satisfy what might reasonably be expected from those to whom the reports are addressed. This in turn normally means compliance with the detailed statutory provisions and also with the Statements of Standard Accounting Practice which guide accountants on the application of principles to various type of situation. However, both authorities may still be overridden if special circumstances required it.

Originally the Companies Acts concentrated more on the quantity of information to be disclosed in accounts rather than the quality but references to basic principles are now included, overlapping with some of the Standards. For instance, the fundamental concepts in SSAP 2 (going-concern, consistency, prudence and accruals) are given statutory recognition, so that all items in a company's accounts must by law be determined in accordance with them, and the accounting policies adopted by a company must be disclosed. Similarly there are requirements about such matters as stock valuation, provisions for depreciation and the treatment of post-balance sheet events which substantially repeat basic sections of SSAP 9, 12 and 17, respectively. Such overlap does not diminish the role of the standards — they continue to be the main instrument by which the accounting profession sets out what is regarded as good practice as the need arises, explaining the rationale and providing guidance for practical application. There are also several important aspects of accounting disclosure which are the subject of standards but not dealt with in the Act — for instance Earnings Per Share (SSAP 3) and Funds Flow Statements (SSAP 10).

As an illustration of how accounting principles are expressed in legal terms the requirement of prudence, referred to earlier in the book, appears in para. 12 of Schedule 4 to the 1985 Act as:

'The amount of any item shall be determined on a prudent basis, and in particular —

(a) only profits realized at the balance sheet date shall be included in the profit and loss account; and

(b) all liabilities and losses which have arisen or are likely to arise in respect of the financial year to which the accounts relate or a previous financial year shall be taken into account, including those which only become apparent between the balance sheet date and the date on which it is signed on behalf of the board of directors in pursuance of Section 238 of this Act.'

16.3   Accounting requirements — form and content

A substantial part of the legislation is concerned with stipulating the minimum amount of information a company must show in its 'published' accounts — those which are received by shareholders and are made available for public inspection by sending a copy to the Registrar of Companies. The annual Profit and Loss account and Balance Sheet prepared for internal use will, of course, include whatever detail the management requires for its own purposes, but making accounts public involves conflicting considerations. On the one hand, a company will be reluctant to reveal too much information to competitors but, on the other, those whose interests and decisions are affected by the financial performance and position of the company have a right to expect disclosure in reasonably adequate detail for their purposes. Successive Companies Acts have increasingly responded to the latter argument, recognizing the needs of various users including shareholders, loan and trade creditors, employees, analysts, government agencies and consumers.

However, the legislation has evolved in a rather *ad hoc* manner instead of being based on a comprehensive study of all these diverse needs, and there is no doubt that further progress still has to be made. The 'stewardship' role of directors who are accountable to the shareholders on whose behalf they act was the dominant influence in early legislation but, more recently, a broader view of corporate responsibilities has been emerging. The trend is also to recognize that for many decisions taken by various users, future expectations — or extrapolations of current results — have more relevance than past history.

Q.16a   Think what sort of information would be most relevant in each of the following cases. Then look through the summary which follows to see to what extent you think it is being provided as part of the minimum statutory disclosure requirements.

   (a) Shareholder with a large holding of ordinary shares deciding whether to vote for the re-election of the directors at the annual general meeting.
   (b) Employees (or their representatives) deciding how large a pay increase they should claim.
   (c) Potential investor deciding whether to buy ordinary shares in the company.
   (d) Potential investor deciding whether to buy preference shares in the company.
   (e) Bank manager deciding how to respond to an application from the company for a loan.
   (f) Financial columnist deciding how to rate the performance of the company in contrast to that of a competitor.
   (g) Potential supplier of materials assessing the creditworthiness of the company.

A distinction is drawn between the accounts sent to shareholders and those filed with the Registrar of Companies. Whilst a full version in accordance with the Acts is always necessary for the former, the level of disclosure in accounts filed with the Registrar depends on the status of the company. For 'small' and 'medium-sized' companies (as defined) there are considerable exemptions and abridged sets of accounts can be presented for this purpose.

If you look at the annual report of one of the larger companies you will usually find that it contains at least the following elements:

Chairman's statement
Directors' report

Profit and Loss account
Balance Sheet
Statement of accounting policies and other notes to the accounts
Statement of sources and application of funds
Auditor's report

The first of these is not mandatory and the sources and applications of funds statement is in response to an accounting standard (SSAP 10). There may be additional explanations and statistics, such as a statement of added value, and the report may be used partly to publicize the company's activities. Where the company is a holding company there will also be consolidated accounts for the group (see Section 16.8).

The DIRECTORS' REPORT must include, where appropriate, these items:

A fair review of the development of the business;
Particulars of important events occurring since the end of the financial year;
The principal activities and any significant changes;
An indication of likely future developments;
Details of directors and their interests in company shares and debentures;
Particulars about the company's purchase of its own shares;
The dividends declared and transfers to reserves;
Any substantial difference between book values and market values of the land and
    buildings and any significant changes in the fixed assets;
An indication of research and development activities;
Company policy regarding disabled employees;
Donations to political and charitable organizations;
Information about arrangements made to involve and consult with employees.

Schedule 4 of the 1985 Act regulates the presentation of the Profit and Loss account and Balance Sheet, though alternative formats are given and some flexibility allowed — for instance, in the extent to which details are shown within the statements or as supplementary notes. On the next page there is an illustration of a company Profit and Loss account and Balance Sheet in approved form but omitting some of the less common items. In addition to the information contained within these statements the company would have to provide supplementary notes, including the following:

A statement of accounting policies (e.g. with regard to depreciation and stock
    valuation)

Relating to the Profit and Loss account
Hire charges for plant and machinery
Auditor's remuneration and expenses
Depreciation of fixed assets
Directors' emoluments (considerable detail to be given, including the chairman's
    emoluments and those of the highest paid director if in excess of the chairman and
    the number of directors in rising bands of emoluments at £5,000 intervals)
Emoluments of highly paid employees (the number receiving more than £30,000 in
    rising bands at £5,000 intervals)
Details about the taxation charge
For each significantly different class of business a description of the type of business,

the amount of turnover and profit before tax, and the amount of turnover for each substantially different geographical market.

The average number of staff employed in total and by different categories, and the amounts paid for wages and salaries, social security costs and pension costs

Details of any extraordinary, exceptional and prior-year items

Details of interest charges and income from investments and rents

Relating to the Balance Sheet

Details of share capital and loan capital — the authorized and allotted share capital to be given including the number of shares and aggregate nominal value for each class and information about redeemable shares

A fixed asset schedule showing changes during the year distinguishing between cost (or revalued amounts) and aggregate depreciation

Information about the basis and amount of fixed asset revaluations and details of all items shown other than at historical cost

Details of investments including the market value of listed investments

Information about large shareholdings in other companies

For each type of stock (as in the balance sheet) the difference, if material, between the balance sheet value and replacement cost

Full details of loans to directors or officers

Changes in reserves and provisions

Information about the payment dates of creditors due after one year

Details of guarantees and future commitments.

COMPACT LTD

Profit and Loss account for the year ended 30 June 19X6

(Historical cost)	£000	£000
Turnover		960
Cost of sales		683
		——
Gross profit		277
Distribution costs	58	
Administration expenses	112	
	——	170
		——
Operating profit		107
Interest payable		10
		——
Profit on ordinary activities before tax		97
Tax on profit on ordinary activities		46
		——
Profit on ordinary activities after tax		51
Extraordinary loss	16	
less Tax on extraordinary loss	4	
	——	12
		——

	£
Profit for the financial year	39
Dividends	25
	—
Retained profit added to reserves	14

Balance Sheet at 30 June 19X6

(Historical cost)	£000	£000
FIXED ASSETS		
Tangible assets		
Land and buildings	105	
Plant and machinery	353	
Fixtures, fittings, tools and equipment	26	
	—	484
CURRENT ASSETS		
Stocks		
Raw materials and consumables	31	
Work in progress	69	
Finished goods and goods for resale	44	
	—	
	144	
Debtors		
Trade debtors	128	
Cash at bank and in hand	12	
	—	
	284	
CREDITORS: AMOUNTS FALLING DUE IN ONE YEAR		
Trade creditors	146	
NET CURRENT ASSETS	—	138
		—
TOTAL ASSETS LESS CURRENT LIABILITIES		622
CREDITORS: AMOUNTS FALLING DUE AFTER ONE YEAR		
Debenture loans		82
		—
		540
		—
CAPITAL AND RESERVES		
Called-up share capital		250
Share premium account		30
Profit and loss account		260
		—
		540
		—

In looking at this illustration note the following points:

(a) Remember that this is not a comprehensive example — some less common headings have been assumed not to apply and therefore are omitted.
(b) Comparative figures for the previous year also have to be given.
(c) The company in this example would qualify as a small company and could submit a very much abridged version to the Registrar of Companies.

(d) For the debtors, as with the creditors, any amounts falling due after more than one year would have to be shown separately.

(e) Alternative formats for both the Profit and Loss account and the Balance Sheet are given in the Act — for instance, the Profit and Loss account costs can be analysed according to types of expenditure instead of by types of operation. Using this format the first part of the account would be shown as:

	£000	£000
Turnover		960
Materials and services		420
Added value		540
Staff costs (i.e. Wages, Salaries, Social Security and Pensions costs)	368	
Depreciation of fixed assets	65	
		433
Operating profit		107

(f) In the Balance Sheet the Debenture loans could have been shown after the Capital and Reserves rather than as a deduction from the assets — the Balance Sheet totals would then have been £622,000.

Q.16b One item to be disclosed by way of note is 'commitments for capital expenditure'. This means sums of money which the company is committed to pay in the future in respect of capital expenditure contracts already signed. Though the contracts have been entered into before the balance sheet date, the sums involved do not appear as liabilities because the work has not yet been carried out. Why do you think there is an obligation to disclose this information?

16.4 Taxation in company accounts

The profits of all businesses are taxable. The net profit revealed by the Profit and Loss account is the starting point for calculating the adjusted profit for tax purposes. Adjustments are necessary because of statutory rules and associated case law which determine what expenses may be allowed or disallowed to arrive at the chargeable profits. For instance, expenses not 'wholly and exclusively' incurred for the purpose of earning profits must be added back to the original net profit, as must business entertainment expenses (except where the customers entertained are from overseas).

The depreciation figure included in the accounts must also be added back but in its place the business can claim capital allowances. These allowances are based on the expenditure on certain fixed assets and a set of statutory rules determine the amount to be allowed.

A simplified version of the adjustment of profits to arrive at the chargeable amount may appear as follows:

Net profit as per P & L account		£35,000
Add back depreciation	£20,000	
Non-allowable expenses	5,000	
		25,000
		60,000
Deduct capital allowances		22,000
Adjusted profits for tax purposes		£38,000

In the case of a sole proprietor the tax on the chargeable profits is assessed on the proprietor personally and will be levied at the rate of Income Tax appropriate to his or her personal situation. This also applies to a partnership, the partners being charged personally on their share of the total profits, irrespective of whether it is withdrawn from or retained in the business. A company is treated as a separate entity for tax purposes (as it legally is). The method of taxation which applies to companies only is *Corporation Tax*. The whole of the adjusted profits are subject to corporation tax, the rate of which is fixed annually for each financial year 1 April to 31 March.

Corporation tax is not an expense in calculating the net profit but an appropriation, because it is a tax based on the profit. It is some time after the end of the accounting period before the actual liability is finally agreed with the Inland Revenue and at least nine months before it becomes payable. An estimate is therefore included as an appropriation in the Profit and Loss account and as a liability in the Balance Sheet, any necessary adjustment being made in the following year. The interval before payment is such that the previous year's liability will often not have been settled and there may therefore be tax liabilities based on two years' profits in the same balance sheet. Where they appear depends on whether the liability falls due for payment within a year (current liability) or after more than a year.

When dividends are paid to shareholders no income tax is deducted from them but following each dividend payment the company must remit to the Collector of Taxes a part payment of the corporation tax liability calculated in proportion to the dividend (known as Advance Corporation Tax). This is then treated by the Inland Revenue as though it had been paid by the shareholders out of their dividends: each shareholder has a 'tax credit' for the amount concerned. Any individual shareholder who is exempt from tax would be able to claim a refund.

When the company pays debenture interest or certain other annual payments income tax is deducted at the source and paid over to the Collector of Taxes. Here the company is acting as an agent (unpaid!) of the Collector of Taxes in a way similar to the deduction of tax from wages and salaries. In the profit and loss account the debenture interest is shown at the gross amount because this is the real amount of the expense — it is of no consequence in the profit calculation that part of the payment goes to the Collector of Taxes.

Here is a simple example to illustrate the treatment of tax in a company's accounts. Remember that this is only an introductory text, so we ignore some aspects such as the entries for Advance Corporation Tax in order to concentrate on the main effects.

Bright Ltd had a credit balance on the Corporation Tax account on 1 January 19X7 of £160,000, representing the estimated liability in respect of profits for the year to 31 December 19X6. In October 19X7 this was settled at the agreed figure of £148,600. The profit before tax for 19X7 was £632,800 and the estimate of corporation tax on those profits was £215,000. During December 19X7 interest on the company's £800,000 10% Debentures had been paid (assume an income tax rate of 25%). The entries would appear as follows:

Corporation Tax account

19X7		£	19X7		£
Oct.	Bank	148,600	Jan.	Balance b/d	160,000
Dec.	Balance c/fwd	215,000	Dec.	Proft and Loss a/c	203,600
		363,600			363,600
			19X8		
			Jan.	Balance b/d	215,000

Debenture Interest account

19X7		£	19X7		£
Dec.	Bank	60,000	Dec.	Profit and Loss a/c	80,000
Dec.	Income Tax	20,000			
		80,000			80,000

Income Tax account

19X7		£	19X7		£
Dec.	Balance c/fwd	20,000	Dec.	Debenture Int. a/c	20,000
			19X8		
			Jan.	Balance b/d	20,000

Profit and Loss account (extract)

	£	£
Profit before taxation		632,800
Corporation Tax on 19X7 profits	215,000	
less Adjustment for overestimate on 19X7 profits	11,400	
		203,600
Profit after taxation		429,200

The amounts owing for corporation tax and for income tax would appear with the current liabilities in the Balance Sheet.

16.5   Sources and structure of capital

In Chapter 9 the methods of raising company capital by shares and debentures were introduced, but it is important to note that much of the additional long-term finance needed by companies comes from retained earnings. The profits that could reasonably be held back by a company to supply these additional funds may still fall short of the total required. Should the extra capital be sought from a further issue of shares or should money be borrowed? If the needs are relatively short term, a bank overdraft could be the answer, subject to the bank being satisfied that the business would be able to clear the overdraft within a given time limit. If the bank can accommodate a company in this way it may be preferable to use this source, depending on how the rate of interest compares with alternatives.

Returning to the question of whether shares or loans are the most appropriate sources of additional finance, consider the following situation:

XYZ LTD

Balance Sheet at 31 December

	£		£
SHARE CAPITAL			
100,000 £1 Ordinary Shares	100,000	FIXED ASSETS	150,000
RETAINED PROFITS	80,000	NET CURRENT ASSETS	30,000
	180,000		180,000

Net Profit before tax last year was £36,000, or 20% of capital employed.

The company now needs an extra £75,000 for long-term projects, and thinks it would be possible to raise it, A, by issuing 50,000 more ordinary shares at a premium of 50p, or, B, by issuing 8% debentures at par for the full amount.

		£
(A)	150,000 £1 Ordinary Shares	150,000
	Share Premium	25,000
	Retained Profits	80,000
		255,000

		£
(B)	100,000 £1 Ordinary Shares	100,000
	Retained Profits	80,000
	8% Debentures	75,000
		255,000

If the company continues to get a return of 20% on the capital employed, the profit of the succeeding year (before tax and debenture interest) will be £51,000. The amount of the profit attributable to each ordinary share, though not necessarily all paid out as dividend, will be as follows (assuming corporation tax at 50%):

			£
(A)	Profit		51,000
	— tax		25,500
			£25,500

= 17p for each of 150,000 shares

			£
(B)	Profit		51,000
	— interest	£ 6,000	
	— tax	22,500	28,500
			£22,500

= 22½p for each of 100,000 shares

The reason for this situation is that in (B) money borrowed at 8% interest is earning 20% profit, and so the balance is available for the shareholders. In (A) an increased number of participants have equal shares in the increased profit, and the amount per share is not therefore materially changed. This advantage of borrowing money naturally applies only where the rate of profit earned by the additional capital is in excess of the interest to be paid for its loan. If the earnings were less than 8%, it would be to the disadvantage of the ordinary shareholders.

Q.16c   The 17p and 22½p can be referred to as Earnings per Share (EPS). Calculate the EPS for both A and B if the profit before tax and interest was 4%; 8%; 12%; and 16% of the capital employed. At what level of profits would you expect the EPS for alternatives A and B to be equal? Plot the results of your calculations on a graph, as below, to illustrate the difference between the two alternatives.

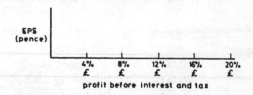

Here is a further example which shows the comparison for different levels of profits between a company having all its capital in ordinary shares and one with a proportion of preference shares.

Company X: £100,000 all in £1 Ordinary shares

	£	£	£	£
If profit after tax is:	2,500	5,000	10,000	20,000
Earnings per share:	2½p	5p	10p	20p

Company Y: £60,000 in £1 Ordinary shares and £40,000 in £1 5% Preference shares

	£	£	£	
If profit after tax is:	2,500	5,000	10,000	20,000
Preference dividend:	2,000	2,000	2,000	2,000
Balance available to Ordinary shares	500	3,000	8,000	18,000
Earnings per share	.8p	5p	13.3p	30p

The proportion of fixed interest capital included in the total capital is referred to as Capital Gearing. In relation to X, Y is a highly geared company because successive increases in total profits create more than proportionate increases in the residue attributable to the ordinary shareholders. Assuming therefore that a company can be reasonably sure of earning more on the money borrowed than the interest charge it is generally advantageous to seek extra capital by borrowing at a fixed rate. There are, however, limits to which the argument can be taken. To have too great a proportion of the total capital provided by loans would be dangerous. It may be disappointing, but not necessarily disastrous, to have a year in which little or no ordinary dividend is paid, but the company cannot survive if debenture interest is withheld. It must be paid, irrespective of profits, and the terms of debenture issues would usually give the holders the right to take some action in protection of their interests if it was not. Notice also that a company's borrowing powers would be limited by the terms of its Articles of Association and that long-term loans are usually contracted on the basis of some identifiable security, so the availability of suitable assets may be a factor.

16.6   Capitalization issues

The nature and use of reserves has already been discussed in Chapter 9. It was noted that profits retained in the business may be used to provide additional resources needed for expansion of the company's activities, and where this applied, they could no longer be regarded as available for distribution. Such retentions are being carried forward as part of the Profit and Loss account balance. The following is a further example of this type of situation:

	£		£
Ordinary share capital		Fixed assets	300,000
(£1 shares)	200,000	Net current assets	150,000
Share premium	40,000	(including cash at	
Profit & Loss account	210,000	bank £10,000)	
	450,000		450,000

Clearly it would not be possible to distribute most of the profits in the Profit and Loss account, and the position is unlikely to change materially. To show that part of the reserves should now be regarded as permanent capital, the company can transfer a given amount to the Share Capital account, and cover the transfer by issuing new shares to existing shareholders *pro rata*. This is termed a Capitalization Issue, or alternatively, a Bonus (or Scrip) Issue. It is the equivalent of partners transferring balances from current account to capital account though for partners no formalities would be necessary. Any reserves can be capitalized in this way. In our example it may be decided to capitalize £200,000, made up of all the share premium account and £160,000 of the Profit and Loss account. This would enable a bonus issue to be made of one new share for each existing share, and the new position would then be:

	£
Ordinary share capital	400,000
Profit and Loss account	50,000
	450,000

The shareholders in this example have had their holdings doubled but this does not mean they are any better off. If before the issue a shareholder, X, had 200 shares, he was an owner of 200/200,000 of the net assets (£450,000). Now his share is 400/400,000 of the same net assets. If the year before the issue the distributed profits were £20,000 (a dividend of 10p per share), X would have received £20. After the issue, if the same total profits are distributed, the dividend is 5p per share, and X will still get £20. If before the issue the market price of the shares was (say) £2.40, it is likely that the price will now be about half of that. In fact, the market price may settle at rather more than half, because a capitalization issue is generally regarded as a favourable sign in the development of a company and the stock market may respond accordingly. Also the greater number of share units at lower prices makes them easier to sell. There will be share issue expenses to be paid, particularly if additional capital has to be registered before the issue can be made. From the company's point of view, the main purpose of such an issue is to bring the balance sheet more into line with reality. It can be thought of as a stepping stone in its development that additional permanent capital has been achieved from reserves. Another reason is to avoid the impression that dividends are more generous than is really the case. For instance, in the above example, before the capitalization issue someone buying 200 shares would pay £480 and get £20 dividend, a yield of 4.2%. As the declared rate of dividend (10%) is based on par value there is quite a big difference, but by adjusting the par value the dividend rate is also brought more into line with reality.

The term Bonus Issue is commonly used, but as this incorrectly suggests that there is an element of gift about it, the more descriptive expression, Capitalization Issue, seems preferable.

16.7   Rights issues

A public company with quoted shares may wish to issue further shares for cash. Usually the existing shareholders would be given an opportunity to subscribe for the new shares in proportion to their existing holdings. This is known as a Rights Issue, and the procedure is justified on the grounds that the present members should be able to increase their stake in the company in priority to outsiders. The price at which the new shares are offered would be below the current market price of the existing shares, and if members wish to renounce the right to take up their allocation, those shares would then be sold and the difference between the preferential price and the amount realized paid over to that member.

16.8   Consolidated accounts

It is not appropriate at this stage for you to make a detailed study of methods of business amalgamations and their effect on the accounting statements. However, it may be useful to offer a brief explanation of the form of accounts published by 'holding companies' if only because most of the published accounts of well-known companies you are likely to be referring to are in this form. A holding company is one which has acquired a controlling interest in one or more other companies, which are then referred to as subsidiaries. This is usually effected by buying all or a majority of the subsidiary company's shares with voting rights.

The Companies Act requires that, whilst both holding and subsidiary companies continue to present their own financial statements, the holding company must also present a consolidated balance sheet and profit and loss account for the group of companies as a whole. The reason is that the holding company controls the affairs of the subsidiary, so there is effectively one economic entity even though they retain their separate identities.

Q.16d   It would be possible for one company to buy all the net assets of another company, the second company going out of existence. That would be an alternative to buying all of its shares and having its separate identity maintained. Can you think of reasons why the holding–subsidiary arrangement is usually preferred?

In a consolidated balance sheet the assets and liabilities of the whole group are amalgamated, as in the following example.

Balance Sheet of Company H

	£		£
Ordinary shares	800,000	Fixed assets	600,000
Reserves	200,000	Investment in S Ltd	400,000
Current liabilities	100,000	Current assets	100,000
	1,100,000		1,100,000

Balance Sheet of Company S

	£		£
Ordinary shares	350,000	Fixed assets	350,000
Reserves	50,000	Current assets	100,000
Current liabilities	50,000		
	450,000		450,000

Assume that H Ltd has just bought all the shares of S Ltd for £400,000 (shown as an investment in H Ltd balance sheet). The consolidated balance sheet would appear as follows:

Balance Sheet of Company H and Subsidiary

	£		£
Ordinary shares	800,000	Fixed assets	950,000
Reserves	200,000	Current assets	200,000
Current liabilities	150,000		
	1,150,000		1,150,000

What has happened in the consolidation process is that the assets and liabilities of S Ltd have been substituted for the cost of the investment. This is shown diagrammatically in *Fig. 14*.

The consolidated balance sheet now summarizes the position of the group as a whole and there would similarly be a consolidated profit and loss account to show the overall performance.

If H Ltd had paid more than £400,000 for the S Ltd shares the balance would be regarded as for the purchase of goodwill which, until it was written off, would appear as an asset in the consolidated balance sheet. Following the date of acquisition any undistributed profits earned by the subsidiary would be added to the group reserves.

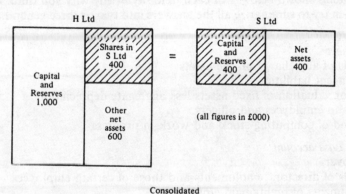

Fig. 14

Where all of the ordinary shares of the subsidiary are not acquired by the holding company, consolidated accounts are still required. The balance sheet would continue to show all of the assets and liabilities for the companies involved but the proportion of the subsidiary's net assets attributable to the minority shareholders would appear separately as a claim.

The example given above is very much simplified in order to illustrate the main idea of a consolidated balance sheet without obscuring it by including many of the complications which arise in practice. It should be sufficient to help you comprehend the basis on which such accounts are drawn up.

16.9   Additional questions

[1]
Section 228 of the Companies Act 1985 requires that the balance sheet must give a true and fair view of the company's state of affairs at the end of the financial year, and the profit and loss account must give a true and fair view of the company's profit or loss for the financial year. The obligation to give a true and fair view is stated as an overriding one. What do you think this means?

[2]
Information which has to be disclosed in a company's annual report and accounts includes the items shown below. For each item say briefly why you think it has to be disclosed. Then try to summarize all the answers into two or three general reasons for disclosure.

Balance Sheet
(a)   Details of any charge on the assets
(b)   Contingent liabilities
(c)   Cost or valuation of fixed assets less aggregate depreciation
(d)   Loans to employees and officers
(e)   Method of computing stock and work in progress

Profit and Loss account
(f)   Turnover
(g)   Details of directors' emoluments and those of certain employees
(h)   Emoluments of highly paid employees
(i)   Expenses for hire of plant and machinery if material
(j)   Any material effect caused by changes in the basis of accounting

Directors Report
(k)   Directors' names and financial interests
(l)   Analysis of turnover and profit between main classes of business
(m)   Contributions for political or charitable purposes
(n)   Particulars of important events occurring since the end of the financial year.

[3]
The following is an abridged version of a company's profit and loss account for the year ended 31 March, year 3:

	£000	£000
Gross profit		800
Miscellaneous expenses	300	
Directors' fees	50	
Depreciation	80	
Debenture interest	40	470
Net profit before tax		330

Of the miscellaneous expenses there was an amount of £10,000 which was not allowable for tax purposes. Capital allowances were agreed at £110,000. The rate of tax for the year was 30%.

Compute the adjusted profits for tax purposes, and the Corporation Tax assessment.

[4]

The following Profit and Loss account and Balance Sheet has been prepared for internal purposes. Show how the published accounts of this company might appear, limiting the information to that which has to be provided by statute. Present both the Profit and Loss account and Balance Sheet in the form required by statute. Omit the corresponding figures for the previous year but where additional information based on the items shown is otherwise required, include hypothetical figures.

GLOSSPORT MANUFACTURING CO. LTD

Profit and Loss Account for Year to 31 March

	£000		£000
Admin. expenses and salaries	1,164	Gross Profit	3,346
Selling and distrib. expenses		Dividend received	20
and salaries	733		
Directors' Fees	120		
Audit Fee	9		
Depreciation:			
Office equipment	22		
Vehicles	47		
Debenture interest	72		
Bad debts and increase in			
provision	6		
Net profit for year	1,193		
	3,366		3,366
Corporation tax	582	Net profit	1,193
Proposed dividend 3.5p per		Balance from last year	72
share	280		
Balance c/fwd.	403		
	1,265		1,265

(i)   The gross profit has been transferred from the Manufacturing and Trading account. The turnover for the year was £10,250,000. Depreciation on the plant and machinery of £455,000 has been charged in the Manufacturing account, and also Directors' salaries of £40,000.

(ii)   Administration salaries and Selling and Distribution salaries include £93,000 and £61,000 respectively for Directors' salaries.

Balance Sheet at 31 March

	£000		£000
Share Capital in 50p		Fixed assets	
Ordinary Shares	4,000	Freehold buildings	750
Share Premium	150	Plant and machinery	3,185
Profit and Loss account	403	Office equipment	198
		Vehicles	188
6% Debentures	1,200	Investment in associated	
Corporation Tax payable in		company	250
21 months	582	Current Assets	
Current Liabilities		Stock of materials,	
Trade creditors	231	finished goods and work	
Corporation Tax payable		in progress	1,953
in 9 months	360		
Proposed dividends	280		
Bank overdraft	85	Debtors and prepayments 777	
		less Provision 10	
			767
	7,291		7,291

[5]

From the following information prepare the Manufacturing, Trading and Profit and Loss accounts for the year to 31 March 19X2. Then prepare a Profit and Loss account and a Balance Sheet for publication.

M. RIVER & CO. LTD

Balance Sheet, 31 March 19X1

	£000	£000
FIXED ASSETS		
Buildings		453
Plant and Equipment		1,360
Vehicles		60
		1,873
CURRENT ASSETS		
Stocks	894	
Debtors	411	
	1,305	

	less		
	CURRENT LIABILITIES		
	Trade Creditors	166	
	Bank overdraft	28	
	Corporation Tax	193	
	Proposed dividend	70	
		457	
			848
	Net Assets		2,721
	50p Ordinary Shares		1,000
	Unappropriated Profit		1,721
	Capital employed		2,721

Other information:

(i) The original costs of the fixed assets were:
Buildings £600,000, Plant and Equipment £2,070,000 and Vehicles £86,000.

(ii) During the year ended 31 March 19X2 a capitalization issue was made of three new fully paid shares for every two held.

(iii) During the year ended 31 March 19X2 new plant and equipment was purchased for £190,000. New vehicles were purchased for £10,000 and old ones (originally costing £12,000) disposed of. The loss on the sale of vehicles (book values at 1 April 19X1, £6,000 less the cash received or trade-in values) was £2,000.

(iv) Plant and equipment is depreciated by 20% and vehicles by 25% on the reducing balance method, a full year's depreciation being charged on new items.

(v) The sales for the year ended 31 March 19X2 totalled £3,.614,000, and items of revenue expenditure during the year were:

	£000
Purchases of raw materials	1,036
Manufacturing wages and expenses	932
Administrative wages and expenses	480
Distribution, wages and expenses	270
Directors' salaries ($\frac{2}{3}$ manufacturing and $\frac{1}{3}$ admin.)	30
Directors' fees	10
Audit fees	2

(vi) The stocks at the two year ends comprised:

	19X1	19X2
	£000	£000
Raw materials	141	193
Work in progress	463	352
Finished goods	290	246

(vii) Capital allowances to be claimed for taxation purposes were estimated at

£303,000; £2,000 of the administrative expenses would not be allowable. Assume corporation tax at 50%.

(viii) A dividend of 5p per share was proposed.

(ix) Near the end of the year the company bought a 30% holding of the shares of another company for £250,000. No income from this source was received or due.

(x) Other balances at 31 March 19X2 were (in £000): Debtors, 452; Bank balance in hand, 13; Creditors, 103.

[6]

Now prepare the Profit and Loss account for M. River & Co. Ltd in the alternative format, showing value added. Assume that the breakdown of wages and expenses was:

	Wages £000	Expenses £000
Manufacturing	761	171
Administrative	375	105
Distribution	202	68

Compare the two formats and the information they convey.

[7]

A new company needs £1m capital and is considering three possibilities:

(a) £1m in Ordinary shares;
(b) £700,000 in Ordinary shares and £300,000 in 6% Debentures;
(c) £500,000 in Ordinary shares, £200,000 in 7% Preference shares, and £300,000 in 6% Debentures.

Calculate the earnings per ordinary share for each of the three possibilities assuming Corporation Tax at 35% and profits (before interest and tax) of:
£30,000;   £120,000;   £210,000;   £300,000.
Plot the results on a graph similar to the one in Q.16c, p. 291.
Note the 'breakeven' points as between A and B, and A and C, and explain their significance.

[8]

In Question 7 which of the three possible capitalization schemes was the most highly geared? What are the advantages of high gearing? What limitations are there to raising the gearing? What type of company would you expect to be suitable for a high gearing capitalization, i.e. what financial characteristics would it have?

[9]

A company with the following balance sheet proposes to make a capitalization issue of one new ordinary share (fully paid) for each existing share.

£1 Ordinary Shares			Fixed Assets	520,000
(Authorized and issued)	300,000		Current Assets	
Share Premium account	40,000		*less* Current	
Profit and Loss account	383,000		Liabilities	203,000
	723,000			723,000

The present market value of the shares is £2.20, and the dividend for the previous year was 12p per share.

(a) Before the issue is made what is the book value of each ordinary share in terms of the net assets as shown in this balance sheet? Mr X holds 400 shares. What is the value of his holding on this basis?

(b) What action in respect of the authorized share capital would be necessary before the issue?

(c) Show the revised balance sheet after the issue. Assume that all the Share Premium account is used. Ignore the costs of the issue.

(d) Recalculate the net assets value of each ordinary share and of Mr X's holding. Compare with the answer to (a) and comment.

(e) Explain to Mr X the possible reasons for making the issue and its effect. Include a reference to the dividend yield change.

[10]

A company with the following balance sheet proposes to make a rights issue of 100,000 shares at £1.40 each.

£1 Ordinary Shares			Fixed Assets	404,000
(Authorized and Issued)	400,000		Current Assets	
Share Premium account	20,000		Stock	291,000	
Profit and Loss account	257,000		Debtors	102,000	
				393,000
				797,000
			less	
			Current Liabilities	
			Bank	27,000	
			Creditors and	
			dividend	93,000	
				120,000
	677,000			677,000

(a) What action in respect of the authorized share capital would be necessary before the issue?

(b) Show the revised balance sheet after the issue. Ignore the costs of the issue.

(c) Mr Y holds 200 shares. Explain the options open to him, and the effect of the issue. Explain why issues are often made in this way rather than making an open invitation to the public to subscribe for the new shares.

[11]

The following is a summary of the capital employed by a company at 1 January 19x6:

	£
Issued share capital	
50p 5% cumulative preference shares	80,000
25p ordinary shares	600,000
Share premium account	40,000
Balance of unappropriated profits	134,000
10% debenture stock (19y5–19y8)	120,000
	974,000
The profit after tax for the year ended	
31 December 19x6 before appropriation was	150,000

An interim dividend of 2p per ordinary share was paid in September and a final dividend of 3p has been proposed. The preference dividend and debenture interest have been paid in full. The company proposed to transfer £10,000 to a reserve for replacement of fixed assets.

(a) Prepare the Appropriation account for the year to 31 December 19X6.
(b) Show the ordinary share dividend account in the ledger.
(c) What additional distribution to ordinary shareholders could legally be made but why is it unlikely that the company would consider using this availability?
(d) If a capitalisation issue of '1 for 4' was made what effect would this have on the position at 31 December 19X6? (restate the summary balance sheet).
(e) If the company was wound up on 31 December 19X6 and the net assets realised £1m how much per share would be repaid to ordinary shareholders?
(f) What do you think is the purpose of making the transfer to a reserve for replacement of fixed assets?
(g) Use these figures to explain what capital gearing means and to show its effect.

[12]
At its year end of 31 December Bright Engineering Ltd had the following balances in the ledger:

Trial balance 31 December (all figures in 000s)

	Dr	Cr
Land and buildings (cost and accumulated depreciation at 1 January)	160	15
Equipment (cost and accumulated depreciation at 1 January)	182	36
New equipment bought during year	34	
Vehicles (cost and accumulated depreciation at 1 January)	49	10
Stocks at 1 January	102	
Trade debtors	204	
Bank balance	23	
Trade creditors		210
VAT		10
10% Debentures		40
Debenture interest	2	
Sales		1,847
Purchases of stock	765	
Manufacturing costs	665	
Administration expenses	172	
Distribution expenses	67	
Directors' fees (10 C.O.G.S.; 6 Admin; 4 Distrib)	20	
Provision for doubtful debts (as at 1 January)		4
Bad debts written off during year	5	
Preference dividend	3	
Ordinary share capital (10p shares)		180
7% Preference share capital		40
Share Premium account		20
Profit and Loss account		47
Proceeds of sale of vehicle		3
Interim dividend on ordinary shares	9	
	2,462	2,462

You will need the following additional information: (all figures in £000s)
  * closing stocks were valued at   138
  * the vehicle sold originally cost 9 and had a book value at the time of
    sale of   5
  * during the year the land was revalued resulting in an increase to the book
    value of   20
    (this should be credited to a revaluation reserve)
  * the buildings (cost 100) are depreciated at 5% straight-line (80% of
    buildings are regarded as factory and 20% administration)
  * equipment is depreciated at 10% of the book value (all equipment can be
    assumed to be in the factory)
  * vehicles (assume all distribution) are depreciated at 20% of cost
  * the provision for doubtful debts is to be increased to   7
  * arising from a dispute with a customer it has been agreed to cancel an
    outstanding charge (inc VAT) of   8
  * corporation tax on the year's profits is estimated at   54
  * a final dividend of 1.5p per ordinary share is proposed
  * a contract has been signed for new garage buildings but work has not
    yet started   23

(a) Prepare the Profit and Loss account and Balance Sheet in published form so far
    as is possible from the above information. Include as part of the notes a schedule
    of fixed assets starting with the balances for cost and accumulated depreciation in
    the previous balance sheet and finishing with the new year-end balances.
(b) Outline the contents of any three additional notes which would have to be given
    relating to the data in the question but for which you had insufficient
    information.

This exercise is a particular opportunity to practice setting out your answer in good
order with notes and workings which will be clear to someone else — an important skill
for an accountant.

Chapter 17

Evaluation of Accounting Reports

17.1 Introduction

In Chapters 12 to 15 we saw how accounting could provide management with a means of guidance and control. To build systems of cost finding and cost control it was necessary to look for detailed information not to be found in the basic set of accounts discussed earlier in the book. We now revert to the statements of overall performance and position to examine how, by analysis, they can yield much useful information which is available to anyone having access to them. It can only be useful, however, if there is also an understanding of the effect of the concepts and conventions used by accountants. All of these aspects were introduced in Chapter 6, and this chapter now extends that discussion.

If you are embarking on a career in banking, you will find this aspect of accounting is given special attention. Businesses of all sizes may look with confidence, hope or anxiety to their banks for part of the funds they need, and in considering granting or extending facilities the profit and loss account and balance sheet will come under very careful scrutiny by the bank. Besides the lending banker, shareholders and prospective shareholders, debenture holders and prospective debenture holders, creditors and prospective creditors, employees' representatives and many others with an interest in the business affairs, may need to glean what they can from the figures. *The Corporate Report*,[1] published in 1975, was an important step in identifying the various users of accounting reports and their different needs. Only by a careful examination of how the contents of accounting reports might influence users' decisions can we judge whether the substance and form of the reports are adequate for those purposes. Improvement in this respect is an on-going process and is effected by individual initiative on the part of more progressive organizations and by national or international measures, either legal or recommendatory. We have already seen how extensions of statutory disclosure requirements partly serve this purpose, and also how publication of accounting standards attempts to reduce the areas of differences in accounting practice and establish more objective reporting standards.

Financial statement analysis is a skill to be developed. All sorts of useful ratios can be learnt, but the skill is in knowing which are the most important in a situation, how

---

[1] *The Corporate Report* — a discussion paper published by the Accounting Standards Committee.

much significance to place on the results and what supplementary questions they should suggest. This adds up to an ability which can only be improved with experience, and which requires a thorough understanding of the basis on which the statements have been prepared. It is perhaps analogous to the doctor's skill in recognizing and interpreting symptoms, and knowing what further enquiries to pursue. Before looking at the analytical methods, we should bear in mind some important considerations arising from the way in which reports are prepared and the effect of the concepts and conventions. It may be useful to look again at Sections 6.2, 6.3 and 6.4 before proceeding.

Remember, when examining financial statements, that:

(1) Whilst working within accepted principles, and preparing 'true and fair' reports, the accountant still has some latitude in deciding such matters as:

> the methods and rates of depreciation;
> stock valuation;
> overhead apportionment, etc.

These all affect the allocation of expense to particular accounting periods. In the long term the results are unaffected but choice of method can be a critical factor in any one year. Whilst accountants follow the convention of prudence this is often a matter of degree and depends upon judgements made about future events.

(2) The statements are historical. Investors and others may be at least equally concerned with prospects. Possibly the day will come when companies are required to submit budgets with their annual reports; but meanwhile, interested parties must rely on whatever portents are available. Financial statement analysis provides some trend indicators, but the balance sheet could still show a sound position when the outlook as evidenced by the state of the order book is depressingly grim.

(3) A balance sheet shows the position at a given date. Because of seasonal characteristics or special circumstances, this may not represent the typical position. For instance, businesses often adopt a year-end date coinciding with the low point in the operating cycle, if there is one. Stocks are then at a minimum and the balances of debtors, creditors and cash may be exceptionally low (or high).

(4) The statements are essentially in financial terms, and incorporate only those items resulting from monetary transactions. Other strengths or weaknesses, such as customer goodwill and human resources, remain undisclosed.

(5) The factor which probably causes most difficulty in appraising financial reports is the effect of the cost concept in a period of changing levels of purchasing power. The profit calculation and assets valuation can be seriously distorted by using out-of-date costs for measuring expense. This aspect warrants fuller treatment and an introductory explanation of the problems of accounting in a period of changing prices is included at Section 17.9.

17.2   Bases for comparison

Examination of any figure in a financial statement must involve comparison, if it is to make sense. To note that the net profit of the business is £50,000, or that its stock is £30,000, is meaningless without having some yardstick by which to assess it. The basis for comparison will depend on what figures are available, and on the nature of the enquiry. Possibilities are:

(1) Figures within the same set of statements, e.g. the adequacy of liquid resources would be examined by reference to the liabilities soon requiring payment shown within the same balance sheet. The relationship between figures in the same statement is sometimes referred to as a 'structural ratio'.
(2) Corresponding figures from the previous year or years, e.g. the turnover, would be compared with that achieved last year. This type of relationship can be referred to as a trend ratio. Companies often show in their annual reports comparative results over a period of five or ten years.
(3) Information from competitors' accounts, or from the figures for the trade as a whole, if available; for instance, how the rate of turnover of stock of a drapery business matches the average rate for the trade. Inter-firm comparisons are often available through trade associations or from a company which specializes in producing this type of information. There are also useful sources of information in some Government statistical publications.
(4) Forecasts — the management will be particularly concerned to see how the actual performance and position measures up to what they had budgeted.

17.3   Case studies

Through the remainder of this chapter we shall be using the final accounts of two companies for illustration and these are set out below. Before getting involved in any detailed analysis it would be useful for you to try to get a general impression of the performance and position of the companies. Would you guess that there are likely to be any particular causes for congratulations — or for concern?

C Legg Ltd is a small company manufacturing special packing cases supplied to shipping agents. The figures for the last three years are given.

C LEGG LTD

Profit and Loss accounts for years to 31 March

	Year 5 £000		Year 4 £000		Year 3 £000	
Sales		800		600		500
Cost of sales		520		360		300
Gross profit		280		240		200
Distribution costs	38		29		24	
Administration expenses	156	194	147	176	118	142
Operating profit		86		64		58
Interest payable		4		4		2

Net profit before tax	82	60	56
Corporation tax	36	26	24
Net profit after tax	46	34	32
Dividends	20	20	12
Profit retained	26	14	20

Note: Depreciation included in expenses	20	18	18

Balance Sheets as at 31 March

	Year 5 £000		Year 4 £000		Year 3 £000	
FIXED ASSETS		164		170		130
CURRENT ASSETS						
Stock	88		72		68	
Debtors	100		60		56	
Cash and bank	4					
	192		132		124	
CURRENT LIABILITIES						
Bank overdraft			2			
Dividend	20		20		12	
Tax	36		26		24	
Trade creditors	60		40		38	
	116		88		74	
NET CURRENT ASSETS		76		44		50
TOTAL NET ASSETS		240		214		180
SHARE CAPITAL (£1 ord shares)		100		100		100
PROFIT AND LOSS ACCOUNT		90		64		50
8% DEBENTURES		50		50		30
		240		214		180

Fassvend plc. is a public company operating a chain of food supermarkets. The figures for the last two years are given.

FASSVEND plc.

Profit and Loss accounts for years to 31 January

	Year 5 £000	Year 4 £000
Turnover	246,820	230,682
Cost of Sales	233,754	218,867
	13,066	11,815
Administration expenses	4,672	3,912
Net operating profit	8,394	7,903
Interest payable	580	480
Net profit before tax	7,814	7,423
Taxation	1,620	1,560
Net profit after tax	6,194	5,863
Dividends	1,392	1,248
Profit retained	4,802	4,615
Note: Depreciation included in expenses	1,620	1,490

Balance Sheets as at 31 January

	Year 5 £000		Year 4 £000	
Fixed Assets		43,240		38,300
Current Assets				
Stock	13,750		12,520	
Debtors	1,086		972	
Cash in hand and at bank	406		832	
	15,242		14,324	
Creditors due within one year	(24,718)		(24,662)	
		(9,476)		(10,338)
		33,764		27,962
Creditors due after one year		(5,800)		(4,800)
		27,964		23,162
Ordinary share capital (10p shares)		2,400		2,400
Share premium		180		180
Profit and loss account		25,384		20,582
		27,964		23,162

Notes: the creditors due within

one year include:	trade creditors	22,008	22,406
	taxation	1,750	1,440
	dividend	960	816

The creditors due after one year
are 10% debentures

17.4   Analysis of working capital

Funds available to the business on a long-term basis provide the fixed assets and the working capital resources.

Source	Use
LONG-TERM FUNDS Share capital Retained profits	FIXED ASSETS
Loans	**WORKING CAPITAL** Current assets − Current liabilities

In this section we look at some aspects of working capital, or net current assets. Adequate working capital is of paramount importance for any business. Too little could mean difficulty in meeting liabilities as they become due, or being unable to replenish stocks at the proper time or in the most economic quantities. Businesses often fail just when their prospects seem favourable because of inadequate working capital to provide extra resources as expansion is taking place. An upward trend in orders received means that more stocks have to be bought or produced before they can be sold. If the existing resources are insufficient for this purpose, they need to be supplemented by introducing fresh capital or by borrowing, and this is not always so easy to arrange. On the other hand, a firm may have more working capital than it really needs, so that a part of it is not being employed effectively. Working capital requirements of businesses in different trades vary considerably. Where a long production cycle is involved, expensive labour and material resources can be tied up over several months before the product is completed and sold. Conversely, a supermarket, such as Fassvend plc., has a very quick turn-round of stock, and sells items for cash often long before the supplier has to be paid for them. For this reason it is not unusual to find net current liabilities instead of net current assets in the balance sheets of supermarkets or even some retail organisations selling goods other than food. The creditors are, in effect, financing the stock holding, and mostly cash trading means that there are few, if any, debtors.

Working capital ratio

In trying to gauge the adequacy of working capital, a starting point is the relationship of current assets to current liabilities, or the working capital ratio. For C. Legg Ltd it is 1.7 in year 5, and 1.5 in year 4. Is 1.7 about right? There is no absolute standard against which to judge the ratio, though it would be useful to compare it with other figures for that particular trade. Ratios between 1 and 3 are typical, though there are many outside this range including the rather exceptional situation of supermarket trading. The real answer is that the analyst must judge the working capital position by looking not only at this ratio and how it compares with previous years and with the trade generally but also by an examination of its constituent parts.

Q.17a   Calculate the working capital ratio for Fassvend plc., and comment on the results.

Liquidity ratio

Can the business pay its way in the immediate future? Some clue may be provided by looking at those current assets which are either in the form of cash, or can be expected to produce cash in the course of a month or so. Against this, set the liabilities which will probably have to be met in the same time span. This relationship is sometimes referred to as the 'acid test' and can be expressed as a ratio — the liquidity ratio. For C Legg Ltd at 31 March, year 5, the quick assets appear to be debtors and cash, totalling £104,000: the stock is presumed not to be an immediate source of cash. The liabilities requiring payment in the immediate future are probably the creditors and the dividend, totalling £80,000: the tax will not have to be paid for another nine months or so. The ratio is therefore 1.3 (i.e. 104,000/80,000). Anything less than 1 may be viewed with some concern depending on the nature of the business, though it would not necessarily be fatal. There may be seasonal factors, or an overdraft may have been negotiated to cover a temporary shortage of liquid assets, as appears to have happened in year 4. A bank overdraft is classified as a current liability, as indeed it is. However, whilst in theory the overdraft is repayable at short notice, in practice many companies are able to rely on bank lending on a continuing basis. If a ratio considerably more than 1 is accompanied by a sizeable cash/bank balance, the question might then follow as to whether the business had more working capital than it could usefully employ.

Q.17b   What is the liquidity ratio for C. Legg Ltd at 31 March, year 3, and at 31 March, year 4? What is the main reason for the change?

Q.17c   Comment on the definition of liquidity in relation to current assets, bearing in mind the Fassvend plc. balance sheet.

Turnover of working capital

The above ratios provide some indication of short-term financial strength: generally speaking, the higher these ratios are, the less vulnerable is the business. However, the safety factor has to be balanced against operating efficiency. Are the working capital resources being utilized effectively? A measure of this is provided by the rate of turnover of working capital — computed by dividing sales by the average working capital. For C. Legg Ltd this gives £800,000 divided by £60,000 = 13.3. Again, to make sense of this ratio, we should need to look at the accounts of other companies engaged in a similar business, and also to compare it with the corresponding ratio for previous years. If the rate increases, this is probably a sign of greater efficiency because more sales are being generated by each one pound of working capital employed. The rate of turnover on some of the elements of working capital can then be separately calculated to show the factors contributing to the overall result. Where the balance of net current assets is immaterial, or where the current liabilities exceed the current assets, this ratio cannot be used.

Turnover of stock

For some statistical purposes this ratio has to be calculated by dividing the sales by the average stock. However, if the cost of sales figure is known, it is better to relate this figure to the average stock because both are expressed in terms of cost price. For C. Legg Ltd the cost of sales in the year ending 31 March, year 5, was £520,000, and the average of opening and closing stock £80,000 (i.e. (£72,000 + 88,000)/2). Therefore, the average stock has been turned over 6½ times during the year, or once every eight weeks (52/6½). For a manufacturer it must be remembered that the stock figure in the balance sheet will comprise raw materials, work in progress and finished goods and the relationship to cost of sales is not as direct as it is with a trader, where both cost of sales and stock valuations are in terms of cost price of goods available for sale.

Q.17d   Calculate the turnover of stock ratios for Fassvend plc. for the two years and comment on the change. (Note that where only two years' accounts are available you cannot calculate average stock for the first year, so, for comparison, the year-end figures have to be used for both years.)

Whether trader or manufacturer, from the management point of view, it is necessary to exercise all possible control over stocks, and there are techniques of varying sophistication to help determine the optimum level. To hold too much of any item ties up money and space unnecessarily, and there is the added risk of deterioration or obsolescence. To hold too little could cause waiting time in the production department, or a lost opportunity to sell the item. Some rough idea of the extent to which the business has been successful in its management of stock levels might be gauged from the year-end figures, though the management would want to have a great deal more than this for control information. The stock-turn ratio is an example of how seasonal factors can make a considerable difference. To get a more realistic average stock figure, we should add the balances at each month end, and divide them by 12, but this is not usually possible for the analyst.

Q.17e   If C. Legg Ltd improved their rate of stock turnover to eight times per annum, and carried the same quantity of stock, by how much would you expect the gross profit to increase (assuming that the improvement is achieved without changing the selling price)?

Turnover of debtors and creditors

The average debtors divided into the annual credit sales shows how quickly debts are settled on average. If we assume that in the year ending 31 March, year 5, C. Legg Ltd has no cash sales, the rate would be 10, i.e.

$$\left(800 \div \frac{60 + 100}{2}\right)$$

which is equivalent to 1.2 months. For Fassvend plc. most of the sales are for cash so this ratio is inappropriate.

The turnover of debtors ratio gives only a general indication of the length of the settlement period and, again, seasonal fluctuations could make a difference. If the year-end figures for debtors have to be used to calculate the ratios there could also be a distortion if monthly sales have been steadily increasing (or decreasing) through the year. From the management's point of view, constant control of outstanding debts is essential and there should be a regular review procedure leading to appropriate action being taken where necessary.

The average settlement period for creditor's accounts can also be calculated by dividing the trade creditors into the total purchases. For Fassvend plc. the year 5 purchases can be found by adjusting the cost of sales for year-end stocks (£233,754,000 + £13,750,000 − £12,520,000 = £234,984,000). The average trade creditors balance is £26,207,000 so the settlement period is 1.3 months (check that you can agree this calculation). Year-end, rather than average, figures may have to be used, depending on the information available, and the cost of sales rather than purchases would give an approximation of the same relationship. Note, however, that cost of sales for a manufacturer includes manufacturing costs other than purchased materials and also that the creditors balance could include amounts owing for fixed assets or other non-trading items. So there may be too many qualifications for this ratio to be of much value in some situations.

17.5   Long-term funds and fixed assets

Some attention having been focused on the working capital sector of the balance sheet, we now look at the overall structural relationships with particular reference to provision of long-term finance and the fixed assets. What proportion of the total long-term finance has been provided by loans? The answer for C. Legg Ltd is 21%. Generally, a low proportion suggests greater long-term financial security because there is less reliance on loans, which must eventually be redeemed, and the interest on which has to be met regularly irrespective of profitability. On the other hand, from the shareholder's point of view, a high gearing is advantageous if the borrowed capital can earn a better rate of return than the interest to be paid on it. On this sort of topic one cannot dogmatize, and much depends on particular circumstances. If the company has a large holding of fixed assets, particularly in the form of property, the issue of debentures is facilitated because of the nature of the security that can be offered. A speculative enterprise with a proportionately small fixed asset base would find difficulty in getting takers for a debenture issue. Again, a large well-established company is in a better bargaining position for raising debt capital than a relative newcomer. If debentures are secured on fixed assets, it is to be expected that there will be a reasonable safety margin of the asset value over and above the amount of the loan. Notice the date for redemption of debt capital. Companies usually have some options about the timing and method of redemption, but if the stated dates are getting close, the question arises as to how repayment will be made. Possibly a sinking fund has been built up with corresponding investments that can be realized, or the company may be intending to issue further debentures for the purpose. The gearing ratio shows the relationship of loan capital (and preference shares if there are any) to the whole of the long-term capital. For example, a company with £800,000 in debentures and £1,200,000 in share capital and reserves would be 40% (800/2,000) geared — which is very high.

Fassvend has a gearing ratio of just over 17% in each year (check the calculation). Though more debentures were issued in year 5 the shareholder's funds have also increased in approximately the same proportion.

Regarding the fixed assets, some general picture of the age might be deduced from the proportion of present book values to original cost. If it appears that plant, equipment or any other fixed asset is substantially depreciated, there may be problems about financing replacements, particularly at an inflated cost.

17.6   Assessing performance

Ratio of profit to capital employed

To see that this year's profit is greater than last year's may provide some initial cheer for shareholders, but there is little consolation if it was achieved only by a disproportionately large increase in the resources employed. Profit must therefore be expressed as a ratio of the resources employed before we can begin to assess the performance. The problem is to decide which figures to use in calculating the ratio. Is the profit the net profit before tax or after tax? By 'resources employed' do we mean all of the assets, or just the net assets after deducting current liabilities? There are many possible and admissible variations in computing both figures, and choice depends upon what we are attempting to demonstrate, what information is available and on personal preference. To make any sense of trends, the same method must, of course, be used consistently. For our purposes we shall use profit before tax, because we want a ratio which will compare the overall efficiency of the company with previous years. Since the amount of tax is beyond the control of the company, to include it as an element of profit calculation would vitiate comparisons, particularly if there was a change in tax rate, or if the incidence of capital allowances varied substantially. To the net profit figure we shall add back the debenture interest because this is a return to the people who loaned that particular part of the capital, rather than an operating expense. Profit will be measured against the net assets employed (i.e. total assets less current liabilities) because it is this amount that is invested in the business on a long-term basis. In our example, it is possible to take the average of opening and closing balances of the net assets employed, and this is preferred because it indicates the level of resources used throughout the year in which the profit was earned, rather than just at the end of it.

Having clarified these issues, we can now analyse the performance of C. Legg Ltd.

	Year 5	Year 4
Net profit (before tax and interest) as a percentage of average capital employed	$\left(\dfrac{86}{227} \times 100\right)$38%	$\left(\dfrac{64}{197} \times 100\right)$32%

Q.17f   Calculate the ratio of net profit to capital employed for Fassvend plc. for each of the two years (note that, again, you will need to use year-end figures rather than averages).

Thinking again about the capital gearing, it is noteworthy that the debenture holders of C. Legg Ltd received only 8% return on the part of the capital that they provided (£50,000), leaving the balance of the earnings from that amount to accrue to the shareholders. The position can be summarized as follows:

£4,000 payable to debenture holders who
provided £50,000 capital   = 8%
£36,000 payable to the Inland Revenue for
Corporation Tax
£46,000 accrues to shareholders who provided
——— £177,000 capital   = 26%
Total: £86,000 was earned by employment of £227,000
——— capital   = 38%

Ratio of profit to turnover

Having established that C. Legg Ltd's overall rate of return has improved since last year, we can now look at some of the contributory factors. The ratio of profit to turnover is about the same as last year.

	Year 5	Year 4
Net profit (before tax and interest) to sales	10.8%	10.7%

but this can be further broken down into:

Gross profit to sales	35%	40%
Expenses to sales	24.2%	29.3%
Net profit to sales	10.8%	10.7%

It appears that the company has increased its turnover by cutting profit margins, and that whilst expenses have increased, sales have increased even more, proportionally.

If a further breakdown of expenses was available, it would be useful to work out for each item the change in its percentage to sales. Overall there is a reduction from 29.3% to 24.2%, but analysing the behaviour of the individual items might reveal some that warranted investigation. Remember that many of the expenses are relatively fixed and their proportion to increasing turnover might be expected to fall.

Ratio of sales to net assets employed

We have already considered the turnover of working capital, i.e. how effectively was it employed? What sales were generated by each one pound of average working capital? As a further step in the analysis, similar ratios may be calculated for total net assets employed, as follows:

	Year 5	Year 4
Ratio of sales to average net assets employed	3.5	3.0
(i.e. sales to £1 net assets)		

The improvement in sales did not therefore require a proportionate increase in resources, or in other words, the resources are being employed more intensively than before. We have already shown that the profit as a percentage of resources has moved from 32% to 38%. The two principal reasons are now seen to be:

(a) Earning power per £1 of resources   increased
(b) Ratio of profit to sales   increased marginally

These key ratios are obviously interlocked in that they use different combinations of the same three elements.

$$\frac{\text{Net Profit}}{\text{Turnover}} (\%) \times \frac{\text{Turnover}}{\text{Capital Employed}} = \frac{\text{Net Profit}}{\text{Capital Employed}} (\%)$$

	$\frac{\text{Net Profit}}{\text{Turnover}}$ (%)	$\times$	$\frac{\text{Turnover}}{\text{Capital Employed}}$	$=$	$\frac{\text{Net Profit}}{\text{Capital Employed}}$ (%)
Year 5	10.8%	$\times$	3.5 times	$=$	38%
4	10.7%	$\times$	3.0 times	$=$	32%

The three ratios may be thought of as being at the apex of a pyramid, suggesting an appropriate sequence of stages for analysis and investigation.

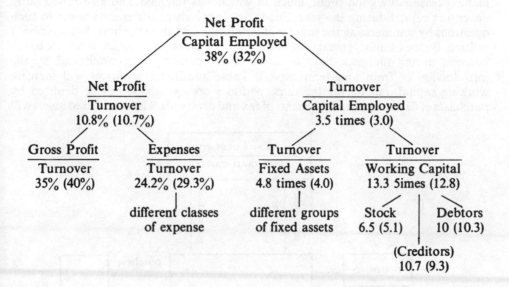

In the above example we used average figures for capital employed rather than those at the beginning or end of the year. An argument for doing this is that it gives a more representative view of the resources available over the whole year in which the profit has gradually accrued. In making trend comparisons from sets of published accounts this would not usually be possible unless the balance sheets for three consecutive years were available, so end-of-year figures may then be the best alternative. In all cases you should look for factors which could distort the ratios. For instance, a company may have raised a significant amount of new capital near the end of the year to finance an expansion of resources which had not begun to be reflected in the profits. Again, some companies revalue their fixed assets from time to time (particularly land and buildings) and create a revaluation reserve to reflect the increase in asset value. This could clearly make a significant difference to the net profit to capital employed ratio and would distort comparisons between companies with different policies in this respect, though it may be possible to make adjustments for the purpose of analysis.

Q.17g Using year-end figures for Fassvend plc. calculate the three ratios at the head of the pyramid (net profit to capital employed has already been calculated in Q.17f). Then proceed with the analysis as far as you think it is useful and summarize your conclusions about the company's performance.

17.7   Analysis of changes in resources (funds flow analysis)

In 17.4 and 17.5 we were particularly concerned with the company's financial structure and strength. In 17.6 the year's performance was analysed. Now we can employ a further analytical procedure to summarize the changes in structure between one balance sheet date and the next, and to relate them to the profit earned in that period. A question arising from the C. Legg Ltd year 3/4 statements is why the working capital position at the end of the year is worse than it was at the beginning when the company made a reasonably good profit, much of which was retained, and also raised more debenture capital during the year. Funds flow analysis provides the answer to such questions by summarizing the sources of new funds, and showing how they have been utilized. By 'new funds' is meant the additional resources that become available to the business during the year, both as a result of operating at a profit and by the introduction of fresh long-term capital. These additional resources will increase working capital, but during the same period working capital will be depleted by purchases of fixed assets, and payments of tax and dividends. The sale of fixed assets will

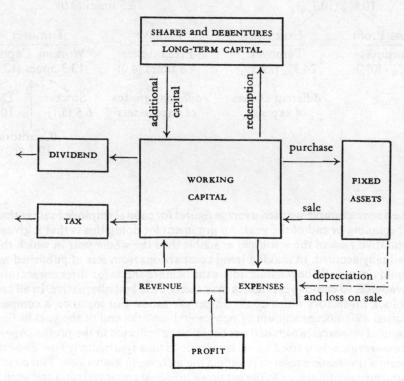

have the effect of increasing working capital, and redemption of debentures will decrease it. All these factors can be summarized diagrammatically (as above).

Notice that whilst depreciation is an expense of the period, it does not represent an outflow of resources: the resources were allocated when the fixed assets were purchased. Therefore the new resources during the period arising from the current operations will be the profit before providing for depreciation.

Consider the following example:

Balance Sheets

	1 January		31 December	
	£	£	£	£
Fixed assets — cost	8,000		11,000	
less Depreciation	3,000		4,000	
		5,000		7,000
Stock	5,000		8,000	
Debtors	10,000		12,000	
Bank	3,000		1,000	
	18,000		21,000	
Taxation	800		1,000	
Dividends	1,700		2,000	
Other creditors	7,500		9,000	
	10,000		12,000	
		8,000		9,000
		13,000		16,000
Share capital		10,000		10,000
Profit and Loss a/c		3,000		4,000
Debentures				2,000
		13,000		16,000

Profit and Loss account for year to 31 December

		£
Gross Profit		12,000
Expenses (including interest)	7,000	
Depreciation	1,000	
		8,000
Net Profit before tax		4,000
Taxation		1,000
Net Profit after tax		3,000
Dividend proposed		2,000
Retained		1,000

The sources of funds were the net profit before deducting depreciation (£5,000) and the proceeds of the issue of debentures (£2,000). Why is there not an extra £7,000 in the bank account at the end of the year? Obviously because funds have been used for other purposes rather than being left in the bank. To begin with, there is the payment of tax and dividend outstanding at the beginning of the year — since we included net profit before tax and dividend as a source any application of that net profit diminishes the amount available for other purposes. Then new fixed assets were purchased and more stock and debtors held. On the other hand, the creditors balance increased, so this was one of the sources from which extra assets were derived. Bringing all of this together we have:

	£	£
Sources of funds		
Net profit before tax and dividend		4,000
add back depreciation		1,000
Total generated from operations		5,000
Issue of debentures		2,000
		7,000
Application of funds		
Payment of tax	800	
Payment of dividend	1,700	
New fixed assets	3,000	
		5,500
		1,500
Increase/decrease of working capital		
Increase in stocks	3,000	
Increase in debtors	2,000	
Increase in creditors	(1,500)	
	3,500	
Reduction in bank balance	(2,000)	
		1,500

It is usual to present statements of sources and application of funds in this format but other variations are possible depending on what needs to be highlighted. There is a Statement of Standard Accounting Practice relating to Sources and Application of Funds statements (SSAP 10).

For C. Legg Ltd, year 4/5, the reconciliation of sources and application of funds is as shown below.

STATEMENT OF SOURCE AND APPLICATION OF FUNDS

SOURCE OF FUNDS	£
Profits before tax	82,000
add back Depreciation	20,000
	102,000
APPLICATION OF FUNDS	
Dividends paid	20,000
Tax paid	26,000
Purchase of fixed assets	14,000

Working capital items:		
Increase in stock	£16,000	
Increase in debtors	40,000	
	56,000	
less		
Increase in Creditors	20,000	36,000
		96,000
Increase in Cash		6,000
		102,000

Q.17h Returning to the question raised at the beginning of this section, explain, with the help of a statement, why the cash position of C. Legg Ltd is worse at the end of year 3/4 than it was at the beginning, despite the profit made during the year and the introduction of new long-term capital.

Q.17i Prepare a Source and Application of Funds statement for Fassvend plc. for year 5 and comment on the result.

Whilst it is interesting and instructive to do this type of analysis for a year in retrospect, it can also be employed for something which is perhaps of more concern to management, that is, in budgeting for the future. The interrelationship of budgeted profit with plans for capital expenditure, the need for extra working capital and the raising (or redemption) of long-term capital can be conveniently expressed as a projected funds flow statement.

17.8 Investors' ratios

In Chapter 9.5 it was shown that the rate of dividend declared on shares could be misleading because it is based on par values. If a 12p (12%) dividend was declared on £1 ordinary shares, and a shareholder paid £2 per share for his holding, the yield is only 6%. The yield is therefore more significant to the holder or prospective holder of shares than the rate of dividend. In the financial press the most recent annual dividend rates are converted to yield percentages on the basis of current market prices: this enables investors to compare the return from different investments on the assumption that the same dividends will be repeated.

The importance of yield compared with other indicators depends on the type of investment. Ordinary shareholders are the real owners of the company, and retained profits, as well as those that are distributed, affect them significantly. Yield is a prime consideration with debenture holders who have nothing more to gain than their return of interest at a fixed rate. The market price of debentures can fluctuate, but usually this would only be in response to changes in interest rates generally.

Q.17j If £100 10% debentures were bought at par at a time when interest rates were generally high, how would you expect the market price to react at a time when 8% was an acceptable yield for that type of investment?

Debenture holders are of course also concerned with the security of their investment and with the certainty of the interest being paid as it falls due. The latter point is of even more consequence to preference shareholders whose fixed dividend depends on there being adequate profits. They would have special regard to the number of times their dividend was covered by the profits out of which it was appropriated. The 'times covered' factor is a measure of the degree of safety.

	£	£
Net profit (after tax)		35,000
Preference dividend	5,000	
Ordinary dividend	15,000	20,000
Retained		15,000

In this case the preference dividend is seven times covered, which seems pretty safe. Ordinary shareholders, whilst not expecting the same margin, may also be interested in this factor.

Q.17k   How many times covered is the ordinary dividend in the above example?

Ordinary shares might be purchased not only for the dividend prospects but also in the hope of a rise in the market price so that they can be resold at a profit. The investor may go for speculative shares, such as those of an Australian mining company, with dreams of spectacular gains around the corner, or he may just be interested in having a hedge against inflation with safer 'blue chip' shares. Ordinary share prices are influenced by a number of factors both external to the company and internal. One factor is the amount of profit retained; or, in other words, the part of the profit which is reinvested on behalf of the ordinary shareholders. In addition to the yield, ordinary shareholders will also be interested in the total earnings which are attributable to them, and this may be expressed as earnings per share. If in the above example there were 150,000 £1 ordinary shares, the earnings per share would be 20p.

We have seen that the relation of share prices to dividends is measured by the yield. In the above example, if the market price of ordinary shares was £2 each, the yield would be 5%. Share prices may also be related to total earnings as an indication of how expensive the investment is when judged by the standards of how much it earns for the holder, in both distributed and undistributed forms. The Price/Earnings ratio is calculated by dividing total earnings available to ordinary shareholders into the current market valuation of all those shares. The result is 10 in our example:

$$\left(\frac{150,000 \times £2}{£30,000} \right)$$

Alternatively the P/E ratio can be found by dividing the current share price (£2) by the E.P.S. (20p).

Q.17l   If the price of a 10p ordinary share in Fassvend plc, was 181p at the end of year 5 calculate the E.P.S., the dividend yield, the earnings yield, and the P/E ratio. Why do you think there is such a big difference between the par value of a share and its market value? On the basis of this share price what is the market valuation of the company?

17.9   Accounting for changing prices

We now return to the problem of changing monetary values and its effect on accounting reports. Whilst the changes could be in either direction we have grown accustomed to inflationary conditions. The difficulties arise because monetary values at which items are brought into account soon cease to represent real values in terms of purchasing power. For instance, you may have invested £100 in a building society one year ago and thought that 6% was a good return. At the end of the year you have £106, so the apparent income (or profit) is £6, but what is your real income if in the meantime inflation has pushed up prices generally by 10%? It now takes £110 to buy the equivalent of what £100 would have bought a year ago, and it appears that from this point of view you have 'lost' £4, though there are probably other very good reasons for making this investment.

Consider the simple business example of a small coach operator who started on 1 January, year 1, with the whole of his £20,000 capital represented by one asset, the coach, which is expected to remain in service for five years. He charges £4,000 per annum depreciation in calculating the net profit, all of which is withdrawn each year, so that the capital remains at £20,000 throughout. If there are no debtors or creditors and no other assets or liabilities, the bank balance should increase over the five years by the equivalent of the depreciation retention to a final figure of £20,000. The balance sheet at the end of the fifth year would show:

	£	£
Fixed asset (cost)	20,000	
less depreciation	20,000	
Bank		20,000
Capital		20,000

Prices have been rising steadily over the five years and a new coach of the same capacity will now cost £30,000. Whilst the capital has been maintained at its original amount it has been eroded in terms of what it will now buy. It follows that the net profit arrived at by using original cost as the basis for charging depreciation was misleading: the proprietor should have withdrawn £10,000 less over the period if he wished to maintain his capital in terms of its purchasing power and finish in the same position as when he started. Notice that we have assumed here that 'in the same position' means that he is able to replace a specific asset of the same capacity without introducing fresh capital or borrowing money. An alternative view of being in the same position could be that the capital at the end of five years has the same general purchasing power as at the beginning. The two are not necessarily the same because coaches may have increased in price at a greater or slower rate than prices generally. We shall return to this distinction later.

A similar problem arises with goods held in stock. Assume that an item of stock is bought for £20 and sold a few months later for £32. In the meantime the cost price increased to £24. Using the historical cost concept we should show a profit of £12, the difference between the revenue earned and the cost of goods sold, but if all the profit calculated by this method was withdrawn the capital would again be eroded: it would not buy as many items of stock. Of the total £12, £4 represents a 'holding gain' and only £8 is an 'operating gain'. Profit is again being overstated and the proprietor should not withdraw more than the aggregate operating gains (taking into account other expenses) if he is to be able to replace the units sold and maintain his capital in terms of its purchasing power. When inflation was high in the 1970s it was estimated that almost half of company profits represented stock appreciation — holding gains that had been realized.

Many companies have long recognized this effect of inflation and tried to ensure that distributions of net profit are restricted accordingly, either by transfers to specific reserves or by just letting the profits accumulate as part of the increasing shareholders' funds needed for capital maintenance. Whilst this action is prudent it does not wholly answer the problem. Net profits are still overstated and, expressed as a return on capital employed, give a misleading impression of progress as the asset values become more out of date. For instance, if the coach proprietor made a profit of £10,000 before charging depreciation, his net profit would be £6,000, which is 30% of the capital employed in monetary terms. If he adjusted his accounts to allow for inflation he would show a profit of £4,000 (£10,000 − £6,000) in the fifth year, and this would be compared with capital employed which had gradually increased to £30,000, giving a 13% return. It also means that tax is being charged on unrealistically high profits, though the burden in this respect has been eased by adjustments to the tax system. Trying to interpret accounts prepared on a historical cost method and to make decisions on the basis of the figures disclosed is rendered extremely difficult unless there is some way of indicating the effects of changing prices. This applies both to decisions based on the annual accounts and to internal management decisions during the year, where the particular danger arises from under-stating costs of production or sales.

Any method of dealing with changing prices needs to adjust balance sheet asset figures to allow for fluctuations since they were purchased, and also adjust the historical profit so as to match current revenues with current costs rather than current revenues with historical costs. The net profit figure provides information for two main purposes — evaluating the year's performance and deciding how much to distribute. A net profit calculation after allowing for the effect of price changes is more relevant to both purposes.

Current purchasing power

Proposals for dealing with the problem have developed around two possible approaches — or a combination of them. One is termed Current Purchasing Power (CPP) accounting. This ignores specific price changes relating to different assets but uses a general price index, such as the General Index of Retail Prices (RPI) to convert the figures in the accounts to their current purchasing power at the end of the accounting period. The aim is to maintain the capital of the business in terms of its general purchasing power, and the adjusted profit is therefore the amount which could be withdrawn and leave the capital intact from this point of view. If at the time the coach proprietor started business the general index was 100, and it was 120 at the end of his first year, his profit should be the amount which, even though it was all withdrawn, would allow his capital to retain its general purchasing power. This would mean an adjusted capital of £24,000 represented by the coach with an adjusted book value of £19,200 (£24,000 less £4,800 depreciation) and the actual bank balance of £4,800. His profit, which is again assumed to have been withdrawn, would be £5,200 instead of £6,000.

There is, of course, much more to the calculation of CPP adjusted profits than is apparent from such a simplified example, and this introduction merely tries to show what the method aims to achieve. One important aspect of CPP calculations is the treatment of 'monetary items' — cash, bank balances or other assets or liabilities where the amounts are fixed by contract and are not affected by general price level changes (such as debtors, creditors and loans). In the adjusted balance sheet these assets and liabilities are still shown at their actual amounts but the profit calculation includes the losses or gains from holding monetary assets or owing money in a period of inflation. The illustration in the opening paragraph of this section reminded us that to hold cash or its equivalent results in a loss of general purchasing power if £1 buys less at the end of the period than it did at the beginning. Conversely, there is an advantage in borrowing money since less has to be repaid in terms of general purchasing capacity than was borrowed, though this would usually be offset by higher rates of interest on the loan.

The current purchasing power method seeks to show everything in a common unit (CPP £s at the date of the balance sheet). It emphasizes the proprietor's or shareholders' viewpoint — their capacity to maintain purchasing power in terms of a general index. Whilst this adjusts profits and valuations for general inflationary effects its serious disadvantage is that it may still be misleading from the management viewpoint of holding and replacing specific assets: for various reasons their values might have fluctuated to a much greater or lesser extent than would be reflected in a general index measurement.

Current cost accounting

An alternative approach concentrates on maintenance of capital in terms of operating capability, emphasizing the business, or entity, position rather than that of the shareholders as individuals. Current Cost Accounting is the term by which this approach has come to be known, though variations have developed, partly influenced by the same sort of reasoning evident in CPP about the effect of changing prices on monetary assets. An important concept is 'value to the business', which is normally the current cost of replacing the asset in its existing condition. For fixed assets such as equipment this means the present cost of buying a new equivalent item less depreciation to date. For stock items it would be the lower of replacement cost and net realizable value. The fixed assets and stocks are adjusted to bring them to their current value to the business in the closing balance sheet, and the operating profit takes into account depreciation and cost of sales amounts based on current values consumed during the year. If, at the end of the coach proprietor's first year, it would have cost £23,000 to replace his coach, he will show £18,400 (£23,000 − £4,600) as the asset value in the adjusted balance sheet and charge £4,600 as depreciation to arrive at the operating profit. Similarly, the cost of sales is the sum of the replacement costs which would be incurred to replace stock as it was used up, which eliminates holding gains from the operating profit.

Q.17m   At 1 January a trader has £500 capital represented by £400 in the bank and ten units of stock just purchased at £10 per unit. All purchases and sales are for cash and there are no other expenses. This is a summary of the transactions:

Date		Units	Total cost £	Cost price per unit £	Replacement cost at that date £
1 January	Opening stock	10	100	10	10
March	Purchased	20	220	11	
July	Sold (£18 each)	15			12
August	Purchased	25	300	12	
November	Sold (£20 each)	30			13
31 December	Closing stock	10			13

Before we use this data to illustrate current cost accounting, work out what the profit would be on a conventional historical cost basis using the FIFO method of valuing cost of sales. Also show the closing balance sheet.

Using the data in Q.17m the calculation of cost of sales at replacement cost is:

		£
July	15 units at £12	180
November	30 units at £13	390
		£570

and the holding gains arise as follows:

Units	Historical cost	in	Replacement cost	in	£
10	100	January	120	July	20
5	55	March	60	July	5
15	165	March	195	November	30
15	180	August	195	November	15
10	120	August	130	31 December	10
Total holding gains (including £10 unrealized)					£80

The calculation of CCA operating profit is:

	£
Sales	870
Cost of goods sold	570
Operating profit	300

This profit is £70 less than the amount you should have calculated using a historical cost basis as the holding gains on items sold (realized holding gains) have been eliminated. This revised profit calculation matches current revenues with current costs.

Following an abortive attempt in 1973–1974 to introduce supplementary financial statements based on CPP calculations it was the arguments for CCA that prevailed over the next decade as tortuous progress was made towards finding a solution that was both sound and practicable. Two adjustments to convert historical cost expenses to current cost have already been illustrated — those for depreciation and cost of sales. Two others also recognized as necessary are now briefly introduced.

The first is the Monetary Working Capital Adjustment. In a period of rising prices a business needs more working capital to finance not only its stock but also its debtors, since amounts owing from customers will be greater for the same volume of activity. Against this, however, can be set the fact that finance provided by creditors will also rise in monetary terms (for the same volume of activity). So these two components of the monetary working capital are considered in conjunction with each other in calculating what extra part of the year's profit should be held back to maintain operating capability. The monetary working capital adjustment is the amount to be deducted from historical cost profits to allow for increased monetary working capital requirements resulting from higher current costs — or added to historical cost profits if current costs are falling. The cash holding may also be included as part of the net monetary working capital if held for the purpose of the day-to-day operating activities.

The final stage is known as the Gearing Adjustment. If part of the total funds required to provide the fixed assets and working capital had been borrowed there would be two relevant consequences. First, interest on the loan would be an extra charge on the profits. Second, it would not be necessary to maintain the borrowed part of the capital in real terms because the loan will be repayable at its original monetary amount. As already noted, a company benefits by using borrowed money in a time of rising prices but, on the other hand, there is interest to be paid and the rate will reflect the level of inflation. If (say) half of the total funds were borrowed, half of the adjustments for depreciation, stock and monetary working capital could be added back, because only the capital attributable to the shareholders needs to be maintained. This assumes that the intention is to continue using borrowed money in the same proportion — that is, to keep approximately the same gearing ratio.

The original CCA standard (SSAP 16) required supplementary current cost statements showing the effect of these adjustments on the historical cost profit together with a current cost balance sheet. However, it was subsequently recognized that the main accounts can hardly represent a true and fair view if an alternative and more relevant version is appended. The proposal was then for current cost information to be incorporated as part of the main accounts, either as a note or by preparing the statements wholly on a current cost basis instead of historical cost. Here is an example of how the adjustment from historical cost profit to current cost profit might be presented in the notes.

		£000
Profit on ordinary activities before taxation (historical cost)		6,894
Cost of sales adjustment	720	
Monetary working capital adjustment	224	
	944	
Depreciation adjustment	316	
		1,260
Current Cost Operating Profit		5,434
Gearing adjustment	(315)	
Interest payable	209	
		(106)
Current Cost Profit before tax attributable to shareholders		5,540

(Then would follow the taxation charge and dividends.)

You will see that there appear to be two current cost profit figures. The first (£5,434,000) is the current cost profit earned by the organization as a whole irrespective of where the long-term funds came from — it is a relevant figure for judging the overall operating efficiency. The second amount (£5,540,000) is after allowing for the effects of borrowing part of the total funds required and can be thought of as a guide to how much (subject to tax) can be distributed whilst maintaining the shareholders' capital in real terms, though, of course, the actual distribution would depend on the company's policy and availability of cash.

Using indices, the annual adjustments can be approximated rather than having to rework all the detailed transactions for the year. Whilst this may suggest that the result will be somewhat arbitrary, it should be remembered that a figure which is relevant though approximate is preferable to one which is misleading though more definite. In any case, we have already seen that some figures in historical cost accounts depend on estimates of future events. The Current Cost Accounting standard (SSAP 16) was withdrawn but the professional accounting bodies continue to encourage companies to 'appraise and, where material, report the effects of changing prices'. A handbook to aid accountants in this appraisal and reporting was produced by the Accounting Standards Committee.

In this text we have dealt only briefly with alternatives to historical cost but, even at this stage, it is important to recognize how changing price levels can affect the financial statement.

17.10   Additional questions

[1]
The most recent set of published accounts of a limited company is made available to each of the following. What main points would each be looking for and what further information (if any) would they try to discover?

(a) A bank manager who is being asked for overdraft facilities.
(b) A potential purchaser of a large holding of ordinary shares.
(c) A debenture holder.
(d) A potential supplier of a large quantity of goods on credit terms.

[2]
Using the following balances and notes as appropriate, prepare:

(a) a Manufacturing and Trading statement for the year ended 31 March, year 3, and a position statement at that date, in a form suitable for presentation to the directors of John Simons Ltd at their next Board meeting;
(b) a 'pie-diagram' for inclusion in the report to the shareholders, showing the analysis of sales turnover broken down into its constituent parts, and a supporting statement analysing each £1 of sales turnover;
(c) calculation of the appropriate return on capital employed, and comment.

	£
Factory expenses	141,870
Selling expenses	45,400
Distribution expenses	32,700
Administration expenses	34,050
Wages incurred in production	85,120
Materials used in production	170,250
Sales during the year	567,500
Tangible fixed assets at cost	230,000
Depreciation provision to 31 March, year 3	83,800
Debtors *less* Provision	102,600
Cash	17,550

Creditors	107,600
Authorized and Issued Ordinary Shares at £1	150,000
Profit and Loss a/c at 1 April, year 2	55,390
8% Debentures	50,000
Stock of material, W.I.P., and finished goods at cost on 31 March, year 3	154,750

Provide for:

(i) Corporation Tax estimated on the net profit for the year which will become payable on 1 January, year 4; £23,000.
(ii) Debenture interest for the year.
(iii) Proposed dividend on ordinary shares of 15p per share.

[3]
Compare the position and performance of the two companies, A Ltd and B Ltd, on the basis of the following information. Both businesses are wholesale clothiers.

Profit and Loss Account, Year to 31 December

	A Ltd		B Ltd	
	£000	£000	£000	£000
Sales		1,000		2,000
Opening stock	200		240	
Purchases	700		1,540	
	900		1,780	
Closing stock	200	700	300	1,480
Gross Profit		300		520
Expenses		220		340
Net Profit		80		180
Dividend for year proposed		60		120
Retained profit added to balance of P & L A/c		20		60

Balance Sheet 31 December

	A Ltd		B Ltd	
	£000	£000	£000	£000
FIXED ASSETS				
Buildings	140		220	
Fixtures, etc.	30	170	80	300

	A Ltd		B Ltd	
	£000	£000	£000	£000
CURRENT ASSETS				
Stock	200		300	
Debtors	190		300	
Bank	110		—	
	500		600	
CURRENT LIABILITIES				
Creditors	80		200	
Bank overdraft	—		10	
Dividend	60		120	
	140		330	
Net Current Assets		360		270
Capital employed		530		570
Share Capital		300		200
Reserves		150		280
P & L A/c balance		80		90
		530		570

[4]

Following is a summary of the results of a trading company for three years, and of the position of the company at the end of each of the years.

Compute the following information and then write a report summarizing the salient features and offering possible reasons for any changes.

	Year 1		Year 2		Year 3	
	£	£	£	£	£	£
Sales		150,000		250,000		300,000
Opening stock	8,000		12,000		16,000	
Purchases	104,000		179,000		213,000	
	112,000		191,000		229,000	
Closing stock	12,000		16,000		19,000	
Cost of Sales		100,000		175,000		210,000
		50,000		75,000		90,000

	Year 1		Year 2		Year 3	
	£	£	£	£	£	£
Wages and Salaries	20,000		26,000		33,000	
Deb. interest,			1,000		2,000	
Depreciation	4,000		7,000		8,000	
Other expenses	14,000		16,000		22,000	
Total expenses		38,000		50,000		65,000
Net Profit before tax		12,000		25,000		25,000
Taxation		5,000		11,000		12,000
Net Profit after tax		7,000		14,000		13,000
Dividend		4,800		6,000		6,000
Retained		£2,200		£8,000		£7,000
Fixed assets		52,000		85,000		95,000
Stock		12,000		16,000		19,000
Debtors		18,000		40,000		48,000
Bank balance		10,000		4,000		—
		92,000		145,000		162,000
less						
Creditors	10,200		28,000		32,000	
Dividends	4,800		6,000		6,000	
Taxation	5,000		11,000		12,000	
Bank overdrafts	—	20,000	—	45,000	5,000	55,000
		£72,000		£100,000		£107,000
Ordinary share capital		60,000		60,000		60,000
Retained profits		12,000		20,000		27,000
10% Debentures		—		20,000		20,000
		£72,000		£100,000		£107,000

	Year 1	Year 2	Year 3
Gross profit to Sales		%	%	%
Expenses to Sales		%	%	%
Net Profit (before tax) to Sales[a]		%	%	%

Average stock	£	£	£
Rate of turnover of stock	times p.a.	times p.a.	times p.a.
Net Profit (before tax) to capital employed[b]	%	%	%
Working Capital	£	£	£
Working Capital ratio	:1	:1	:1
Liquidity ratio	:1	:1	:1
Rate of turnover of Capital Employed[c]	times p.a.	times p.a.	times p.a.
Debtors average settlement period (assume all sales were on credit terms)	months	months	months
Creditors average settlement period (assume all purchases were on credit terms)	months	months	months

(You can check some of the arithmetic by showing that $(a) \times (c) = (b)$.)

[5]
John Clark and Peter Dobson entered into a partnership three years ago to operate a garage business. Initially they sold petrol and oil and second-hand cars. More recently they have commenced servicing and repair work. They share profits in the same ratio as their capitals (Clark 4/7, Dobson 3/7).

They are now having discussions with Ron Eden about the possibility of his entering the business. A capital of about £40,000 has been suggested but, so far, no revised profit-sharing ratios have been mentioned. Eden would probably have to make an extra payment for goodwill.

Eden has asked you for advice. He has been given the information shown below and opposite. You are required to evaluate the performance and position of the business and outline the main points you would make to Eden. Mention any matters you think he should investigate further.

TRADING AND PROFIT AND LOSS ACCOUNTS

	Year 1 £000	Year 2 £000	Year 3 £000
Sales	632	759	1,023
Closing stock	51	92	164
	683	851	1,187

	Year 1 £000	Year 2 £000	Year 3 £000
Opening stock		51	92
Purchases	580	679	917
Wages, NI	43	52	83
Rent, rates	7	7	7
Admin. and miscellaneous	7	8	10
Heat, light and power	3	3	4
Depreciation	1	1	2
Interest			3
Net Profit	42	50	69
	683	851	1,187

BALANCE SHEETS			
Plant, equipment, pumps	23	27	35
Stock	51	92	164
Debtors	10	10	21
Bank	14	5	
	98	134	220
Creditors	21	25	42
Bank overdraft			4
Current accounts — Clark	2	8	12
Dobson	5	3	4
Capital accounts — Clark	40	56	56
Dobson	30	42	42
Loan			60
	98	134	220

[6]

From the balance sheets of a company summarized below prepare statements to show:

(a) sources and application of funds during the year, and
(b) why the bank balance has improved.

	Position at 31 March			
	Year 8		Year 7	
	£000	£000	£000	£000
FIXED ASSETS				
Freehold property		180		180
Plant and equipment at cost	1,236		987	
less aggregate depreciation	302		196	
		934		791
		1,114		971

	Position at 31 March			
	Year 8		Year 7	
	£000	£000	£000	£000
CURRENT ASSETS				
Stocks	285		237	
Debtors	117		83	
Bank	68			
	470		320	
less				
CURRENT LIABILITIES				
Creditors	64		58	
Bank			39	
Tax	107		48	
Dividend	72		72	
	243		217	
		227		103
NET ASSETS		1,341		1,074
Ordinary Share Capital		600		600
Reserves		541		474
6% Debentures		200		
		1,341		1,074

No plant and equipment was sold during the year.

[7]
Using the data in Question 5 (Chapter 16), p. 298, and in your answer to that question write a report on the results of the year and on the changes in financial structure. Support your answer with appropriate ratios and a funds flow statement.

[8]
Hall Ltd and Watt Ltd are two companies manufacturing and selling similar products. From the following financial statements calculate the main ratios and see what inferences you can draw from a comparison. In what respects is the information given inadequate for this purpose?

Profit and Loss accounts

		Hall		Watt
		£000		£000
Sales		480		360
Net profit before tax		44		42
after charging				
depreciation	(12)		(15)	
interest	(6)		(1)	
Taxation		18		16
Net profit after tax		26		26
Dividends		12		8
Retained		14		18

Balance Sheets (at end of year)

		Hall		Watt
Fixed assets		90		110
Current assets				
Stock	108		138	
Debtors	42		60	
Bank			10	
	150		208	
Current liabilities				
Creditors	30		24	
Tax	18		16	
Debtors	12		8	
Bank	20			
	80		48	
	—	70	—	160
		160		270
Ordinary share capital (25p shares)		60		80
Reserves		70		180
		130		260
Loans		30		10
		160		270

[9]
The following information is extracted from the accounts of a company.

	£000
Net profit before tax and interest	420
Debenture interest	20
	400
Corporation tax	200
	200
Proposed dividend of 10%	100
Retained	100
Ordinary share capital (£1 shares)	1,000
Reserves	1,250
5% £1 Debentures	400
Capital employed	2,650

At the same date the market values of the shares and debentures were £2.50 and 90p, respectively.

(a) Calculate the yields for the shares and debentures. Explain the difference between the declared dividend/interest and the actual yields and why the difference is greater for the shares than for the debentures.
(b) Calculate the earnings per share and the P/E ratio. You have noted that another company in the same industry has an after-tax profit of £300,000. There are 1.6m shares and the market value is £2.15. Compare the two companies on the basis of these ratios and comment.

[10]
Obtain three sets of accounts for companies trading in the same sector. Examples of suitable sectors for this purpose include: Builders, Breweries, Mail Order, Department Stores, Hotels. Try to avoid companies which are very diversified in their activities. Prepare a summary in tabular form to show the key figures from the accounts and also the key ratios. Include the market value of the shares. Prepare a report to summarize and comment on features which the companies have in common or which show distinct differences.

[11]
If the students in a group have chosen different sectors for the purpose of the previous assignment they can now compare and contrast their findings (possibly three or four students working together for this purpose). Try to find explanations for the main differences.

[12]
Charles and Henry have been trading in partnership for three years. Business has steadily increased but the liquidity position has worsened and overdraft facilities had to be arranged. The partners are puzzled by this apparent paradox and have asked you to

analyse the accounts and suggest possible reasons. The following information is provided:

Trading and Profit and Loss Accounts

		Year 1 £000		Year 2 £000		Year 3 £000
Sales*		300		320		480
Cost of goods sold		180		192		312
		120		128		168
Wages	40		44		52	
Rent, Rates, Insurance	16		16		16	
Delivery expenses	8		11		16	
Misc. expenses	12		12		12	
Depreciation	8		8		12	
		84		91		108
Net Profit		36		37		60

* In the first two years about half of the sales were for cash and the other half on credit but for the third year about two thirds are credit sales.

Balance Sheets

		End of Year 1 £000		End of Year 2 £000		End of Year 3 £000
Fixed Assets		88		92		80
Stock		20		28		76
Debtors		24		26		56
Bank		4		—		—
		136		146		212
Creditors	16		20		60	
Overdraft	—		2		16	
		16		22		76
		120		124		136
Capital Accounts						
Charles		60		60		60
Henry		60		60		60
Current Accounts						
Charles		—		2		6
Henry		—		2		10
		120		124		136

Draft a report evaluating the performance and position of the business.

[13]
Outline the main problems which arise from using the historical cost concept in a period of inflation and briefly summarize possible approaches to the solution.

[14]
'The rate of gross profit to sales could be very misleading unless the trading account is adjusted for the effects of inflation.' Prepare figures for two years which will illustrate this effect and explain why it is important for the trader to understand the implications.

[15]
John Wise commenced business on 1 January, year 1, with a capital of £20,000 which was all invested in packaging equipment. He buys goods in bulk, packs and resells them. In year 1 his sales are £240,000, and he buys goods for £210,000 of which £30,000 are still in stock at the year end. He depreciated the equipment over five years on a straight-line basis and his other expenses are £26,000, all paid in cash. There are no debtors or creditors. Calculation of the cost of goods sold at replacement cost would give £192,000 and the closing stock would cost £36,000 to replace. At the end of the first year similar equipment would cost £25,000 (new). Show his summarized Profit and Loss Account and Balance Sheet using both the historical cost method and also adjusting for inflation on a current cost basis. Show your calculation of the holding gains and assume that these are put to a separate reserve account. Explain the implications of the result.

[16]
Explain why the ordinary shareholders in a company which is highly geared may feel that they have an advantage in a period of inflation over shareholders in a similar company which has a low gearing. Would you agree that there is an advantage?

Chapter 18

Accounting for Different Types of Organization

18.1 Classifying organizations

Until now we have concentrated our attention on the accounts of *profit*-orientated business organizations. In the early chapters we looked at the form of accounts which might be kept by the sole proprietor of a business. In Chapter 9 we looked briefly at the form of partnership accounts. The Partnership Act 1890 defines a partnership as consisting of 'two or more persons trading in common with a view to *profit*'. Most larger-scale businesses are organized as limited companies. Chapters 9 and 16 have been concerned with the accounting requirements of companies. As we saw, one of the overriding legal requirements is that the accounts should give a true and fair view of the company's *profit* or *loss* for the financial year.

For a number of reasons it seems appropriate to extend our discussion of 'business' accounting to consider the accounting problems of other types of organization which lie outside the private commercial sector. *All* organizations, whether they are profit orientated or not, need to keep proper accounts. Sports clubs, trades unions and charities need to keep accounts of their income and expenditure and to draw up balance sheets to show their financial position. Government agencies need to account for the way they are making use of public money.

From a practical point of view, many examining bodies require an understanding of the accounting principles of several different types of organization. For instance, BTEC courses in public administration are classified under the general heading of business studies. As we have already seen in Chapters 12 and 14, it is as important to apply costing and management accounting techniques in the public service as in private business if these services are to be efficiently managed.

Variations in the accounting requirements of different organizations may arise from a number of causes.

(1) Differences between the public and the private sectors.
(2) Differences in objectives.
(3) Different legal requirements.
(4) Differences in basic operating systems.

To some extent these categories overlap. For instance: legal requirements will vary because there are differences in objectives between say a public limited company and a

337

local authority. Nevertheless it should be helpful to look at each of these categories in turn.

Central government departments, local authorities and public service agencies, such as the National Health Service, are publicly controlled bodies providing social and welfare services. There is, however, a whole range of other publicly owned organizations which operate as though they were commercial undertakings although they usually have to meet certain additional social obligations. The most important of these are such public corporations as the National Coal Board and the British Railway Board. In many respects these organizations follow normal business accounting practices. They sell goods or services to the public and must show the results of these trading activities in a profit and loss account. See the *British Railways Board* case as an example (18.5). As public corporations they must present their accounts in the form laid down by Parliament, and in general they must make more information available to the public than a public limited company.

In the UK the situation is further complicated by the Government's policy of 'privatisation'. Organizations such as British Gas and British Telecom which were formerly in the 'public' sector have been transferred to the 'private' sector. From a legal point of view they were public corporations but are now public limited companies.

1 The public and private sectors

A broad distinction is often drawn between privately owned and publicly owned organizations. The dividing line is sometimes blurred but the private sector–public sector categorization remains a useful one. Private-sector organizations are owned by people who choose to become involved: they provide the risk capital, have overall control and participate in the distribution of profits if there are any. Public-sector organizations are owned on behalf of the whole population, national, regional or local.

2 Objectives

Again we make a very broad distinction, this time between organizations producing and/or selling goods or services on a commercial basis and those which are not profit orientated. The former aim to cover the expenses incurred by the revenue earned through the market, the latter finance their operations from sources such as taxes, rates, grants, subscriptions or donations. Examples from the 'private sector' would include such voluntary organizations as churches, charities and clubs. Within the 'public' sector we might include the public organizations which provide health, social security, education, defence and police services (see the National Health Service case as an example (18.7)). Health and education services are, of course, also provided by private sector organizations working for profit.

The table shows how these categories overlap (*Fig. 15* on p. 339).

3 Different legal requirements

We have already seen that partnerships and limited companies are governed by different Acts of Parliament. Where a public limited company controls subsidiary companies we have seen that there is a legal requirement to prepare consolidated accounts for the groups. Local authorities, health authorities and similar public bodies must present their accounts in the manner laid down by Parliament.

Certain types of businesses must prepare their accounts in a particular format.

Examples of Organizations

SECTORS

<table>
<thead>
<tr><th></th><th></th><th>Private</th><th>Public</th></tr>
</thead>
<tbody>
<tr><td rowspan="6">O
B
J
E
C
T
I
V
E</td><td>Commercial</td><td>Sole traders

Partnerships

Limited companies</td><td>Publicly owned business
e.g. Coal, Post Office,
HM Stationery Office

Parts of local government operating
on a commercial basis — e.g. direct
labour organizations</td></tr>
<tr><td>S</td><td>Non-profit
organizations</td><td>Voluntary
organizations e.g.
trade unions,
churches, charities,
sports clubs</td><td>Central and local government
services e.g. the armed forces,
education authorities.

District health authorities.</td></tr>
</tbody>
</table>

Fig. 15

Financial institutions, in particular, are subject to statutory control over the form of their accounts in order to protect the actual and potential customers who need to be assured that their money is likely to be safe with the bank, building society or insurance company. The insurance company case 18.3 is an example.

4 Different operating systems

When we consider the wide range of business organizations — manufacturers, transport organizations, retailers, financial institutions, providers of leisure services etc. — it is clear that there must inevitably be variations in the style of reporting financial information. In the case studies which follow it will be of value to consider the basic operating systems of the organization first before looking at the form of the accounts. Look, particularly, at the insurance company case 18.3 and Central Television 18.6.

As a further exercise, obtain the published balance sheets of three organizations with entirely different operating systems e.g. a bank, a major retailer and a manufacturing business. Examine the form and content of the Balance Sheets and Profit and Loss Accounts of the three organizations. Comment on the differences in presentation which are apparent in these published accounts by virtue of the different nature of the businesses.

18.2 Introduction to the case studies

All organizations prepare annual operating statements, but there is a difference between commercial and non-commercial organizations with regard to their purpose and composition. Commercially-orientated organizations both in the private and in the public sectors use the accruals (matching) basis for measuring and reporting results. You will recall that this involves setting against the revenue earned in a period all expenditure deemed to have been consumed in earning that revenue, including a proportion of capital expenditure in the form of depreciation. The resultant 'bottom-line' figure of net profit provides two types of information — it is an indication of overall operating efficiency and it represents the amount available for distribution or capital accretion.

Social or welfare-orientated organizations do not *sell* services to users and so the notion of profit does not apply. The purposes of the annual operating statement in their case is to report how money has been made available and how it has been used. The bottom-line amount of surplus or deficit does not purport to be a measure of operating efficiency since the objective is to provide as good a service as possible within the constraints of resources available. Many local authorities match *current* income with expenditure relating to the period but account for capital items separately and do not include depreciation as an expense. The National Health Service also uses the current accruals method whilst government departments operate on a predominantly cash receipts and payments basis. With voluntary organizations the full range from receipts and payments accounting to full accruals accounting can be found.

These variations are reflected in the end-of-year position statements which, unlike the balance sheets of commercial organizations, do not usually purport to show what total resources are held as assets for future use and the corresponding sources to which they are attributable. For instance, most local authorities' balance sheets include capital expenditure items only to the extent that the loans raised for their purchase are still outstanding. Such balance sheets will, however, still show current assets and liabilities if the operating statements were prepared on a current accruals basis.

We are obviously thinking here about very diverse types and sizes of organization but, as we saw in Chapter 14, one thing they generally have in common is that the budgeting process is of crucial importance. Spending requirements or aspirations and prospective sources of income are then manoeuvered into line, and it is then that key decisions are taken about the level of taxes (central government) or rates (local government) or subscriptions (voluntary societies or clubs) and what spending limits are to be imposed. Financial accounting activities thereafter have a mainly controlling and reporting function. We have given no more than a glimpse of the many varied accounting arrangements within non-commercial organizations, but it may be sufficient to illustrate how accounting methods and reports respond to differences in organizational objectives.

For the remainder of this chapter we shall examine a range of organizations which need to keep accounts in a proper manner but which differ from the private trading or manufacturing businesses with which we can have been largely concerned in this book. We shall be adopting a 'case study' approach by selecting important and (we hope) interesting examples of actual organizations rather than attempt the impossible task of covering the whole field.

Some organizations (e.g. Royal Insurance and British Gas Corporation) are clearly commercially-orientated, but the form and content of their accounts merit special consideration. The professional football club is chosen because, although registered as a limited company, it is not *primarily* a profit-orientated organization. The hospital accounts are given as one example of public service accounting. Most of these case studies raise questions about the form, content and interpretation of the accounts. The reader is invited to consider each of these extracts in the light of the objectives of the organization. A well-presented set of accounts should reflect the activities undertaken by the organization, whatever its basic purpose. Any set of accounts should enable a reader to reach an informed judgement about the success or failure of an organization in reaching these objectives. Variations in the form of accounts are simply a reflection of the wide differences in objectives and activities between different organizations.

Although the examples are taken from actual published accounts, the years to which the figures relate have been omitted. The intention is not to consider the business issues arising from a particular set of business conditions but to examine the basic form of the published accounts.

18.3 Royal Insurance (UK) Ltd

Because of the special nature of their business, insurance companies have to comply with certain regulations designed to protect the interests of policy holders as well as shareholders. The nature of an insurance business and the way in which its overall profit is earned and distributed is clearly illustrated in the Consolidated Revenue and Profit and Loss accounts.

Revenue Account

	Year X
	£000
Premiums earned	518,947
Claims incurred	377,320
Commission and Expenses	164,524
Underwriting Balance	22,897
Investment Income on Insurance funds	56,395
Insurance Profit	33,498

Profit and Loss Account

	1983
	£000
Insurance Profit	33,498
Other Investment Income	15,925
Profit before taxation	49,423
UK and Overseas Taxation	20,410
Profit after Taxation	29,013
Dividend — Interim	7,600
— Proposed final	11,400
Transfer to Retained Profits	10,013

Discussion topic

Explain how the insurance profit for the year is calculated. Note that the investment income included in the insurance profit represents the earnings from the investment of insurance funds received from policy holders. Why is it necessary to distinguish between insurance profit and 'other investment income'.

In the Balance Sheet of an insurance company, the most important group of assets will be its investment portfolio and the most significant liabilities will be the provisions made against insurance liabilities. The provision for unearned premiums represents the proportions of premiums received which relate to periods of insurance subsequent to the Balance Sheet date. Outstanding claims include the estimated cost of all claims incurred but not settled at the Balance Sheet date.

Consolidated Balance Sheet as at 31 December Year X

	1983
	£000
CAPITAL AND RESERVES	
Share Capital	
Authorized: £2,000,000	
Issued: 1,000,000 shares of £1 each	
fully paid	1,000
Retained Profits and Other Reserves	44,497
	45,497
Investment Fluctuation Account	221,206
	266,703
SECURED LOANS OF SUBSIDIARIES	3,739
INSURANCE FUNDS	
Unearned Premiums	241,938
Outstanding Claims	383,441
DEFERRED TAXATION	10,292
SUNDRY LIABILITIES AND PROVISIONS	75,164
	981,277
Represented by	
INVESTMENTS	
British Government Securities	344,041
Overseas Government Securities	32,792
Local Authority Securities	1,802
Debentures	4,734
Preference Stocks and Shares	20,901
Ordinary Stocks and Shares	198,313
Mortgages and Loans	19,749
Freehold and Leasehold Property	136,432
	758,764
OTHER ASSETS	222,513
	981,277

Discussion topics

(a) Why does the portfolio of investments include a number of different types of securities, loans, shares and property investments? What is the reason for including each type of investment in the portfolio?

(b) The investments are shown at market value at the balance sheet date and properties at professional valuation. What would be the effect on the balance sheet if, because of a slump in stock market prices, the investments are revalued at £550m?

(c) 'Other Assets' include bank balances, debtors and fixtures and fittings but do not include a figure for premises, even though the company occupies a number of branch offices, most of which are located on valuable sites in city centres. Comment on this position.

18.4   British Gas

The overall efficiency of the business may be assessed by examining the published set of performance ratios over a period. The table on page 344 is a selection of some key ratios over five years to indicate trends.

Discussion topics

(a) Notice that return on profit is calculated on both a 'current cost' basis. Explain this term and comment on the significance of the results.

(b) Comment on any trends in total operating costs and the consistent elements in those costs.

(c) Comment generally on the performance of British Gas Corporation over this period.

18.5   British Railways Board

According to the Transport Act 1968 the British Railways Board is under a statutory obligation to ensure that revenues should be 'not less than sufficient to meet ... charges properly chargeable to revenue account, taking one year with another'. In less legal language the Board must try to keep out of the red. At the same time the Board has to meet other objectives which limit its ability to run the railway system on strictly commercial lines even if it wanted to do so. Although inter-city and busy commuter passenger business could be run profitably, many other lines can only be justified in terms of their value as a public service.

The extract on page 345 is a simplified version of the published accounts for year X. The commentary shows how the form of the accounts highlights some of the main issues which this public corporation has to face, in particular the need to account for its unremunerative passenger services.

		Year 1	Year 2	Year 3	Year 4	Year 5
				RATIOS ON THERMS SOLD		
Turnover	Pence per therm	37.01	38.96	41.11	40.28	39.37
Operating costs:						
Gas prime materials	Pence per therm	13.08	15.95	18.05	16.01	14.52
Gas levy	Pence per therm	3.05	2.84	2.78	2.66	2.51
Gas prime materials plus gas levy	Pence per therm	16.13	18.79	20.83	18.67	17.03
Other operating costs	Pence per therm	16.00	16.44	16.50	16.31	16.71
Total operating costs	Pence per therm	32.13	35.23	37.33	34.98	33.74
Current cost operating profit	Pence per therm	4.88	3.73	3.78	5.30	5.63
Gas prime materials plus gas levy per therm as an index	(Year 1 = 100)	100	116	129	116	106
Other operating costs per therm as an index	(Year 1 = 100)	100	103	103	102	104
Retail price index	(Year 1 = 100)	100	105	111	115	119
				EMPLOYEES		
Therms sold per direct employee	000 therms	174.0	185.7	203.5	213.6	220.3
Therms sold per employee (direct and contractor)	000 therms	155.0	164.9	179.9	186.0	191.9

BRITISH RAILWAYS BOARD

Group Profit and Loss account: year X

	Total £m
TURNOVER	
Turnover, excluding Government grant	2,255.4
Government grant	933.4
	3,188.8
Operating expenditure	3,113.2
Other income (net)	11.0
SURPLUS BEFORE INTEREST	86.6
Interest payable and similar charges	75.3
SURPLUS ON ORDINARY ACTIVITIES	11.3
Extraordinary surplus	0.4
GROUP SURPLUS FOR THE FINANCIAL YEAR	11.7
Amounts transferred to reserves	(3.9)
GROUP SURPLUS AFTER TRANSFERS FROM RESERVES	7.8

Commentary

(1) Under the Railways Act 1974 the Board receives a grant for providing unremunerative passenger services (£933.4m in Year X). This compensation for carrying out its 'social' obligation is added to the Board's 'commercial' turnover to give a total turnover for the rail businesses of £2,925.0m.

(2) A public corporation does not have shareholders and therefore does not declare dividends. As a result of the legislation setting up the BRB and subsequent transactions, the Board now has capital liability to the Government of £435m repayable at various dates. It has also to pay interest on other loans. The total interest payable on these debts has the effect of reducing the surplus on current operations from £86.6m to £11.3m.

Discussion topic

The permanent way and stations which were built in the nineteenth century comprise the basic structure of the British railway network and the British Railways Board is, in effect, the 'heir' to all these assets. Comment on the Board's current depreciation policies (see the following extract) in the light of this historical situation and what you know of the railway modernization programme.

Extract from Statement of Accounting Policies

(1) *Depreciation-type assets*

Depreciation is provided on the cost of the assets over periods related to their estimated useful lives and normally commences from the beginning of the year following entry into service. Lives used for the major assets are:

Locomotives	20 years
High-Speed Trains	15 years
Electric multiple units	25 years
Passenger carriages	20 years
Wagons	15 years
Plant and equipment	4–20 years

Alterations and modifications to assets are charged to Revenue Account as incurred.

(2) *Buildings, way and structure-type assets*

Expenditure on additions, alterations and replacement of buildings above the minimum monetary level, and certain expenditure on track works in connection with major additions to routes and new electrification schemes, is capitalized.

Expenditure on replacements and alterations to all other way and structure assets including track works and all signal and telecommunications equipment is charged to Revenue Account as incurred.

The expenditure capitalized over periods fixed with due regard to the useful lives of the assets but with a maximum of 33 years. As regards rail assets, expenditure prior to 1963 was written off at 1 January 1969 and certain further expenditure was written off at 1 January 1975.

(3) *Land*

A nil value is attributed to rail operational land.

18.6 Central Independent Television plc

Central Television holds the franchise to operate an independent or 'commercial' television service for the East and West Midlands. As a public limited company, its shareholders will be looking for an adequate return on their investment. At the same time the company must observe certain standards and meet certain conditions under the terms of its contract. In simple terms, if Central were to screen little else apart from quiz shows, old American films and pop music programmes, the Company's present contract would be unlikely to be renewed after it expires. The company therefore makes a number of documentaries, educational and minority-interest programmes which may not secure as large an audience as 'soap operas' and which may be expensive to produce compared with some more popular programmes. Indeed, Central makes the proud claim that 'it has continued to make both a greater number and a greater variety of documentaries than any other ITV company'.

The following extracts from Central's report and accounts for Year X should be largely self-explanatory.

Consolidated Profit and Loss Account for the year ended 31 December Year X

	£000	£000
Net income (see Note 1)		129,235
Expenditure of transmitted programmes	(42,701)	
Operating charges (see Note 2)	(79,240)	
		(121,941)
Profit on ordinary activities before Exchequer levy		7,294
Exchequer levy		(465)
Profit on ordinary activities before taxation		6,829
Tax on profit on ordinary activities		(2,883)
Profit on ordinary activities before taxation		3,946
Extraordinary items after taxation		147
Profit for the financial year		4,093
Dividend proposed		(1,625)
Retained profit for the year		2,468
Loss brought forward		(685)
Retained profit carried forward		1,783

NOTES TO THE ACCOUNTS

1. *Net Income*	Year X
	£000
Advertising revenue less discounts	131,982
Sales of programmes	14,684
Sundry income	2,741
Turnover, exclusive of value added tax and intra-group sales	149,407
Advertising agency commissions	(20,172)
Net income	129,235

2. *Operating Charges*	Year X
	£000
Staff costs	30,377
Depreciation	4,039
Rental payable to the Independent Broadcasting Authority	6,911
Channel Four subscription	15,864
Hire and leasing costs of plant and equipment	2,036
Auditors' remuneration	34
Other operating charges	20,268
Interest payable on borrowings repayable within five years	311
Interest receivable	(600)
	79,240

The average number of persons employed by the Group during the year was:	Number
Production staff	1,337
Management and office staff	453

EXTRACT FROM THE GROUP BALANCE SHEET

Programmes and film rights

Untransmitted programmes, including programmes in the course of completion, and film rights are carried forward at direct cost less such amounts as are necessary to reduce these assets to their estimated realizable value.

The costs of own production and film rights are wholly written off on first transmission.

Valuation of programmes and film rights at 31 December Year X
(Included in current assets)

	£000
Completed programmes	3,671
Uncompleted programmes	6,958
Film rights	4,910
	15,539

Discussion topics

(a) From an analysis of the above extracts from the published accounts, explain in as much detail as you can the nature of Central's business activities. What are its actual and potential sources of income?

(b) In addition to its liability to corporation tax, the Company is liable to pay an Exchequer levy in accordance with the provisions of the Broadcasting Act 1981. Why do you think that these extra charges are levied on these bodies?

(c) What other information would you require in order to evaluate the long-term prospects of the company?

18.7   The National Health Service

The Nottingham District Health Authority, which is part of the Trent Regional Health Authority, is responsible for all National Health Services provided within the City of Nottingham and the surrounding area, including hospitals, community health services, ambulances, general family practitioners, pharmacists, dentists and opticians.

The annual accounts of the Health Authority provide a detailed analysis of the capital and revenue expenditure and records its sources of funding (mainly cash advances from central government within an approved cash limit).

The following extract summarizes the revenue expenditure on hospital services for the financial year ended 31 March Year X.

National Health Service Annual Accounts — year ended 31 March Year X
Hospital Services Account — Nottingham District Health Authority

	£000	Items of Net Expenditure as % of total Net Expenditure
PATIENT CARE SERVICES		
Direct Treatment Services and Supplies		
Medical staff services	10,008	9.99
Dental staff services	204	0.20
Nursing staff services	30,948	30.89
Medical and Surgical Supplies:		
Equipment and Services	5,458	5.45
Pharmacy	5,103	5.09
Miscellaneous Direct Treatment Services	599	0.60
TOTAL Direct Treatment Services and Supplies	52,320	52.22
MEDICAL AND PARA-MEDICAL SUPPORTING SERVICES		
Radiology	2,706	2.70
Pathology	3,963	3.96
Electrocardiography, Medical Physics and other diagnostic services	1,080	1.08
Radiotherapy	195	0.19
Physiotherapy	1,194	1.19
Occupational Therapy	831	0.83
Other Services	1,321	1.32
TOTAL Medical and Para-Medical Supporting Services	11,290	11.27
TOTAL PATIENT CARE SERVICES	63,610	63.49
GENERAL SERVICES		
Administration	6,214	6.20
Medical Records	1,032	1.03
Training and Education	767	0.77
Catering	3,990	3.98
Domestic/Cleaning	6,686	6.67
Portering	1,671	1.67
Laundry	1,186	1.18
Linen Services	1,344	1.34
Transport	294	0.29

	£000	%
Estate Management:		
Engineering Maintenance	2,653	2.65
Energy and Utility Services	4,945	4.94
Building Maintenance	2,136	2.13
Grounds and Gardens	308	0.31
General Estate Expenses	2,483	2.48
Miscellaneous Services and Expenses	875	0.87
TOTAL General Services	36,584	36.51
TOTAL PATIENT CARE AND GENERAL SERVICES	100,194	100.00

The above account records total expenditure on all the general and psychiatric hospitals in the district, including a large modern teaching hospital. The percentage figures in the final column will therefore give an *average* picture of the relative importance of the main elements in hospital costs.

Discussion topics

(a) Taking the Nottingham Health Authority percentages for the main elements of health care as an average figure for all types of hospital, give an estimate based on 'intelligent guesswork' of the equivalent percentages for the following main services:

   Medical staff services
   Nursing staff services
   Medical and surgical supplies, equipment and services
   Medical and para-medical supporting services
   Administrative and medical records
   Catering
   Domestic/cleaning
   Estate management
   in *each* of the following special types of hospital
   (i) a large psychiatric hospital;
   (ii) a major teaching hospital undertaking a substantial programme of research and treatment into several branches of 'high-technology' medicine.

(b) In accordance with current practice in the NHS, the published accounts of Nottingham District Health Authority contain the following statement: 'There is no record in the balance sheet of capital assets, nor is there any provision for the depreciation of such assets in the revenue accounts.' In the same way, local authorities do not attempt to value the schools, old people's homes, fire stations, etc. under their control. Discuss fully the reasons for the omission of capital asset values in public-service accounts.

18.8   A professional football club

We do not usually measure the success or failure of a professional football club in financial terms. Success on the playing field will be seen as the club's main objective by supporters and directors alike. In practice, however, the financial and footballing fortunes of a club are often interrelated, and many clubs have been caught in the following 'vicious circle': disappointing results lead to a drop in attendances, forcing the club to sell good players to raise cash, resulting in even poorer footballing performances.

Although we often associate these problems with smaller clubs, even well-established successful First Division clubs are not immune from financial difficulties.

The position of this club is typical. The following extracts from the accounts should be largely self-explanatory.

Profit and Loss Account
for the year ending 31 May 19X8

	Footballing Activities £000	Transfer fees £000	Other activities £000	Total £000
Turnover	1,549	875	373	2,797
Staff costs	940	—	56	996
Depreciation	205	—	—	205
Other operating charges	579	760	172	1,511
Interest payable	260	—	—	260
Profit/(loss) on ordinary activities before taxation	(435)	115	145	(175)
Tax credit				100
(Loss) on ordinary activities after taxation and amount set aside to reserves				(75)
Year ended 31 May 19X7				
Turnover	1,661	1,634	481	3,776
Staff costs	1,060	—	57	1,117
Depreciation	206	—	—	206
Other operating charges	677	1,836	236	2,749
Interest payable	303	—	—	303
Profit/(loss) on ordinary activities before taxation	(585)	(202)	188	(599)
Tax credit				280
(Loss) on ordinary activities after taxation and amount set aside to reserves				(319)

Balance Sheet 31 May 19X8

	£000
Tangible fixed assets (Mainly short-leasehold land and buildings)	2,695
Current assets	
Stocks	15
Debtors	205
Cash at bank and in hand	5
	225
Creditors (Amounts falling due within one year)	1,682
Net current liabilities	1,457
Total assets less current liabilities	1,238
Creditors (Amounts falling due after more than one year)	900
Provisions for liabilities and charges	—
	338
Capital and reserves	
Called-up share capital (£209)	—
Capital reserve	413
Profit and loss account	(75)
	338

NOTES TO BALANCE SHEET

1. Creditors (Amounts falling due within one year)

Bank loans and overdrafts (Note 3)	1,214
Trade creditors	150
Other creditors	16
Taxation and Social Security	57
Accruals and deferred income	245
	1,682

2. Creditors (Amounts falling due after more than one year)

Bank loans and overdrafts (Note 3)	900

3. Bank loans and overdrafts

Included in bank loans and overdrafts is a bank loan amounting to £1,050,000 at 31 May 19X8 secured by guarantee from a local authority. The loan is repayable at £150,000 per annum as follows:

	£000
Within one year (Note 1)	150
After one year, of which £150 is repayable after five years (Note 2)	900
	1,050

The bank overdraft is secured on the company's freehold land and buildings.

At 31 May 19X8 guarantees totalling £225,000 had been given by nine directors to the company's bank.

Extract from the Chairman's Report

'To turn to the accounts the backcloth was one of the lower season ticket sales, lower attendances and less commercial revenue. This meant we had to cut our costs, not an easy task to achieve, since wages are such a high proportion of our expenses and players are usually on term contracts thus we have had to transfer players causing our Manager to have a very small playing staff. We are fortunate to be invited to tour overseas and welcome the revenue from this source.

'We have made economies in every area of the Club except perhaps in the search for and recruitment of young players with a view to apprenticeship with the Club. This is the positive side of our long-term plan for the future.'

Discussion topics

  (a) Explain how the transfer of players is recorded in the accounts. Why is the value of players under contract not included in the Balance Sheet?
  (b) Supporters often believe that they know better than the directors and the manager how their team should be run. Now is your chance! Write a report to the Board, setting out your recommendations about how the financial future of the club might be secured whilst retaining its high footballing reputation.

18.9   The accounts of two charities

As will be seen from the following extracts from their annual report and accounts, Oxfam and the British Heart Foundation are charities with widely differing objectives, organization structure and methods of fund raising.

(1) Objectives

British Heart Foundation: 'The principal activity of the Foundation continues to be to encourage and finance research into the causes, diagnosis, treatment and eventual prevention of cardiovascular disease.'
Oxfam: 'Its main objective is to raise funds in the UK, the Republic of Ireland and throughout the world in order to fund relief and development projects in developing countries. Oxfam's funds have again been used to fund social development, health, agricultural and humanitarian projects and emergency programmes in some 80 developing countries. A small part of its income is allocated to increasing public awareness in the UK concerning the problems of the developing countries.'

(2) Investments

Investments are included in the respective balance sheets at the following values:

British Heart Foundation	£13,607,793
Oxfam	£639,000

(3) Patterns of income and expenditure

Oxfam Group
Income and Expenditure Account 30 April 19X8

		19X8
		£000
INCOME		
Donations		7,633
Oxfam Shops		6,755
Oxfam Activities Limited		929
Contributions from Other Agencies		1,833
Contributions from UK Government and EC		2,022
Miscellaneous		530
TOTAL INCOME RAISED BY Oxfam		19,702
EXPENDITURE		
Fund raising		2,897
Administration		595
Irrecoverable VAT		65
		3,557
NET INCOME AVAILABLE FOR ALLOCATION		16,145
		16,145
Overseas Aid Programme	14,917	
Education Programme	742	
		15,659
SURPLUS OF INCOME FOR YEAR		486
RELIEF AND OVERSEAS AID FUND		
Balance at 30 April 19X7		1,594
Deduct Prior year adjustment		209
		1,385
Surplus of Income over Expenditure for year		486
		1,871
Deduct Transfer to Capital Fund		691
Balance at 30 April 19X8		1,180

British Heart Foundation
Income and Expenditure Account for the year ended 31 March 19X8

	19X8 £	19X8 £
Subscriptions, donations and fund raising	2,854,236	
Legacies	3,163,447	
		6,017,683
Fund raising and publicity costs	830,568	
Administration expenses	312,752	
Staff pension scheme	103,222	
Provision for building works —		
no longer required	(60,000)	
		(1,186,542)
		4,831,141
Other income	7,161	
Subsidiary company — covenanted donation	23,008	
		30,169
		4,861,310
Interest and dividends		1,343,918
Amounts written off investments — no longer required		61,190
Profit on sale of investments		615,487
Disposable income		6,881,905
Medical department	89,974	
Education	137,390	
Research awards, fellowships and		
cardiac care equipment	4,156,527	
Expenditure on established University		
Chairs of Cardiovascular Disease:		
Maintenance	743,450	
Endowment	95,000	
Provision for Chairs of Cardiovascular		
Disease	750,000	
		5,972,341
Surplus for year		
		909,564
Transfers:		
Chairs Maintenance Fund	1,377,496	
G. M. Yule Bequest Fund	3,682	
		1,381,178
Transfer (from) to Accumulated Reserves		(471,614)

Discussion topic

From the information given in the above extracts, describe and explain the relative importance of different methods of fund raising for the two charities. How will expenditure be planned and controlled in each case?

Answers to Questions within the Text

Chapter 2

Q.2a £2,000 + 16,400 − 10,150 − 7,000 = £1,250.

Q.2b

Balance Sheet of Grieg Enterprises at 30 April

Assets	£
Equipment	420
Stock	1,500
Cash at bank	1,080
	3,000
Liabilities	
Creditors	670
Capital	2,330

Q.2c

Balance Sheet at 31 March

	£		£
CAPITAL		FIXED ASSETS:	
R. Simon	130,536	Freehold Buildings	120,000
		Machinery and	
LONG-TERM LIABILITY		Equipment	36,000
Loan	36,000	Delivery Van	7,200
CURRENT LIABILITIES		CURRENT ASSETS:	
Creditors	1,524	Stock	4,107
Bank overdraft	638	Debtors	1,375
		Cash	16
	£168,698		£168,698

Q.2d   Capital £1,095, Creditors £100 (£1,195), Equipment £350, Stock £100, Debtors £160, Bank £585 (£1,195).

Q.2e   Valuation of business depends on what someone else would pay to take it over as a going concern or to buy the assets separately. As a going concern the value would depend on the established reputation and future prospects. Asset values based on original cost may not be good guide (topic developed in Chapter 6).

Chapter 3

Q.3a

	£
Total REVENUE (£800 + £2,000)	2,800
Total EXPENSE (£1,900 + £400)	2,300
PROFIT	500

Purchase of stock for cash £600 and receipt of £1,000 from debtors do not affect profit calculation as in each case they result in one asset being substituted for another.

	£
Total RECEIPTS of cash (£800 + £1,000)	1,800
Total PAYMENTS of cash (£400 + £600)	1,000

These answers can be reconciled as follows:

Assume that the £1,900 stock was the only asset at the beginning of the period. The opening balance sheet would be:

Capital	£1,900	Stock	£1,900

The closing balance sheet is then:

		£		£
Capital	1,900		Stock	600
+ profit	500		Debtors	1,000
		2,400	Cash	800
		2,400		2,400

Q.3b   By more than 10%. Gross profit increases by 10% (£1,780) but assume wages and rent and rates unchanged. Net profit increased by £1,780 (37%).

Q.3c   £11,000.

		£	£
Q.3d	Revenue — Sales		32,600
	Expenses — Stock used	17,800	
	— Wages	9,600	
	— Bad debt	120	27,520
	PROFIT		£5,080

Balance sheet entries:	£
Assets — Debtors	2,080
— Stock	2,000
Liability — Creditors	300
(deposits in advance)	

Q.3e   £600 chargeable as expense against profit to 31 December 19X5 and £600 liability shown in balance sheet.

Q.3f   No. Quantity and value of stock estimated. Depreciation of lorry still to be considered. Other debts may be doubtful or bad.

Q.3g   Some assets purchased but not yet charged as expenses. Rent paid in advance. Some of profit withdrawn.

	£	
Opening bank balance	18,000	
Profit	23,800	
	41,800	
Used for:		
Drawings	£20,000	
Assets unused (net)		
(£10,000 + 2,400 + 6,600		
+ 1,200 − 2,400)	17,800	
		37,800
Closing bank balance		4,000

Q.3h   Balance Sheet is that of the business. Black may have other assets or liabilities. Some valuations uncertain and there may be goodwill.

Q.3i   Almost 50% (£39,400 on £79,600).

Q.3j   Higher contribution per table sold (£5.63 instead of £5) because of lower than expected material costs. 820 × extra 63p = £520, less 80 × £5 = £120. Further £10 saved on other expenses.

Chapter 4

Q.4a

Jan. 22 Debit Office Equipment a/c
Credit T. Abel Ltd a/c
Jan. 24 Debit Rent a/c
Credit Cash at Bank a/c

Q.4b   Kay Ltd is a creditor of A. Booth for £2,400. Booth owes Kay Ltd that amount. In Kay Ltd's books Booth would be shown as a debtor.

Q.4c   Situation (iii) would not affect the balancing of the trial balance — the posting is to the correct side of the ledger but in the wrong account. As a result of (i) the credit side would be greater than the debit side by £20 (the posting should have been to the debit of Discounts Allowed account). As a result of (ii) the credit side will be understated by £76.86. The net effect is therefore £56.86 greater on the debit side.

Q.4d   On the debit side M. Wye and C. Dee are assets (debtors), Bank, Cash and Shop fittings are also assets. Wages and Miscellaneous Expenses are expenses. Purchases is partly an expense and partly an asset, depending on how much is still in stock. On the credit side, Sales is a revenue account and the other two are liabilities.

Q.4e	*Debit*	*Credit*
	£	£
Cash in hand (asset)	36	
J. Small (asset)	425	
Sale of goods (revenue)		112,680
Furniture and Fittings (asset)	3,000	
Wages and Salaries (expense)	42,840	
Capital (capital)		220,000
Drawings (reduction of capital)	18,529	
C. Large (liability)		350
Purchases (expense)	79,600	
Vehicle (asset)	9,200	
Vehicle running expenses (expense)	1,390	
Land, buildings (asset)	159,400	
Bank balance (asset)	110	
Admin. expenses (expense)	18,500	
	£333,030	£333,030

Q.4f   See Chapter 7.3.

Q.4g

Maintenance of equipment a/c

Year 1		£	Year 1		£
Oct.	Bank	80	Dec.	P & L a/c	320
Dec.	Balance	240			
		320			320
Year 2			Year 2		
Feb.	Bank	240	Jan.	Balance	240

Q.4h

D Major a/c

	£		£
Returns	50	Purchases	900
Cash discount	17		
Bank	833		
	900		900

Purchases Returns a/c

		£
	D Major	50

Discount Received a/c

		£
	D Major	17

Chapter 5

Q.5a

Provision for Doubtful Debts a/c

Year 3		£	Year 3		£
Dec.	P & L a/c	100	Jan.	Balance	900
Dec.	Balance	800			
		900			900
			Jan.	Balance	800

Q.5b Reduces working capital requirement and possibly interest on overdrafts. Reduces risk of debt becoming bad. If Brown & Co. pay 12% p.a. on overdrafts it would cost about £1.50 to borrow £100 for six weeks, which is less than cost of cash discount. However, other considerations may still justify offer, particularly limited availability of working capital.

Q.5c The closing stock valuation may be less (and therefore the cost of goods sold greater) because of items being lost or damaged or otherwise becoming worth less than the original cost.

Q.5e

Item	Stock valuation
	£
a	1,160
b	360
c	700
d	5,000
e	1,000
f	100
	£8,320

Q.5f

	A	B	C
	£	£	£
Selling price	3,650	4,200	2,850
Reduced items		800	
		3,400	
Cost price equivalent	($\frac{4}{5}$) 2,920	($\frac{3}{4}$) 2,550	($\frac{2}{3}$) 1,900
Reduced items		800	
		3,350	

Total stock value at lower of cost or net realizable value £8,170.

Q.5g a Fixed; b Fixed; c Fixed; d Current; e Fixed; f Current; g Current; h Fixed.

Q.5h

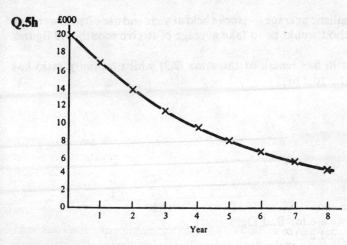

Q.5i $38\frac{1}{2}$%.

Q.5j   (i) £2,400 p.a.   15%
(ii) Balance sheet entry 31 December year 2

Delivery Van	£16,000	
less depreciation	4,800	
	——————	11,200

£11,200 represents the proportion of the original cost equal to another three years' usage plus the expected residual value.
(iii) Book value at 31 December year 3 is £8,800. Therefore £2,800 will be treated as an expense in year 4.
(iv) In year 1 only £2,000 was charged as depreciation so the book value will have remained £400 greater than the original figures since then. £3,200 will now be treated as an expense in year 4.

Chapter 6

Q.6a It would be inappropriate to recognize the whole of the hire purchase price as being earned at the time of the sale because of the inclusion of interest and the risk of default before payments are completed. A proportion of the total profit, including interest may be taken into account for each period concerned but practice varies according to the circumstances.

Q.6b Answered within Chapter 6.7.

Q.6c Reasons such as: lower selling prices because of competition, bad buying policy, some stock deteriorated, less demand for goods with higher margin, etc.

Q.6d It may not give a realistic average — stocks held at year end are often lower than at other times. Better method would be to take average of twelve month-end figures.

Q.6e Working capital ratio has remained the same (2.3) whilst liquidity ratio has marginally strengthened (1.5 to 1.6).

Chapter 7

Q.7a

	Dr £	Cr £
G. Steele	10	
Bad Debts a/c (or Bad Debt Recovered a/c)		10
Cheque from Steele in respect of debt written off last year.		

Q.7b

	Dr £	Cr £
Office furniture	700	
W. Irons		700
Office furniture accepted in full settlement of debt		

Q.7c

	Dr £	Cr £
Suspense a/c	79.32	
H. Hall		79.32
Correction of omission in posting purchase invoice		

Suspense a/c

	£		£
Balance	820.68	Equipment a/c	900.00
H. Hall	79.32		
	900.00		900.00

Q.7d £80 overdrawn (credit balance in bank account).

Q.7e

Debtors' Ledger Total Account

	£		£
Opening balance	63,425	Allowances	1,314
Sales	42,108	Bank	45,275
Bad debt recovered	260	Bad debts	138
		Transfer	80
		Closing balance	58,986
	105,793		105,793
Opening balance	58,986		

Creditors' Ledger Total Account

	£		£
Opening balance	120	Opening balance	48,914
Allowances	90	Purchases	31,242
Bank	39,403	Bank	120
Transfer	80		
Closing balance	40,583		
	80,276		80,276
		Opening balance	40,583

Q.7g

	DLTA			List of DL balances	
	£	£		£	£
	+	−		+	−
(i)				30.00	
(ii)		383.24			
(iii)					277.82
(v)		324.80			
(vi)	68.54	68.54			
(vii)	100.00				
(viii)				9.00	
(ix)		64.50			
	£168.54	£447.74		£432.34	£277.82
		−£279.20			+£154.52

Correct balancing figure £18,408.20. (v), (vi) and (ix) are most serious and need improvements to system.

Q.7h

(a)

VAT a/c			
	£		£
Equipment	360	Balance	200
Audit	90	Sales	600
Cash	160		
Stock	120		
Balance	70		
	800		800
		Balance	80

(amount owing to revenue authorities for net amount of tax collected)

(b)

Debtor	4,600	Sales	4,000
		VAT	600
Equipment	2,400	Creditor	2,760
VAT	360		
Audit	600	Bank	690
VAT	90		

Chapter 8

Q.8a   Were any goods bought for cash — out of the takings?
Were any goods taken for personal consumption? (trader's drawings)
Were all the invoices for goods or did they include capital items or services?
Were any goods received during the year which have not yet been invoiced?
How was the closing stock valued?

Q.8b   Sales £55,812. Doubts particularly about cash receipts and outstanding debtors.

Q.8c   Estimated profit £19,080 (£7,080 + 18,000 − 6,000).

Q.8d   Show receipts and payments directly related to each of the two productions separately. Give corresponding figures for previous year.

Chapter 9

Q.9a

	Total £	Freeman £	Grant £
Interest	4,000	3,200	800
Salary	12,000		12,000
Balance of profit	21,000	7,000	14,000
	37,000	10,200	26,800

Q.9b

Appropriation Account

	£	£		£
Interest:			Net Profit	32,000
Coles	600			
Dawson	500			
Edrich	300	1,400		
Profit				
Coles	10,200			
Dawson	10,200			
Edrich	10,200	30,600		
		32,000		32,000

Current Account

	C	D	E		C	D	E
Drawings	10,890	10,780	10,510	Balances	120	20	70
Balance c/fwd	30		60	Interest	600	500	300
				Profit	10,200	10,200	10,200
				Balance c/fwd		60	
	10,920	10,780	10,570		10,920	10,780	10,570
Balance b/d			60	Balance b/d	30		60

Balance Sheet at . . .

Capital Accounts:
Coles	12,000	
Dawson	10,000	
Edrich	6,000	28,000

Current Accounts:
Coles	30	
Edrich	60	
	90	
less Dawson	60	30

Q.9c $6\% \times \dfrac{100}{105} = 5.7\%$

Chapter 11

Q.11b   (a) FIFO. Closing stock value, £550.
(b) LIFO. Closing stock value, £475.
(c) Weighted average. Closing stock value, £506.

Q.11c   Stock discrepancy of £3,930.

Q.11d   £47.5. *See* discussion on manufacturing overhead in Chapter 12.4.

Q.11e   (a) Fixed costs: Rates, Insurance, Depreciation (factory buildings).
(b) Variable costs: Raw materials, Direct wages.
(c) Semi-variable costs: Indirect wages, Indirect materials, tools, maintenance, repairs, power, light, heat, depreciation of machinery.

Q.11f   The closing balance of the Profit and Loss Account is now £67,100.

Q.11g   Gross profit for the year:

Model 1	£93,060
Model 2	162,040
Total	255,100

Chapter 12

Q.12a

Cost clerks salaries	Labour	Admin. O/H

Stationery (Sales)	Materials	Selling O/H
Overtime allowance	Labour	Manufacturing O/H
Interest on bank overdraft	Other cost	Financial O/H
Fire insurance	Other cost	Manufacturing O/H (in so far as it relates to the insurance of factory, plant and buildings)
Fee to advertising agency	Other cost	Selling O/H
Depreciation on cars used by salesmen	Other cost	Selling O/H
Directors' fees	Other cost	Admin. O/H
Electricity account	Other cost	O/H (mainly manufacturing)
Subcontractor's charge	Other cost	Prime cost
Employers' National Insurance contribution	Other cost	Manufacturing, selling and admin. O/H (based on numbers of employees)

Q.12b High cost may mean high quality of service.

Q.12c Total FTE students $= \dfrac{\text{Total hours on all short courses}}{20} \times \dfrac{150}{100}$

Q.12d (a) Cost per patient or per bed with appropriate weightings.
(b) Cost per bed/night.
(c) Cost per tonne of coal mined.
(d) Cost of service per 1,000 population.
Cost per book issued.
Average cost per book purchased.

Q.12e Cumulative unit cost of Process 5, £201.

Chapter 13

Q.13b Price variance £0.4 (favourable).
Usage variance £2.5 (unfavourable).

Q.13c Wage rate variance $=$ £212.5.
Labour efficiency variance $=$ £187.5.

Q.13d (1) Efficiency percentages show the proportion of time in the factory actually spent working. The final column gives reasons for any idle time. The figures suggest that 'waiting for work' and 'waiting for materials' are the major causes for idle time. Perhaps the production control system needs strengthening.

(2) Productivity percentages show the efficiency of individual workers in producing the actual output. The ratios vary from 83% (Wilson) to 33% (Dennis). Supervision may be lax, and the policy of letting experienced workers teach newcomers on the job may need re-examination. Both the instructor and the trainee have a low productivity; it may be more efficient to provide 'off the job' training.

Chapter 14

Q.14a Overdraft at 31 Dec.: £4,700.
Maximum overdraft at 30 Sept.: £8,400.

Chapter 15

Q.15a (a) Straight-line method: depreciation treated as a fixed cost.
(b) Hours worked: depreciation treated as a variable cost.

Q.15b The curve is of equal 'steps' of £8,500 for every 100 units produced.

Q.15c A high proportion of a railway's costs are fixed in relation to the volume of traffic. Excursion trains do not affect the regular scheduled services, and therefore any income in excess of the variable costs of running these trains will make a contribution to the fixed costs incurred by British Rail. As there is intense competition from coach operations, the price must be considerably below the 'full cost' of running train services if maximum contribution is to be achieved.

Q.15d Policy (3) would be followed because, although profits are equal under policies (1) and (2) (£45,000), policy (3) gives a lower breakeven point (2,500 units).

Q.15e The differential cost is £0.015 per unit in favour of keeping the old power press. This is not significant financially, and so the decision would be taken on other grounds, such as quality, reliability and ease of maintenance.

Q.15f The differential costs are negative (−£173). Lathe B would be purchased.

Chapter 16

Q.16b Because it represents an obligation to pay sums of money other than out of the normal trading income. It would influence opinions about the adequacy of the company's finances, particularly if the amount was relatively substantial. If the liquid position shown in the balance sheet was weak the question would arise as to how the new capital expenditure was to be financed. It also helps users of the statements to form an opinion about future developments.

Q.16c

Rate of return	Profit before tax and interest £	A EPS	B EPS
4%	10,200	3.4p	2.1p
8%	20,400	6.8p	7.2p
12%	30,600	10.2p	12.3p
16%	40,800	13.6p	17.4p
20%	51,000	17.0p	22.5p

Had the reserves been proportionate to the share capital (or if there were no reserves) you would expect the EPS to be equal when the rate of return was equal to the interest rate.

e.g. X Share capital £200,000 in ordinary ahares
Y £150,000 in ordinary shares and £50,000 in 6% debentures.
At a 6% rate of return the profit less tax and interest is X £6,000 (EPS 3p) and Y £4,500 (EPS 3p)

In this example the reserves did not remain in proportion to the ordinary shares in A and B, so the breakeven point does not tally exactly with the interest rate of 8 per cent, but it still approximates to that level.

Q.16d Retention of company name and structure usually an advantage for goodwill and organizational reasons.

Chapter 17

Q.17a Year 5 .62:1 Year 4 .58:1. Current liabilities only partially covered by current assets but this is typical of supermarket trading. Results from fast turnover of stock compared with settlement period for creditors.

Q.17b C. Legg Ltd

Liquidity ratio, 31 March, year 3   1.12
31 March, year 4   0.96

Reason for deterioration of liquid position is probably purchase of fixed assets during the year, temporarily depleting liquid resources. See also Chapter 17.7.

Q.17c Cannot always be assumed that stock is not liquid for purposes of liquidity ratio. Fassvend's stock is certainly liquid, being turned into cash on average well before it has to be paid for. Liquidity ratio would be the same as working capital ratio. In other cases, debtors may include some debts which will not be collected for several months.

Q.17d   Year 5 17 times. Year 4 17.5 times (both approximately 3 weeks on average). Management would be concerned that stock not being turned over quite as quickly. Compare the average period goods are in stock with the settlement period for creditors — see next section in Chapter 17.4.

Q.17e   If average stock remains at £80,000, and rate of stock-turn increases to eight times p.a., goods costing £640,000 would be sold. Gross profit would be

$$£280,000 \times \frac{649}{520} = £345,000, \text{ an improvement of } £65,000.$$

Q.17f   Year 5 24.9% (8,394/33,764). Year 4 28.3% (7,903/27,962).

Q.17g $$\frac{NP}{Turnover} \times \frac{Turnover}{Cap. \ employed} = \frac{NP}{Cap. \ employed}$$

Year 5 3.40%	×	7.31	=	24.86%
Year 4 3.42%	×	8.25	=	28.25%

Significant fall in profitability in year 5 due largely to turnover of capital employed but also to slight worsening of margin on sales. Slower turnround of stock already noted. Also more fixed assets now needed to generate equivalent sales (turnover of fixed assets 5.71 times in year 5 from 6.02 times in year 4) though revaluations or new store acquisitions could have affected this.

Q.17h   C. LEGG LTD, years 3/4

Source and Application of Funds

Source of Funds		£
Issue of debentures		20,000
Profits before tax		60,000
add back depreciation		18,000
		98,000
Application of Funds		
Dividends paid	12,000	
Tax paid	24,000	
Purchase of fixed assets	58,000	
Increase in stock	4,000	
Increase in debtors	4,000	
Increase in creditors	(2,000)	
		100,000
Decrease in cash		£2,000

Q.17i

Sources of funds		£000
Net profit before tax and dividend		7,814
Depreciation		1,620
Generated from operations		9,434
Issue of debentures		1,000
		10,434
Application of funds		
Purchase of fixed assets (43,240 − 38,300 + 1,620)	6,560	
Tax paid (1,440 + 1,620 − 1,750)	1,310	
Dividend paid (816 + 1,392 − 960)	1,248	9,118
Increase in working capital		1,316
Increase in stocks	1,230	
Increase in debtors	114	
Decrease in creditors	398	1,742
Decrease in cash		426

Note the large proportion of new funds needed for additional fixed assets. Also increase in stocks not funded at all by creditors.

Q.17j £125 (£10 interest = 8% yield on £125).

Q.17k Twice $\left(\dfrac{£35,000 - £5,000}{£15,000} \right)$

Q.17l Div per share 5.8p: Earnings per share 25.8p:
Dividend yield 3.2%:   Earnings yield 14.3%:
P/E ratio 7
Market value of shareholders' interests is £43,440,000 (compared with book value of £33,764,000).

Q.17m

Sales (15 × 18 + 30 × 20)	£870	
Cost of sales (155 + 345)	500	
Profit	370	

Index